WATCHING

WHILE BLACK

WATCHING WHILE BLACK

Centering the Television of Black Audiences

EDITED BY

BERETTA E. SMITH-SHOMADE

RUTGERS UNIVERSITY PRESS

New Brunswick, New Jersey and London

Library of Congress Cataloging-in-Publication Data

Watching while black : centering the television of black audiences / edited by
Beretta E. Smith-Shomade.

    p. cm.

Includes bibliographical references and index.

ISBN 978-0-8135-5387-0 (hardcover : alk. paper) — ISBN 978-0-8135-5386-3
(pbk. : alk. paper) — ISBN 978-0-8135-5388-7 (e-book)

    1. African Americans on television.   2. African American television viewers.
3. Television broadcasting—Social aspects—United States.   I. Smith-Shomade, Beretta E.,
1965–

  PN1992.8.A34W38   2012

    791.45'08996073—dc23

2012005040

A British Cataloging-in-Publication record for this book is available from the British Library.

Visit our website: http://rutgerspress.rutgers.edu

Manufactured in the United States of America

For Teshome Gabriel
Thank you

Contents

Acknowledgments — ix

Introduction: I See Black People
BERETTA E. SMITH-SHOMADE — I

Part I   Producing Blackness

1   The Importance of *Roots*
ERIC PIERSON — 19

2   Two *Different Worlds*: Television
as a Producer's Medium
ROBIN R. MEANS COLEMAN AND
ANDRE M. CAVALCANTE — 33

3   A Black Cast Doesn't Make a Black
Show: *City of Angels* and the Plausible
Deniability of Color-blindness
KRISTEN J. WARNER — 49

4   Blacks in the Future: Braving the
Frontier of the Web Series
CHRISTINE ACHAM — 63

Part II   Blackness on Demand

5   "Regular Television Put to Shame by
Negro Production": Picturing a Black
World on *Black Journal*
DEVORAH HEITNER — 77

6   "HEY, HEY, HEY!" Bill Cosby's *Fat Albert*
as Psychodynamic Postmodern Play
TREAANDREA M. RUSSWORM — 89

7   *Gimme a Break!* and the Limits of the
Modern Mammy
JENNIFER FULLER — 105

8   *Down in the Treme . . .* Buck Jumping and Having Fun?:
The Impact of Depictions of Post-Katrina New Orleans
on Viewers' Perceptions of the City
KIM M. LEDUFF ⸺ 121

Part III   New Jack Black

9   Keepin' It Reality Television
RACQUEL GATES ⸺ 141

10   Prioritized: The Hip Hop (Re)Construction of
Black Womanhood in *Girlfriends* and *The Game*
NGHANA LEWIS ⸺ 157

11   Nigger, Coon, Boy, Punk, Homo, Faggot,
Black Man: Reconsidering Established
Interpretations of Masculinity, Race, and
Sexuality Through *Noah's Arc*
MARK D. CUNNINGHAM ⸺ 172

12   Graphic Blackness/Anime Noir: Aaron McGruder's
The Boondocks and the Adult Swim
DEBORAH ELIZABETH WHALEY ⸺ 187

Part IV   Worldwide Blackness

13   Resistance Televised: The TV da Gente Television
Network and Brazilian Racial Politics
REIGHAN ALEXANDRA GILLAM ⸺ 207

14   South African Soapies: A "Rainbow Nation"
Realized?
NSENGA K. BURTON ⸺ 220

15   Minority Television Trade as Cultural Journey:
The Case of New Zealand's *bro'Town*
TIMOTHY HAVENS ⸺ 232

Notes on Contributors ⸺ 247
Index ⸺ 251

Acknowledgments

The space between when you conceive a project and its fruition can sometimes be a long one. Such is the case with this anthology.

I thank the two anonymous readers for their support and critical insights into the workings of the articles and the book as a whole. Your critiques have made the work much stronger. I appreciate my wonderful and patient press editors as well, Leslie Mitchner and Lisa Boyajian, who persevered even when I made their lives admittedly, a bit difficult. Thank you.

I thank my Tulane Sistah Circle writing group, Katie Acosta, Rebecca Chaisson, and Nghana Lewis, for their support and encouragement, critique and response. With hectic lives and even more hectic commitments, you find time to share your wisdom and yourselves. For this, I'm very grateful.

I thank Bambi Haggins and Deborah Elizabeth Whaley for their constant intellectual support and Oyinlola Longe for her hard work.

I thank Timothy Rodriguez for finding stills for the book and India Cooper for her meticulous copyediting.

I thank my children and husband for their constant patience with and support of me in doing "mommy's work," especially when I'm cranky in the morning after staying up way too late. I especially appreciate my husband's willingness to continue membership in the honeydo club!

Finally, I offer many thanks to all of the smart, engaged and wonderful contributors of this text. I appreciate each of you for not only the hard work and necessary engagement with your chapters but for allowing me to ask, and ask, and ask for more and for giving it back to me with such grace and good spirit. I thank you all for your constant encouragement and for being stalwart in your tasks.

In the process of putting this book together, we lost a most generous spirit and guiding force for so many of us, Dr. Teshome Gabriel. While I will never be able to replicate his mastery of touch and the word, I dedicate this book to him to remember and constantly return to the magic that he shared and he was.

WATCHING
WHILE BLACK

Introduction

I SEE BLACK PEOPLE

BERETTA E. SMITH-SHOMADE

This project has been engaging my thoughts for nearly a decade. I was forced to actually address it while sitting in our temporary home in Ile-Ife, Nigeria, watching world satellite TV with virtually no Blacks on it. In Nigeria, I became acquainted with Paris-based Fashion TV, U.S.-based Style Network, and the Australian production *McLeod's Daughters*. Outside of M-Net's Africa Magic, a network dedicated to showing Nollywood productions primarily, television was anything but Black. This whitening of the televisual frame, even in Black Africa, made me begin to consider the dearth of knowledge circulating about Black television programming, even when abundance exists—of how this lack of knowledge could contribute to programming selections. Closer to home, I thought about how that same "whiteout" existed in U.S. scholarship on television production and viewership and their cultural flows. I realized that I needed to move from reflections to response.

Discussions about the transforming reception/audience/user landscapes pervade every mediated outlet—whether scholarly engagement within Media Studies or Communications, journalistic pieces from technology sectors and from new media theorists and practitioners, or within business, public-sphere, and institutional spaces. Evidence of the divergent and fragmented deluge of media consumption and production demands attention but is often invoked as if a coherency exists. Moreover, acknowledgment that certain aspects of this media landscape have *always* been fractured, minimized, and ignored rarely surfaces.

In 1990–1991, Nielsen Media began to demarcate the viewing patterns of African American audiences from other American demographics. Nielsen's ability and desire to bring into focus taste and cultural preferences according to discrete identity categories (race, gender, age, class, and sociopolitical orientation), all for the benefit of corporate advertising, remains a source of consternation and fascination. Yet differences between *what* Black viewers watch and what "all others" watch has not received much critical examination beyond parenthetical variations of "oh yeah, *they* watch different stuff." This dearth of incisive examination points to a critical gap and negation in discourse—both past and present.

More poignantly, the discrepancy suggests a glaring disjuncture between the discourses of postracialism and the media taken up by identifiable "Other" audiences.

Watching While Black aims to address this omission by centering the viewing choices of Black audiences and the programs directed at a Black viewership. While Black Entertainment Television (BET) celebrated its thirty-first year (and its very first season of original series production) in 2011, and TV One and others (intermittently) dot the U.S. television landscape, most Black representation comes from mainstream (read white) cable and broadcast networks that primarily target different, non-Black audiences. This national phenomenon is examined in two sweeping histories: *Blacks and White TV: African Americans in Television Since 1948* (1992) and *Prime Time Blues: African Americans on Network Television* (2001). Television scholarship in general, however, continues to ignore programming aimed at Black audiences—both at large and in the margins, at home and abroad.

An easily countable number of academic texts give evidence to Black-watched, Black-targeted television narratives. Ironically, these are essentially the same studies mentioned in the introduction of my last book—*Pimpin' Ain't Easy*—even as our televisual choices and opportunities continue to explode. The now canonical works by Herman S. Gray, *Watching Race* and *Cultural Moves*, established the parameters by which we can approach Black television narratives through both their sophistication and their centering of Black narratives as theoretical objects of study. *Watching Race: Television and the Struggle for Blackness* (1995) troubles the ground of Black cultural politics and representation. It examines early 1980s and 1990s television programs such as *Frank's Place* (1987–1988) and *In Living Color* (1990–1994). *Cultural Moves: African Americans and the Politics of Representation* (2005), while much more about the deployment of Blackness through a variety of cultural production practices, signs, referents, and strategic political maneuvers, still privileges Black viewing space as a site for critical interrogation.

My own works, *Shaded Lives: African-American Women and Television* (2002) and *Pimpin' Ain't Easy: Selling Black Entertainment Television* (2007), center Black narratives as sites for explicit examination. Through the lens of gendered and racialized confluence, *Shaded Lives* attempts to rethink the pulls of progressive and regressive representations of Black women throughout various television genres. Utilizing macro/structural/industrial lenses, *Pimpin' Ain't Easy* explicitly interrogates the strategic deployment of Black televisual processes. *Pimpin' Ain't Easy* engages with the idea of BET as an interlocutor and examines the conundrum posed between Black expectations and the realities of market capitalism on the first network for Black folks. Kristal Brent Zook's *Color by Fox: The Fox Network and the Revolution in Black Television* (1999) was a forerunner to *Pimpin' Ain't Easy*—leading the industrial charge against Fox and its spate of programs strategically deployed to lure Black audiences. Christine Acham (a contributor in this text) made televisual Blackness a site of political disruption in her book *Revolution Televised: Prime Time and the Struggle for Black Power* (2004). Robin Means Coleman (also a contributor here) offers *African American Viewers and the Black Situation Comedy* (2000) and *Say It Loud! African-American Audiences, Media, and Identity* (2002) to give voice to the ways race is articulated across media platforms and how the confines of the media shape what we see as Blackness, and how. Darnell Hunt's *Channeling Blackness* (2004) deftly makes the case of Black representation through critical, canonical essays over the past nearly forty years. Yeidy Rivero's *Tuning Out Blackness: Race and Nation in the History of Puerto Rican Television* (2005) excavates and translates facets of culture that turn on a myriad of agendas—economic, racial, and political. She carefully weaves the historical context, cultural mixing, and economic imperatives of the Caribbean's engagement with media. And finally, *Black Television Travels: Media Globalization and Contemporary Racial Discourse*, forthcoming by contributor Timothy Havens, promises to open up ground surrounding the myth of Black television marketability beyond U.S. borders.

Surprisingly, this handful of books constitutes the existing long-form studies done for and about Black folks' television programming. The one-off articles notwithstanding, it is as if Media Studies scholars do not know (or do not care to know) that target "Black" shows exist, or conversely fail to value their existence, or both.[1] This matters because when my mostly white and privileged students teach media literacy in the New Orleans public (code Black) schools (or any other urban system), they bring a distinct disadvantage, disconnect, and cultural illiteracy by not only *not* having seen *The Game* but also not knowing that such shows and the culturally specific codes they play with exist.

In the second decade of the new millennium, texts such as *Thinking Outside the Box: A Contemporary Television Genre Reader* (2008), *Television Studies After TV* (2009), and *The Politics of Reality Television: Global Perspectives* (2011) (produced by scholars and publication places known for their depth and rigor) fail to mention *any* program with a predominance of Black characterizations—including the flamboyant and widely popular *Flavor of Love*. These omissions allow for substantive address of race, class, and gender confluence to go undone. Such an absence of discourse serves to perpetuate the idea of a homogeneity of taste, experience, desire, and outlook that does not exist. It fails to acknowledge the exploitation and co-opting of heterogeneity—even in the face of explosive writings about difference, hybridity, multiple identities, globalization, and plurality. This disjuncture should matter to all interested in transforming the United States and the larger world—from an increasingly duplicitous, insular, and fragmented place to one where possibilities for respect of and appreciation for difference exist beyond written and verbal rhetoric. *Watching While Black* works to forward this ideal.

The "Black" in Black Audiences

Who is this Black audience that watches programming labeled as Black and targeted to Blacks? The projected 2012 Nielsen Media figures suggest almost 115,000 total U.S. households. African American audiences represent over 14 percent of these households, or nearly thirty-eight million viewers aged two-plus.[2] Black folks' television usage far outpaces viewing in "other" households, and Blacks have a higher percentage of homes with multiple sets. Young African Americans in general and African American men in particular watch more ad-supported cable and less network affiliate programming compared to women and older demographics. Seventy-two percent of viewing for Black children (two to eleven) goes toward cable. African American teens (twelve to seventeen) watch cable 65 percent of their viewing time, while Black men of all ages and Black folks eighteen to thirty-four have a 56 percent cable share of viewing. Black folks watch more on the go than any other group as well—six hours per month on mobile phones and other handheld media devices.[3]

These figures tell us that Black people watch a lot of television but also that their viewing preferences, both discriminately and indiscriminately, give credence to the idea that there is nothing postracial about living while Black. Beginning in 2007, Black-owned TV One's promotional tagline was "I See Black People." This seemingly innocuous phrasing resonates powerfully within Black communities. It implies (and is later directly expressed within the promotion) that Black folks are seen on the network loving, living, laughing, and even "celebrating a great literary saga" (referencing the airing of a special on Broadway's version of *The Color Purple*). Kristal Brent Zook employs the tagline in the naming of her book about Black-owned television and radio entities. She argues that ownership, in this case, matters because "the perceptions and life experiences of people of color are often wildly divergent from those of the general population. As one writer noted, white people are always horrified and gasp aloud when she confesses to them that her grandfather was a Klansman. Black people, she says, don't even bat an eye."[4] This same notion of divergent lives is equally true for the visualization (and qualification) of Black life on the televisual screen. These different ways of seeing impact our ability to imagine the world in any other way than it exists right now. And that, to put it quite simply, is untenable.

Unpacking the Notion of Watching While Black

Apparently seeing Blackness continues to be a gargantuan task in scholarly endeavors and everyday mainstream life across the world. Ralph Ellison addressed this challenge in his 1952 prologue of *Invisible Man* when he wrote: "I am invisible, understand, simply because people refuse to see me."[5] Contemporary iterations of this invisibility are resilient even in the face of hypervisibility.

The same students, the same staff, the same faculty members in your own department who talk with you for what seems like hours on the most intimate of things will look directly at you outside of that space and not acknowledge you, literally not see you and thus not see your humanity. When you ask these colleagues why they failed to speak or acknowledge your presence, their honest answer is *"I didn't see you."* This *conditioned* and supported response to not seeing Black humanity undergirds and supplies the subtext to the dearth of writing about racialized texts within television scholarship.

The 1980s and 1990s postmodernist push to challenge common notions of race and gender has waned in the decades following—as we become, reportedly, postracialized and postfeminist. Critical code words deployed when Marlon Riggs's *Color Adjustment* appeared in 1991—hybridity, postmodernism, and pastiche, hyphenated identities and essentialist tropes—continue to resonate in Television and Media Studies, Cultural Studies, and American Studies. Yet this once critical terminology exists more as nods to the past rather than with any kind of agency or urgency. Criticality is quietly returning from the streets to the hallowed grounds of academia, despite the blogs, podcasts, guest network appearances, and Facebook protests to the contrary (as we see with the Occupy Wall Street activism).[6]

A part of that dissolve comes from the discrepancy between the theoretical expectation and the lived problematic of race and ways of seeing. Even while Arjun Appadurai projects the ability of mediascapes' distant audiences to imagine "worlds that are chimerical, aesthetic, even fantastic objects," Marwan Kraidy exalts hybridity (finding cultural bleed in every artifact), and Amy Villarejo tarries with the normative to find compatriots in life's identity wars, the continuing impact of Bakke nationwide, Proposition 209 in California, 9/11, Hurricane Katrina, the Haitian earthquake, and the election of Barack Obama as U.S. president, all bring thinking squarely back to a stultified and enduring construction of race grounded in phenotype. Naomi Klein has argued that the focus on the external manifestations of identity distracted consumers and audiences and allowed corporations to merge and acquire the rights to all mediated spoils. Yet Klein's thinking presumes a world differently, better articulated in the land of color now and before. This post notion quite literally dominates U.S. television (and other mediated forms and locales outside the United States), across genre, day part, production process, and distribution window.

The evidence of what Blackness means (or fails to mean) *reflects* in both visual offerings and scholarly discourses. *Watching While Black* provides audiences of Black television (and those who purportedly have never watched or seen race) an opportunity to consider some of these programs and what they mean (and can mean) to this century's thinking about and engagement with Blackness, television, history and our real-lived engagement with one another.

Figure I.1   Democratic presidential candidate Barack Obama (2007). Courtesy of PhotoFest.

Television Done and Undone

The works in this anthology understand the centrality of television as a cultural barometer in the lives of Black folks. Television and Media Studies has been increasingly self-reflective about its very existence as Television Studies positions in the academy shift and disappear and tales of the death of television reemerge. However, agreeing with Elana Levine, "Perhaps the designation of today's television as 'postnetwork' functions quite similarly to designations such as postfeminist and postracial. In this respect, postnetwork logic would argue that with the dominance of the Big Three broadcast networks reportedly behind us, there is no longer a need to think about television as a site of cultural struggle."[7] But indeed, television continues to be a necessary and viable site for struggle for those now appearing more pervasively on it.

Aniko Bodroghkozy reminds us that television was once the "new" media and relegated radio to near invisibility. Yet "radio was and is still everywhere in the socio-cultural-political environment."[8] Radio's significance to Black audiences and Black communities is measurable and is still taken up by non-profits and businesses aiming for Black consumers. Television, even through it constitutes variant platforms, exists in this same capacity for many Black viewers. Thus, this anthology presumes not only a predominately Black viewing

Figure I.2 *The Wire*. Courtesy of PhotoFest.

audience but also a Black audience that networks target. For example, while critically acclaimed series such as *The Wire* exist largely in the world of the urban Baltimorean (in this case, a Black and illegal working class and the fall-out from that illegality), it is not included here because of its overall projection. The series never pretended to address Black folks per se. The lingo, the accents and the references reflect a cultural specificity to the area. Its presentation, however, did not suggest a Black target audience demographic but more spoke of and about a Black experience to an audience culturally unfamiliar with any part of that experience. The way that the well-written *The Wire* explains itself and supports a mixed-race cast overdetermines its target audience. In fact, because HBO courts a white middle- and upper-class sensibility, many Black audiences (and larger mainstream audiences) only came to know the series post its airing. Its premium programming status on HBO ultimately comes at a premium price.

While *Treme* and the documentaries by Spike Lee on Hurricane Katrina carry this same limitation by appearing on HBO (and are included in this text), their presumed reach moves differently because of what they are (documentaries that circulate in schools, nonprofits, etc.) and people's interest in everything New Orleans at this juncture (at least in the first half of *Treme*'s inaugural season). These programs function as almost historical texts and are taken up and marketed as such. Thus, their reach has been significantly greater.

A couple of critical areas of Black representation do not receive examination in this anthology: neither the pervasiveness and presence of Black athletes demonized, defined, and denatured on television, nor the range of Black tele-evangelical ministries, music videos, talk shows, networks, and, now, gospel competitions. A central rationale for these absences returns us to the heart of the need for this text—too few scholars working on things that Black folks watch. Another part, more strategically, is recognizing the amount of work, at least in journals, that has already been done in some of these cases. I reference them here, as they exist as additional spaces where Black audiences gather and, in the case of religious programming, where they gather under the presumption of directedness. I hope the mentioning of such scholarly directions will as well encourage interrogation into these equally important areas.

Finally, I must discuss the phenomenon that is Tyler Perry. Perry has transformed a theatrical cottage industry for Black audiences into a multimedia empire. In fact, *Forbes* named him Hollywood's highest-paid man in September of 2011, earning $130 million from May 2010 to May 2011. His cinematic work has yielded tremendous financial success and fierce fan loyalty while remaining fundamentally underexamined by cultural and media theorists. His 2006 deal with Debmar-Mercury, Lionsgate, and TBS for one hundred television episodes of *House of Payne* upfront put the industry on notice (at least for Black programming) that a new model was afoot. The newness of his complete transformation of Black televisual possibilities, however—especially in terms of industrial models—makes for limited consideration at this moment. While we have recently begun to see a number of critical essays and texts about his film work,[9] Perry's television forays, *House of Payne* and *Meet the Browns*, have not been examined by media scholars (or even journalists to any great extent).

Figure I.3   *House of Payne*. Courtesy of PhotoFest.

But what must be noted for this anthology is the knowledge Tyler Perry has (and uses) about his audience. Steve Koonin, president of TNT, the network that houses both of Perry's series, remarks: "[Perry] understands who he is trying to make laugh . . . He doesn't try to please other constituents. That clarity is the reason he is so successful; he is not trying to be all things to all people. He is incredibly strategic . . . I've never had the privilege to work with somebody who understands who their brand and who their audience is more than Tyler does."[10] Perry must be referenced here so readers do not miss the significance of what he's doing industrially and narratively. While many may disagree with and/or dislike the stories he tells, he's one of the very few Black producers/writers who is getting to tell them at this televisual moment. It is my hope that readers of *Watching While Black* will critically engage Perry's work in order to paint a fuller picture of what Blackness can mean (will mean) in our future mediated landscape.

Black TV

In singer Alicia Keys's song "Unbreakable" (2005), Black love is defined through fictionalized and live-action celebrity African American couples. How we are supposed to love is exemplified by how these couples love and make money and perform their love. The music video visualization of this idea ushers viewers into a warm and reminiscent feeling about these familiar extended-family members. So the dream, at least in the words of this pop culture phenomenon, is love solidified through fictional, pop cultural referents. And I thought, "Wow, is this what living our dream means now?" Yet this example, both the song and video, seemed apropos for rethinking a number of programs in our recent past and their relationship to Black audiences' negotiation of mediated references.

Thus, the four parts of this book reflect an organization of promise and possibility. The individual chapters cover a wide swath of work done by and about Black folks for both Black audiences and, secondarily, a general audience. The contributors stand out for the fire of their analysis, their freshness, their unique and unexpected perspectives, and their ability to navigate critical areas of contest. In so doing, their chapters should encourage readers to pause and reconsider our everyday experiences in new and, hopefully, more progressive ways. The chapters span time periods, genres, and scope and speak to one another across programs, players, and approaches.

The anthology opens with discussions of the entertainment industry— structural concerns around producing, writing, casting, and Web distribution. The industrial processes of ownership and regulation shape viewing practices even before one can delve into a textual analysis of television programming crafted to appeal to Black audiences—historic and contemporary, domestic and worldwide. In part 1, "Producing Blackness," several macro areas of television production are addressed, including the role of producers, writers, casting, and Internet distribution, alongside the economies of programming for Black audiences.

The part opens with Eric Pierson's examination of the miniseries *Roots* to introduce some of the ways in which Black programming moves through the television system. Pierson situates the dynamic expectation and promise of the program against competing discourses operating within the writing, producing, casting, and scheduling of the *Roots* series. Furthermore, he illuminates why these expectations failed to materialize. In so doing, Pierson gives readers the opportunity to revisit (and others to be introduced to) this uniquely significant thirty-five-year-old series. The work foregrounds the chapters following it by addressing how various production processes operate.

Much like Pierson's *Roots* chapter, chapter 2 illuminates the central role of the producer and the ways in which that vision dominates (and can transform) a televisual space. Robin Means Coleman and Andre Cavalcante explore *The Cosby Show*'s 1987 spinoff, *A Different World*, to specifically highlight where race and culture coalesce to shift the stories told. They argue that changing the vision and terrain of a text can significantly impact the culture, success, and "structure of feeling" of a narrative—even one hemmed in by genre. Specifically, they address how white producer Anne Beatts imagined the fictional Black college tale and how Black producer Debbie Allen reimagined it. Centering a Black cultural perspective, this chapter rethinks what audience grounding means in television production. Moreover, the chapter rehearses some of the vision arguments made later by Nghana Lewis in her focus on the contemporary series *Girlfriends* and *The Game*.

Kristen Warner reiterates the intensity and high-stakes environment of Black-cast programs in the front office. She does this by offering a unique and wholly understudied area of the production process—casting. She argues that the contemporary reification of blindcasting, as articulated both in stage productions and in television, actually relies on the old measures of typical casting— phenotype, fit, and familiarity. Looking at the short-lived series *City of Angels*, she suggests that these culture-light discourses of blindcasting may, in fact, paradoxically center the racialized articulations that they seek to destabilize.

The final chapter in part 1 looks to the future. Christine Acham explores one of the strategic latest developments in finding ways to bring Blackness to screens—webisodes. In her chapter "Blacks in the Future: Braving the Frontier of the Web Series," Acham discusses the conditions that led Black producers, writers, and actors to seek the Web as a viable space to practice their craft. Combining interviews, audience online responses, and textual analysis of two series, Acham describes what might indeed be a "webtopia" for Black visual production.

Part 2, "Blackness on Demand," allows scholars to revisit critical Black television programs of the twentieth century. Inaugural Black series such as *Amos 'n' Andy* and *Beulah* receive less attention due to the preponderance of work that centers these texts. The same rationale exists for not rehashing the legacy and meanings of *The Cosby Show*.[11] Pivotal Black-centered narrative programming, however, is its focus. Moreover, documenting Black representation in this era must include public affairs programming and documentary due to their position in television lore as truth-teller and central harbinger of the realities of "living while Black."

The part begins with Devorah Heitner grappling with the 1970s public affairs program *Black Journal* and its explicit centering of Black audiences, issues, and visions. Through interviews, overviews, and analysis, Heitner gives credence to the ways in which producers attempted to reframe, recenter really, the mediated discussions of Black folks' lives worldwide. She revisits the show's impetus and situates that as a speaking back to mainstream news media's constant structuring of who and what Black people were and wanted without direct consultation or reference. She allows us to recognize the power media producers actually have and harks back to Coleman and Cavalcante's examination of producers' roles in *A Different World*.

In a similar way, TreaAndrea Russworm explores Bill Cosby's early children's television foray, *Fat Albert and the Cosby Kids*. While Heitner traverses the exterior Black world, Russworm focuses on the interiority of Blackness. She argues convincingly that the program serves as a renunciation of the 1960s and 1970s rhetoric of Black pathology and dearth, especially as associated with Black children. Employing the framework of psychoanalysis, she valuates Cosby's transforming notion of the interior life of Black children. In so doing, she provides a level of insight into Black audiences and the pervading cultural commentary of the time while also speaking back to the particularities of that commentary.

The twentieth-century-contesting texts of *Black Journal* and *Fat Albert and the Cosby Kids* on behalf of balancing out television offerings were not without their throwbacks, or at least ones perceived that way. In *"Gimme a Break* and the Limits of the Modern Mammy," Jennifer Fuller resuscitates and contextualizes the early 1980s controversial sitcom *Gimme a Break*. Fuller argues against the narratives of this six-season series that suggest it should be only considered in derisive terms. She makes a claim for thinking about the program in conversation with early expectations of Black audiences (although this was a program targeted at main-stream—all—audiences) and the subsequent competing discourses ushered in with the success of *The Cosby Show*. Her project is not to reclaim the mammy trope but to complicate its meaning across time and medium. This same type of complication, though for very different aims, is what connects the final chapter of part 2.

Chapter 8 focuses on three different programs and their relationship to New Orleans. Kim LeDuff looks at Spike Lee's documentaries about the aftermath of Hurricane Katrina: *When the Levees Broke* (2006) and *If God Is Willing and da Creek Don't Rise* (2010) as well as the fictional narrative about New Orleans, *Treme* (2010–). These texts, though all situated in the twenty-first century, bridge the discourses surrounding authenticity, reality, and culture—theoretical and lived concepts that exploded in the 1970s and 1980s and began to metamorphosize in the 2000s. LeDuff employs communication theory to examine audience perceptions of the Katrina tragedy—economically, politically, narratively, and visually. Rightly, she notes the repositioning of documentaries and reality-based narrative that now serve as historic artifacts. Inasmuch, interrogating/knowing/exploring what and how audiences interpret and process visual information becomes paramount. This final chapter also transitions us to contemporary examples of Black programming and their viability for target market Black.

Part 3, "New Jack Black," looks to the most recent programming offered on U.S. television but not necessarily in traditional ways. Chapters in this section address their televisual objects from a myriad of perspectives and embrace programming that reflects the significant changes occurring within the television industry itself and the narrative and aesthetic possibilities that become available with developing technologies and expanding needs for programming. In chapter 9, Racquel Gates asks readers/watchers/audiences to reconsider meaning of the "real" aspect of reality television. Reading disruption over the tradition of racist, gendered, and classist performance, Gates forces us to think again about the actions and narratives of key reality programs appearing at the beginning of a new century. She seeks to undo, or at least loosen, the stranglehold that respectability and uplift have had on critiques of Black representation in order to forward a more culturally centered, or at least considered, understanding of what and why Black folks watch.

Likewise, Nghana Lewis in chapter 10 asks that Black audiences and others understand the social and cultural implications and significance of particular narratives directed at Black audiences. In her examination of Mara Brock Akil's *Girlfriends* and *The Game*, Lewis selects and privileges one significant aspect of Black women's lives—their mental and physical health in the age of HIV/AIDS and hip hop. In this chapter, she demonstrates how Brock Akil's series deals with these mutually affecting and mushrooming phenomena unlike any other televisual narratives and why Black audiences support these works. Moreover, she allows for a consideration of how Black women's health can be prioritized in fictional narratives and, in many ways, why it *needs* to be recognized within these narratives.

Mark Cunningham's reading of *Noah's Arc* in chapter 11 treads similar ground but for a vastly different purpose. This program ushered in a way of seeing Black gay life beyond the fractured laughter of Fox's *In Living Color*'s "Men on Film" skit and the lyrically meditative documentaries of Marlon Riggs.[12] Cunningham walks us through the life of *Noah's Arc*, its viewership, and its institutional worth. His critical analysis sheds light on the ongoing negotiations audiences and programmers make in twenty-first-century television. Foregrounding Black gay men and their lives helps audiences recognize the continually changing landscape of representation and industry, both on- and off-screen.

And finally in chapter 12, Deborah Elizabeth Whaley takes on Aaron McGruder's *The Boondocks* in its move from comic strip to anime on the Cartoon Network's late-night programming, Adult Swim. She theorizes about the necessary navigation of Black cultural politics within the aesthetic and narrative boundaries of television. Rethinking the ideas of respectability that opened this unit with Racquel Gates's chapter and were addressed again in the work of Nghana Lewis, Whaley situates *The Boondocks* in dialogue with the most pressing social and political issues of the twenty-first century. A part of her discourse is to unpack the cultural commentary McGruder levels throughout the series. In her deconstruction of one episode, for example, Whaley makes connections to Mark Cunningham's chapter with her examination of the complexity of televised sexuality and race—complicating the ideas of masculinity, sexuality, Blackness, and representation.

Part 4, "Worldwide Blackness," takes up networks, specific programs, and larger sociopolitical issues in the reception and articulation of Blackness worldwide. Dual needs exist for a section like this in a book that mostly centers Blackness inside the U.S. television context: the first being connection. For example, I've been considering the similarities between how Nigeria's Nollywood and African American media producers distribute their product. "Taking it to the streets" appears as the mantra in both cases. But those ties, those connections that bind African Americans, Ghanaians, and Nigerians historically, culturally, ideologically, and now technologically, have received virtually no critical examination. Discerning connections of African diasporic peoples in a mediated context is important and one purpose for including this section. Secondly, globalization rhetoric merit attention in a book that centers Black television viewership. Black watchers are always-already implicated worldwide due to television's conveyance of information and possibilities of exchange, the whimsies of televisual flow, and the call and response of television formatting (think *Big Brother Africa*). Thus, *not* having a section on Black audiences across the globe would delimit the ways in which we can and should visualize televised Blackness.

Reighan Alexandra Gillam unpacks the connections between Blackness, television, and Brazil's culture of racial denial in chapter 13. She introduces readers to Brazil's cultural positioning of "racial democracy" and its encounter with Afro-Brazilians who deny its existence. In her chapter on TV da Gente, Gillam centralizes Blackness as the medium of exchange in that television network's effort to create programming for, about, and by Black folks. Similar to the efforts discussed in Heitner's *Black Journal* chapter, TV da Gente sought to make a significant dent in selling racial equality.

As opposed to forcing recognition of racial inequality, Nsenga Burton looks at South African soap operas from the viewpoint of a country that legislated its racism and is attempting to help rectify it through television. Specifically, in chapter 14, Burton discusses South African "soapies" as part and parcel of the country's transforming identity. She traces the development of South Africa's national television networks and their utilization of the soap opera as a vehicle for modeling societal and political change.

Chapter 15 of this text pursues ideas about televised global Blackness in an entirely different way. Timothy Havens connects the relationship between Blackness and other peoples of color through the New Zealand series *bro'Town*. Concluding the book, this chapter traverses ground that on first blush seems ill suited to a book on Black programming and Black audience preferences. However, his interrogation of the television industry's developing credo of "cultural journeys" and the ways that this particular series connects with Black sociopolitical stances makes it uniquely complementary and appropriate as we consider the future of watching while Black.

This anthology collectively paints a decidedly introspective picture of the programs Black audiences have watched and supported over the last few decades. The viability of these assessments can be accounted for in a myriad of contexts—thus serving several different audiences. The chapters critically engage historic and contemporary texts taken up by Black audiences. This project is intended to illuminate an important swath of an underexamined area, Black television viewership; to broaden common considerations of Black audiences; and to recognize the preferences of Black audiences and producers of Black-targeted programming.

I hope that by clarifying and complicating issues around Black viewership, *Watching While Black* will become a resource for scholars, students, and all interested in Black programming. I see the humanity of Black people in live action and on screens and think it not too much to ask for all others to see it too. Thus, if the works here allow the world to be more informed about, more engaged with, more considerate of the representation of Black folks' lives—and how that consideration must resonate in *their* lives—the labor to bring it forth will be well worth it.

NOTES

1. Meghan Sutherland recently released a small monograph on *The Flip Wilson Show* (Detroit: Wayne State University Press, 2008).

2. Jeanne Frazer, "TV Viewing Habits Are Changing," http://www.business2community .com/trends, June 13, 2011 (accessed July 8, 2011).

3. "Nielsen: Blacks Watching More Video on Mobile Phones than Other Groups," *Target Market News*, June 16, 2011, http://targetmarketnews.com/storyid06171101.htm (accessed July 8, 2011).

4. Kristal Brent Zook, *I See Black People: The Rise and Fall of African American-Owned Television and Radio* (New York: Nation Books, 2008), xvi.

5. Ralph Ellison, *Invisible Man* (New York: Random House, 1952), 3.

6. If interested in one rationale for why Black folks are visualized as absent from the Occupy Wall Street movement, see Greg Tate, "Top Ten Reasons Why So Few Blackfolk Appear Down to Occupy Wall Street," *Village Voice*, October 19, 2011.

7. Elana Levine, "Teaching the Politics of Television Culture in a 'Post-television' Era," *Cinema Journal* 50, no. 4 (2011): 180.

8. Aniko Bodroghkozy, "Teaching Television History: The Textbook," *Cinema Journal* 50, no. 4 (2011): 189.

9. See, for example, Robert J. Patterson, "'Woman Thou Art Bound': Critical Spectatorship, Black Masculine Gazes, and Gender Problems in Tyler Perry's Movies," *Black Camera* 3, no. 1 (Winter 2011); Timothy Lyle, "'Check With Yo' Man First; Check With Yo' Man': Tyler Perry Appropriates Drag as a Tool to Re-Circulate Patriarchal Ideology," *Callaloo* 34, no. 3 (Summer 2011); Robin R. Means Coleman, "Tyler Perry and Black Cyber-Activism in the 21st Century," *Black Communicator* 250 (October 25, 2007), http://hdl .handle.net/2027.42/60138; and Patrice A. Harris, "Black Masculinity in Tyler Perry's 'Diary of a Mad Black Woman'" (MA thesis, University of Central Missouri, 2010).

10. As found in Rupal Parekh, "How Tyler Perry's House of Hits Was Built," *Advertising Age*, May 18, 2009, 24, http://www.*ebscohost.com* (accessed March 19, 2011).

11. For information on scholarly engagement with these works, see Sut Jhally and Justin Lewis, *Enlightened Racism: The Cosby Show, Audiences, and the Myth of the American Dream* (Boulder, CO: Westview Press, 1992) and Melvin Patrick Ely, *The Adventures of Amos 'n' Andy: A Social History of an American Phenomenon* (Charlottesville: University Press of Virginia, 2001).

12. Keenan Ivory Wayans's *In Living Color* (Fox, 1990–1994) featured an ongoing skit called "Men on Film." Filmmaker and scholar Marlon Riggs produced several documentaries on the lives of Black gay men for PBS: *Tongues Untied* (1989) and *Black Is, Black Ain't* (1995)—both of which complicated viewers' understanding about Blackness, homosexuality, disease, and acceptance.

PART I

PRODUCING BLACKNESS

1   The Importance of *Roots*

ERIC PIERSON

In January 1977, I, along with over ninety million other Americans, watched at least one episode of the television miniseries *Roots: The Saga of an American Family.* Over the eight days of the broadcast, the audience grew, and debates regarding its impact filled media outlets. In the weeks and months after the show aired, the impact was measurable as many families sought out genealogists to research family histories and college campuses saw increased interest in African American Studies. Vernon Jordan, executive director of the National Urban League, commented, "*Roots* was the single most spectacular educational experience in race relations in America."[1]

Congratulations were in abundance as the network executives at ABC presented their involvement as a stroke of genius: they had the foresight to hire David L. Wolper to produce and the vision to challenge the conventions of program scheduling. Criticisms centered on the historical accuracy of the program were drowned out by the high praise in the popular press, while the academic press generated numerous research projects domestically and abroad. There was speculation that many of the rules that governed representation of the African American family in network television were about to change. "It looked like TV had entered a new era where Blacks and Black themes could receive full dramatic treatment and be accepted by a mass public. Black actors were particularly hopeful that new opportunities for major roles would open up to them."[2] There is little question that *Roots* impacted the landscape of television in 1977.

Did *Roots* fundamentally alter television, or did it fade and collapse under the weight of unrealized expectations? Did *Roots* challenge the status quo in network television programming, or did it in many ways conform to the traditional television narrative? Can a closer examination of the production process of the program allow a more critical reflection on the significance of the program? In retrospect, was it even realistic to believe that a single program could be the catalyst for real and lasting changes in network television programming? In 2007, *Roots* celebrated its thirtieth anniversary with a commemorative DVD collection. This release and celebration presents an excellent opportunity to revisit the importance of *Roots* for network television culture.

The relationship between television's African American audience and the institutions associated with television programming has always been tenuous. When African Americans complained about their lack of visibility on television programs in the 1950s, network executives responded with *Amos 'n' Andy*, a program based on demeaning caricatures and stereotypes. It took a strong campaign mounted by the NAACP to remove *Amos 'n' Andy* from the air, but the images that replaced it were only a mild improvement, as Blacks appeared almost exclusively in comedies or as secondary characters in dramas.[3]

Throughout the 1970s and 1980s, African Americans saw little change in their depiction on network television, despite a number of research studies indicating that African Americans watched network television programming at a higher rate than any other demographic. Yet the Nielsen rating system, the vehicle used by the networks to assess program popularity, did not institute a plan to accurately tabulate the viewing habits of the African American audience until 1991. This change came about after years of protest from Black communities believing that network programmers were not hearing their voices.

The novel *Roots* began its transition from page to screen during an extremely volatile period in network television programming. Changes in the Nielsen rating system and the concentration of network programming power into the hands of a few men had a profound impact on the programming landscape. In the early 1970s, Nielsen began to provide overnight ratings based on viewership in New York, Chicago, Los Angeles, and San Francisco. This change created a climate of ratings obsession, where programs were being judged not on their performance across an entire season but on a single evening. The switch also allowed the large urban markets to have a greater impact on programming than they normally would have prior to this focus on the overnights.

The new focus on overnights forced networks to cater to large pockets of urban consumers, consumers that advertisers saw as much younger and more affluent than the audience for programs such as *The Beverly Hillbillies*. Fred Silverman took over the programming division of CBS in 1970, and by the end of the 1971–1972 television season CBS had canceled *Mayberry RFD*, *Hee Haw*, *The Glen Campbell Goodtime Hour*, *The Jim Nabors Show*, and *The Beverly Hillbillies*, all of which had been top twenty-five programs during their tenure at CBS, but with narratives affiliated with rural America.

The manner in which Silverman could single-handedly change the face of CBS highlights the volatility of network programming during the time, as well as the power held by those who ran the networks. Silverman took a network that had built a solid foundation with programs that appealed to rural audiences and shifted it to one that catered to a more urban demographic with the addition of programs such as *The Mary Tyler Moore Show*, *All in the Family*, *Maude*, *The Jeffersons*, *Kojak*, and *M.A.S.H.* The ability of a single individual to control a network's programming schedule served as a crucial element in the production process for *Roots*.

Fred Silverman left CBS in 1975 to become the president of ABC Entertainment. In his short three-year tenure at ABC, Silverman would once again radically change the identity of a network. ABC would go from last place to first in the network ratings race under Silverman's leadership. He is also given credit for overseeing two of television's most successful miniseries, 1976's *Rich Man, Poor Man* and *Roots* in 1977. *Rich Man, Poor Man* was the second-highest-rated series of the 1975–1976 television season. Silverman made the decision to air *Rich Man, Poor Man* in weekly one-hour installments, beginning at the start of the February sweeps period and running for twelve weeks. He created a format that yielded a success, a level of success that makes the manner in which he chose to schedule the broadcast of *Roots* worthy of closer examination.

Roots first came to the attention of the American public in the form of pre-publication excerpts from Alex Haley's book and articles highlighting his research. The book excerpts appeared in the May and June 1974 issues of *Reader's Digest* along with a piece entitled "My Search for *Roots*." *American History Illustrated* also published an article entitled "In Search of the African" in its fall 1974 issue. Haley received funding from *Reader's Digest* to do much of his research. The book would take over a decade to reach the publisher, and during this period Haley often found himself short on funding. Thus he supplemented his income with appearances on college campuses. It took until August of 1976 before *Roots* was presented to a primarily African American audience through an article that appeared in *Ebony* magazine as part of an issue focusing on Africa. Upon the completion of the television series, *Ebony* dedicated the cover to Alex Haley and his return to Africa.

Prior to the *Roots* project, Haley was best known for his work in *Playboy* magazine. During the 1960s, he conducted interviews with some of the most influential cultural leaders of the period. Among those Haley interviewed were Muhammad Ali, Quincy Jones, Miles Davis, Martin Luther King Jr., and Malcolm X. The interviews with Malcolm X would serve as the basis for *The Autobiography of Malcolm X*, published just a few short weeks before Malcolm X was assassinated. Haley claims that the book was the product of over fifty hours of in-depth interviews he conducted with Malcolm during the 1960s.[4] The success of the book provided Haley with the resources to begin the project that would eventually become *Roots*.

While the story was still being written and marketed as a forthcoming book, the project had begun to garner the attention of both television and film producers. The first company to seriously consider turning *Roots* into a film project was Columbia Studios, which held an option on the story until 1972. It is unclear why Columbia let the option expire; however, Haley's penchant for missing deadlines may have been a contributing factor. It is worth noting that 20th Century Fox Studios had experienced box-office success in 1972 with the release of *Sounder*, a film that covered some of the same thematic elements as *Roots*.

Roots ultimately landed in the hands of producer David L. Wolper. Prior to *Roots*, Wolper was best known as a producer of documentary films and television programs with a historical focus. He first became aware of Haley's project through a conversation with actress Ruby Dee in 1972.[5] In 1974, shortly after receiving the rights to the novel, Wolper held a meeting with Barry Diller, head of ABC's Movies for Television division. Diller would take some convincing to undertake the project—one that initially appeared to have very little potential for success on television. However, through his enthusiasm and his experience in putting together historical documentaries, Wolper eventually obtained a commitment from ABC.

Wolper speaks about his attraction to the story: "Alex Haley's *Roots* was a magnificent story. Not a magnificent Black story, but the kind of universal story that I believed would appeal to people of all races."[6] His attitude regarding the "universal" nature of the story would be critical in the creative process. Yet the question remained, how was he going to take a story that focused on the history of a Black family punctuated with rape, torture, violence, brutality, and cruelty and put it on television?

The desire to universalize the narrative for television was made easier by the unfinished status of the book and the support of Alex Haley. As the story outlines for the television program were being written, Haley was still writing the novel. Incomplete material provided the screenwriters with significant latitude to shape the narrative. In fact, they were given great freedom to change characters and much more. Some of the characters that appeared in the drafts of the book were used in the television series only to find themselves eliminated from the final draft of the novel. Haley appeared to be either unwilling or unable to involve himself with the adaptation process. A notoriously slow writer, he had already missed several deadlines for the delivery of the novel to the publishers and had never had one of his stories adapted for television. Both of these circumstances would certainly have impacted his ability to actively participate in the adaptation.

Though Haley had some screenwriting experience, having co-written the screenplay for *Super Fly T.N.T.*, he declined to participate in the scripting process. It appears that he only made one substantive suggestion to the series: that someone with dark skin play the lead character of Kunta Kinte and that lighter-skinned actors could be used as the story progressed. Though Haley was very visible on the set during the filming, nothing indicates that he took an active role in shaping the overall narrative. His input was primarily with the actors playing members of his family. Because the novel was still a work in progress, the actors relied on Haley for insights into their characters.

The producers made it clear from the beginning that Roots was going to be designed to appeal to the widest audience possible. The program would have to find a way to appeal to both Black and white audiences without alienating either.

During the initial scriptwriting phase, a strategy was adopted to soften many of the harsh realities of the slave trade and slave life in America, a softening of history that received significant criticism when the series aired.[7]

The novel, however, contained many graphic depictions of the slave trade. One example is the description of the journey from Africa to America aboard the *Lord Ligonier*. These passages highlight the smell, taste, rage, and despair of the journey. Haley writes:

> For three days Kunta lay among them [dying men] in a twilight of pain, vomiting, and fever, his cries mingled with theirs. He was also among those racked with fits of deep, hoarse coughing. His neck was hot and swollen, and his entire body poured with sweat. He came out of his stupor only once, when he felt the whiskers of a rat brush along his hip; almost by reflex his free hand darted out and trapped the rat's head and foreparts in its grasp. He couldn't believe it. All the rage that had been bottled up in him for so long flooded down his arm and into his hand. Tighter and tighter he squeezed— the rat wriggling and squealing frantically—until he could feel the eyes popping out, the skull crunching under his thumb. Only then did the strength ebb from his fingers and the hand open to release the crushed remains.[8]

The television production avoided a vivid and graphic presentation of the Middle Passage to undercut the pain and suffering described in the novel.

While the historical accuracy of the Middle Passage could be toned down for broadcast, maintaining realism in other elements of the novel was seemingly worth fighting for. For example, the production company, under the guise of authenticity, fought very hard to include bare-breasted women in the narrative. The producers had to assure the Broadcast Standards Department at ABC that all the women cast would be of age and sport an acceptable breast size. They would also monitor how close the women would be to the camera. Even with this high level of breast-related scrutiny, the program encountered a problem during the postproduction process when it was discovered that one of the actresses used was in fact underage and should not have been allowed to appear topless.

One of the more sensitive issues that the producers had to address was how to present the number of sexual assaults that appear in the novel. Ron Taylor, a young Black man working in ABC's Broadcast Standards Department, was very vocal about his concerns regarding the script: "How do you depict the sexual ravagement of slave women by white men in a way that is historically accurate but not too viscerally overpowering for the viewing audience?"[9] Though the novel is sometimes graphic in describing the physical and emotional impact of the assault, the producers chose to move much of this action off-screen, and in the cases when presented, it is depicted in a sanitized fashion devoid of the level of fear and violence that readers of the novel would experience. Also removed for television audiences were scenes that focused on the emasculation of Black males as they found themselves unable to protect Black women. The producers did not have an outside consultant to help them deal with issues that may have been culturally sensitive; whatever input they received came from people on the periphery of the project like Ron Taylor.

While working to finish the script in the summer of 1975, ABC changed leadership; Fred Silverman was hired as vice president, putting him in charge of all prime-time programming. One of the first items on Silverman's agenda was to commit to broadcasting *Roots* in a twelve-hour format at a budget of six million dollars. Prior to his arrival, ABC had only committed to a six-hour broadcast. In coming to ABC and supporting the series, Silverman created a win/win situation for himself and his team. If the program failed, Silverman could connect the failure to the previous regime; if the program succeeded, Silverman would receive the credit. The firm commitment by ABC allowed the production to move ahead with several areas of production, the most important of which was casting.

The casting of *Roots* was a critical component in creating a universal, familiar, and more palatable narrative. "So in casting actors—here I'm talking about white actors—we decided we had to use white television stars to reach the white viewing audience (over 90% of the American viewing audience)."[10] This quote from producer Wolper reflects the pressure that the program was under to appeal to the widest possible audience. The producers wanted to populate the narrative with white actors who were very familiar to and well liked by television audiences. For example, Edward Asner was signed to play Captain Thomas Davies, the captain of the slave ship the *Lord Ligonier*, a role that was significantly expanded in the transition from novel to television. Asner was well known to white audiences for his portrayal of the lovable Lou Grant, a character that was so popular, it was transplanted from *The Mary Tyler Moore Show*, a half-hour comedy, to a successful drama, *Lou Grant*. By the time *Roots* aired, Asner had played Lou Grant for over 150 episodes and won four Emmys.

Ralph Waite was cast as the callous Mr. Slater, who had made numerous slave transport voyages and was seen as an expert in the area of the slave trade. Waite was well known to audiences as Pa Walton from the long-running program *The Waltons*. While Captain Davies was presented as morally conflicted by the idea of slavery, Mr. Slater had no such conflict. To Mr. Slater, slaves were cargo that had to be transported. They were not people. Waite was very convincing in his role, offering advice on the advantages and disadvantages of packing the slaves tightly together. He also encouraged the sexual assault of the slaves as a recreational activity. This narrative strategy of presenting a good and evil character as foils for one another was effective in removing the narrative focus from slavery as an institution and getting the audience to focus on the behaviors of individuals within the narrative.

The Mr. Slater/Captain Davies dynamic would be mirrored throughout the television program. The narrative consistently presented a character that wanted

Figure 1.1   *Roots*: Kizzy (Leslie Uggams) and Sam Bennett (Richard Roundtree). Courtesy of PhotoFest.

to treat the slaves well and then offered a contrasting character that treated them harshly. Lorne Greene and Robert Reed, well-known television fathers from *Bonanza* and *The Brady Bunch* respectively, were cast as brothers and benevolent slave owners. They treated their slaves well and would only treat them harshly when circumstances and economics dictated they do so. This is the case when Dr. William Reynolds, played by Reed, is forced to sell Kizzy (Leslie Uggams) and consent to the beating of Noah (Lawrence Hilton-Jacobs), the man she loves, to maintain order on the plantation. He explains that he has no other choice and goes into another room so as not to be part of their painful separation. The overseer characters are charged with administering the punishment, which is always done out of the sight of the master and allows the master to maintain his benevolent position.

The casting of Black actors created a difficult challenge for the producers due to the emotional nature of the roles they were asked to play. The script called for a number of actors to play subservient roles, and many found this challenge extremely difficult. For example, Redd Foxx, who would have been well known to television audiences, refused to accept the role of an old slave. He felt that the part would be demeaning and was very vocal in the press regarding his distaste for the project. Though the series featured numerous Black actors, a good number of prominent ones did not participate in the project for a variety of reasons.[11] Even those who accepted roles had trouble with the emotional demands of the script. Richard Roundtree, in his role as Sam Bennett, had a very difficult time playing the scene where he is forced to beg his master for forgiveness in the presence of Kizzy, his romantic interest. In fact, Roundtree at first refused to play the scene and only agreed to do it after some conversation with the producers. Assuming the emotional demands of the roles for the Black cast was paramount when it came to their casting—not only did they have to embody these emotionally charged moments, they had to be willing to do so.

"Roots was perceived from its inception to be a mass audience production, a drama that could be both entertaining and informative. It was not perceived to be a Black Journal, total Black history—a lesson for Blacks and white intellectuals."[12] Throughout the production, ongoing conversations focused on how the Black audience would respond to the narrative.[13] Roots did not need the Black audience to be successful, but it could also not risk offending them. As mentioned, one strategy that the production used was to soften the brutality of the novel. Another was to make the production less overtly political. A full examination of slavery as an institution and racism as part of the accepted social order would have made the narrative much more controversial and very difficult to sell to a television audience. The most effective strategy in the presentation of Roots was to construct and present the story as an immigrant narrative. "This powerful television epic effectively constructed the story of American slavery from the stage of emotional identifications and attachments to individual characters, family struggles and the realization of the American dream."[14]

In building the story around the quest for the American dream, Roots moved audiences by focusing on the gains in Blacks' quest and ignoring what was lost. The producers, however, took the immigrant narrative to extremes, and the end result was a narrative of complete and unapologetic assimilation. The traditional immigrant narrative would highlight the ways in which the immigrants adapt to their new country while maintaining important elements of their cultural identity. Those elements often include language, spiritual practices, fashion, and ties to family members who do not immigrate. The creative ways in which immigrants blend the new cultural elements with parts of their old cultures is a complex process, often spanning many generations. In Roots, no room existed for the blending of cultures. It told a story that required the family to completely give up their culture and assimilate into the dominant culture. The program cleverly presents this cultural transition as a positive one—one embraced by the participants. Over the course of the twelve-hour program, Africans from various countries give up their language, their spiritual practices, and all connections to Africa.

Alex Haley created a dense and detailed story from which the television series could pick and choose what elements it would highlight. One of the most effective tactics for creating a more universal narrative was to move the narrative as quickly as possible into a part of the world that would be familiar to the U.S. audience. The program spends only two of the broadcast twelve hours in Africa. Because the narrative spends so little time there, it does not leave the audience with a real sense of what Kunta's life was before his abduction. The narrative also never returns to Africa. Without this real sense of home provided to the audience, it minimizes the understanding of what was lost. In the Africa portion of the narrative, time is condensed. We view Kunta's birth and then are fast-forwarded to him as a young man. We see the village as a place of community and order but get little information about the day-to day life of the young Kunta Kinte (LeVar Burton).

The audience is left with a limited sense of the spiritual dynamic of the village as well. These villagers practice a monotheistic concept of God, and they mention Allah often in their conversations. One of the film's most powerful spiritual motifs occurs when the newborn infant is presented to the heavens as a sign of submission and worship. This motif becomes important, as it is one of the few connections to Africa that remain once the story moves to America. With so little

Figure 1.2   *Roots*: "Behold." Frame grab.

of the story rooted in Africa, the transitions that the characters must make in coming to America seem simple and natural.

Over the next ten hours of narrative, the Kinte/Haley family gives up their native language, with the exception of a couple of phrases. The worship of Allah will be replaced with a belief in a Christian god. Their spiritual ritual that calls for the family to "behold the only thing greater than thyself" is no longer practiced.[15] In some cases, important family spiritual traditions become the object of ridicule and mockery, as in the case of Toby/Kunta's belief that if you take dirt from the footprint of someone who leaves, the person will return.

When the television series reaches its conclusion, the family is fully assimilated into the culture. They are Christian worshipping, English speaking, law abiding landowners. Chicken George (Ben Vereen), the family patriarch, is symbolic of all the benefits of being assimilated into the culture. He is biracial, so he is no longer fully African. He has used his education to earn enough money to buy land and his own freedom. As the family begins their new life, they have acquired white friends. The family serves as an exemplar of what one should aspire to. Roots demonstrates that when attempting to explore issues of racial conflict, the process of assimilation becomes the overly utilized narrative trope of television and film.

Figure 1.3   The assimilated immigrant African American family. Frame grab.

Throughout the production process of *Roots*, the network was concerned that the program could, despite their best efforts, end up a very expensive ratings disaster. Audience size would be the ultimate arbiter of the program's success. Although ABC had invested a great deal of money in the production of the program, its promotion and scheduling certainly raise questions regarding the network's faith in it. Stan Margulies, one of the producers of *Roots*, recalls telling a trepid ABC, "What have you got to lose? You're number three. If *Roots* fails, you'll still be number three."[16] The network made a series of decisions that, given the standards and conventional practices of program promotion at the time, would be confusing.

For example, ABC had been very successful in using the miniseries format it established for *Rich Man, Poor Man*. Conventional wisdom dictated that it broadcast the series during a sweeps period and extend the program over as many weeks as possible. *Rich Man, Poor Man* aired beginning February 2, 1976, with the last episode airing on March 15. This scheduling strategy made it possible for ABC to use the program as a ratings booster for over a month, dominating the February 1976 sweeps period and providing the network with a blueprint for success. The *Rich Man, Poor Man* strategy allowed the program to become the number-two-rated television series of the season. Yet though *Roots* and *Rich Man, Poor Man* were similar in genre, the network could not have handled them more differently.

Silverman made the decision to air *Roots* over eight consecutive nights, beginning January 23 and concluding on January 30. The scheduling reflected a serious concern about the likely success of the program; if Roots failed to attract a large audience, the impact on other network programs would be minimal. This scheduling had an adverse impact on potential advertisers, forcing the network to sell advertising at a discount. The unusual scheduling coupled with the difficulty in attaching sponsors led many to see the January programming as a sign that the network wanted to dump the show and move on. Once the show aired, the Nielsen ratings were stronger than the network or the sponsors expected. It began with strong ratings and only got stronger as it moved to its conclusion, garnering a 71 share for the final episode. While Silverman presented the scheduling as a stroke of genius, the network lost significant revenue because it had been forced to sell spots at a reduced rate to entice participation. If *Roots* had been scheduled over eight weeks instead of eight days, the network would have experienced significantly higher advertising revenue and overall ratings impact.[17]

Beyond the ratings success, the program received critical acclaim. *Roots* was nominated for thirty-nine Emmy awards, winning in several categories. Among the winners of note were David L. Wolper and Stan Margulies as producers, Ernest Kinoy and William Blinn for writing, and Louis Gossett Jr. for his portrayal of Fiddler. The program would have collected more Emmys if it had not been competing with itself in several categories—for example, in the category of

Outstanding Lead Actor, four of the five nominees were from the *Roots* cast. During the Emmy broadcast, *Roots* was celebrated as the cast and many of the creative team took the stage to a standing ovation from their peers. Wolper also received a Peabody Award for his role as producer. There was hope that the momentum generated was going to alter the network television landscape. A dramatic program featuring Blacks in lead roles, encased in a narrative that highlighted their experiences, had proven an unparalleled success. Network television would now eagerly begin to produce similar programs. The success of *Roots* left many thinking that change was imminent and new ways of presenting Blacks on network television were on the horizon. Richard E. Wiley, chairman of the FCC, commented, "The ratings of *Roots* were so phenomenal that they may require a fundamental reevaluation to the traditional TV programming and scheduling concepts."[18]

However, the exuberance of the *Roots* broadcast was quickly tempered by the realities of the period and the industry. Gilbert Moses, who received an Emmy nomination for his direction of part six of the series, commented on his post-*Roots* experience: "So far nothing has happened to me. One would think it would open doors, but I'm not so sure that it has. It's easier now to be considered for a project when somebody knows what I've done. But in terms of my being considered a director and not just another Black director, there is no change. There is still the same problem."[19] In the months that followed, all three networks added Black-themed dramas to their schedules. However, these programs were all quickly canceled, and the universal reason given was low ratings.

In the end, the expectation that one program could somehow single-handedly transform decades of network television practices was misplaced. Because positive or even progressive presentations of the Black experience are so infrequent, there is often the desire to see these presentations address myriad problems and concerns. *Roots* reminded network programmers that America was willing to watch Blacks in something other than comedy programs. Black Americans were reminded of the struggles of generations past and could feel a sense of pride in the accomplishments of their own families.

For eight days in January the strength and resilience of the Black family was on display and celebrated. During this time of celebration, universities around the country used this moment to either implement or expand Black Studies programs. The program forced many in America to engage a very difficult period of American history. So, though the direct impact on television programming did not occur, the impact on American culture was significant. The scope and force of that impact would not have been the same without the reach and influence of television. Television took the power of Haley's novel and multiplied its reach exponentially, bringing it to millions more than those who would access the novel.

Some thirty years after the broadcast of *Roots*, it is disappointing that we continue to have many of the same conversations regarding images of the Black family in network television programming. Blacks keep calling for more positive or at least complex presentations of their experiences. Yet when it comes to successful network programs, Blacks continue to appear primarily in comedies—even with expanded channel offerings provided by cable and satellite. Images of Black America continue to be dominated by those created and distributed via network television. Though we can point to individual characters within the framework of selective programs, the Black family as a loving, supportive unit has never been the focus of a network drama. In sixty years of network television programming, *Roots* remains the standard of excellence for television's dramas focused on the Black experience. Because of this glaring omission in the lexicon of network television programming, *Roots* will continue to be an important television milestone as well as a reminder of the continuing void in network television offerings.

NOTES

1. David L. Wolper with Quincy Troupe, *The Inside Story of TV's "Roots"* (New York: Warner Books, 1978), 251.

2. Kathryn Montgomery, *Target: Prime Time* (New York: Oxford University Press, 1989), 126.

3. The program *I Spy* (1965–1968) is worthy of mention as a program that challenged stereotypes by having Bill Cosby and Robert Culp share equal billing.

4. Alex Haley, "Alex Haley Remembers," in *Malcolm X as They Knew Him*, ed. David Gallen (New York: Ballantine Books, 1995), 266.

5. Wolper with Troupe, *Inside Story*, 34.

6. David L. Wolper with David Fisher, *Producer: A Memoir* (New York: Scribner, 2003), 229.

7. Significant debate surrounded the historical accuracy of *Roots*, both as a novel and a television program. These debates were conducted in academic and popular culture settings. An interview with historian Arvarh Strickland in *The Christian Century*, March 2, 1977, offers an assessment of the value of *Roots* as both an academic and popular text.

8. Alex Haley, *Roots* (Garden City, NY: Doubleday, 1976), 182.

9. Wolper with Troupe, *Inside Story*, 73.

10. Ibid., 56.

11. Notable Black actor Sidney Poitier refused to participate in the project. James Earl Jones and Billy Dee Williams were also offered roles in the program but declined them.

12. Wolper with Troupe, *Inside Story*, 57. [Editor's note: For more insight into the significance of that reference, see Devorah Heitner's chapter on *Black Journal* in this volume.]

13. No evidence suggests that the production company or the network solicited input from the Black community. There was no organized protest from the Black community. However, the Black community would be organized and influential in the production process of *Beulah Land*, a miniseries on NBC set during the Civil War. Kathryn Montgomery's *Target: Prime Time* provides a detailed presentation of the Black community's influence during the production of *Beulah Land*.

14. Wolper with Troupe, *Inside Story*, 78.

15. The presentation of the newborn to the heavens is one of the moments that link the generations. When it disappears from the narrative, it reflects a significant change in the family dynamic.

16. Todd Gitlin, *Inside Prime Time* (New York: Pantheon Books, 1983), 162.

17. *Rich Man, Poor Man* was allowed to have influence over a large potion of the prime-time schedule. ABC was able to charge increasing advertising rates based on its performance.

18. Wolper with Troupe, *Inside Story*, 253.

19. Ibid., 164.

2 Two *Different Worlds*

TELEVISION AS A PRODUCER'S MEDIUM

ROBIN R. MEANS COLEMAN

ANDRE M. CAVALCANTE

> *But to the extent that freedom exists and values are*
> *expressed, it is the producer who is the catalyst, the*
> *one responsible for the decisions . . . As facilitator,*
> *the producer is striving for the highest number of*
> *those moments when one "flirts with the edges of art"*
> *while addressing the nobler sentiments of humanity.*
> —Horace Newcomb and Robert S. Alley (1983)

Although discourses regarding 1980s representations of Blackness on television heavily focus on *The Cosby Show*, its NBC spin-off series, *A Different World*, depicting student life at a historically Black college, was equally groundbreaking and deserving of critical attention. Looking to transfer the appeal and audience share of *The Cosby Show* to *A Different World*, the spin-off show's first season centered on the life of *The Cosby Show*'s star Denise Huxtable (Lisa Bonet) at Hillman College. *A Different World*'s story provides an illuminating case study of the role and power of television producers, highlighting their influence over a show's narrative and cast ethos. One of the most compelling aspects of *A Different World* is how audiences were presented with two distinctly disparate versions of the series, the first under the direction of Anne Beatts, a white woman, and the second under the guidance of Debbie Allen, a Black woman. Each woman had her own distinct vision for and approach to the show informed by subjective tastes, personal history, cultural literacy, and experience in the entertainment industry. As Horace Newcomb and Robert Alley offer, television is a producer's medium in that the producer takes on the multiple responsibilities of supervision of cast and crew, dictating the creative direction, working within budgetary constraints, and engaging in negotiations between the business (the network) and creative (the writers) ends of a show. All of this takes place while the producer may have the additional goal of offering up innovative shows—content that may press genre boundaries while still working within generic conventions. Considering the complexities of the medium, Newcomb and Alley explain, "the problems faced by these individuals assume overwhelming proportions," and in such a dynamic, unstable, and demanding industry "the composure of the most sanguine creative talent could be shattered."[1]

A "Mundane" World: Anne Beatts's Vision

One may question the decision to grant Anne Beatts the producer role for *A Different World*. Yet when understood in the context of the television industry, the choice makes more sense. Beatts was well known to NBC executives. In 1973, she was a writer for the *Lemmings* (a.k.a. *National Lampoon's Lemmings*), an Off-Broadway musical comedy revue featuring soon-to-be *Saturday Night Live* (NBC) stars John Belushi, Chevy Chase, and Christopher Guest. In 1975, she joined the *Saturday Night Live* production crew as a writer and appeared (often uncredited) as an extra cast member in skits alongside Belushi and Chase. Beatts's tenure at *Saturday Night Live* lasted for five years, ending in 1980. In 1982, the writer-turned-producer jumped to the CBS network, which picked up her situation comedy creation *Square Pegs*, a series inspired by her own high school and early teen experiences and credited with launching the career of Sarah Jessica Parker (*Sex and the City*). *Square Pegs* focused on a group of "outsider" freshmen—hence the "square peg in a round hole" metaphor—at the fictional Weemawee High School. In spite of a guest appearance by the New Wave band Devo, the series performed poorly in the ratings, and after just one season *Square Pegs* was canceled.

The production of sitcoms is, at best, a venture fraught with risk due to the possibility of losing large sums of money and other capital. Because the stakes are high, as David Marc explains, "throughout sitcom history, production has been kept under strict corporate patronage. There is no such thing as a 'small-time' sitcom; a show either makes it coast-to-coast or disappears into the effluvia."[2] This fact makes networks and industry professionals often rely on what Brett Mills identifies as a "family tree" of sitcom production: "the continued use of the same writers, producers, actors, and production companies, in both Britain and America, demonstrates the networks' reliance on trusted bankers."[3] Thus, since Beatts was already known for her (albeit failed) work with *Square Pegs*, she was a member of the "family tree" of television production and remained a go-to producer for industry executives.

The first season of *A Different World* in 1987, governed by the production leadership of Beatts, revolved around jokes stemming from misunderstandings, pranks and pratfalls, miscued romances, competition, and jealousy. Scathing reviews were heaped upon the show, citing it as "boring,"[4] "juvenile and unrealistic,"[5] and "sitcomville, a place we've visited many times before."[6] According to actress Jasmine Guy, who starred in the series as the entitled southern belle Whitley Gilbert, bringing in Beatts resulted in *A Different World* becoming a

"*Square Pegs* junior."[7] Elvis Mitchell in a *Rolling Stone* feature argued, "Beatts's sensibility doesn't fit this show . . . The students at the severely underpopulated Hillman College look more like kids at some San Fernando Valley junior college."[8] Though the setting of *A Different World* was a college, and a predominately Black one at that, students were rarely seen in the classroom. Education was an absent topic of discussion, and the historically Black college setting was incidental to the overall plot.

While the show had more Black faces than many series on network television before it or since, the backdrop that was Hillman College was presented as racially contrived. Denise, Lisa Bonet's character, roomed with and befriended Maggie, a white transfer student played by Marisa Tomei. The clusters of students seen gathering in the school's cafeteria were almost always presented in equal ratios of white to Black students, and as such, *A Different World* presented a harmonious cultural collective that was not often seen outside of the television imaginary.[9] Absent from the visual landscape of the show were those fiercely independent, stylized selves that pepper most college campuses. Bohemians, grunges, hippies, punks, Greek-letter organization members, fashionistas, or those clothed in Afro-centric styles simply did not exist. Also absent were a Black diasporic informed curriculum and an attention to racism and the American history that necessitated the advent of Black colleges and universities in the first place. All were imperceptible, further illustrating a deficit in the show's authenticity.

David Ehrenstein lamented the first season's inattention to the racial contexts it was to represent, writing, "The show's action invariably revolves around such heart-stopping issues as unfinished term papers and borrowed money—at a time when black students at 'liberal' schools like the universities of Michigan and Massachusetts are subjected to racial harassment."[10] Indeed, *A Different World* emerged when news headlines were rife with incidents of campus racism, and yet it failed to mirror and comment on the lived experiences of Black college students in the United States. According to a lengthy 1989 *New York Times* report on the state of race relations at America's colleges and universities, "more than 250 colleges [had] reported racial incidents, some of them violent. At the University of Massachusetts at Amherst, up to 3,000 white students chased 20 black students and beat one nearly to death following a 1986 World Series game. [At the University of Mississippi in 1988] arsonists burned down what was to be a fraternity house for blacks . . . And at the University of Wisconsin at Madison, white members of the Zeta Beta Tau fraternity wore Afro wigs and blackface and held a mock slave auction."[11]

Beatts, nevertheless, seemed indifferent to, or maybe unaware of, the absence of a full and complicated representation of Blackness on the series, even with *The Cosby Show* as its benchmark. Narratively, conspicuously missing from *A Different World*, though particularly present on *The Cosby Show*, was the long and storied tradition of Black humor. Hallmarks like call and response, humor born of pain, and race-related comedy were nowhere to be found. The absence was purposeful. When comedian Sinbad, a former guest star on *The Cosby Show*, was added to the *A Different World* cast in 1987, while concurrently hosting the iconic Black talent competition *Showtime at the Apollo*, Beatts revealed her "specific conceit" about her inattention to Blackness.[12] She admonished, "Sinbad can't do his act on my program."[13]

Certainly, there are countless people involved in the creation of a television program, and many of them will accept the credit of a series' success. When a series fails, the responsibility often lands squarely on the shoulders of its producer. Compared to British industry practice, where creative control lies more in the hands of the writers, in America "producers usually create and control programmes and employ writers to write them, retaining the artistic control . . . The American sitcom writer is a much smaller part of a much larger process, whose overall control is in the hands of the producer."[14] In the end, Beatts as producer presented, plainly, a bad sitcom because little creative investment was made in its writing. For example, in the episode "Porky de Bergerac," timeworn themes of personal embarrassment, impression management, and quickly resolved, banal interpersonal conflict characterized the story. Here, dorm monitor Jaleesa (Dawnn Lewis) enacts a punishment for littering that includes wearing a pig nose for one day. Of course, the first victim of this policy becomes Denise, and her punishment falls on the same day as her date with a new beau, Michael (Reggie Johnson). Denise begs Jaleesa to excuse her from wearing the nose. But Jaleesa refuses to capitulate, saying, "Huxtable, you are not living in your parents' house anymore, so for once you're going to have to deal with your trash. Now grow up and put on the pig nose!" The couple's first date, to a wine and cheese party, concludes, as does the episode, with Michael happily joining Denise in wearing the pig nose.

Though the show was prominently branded with the Bill Cosby stamp, Cosby himself adopted a strict hands-off approach to *A Different World* by staying completely away from the series' West Coast production studio. However, a first-season crossover appearance by Phylicia Rashad as Clair Huxtable gave the Cosby Show actress an opportunity to take careful inventory of *A Different World*, which had publicly drawn the scorn of critics. Rashad flew back to New York from her taping and immediately reported to Cosby that *A Different World* was far from quality and that the cast was disaffected and simply waiting for the series to be canceled. Rashad urged Cosby, as the creator and executive producer, to care about what was happening internally with the series because "his name was on it."[15] Consequently, Beatts's contract was not renewed at the end of the first season.

Debbie Allen's *A Different World*: A Road Less Traveled

Season two brought with it a new *A Different World* producer in Rashad's sister, Debbie Allen, a Black woman, a talented artist, and an alumna of a historically Black university. Bill Cosby asked Allen to take the reins in 1988, as she recalls: "I'd been told to get my broom and go clean house."[16] Operating from *within* Blackness, Allen's show was worlds apart from Beatts's. She gave the series a much-needed insider perspective on Black college life that spoke intimately to both Black and non-Black audiences.

Allen's professional accomplishments at the time she took over *A Different World* were already lengthy; she had appeared in over a dozen television series and half a dozen films. Prior to joining *A Different World*, Allen had starred in and co-produced the hit NBC television series *Fame*. An accomplished dancer, she also choreographed and performed in two dozen televised specials including the Tonys, Golden Globes, and Academy Awards. Her artistic sensibility and acute expertise brought immediate, recognizable change to *A Different World*. Allen summarized her changes bluntly: "The show was too White. I said 'Come on, honey.' This is a college where you go to the cafeteria and they have fried apples and grits for breakfast."[17] The question becomes, then, how was Allen able to create new counternarratives that focused on and cast Blackness as sociopolitically provocative and relevant given the historically poor treatments of African Americans in media, the confines of the situation comedy genre, and the strictures of commercial network television?

Venita Kelley, as part of her 1995 dissertation "Revealing the Universal Through the Specific in *A Different World*," conducted interviews with Allen's crew members. Kelley reports that one of the first things Allen did when bringing her unique direction to *A Different World* was to create a series "bible," an expansive document that would ultimately serve as the overarching treatment for the show. Kelley summarizes the bible's content:

> Hillman was established in 1880. Its motto is "Deus Nondum Te Confecit-Hillman 1881," "God is not through with you yet." The college, established first in a residential home, had been a station in the Underground Railroad. Josiah Hillman, an abolitionist, was its founder . . . Women outnumber men three to one . . . Besides the regular undergraduate curriculum, Hillman has a five year MBA program, a pre-med, a pre-law, and (a) criminal justice program(s). It also provides a chemistry and engineering degree and has lab facilities to support their study. Hillman has its own Medical school and Law school . . . Hillman graduates as many PhD's as most top ranking Ivy League schools . . . The "top" fraternity on campus is Kappa Lambda Nu (fictitious), and the "top" sorority is Alpha Delta Rho, Inc. (also fictitious, but containing one name each from three national African American women's sororities) . . . Hillman's current president is the first woman president (as Dr. Johnetta Cole was of Spelman College).[18]

A 1971 cum laude graduate of (the historically Black) Howard University in Washington, D.C., Allen appreciated firsthand the experience of student life and activity at historically Black colleges and universities (HBCUs). The *A Different*

World bible marked Allen's overt strategy to refocus the series in an informed, substantive way toward the Black college experience.

Although each HBCU has its own distinct history, they all share a common background, as the Civil War, Reconstruction, and laws like "Separate but Equal" mandating racial segregation necessitated their formation. According to G. M. Sawyer, during their creation in post–Civil War America, Black colleges were understood by many Whites as serving a particular social function: harboring Blacks who would otherwise become "community liabilities."[19] With little to no help coming from state and federal institutions, many HBCUs originated in Black churches or private homes during Reconstruction and were predominantly a local, community effort, as dedicated members of the clergy and other community members served as the major organizing forces behind the development of Black education.[20] Established by Congress in 1865, the Freedman's Bureau, founded to protect and aid former slaves, cooperated with church organizations and missionary societies to help establish Black educational facilities throughout the United States. The second Morrill Land-Grant Act of 1890, which gave assistance to colleges, mandated that states spending federal funds funnel money to historically Black colleges and universities or allow unrestricted access to schools for both Black and white students. In the absence of fervent state support, philanthropy became an important source of funding for Black colleges; for example, the George Peabody Fund (1867), the Julius Rosenwald Fund (1917), the United Negro College Fund (1944), and countless contributions and gifts by alumni all greatly benefited Black education. In fact, in the season two episode "A Stepping Stone," Allen acknowledges this tradition when she introduces the character Mrs. Pruitt, one of Hillman's eldest alumni and most wealthy contributors, who pays a visit to the campus.

As innovative as Allen was with retooling the series, she, much like Beatts before her with *Square Pegs*, had her own textual template in addition to her real-life experiences to draw upon. In 1988, filmmaker Spike Lee released his second feature film—*School Daze*, a film reflecting his own experiences while attending Morehouse College. Focusing on events surrounding the fictional Mission College's homecoming weekend, the film, a music-infused drama, presented several controversial plot points, including the tension between those invested in Black nationalism versus those who explicitly reject it, the call for divestiture from the apartheid-segregated South Africa, the function and occasional bad behaviors of Black Greek-lettered organizations, strife-ridden "town and gown" relationships, and intraracial conflicts such as colorism. More, a great many of *A Different World*'s cast had first been featured in *School Daze*. Core *A Different World* cast members Jasmine Guy, Kadeem Hardison, and Darryl M. Bell had all starred in the film. *School Daze* also contributed recurring performers and guest stars to the television series, including Tisha Campbell, Art Evans, Dominic Hoffman, and Roger Guenveur Smith. The near-simultaneous mainstream presentations of *School Daze* and *A Different World*, with their overlapping casts, forever linked the two offerings. As one reporter wrote, *"A Different World* played good cop to *School Daze's* bad cop. And, between the two, the previously Southern regional phenomenon of the HBCU . . . went nationwide."[21]

A Different World soon became a complex and dynamic show reflecting a diverse set of characters and a broad range of often competing viewpoints concerning pressing social issues and struggles. Commenting on this trend, Emily Nussbaum explains that "it had forged something more groundbreaking than 'Cosby' ever had: a diversity of black perspectives . . . 'A Different World' had no one moral perspective, no character hogging the role model mike."[22]

Nevertheless, almost immediately Allen's vision came into conflict with lingering racial antagonisms, as well as corporate strictures, when she pitched to the network an interracial romance storyline for Marisa Tomei's leading character, Maggie, Denise's white roommate:

> I thought that [Maggie] and Dwayne would be really good friends and we could do an episode where she eventually goes home with him for Thanksgiving, and it would be 'Guess Who's Coming to Dinner.' And then his mama would not like him coming home with a little white girl. I thought this would be great to show the reverse racism and those kinds of challenges. Well, they [the execs] didn't like that idea. I said, "How can you have one white character in an all-black dorm and you don't deal with that?"[23]

Not only was the story rejected, the network's response serves as an important reminder of how media corporations place preeminence on commercial interests. Fearful of a miscegenation-centered story, network executives removed Tomei from the series entirely,[24] a decision that left the actress in tears.[25]

By the show's second season, Allen also lost the show's star, Lisa Bonet. Bonet's well-publicized personality conflict with Cosby, her pregnancy with husband-rocker Lenny Kravitz (somewhat problematic considering she portrayed a teen on TV), and her erotically charged appearance in the 1987 film *Angel Heart* were all cited as reasons for placing the series in jeopardy. Allen reimagined and regained the esoteric nature and beauty lost with Bonet's departure by adding actress Cree Summer as the biracial, earthy, bohemian Freddie Brooks, hailing from New Mexico. Allen also recuperated the academic excellence and enthusiasm represented in Tomei's Maggie by adding Charnele Brown as the level-headed and diligent premed student Kimberly Reese. Additionally and notably, in season four Allen was finally able to present her theme of interracial dating by reversing the couple's race (i.e., white male/Black female) through Kimberly's brief relationship with Matthew (Andrew Lowery), a white student from Emory University. Allen kept several original cast members: the self-involved southern belle Whitley Gilbert (Jasmine Guy), the studious and suave Dwayne Wayne (Kadeem Hardison), the relentless ladies' man Ron Johnson Jr. (Darryl Bell), and the nontraditional-aged student/divorcée Jaleesa Vinson (Dawnn Lewis). With her cast in place, Allen led the series into television history. Her *A Different World* racked up accolades in the form of over sixteen industry award nominations as well as an Emmy Award, a People's Choice Award, and numerous NAACP Image Awards in a variety of categories.

An African American Auteur: Expressing a World from Within Blackness

A Different World, under Allen, became a show that displayed its leader's worldview, timbre, and style. Allen participated in script development, oversaw postproduction, managed the technical crew, and even held veto power over the set designs. She became what David Marc would call a *moral interlocutor*,[26] inserting her vision regarding class, love, race, and historical lessons and messages into the show's narrative.

For Allen, *A Different World* was about more than offering up a unique experience for viewers, it was about inviting her audience to understand and experience Blackness. She exploited the knowledge function[27] of television by presenting forms of cultural knowledge and political struggle in new ways, accessible to both Black and non-Black audiences. Allen's approach to the series was marked by a Reithian "edutainment" quality, presenting situational comedy infused with relevant social topicality and political commentary. For example, the series taught its audience about things like the connection between the linguistic jousting of "playing the dozens" and how "lower quality" slaves were described as they were auctioned off in lots of one dozen, or the link between African boot dancing and African American fraternal stepping.

As a polysemic text, *A Different World* invited its audience members to decode and appreciate its narrative and imagery on multiple levels. The program was able to strike a difficult yet successful balance between displaying material encoded primarily for African Americans and content identifiable and palatable to a larger audience. On other occasions, culturally specific jokes, icons, art, dress, style, and the like were left undefined for the unschooled. In short, the series resisted the impulse to be the "Blackness tour guide." Instead, what it often did focus upon was a variety of social, economic, romantic, and educational topics that were complicated by the effects of race relations and racism—effects that were glaringly absent from *The Cosby Show* narratives and from most situation comedies before and since. Given the televisual medium within which she worked, Allen's contributions, in a purist sense, were not on par with the auteurist contributions most noted in film and literature. Working within the extreme confines of commercial network television and the genre of situation comedy severely limited the range and intensity of Allen's innovation.

Nevertheless, Allen was able to revive the show and breathe new life into it. *USA Today* TV critic Monica Collins, writing in 1989, was one of the first to note a shift in the series toward quality and relevant topics. As evidence, Collins points toward the episode "No Means No," which focused on date rape, as proof that consciousness raising around political and social issues was just the "new attitude of responsibility" the series needed. Allen's timely turn toward relevancy and topicality regularly received a nod from critics. Richard Stevenson wrote: "Social issues are increasingly good material for dramatic and comedic situations as well as a positive use of television's immense influence ... The NBC series 'A Different World' used a continuing plot line this season exploring whether the character Kim should accept a scholarship from a company that does business in South Africa."[28]

Toward this end, Allen surrounded herself with other talented African Americans, thereby seriously challenging assertions that locating outstanding people of color to work behind the camera was a difficult prospect.[29] For example, Susan Fales, a Black woman, climbed the ladder on *A Different World* from writer to story editor, co-producer, supervising producer, and finally co-executive producer, and all by age twenty-seven.[30] Allen's controlling position in production, as well as Fales's, was notable given the rarity of its occurrence. According to Darnell Hunt, the first African American "showrunner" was Bill Cosby in 1969 for *The Bill Cosby Show*.[31] Between 1969 and 1990, Black control rose only minimally, remaining between zero and 5 percent, with the most modest of gains seen when upstart networks UPN and WB arrived on the scene in the 1990s with a lineup of Black situation comedies.

The widely hailed qualitative and quantitative improvements that *A Different World* experienced upon the departure of Beatts and with the arrival of Allen bear witness to the fact that a Black image-maker is a significant factor in producing quality Black imagery. However, it is the introduction of an image-maker from within Blackness that prompts a new set of questions regarding whether cultural proximity and even ideological allegiance are sufficient to overcome the hegemonic power of the split image—a resulting constant diet of mainstream media products that present and reward presentations of Blackness as Other.

Two Introductions, Two Truly Different Shows

By comparing the thematic elements within each producer's opening credits, their two distinct visions become legible. Accompanied by a song that sets the mood for the program, opening credits and the introductory montage function as a symbolic first impression and typically introduce the characters, setting, and context of the show. The first season's opening montage of Beatts's *A Different World* set the tone of what audiences were to expect, and what they were not going to get, from the show. As the show's title appears against the background of a colorful graffitied wall, the sound of a harmonica initiates the soulful theme song written by Bill Cosby, Stu Gardner, and Dawnn Lewis, stylized by Phoebe Snow's vocal performance: "I know my parents love me, stand behind me come

Figure 2.1   *A Different World* cast under Anne Beatts. Courtesy of PhotoFest.

what may. I know now that I'm ready, because I finally heard them say: It's a different world from where you come from. Here's a chance to make it, if we focus on our goals. If you dish it we can take it, just remember you've been told: It's a different world from where you come from. It's a different world from where you come from."

A Different World's opening depicted Denise, along with co-stars Dwayne Wayne, Jaleesa Vinson, and Maggie Lauten, in long shots, joyfully romping through the streets of a small town. The opening credits sequence reveals neither omission nor distortion. Rather, the opening's narrative simply depicts "a day in the life" of the characters as they traverse a cultural geography that rejects any clear identity. The opening montage, by indicating that the stars of the show are African American by simply showing them, demonstrates a failure to situate the characters within the unique cultural tropes of Blackness.

To its credit, the very first scene shows Jaleesa jumping double-dutch rope with two young Black girls. In presenting double-dutch as the signifier, Beatts's *A Different World* resists the impulse to do as so many Black situation comedies have done—to signal Blackness through, for example, deficiency and / or poverty as marked through junkyards (*Sanford and Son*) or urban decay (*Diff'rent Strokes, Fresh Prince of Bel-Air, Good Times*). In addition to double-dutch, the show's theme song, which resembles a bluesy, soulful melody, offers a nod to the African American musical tradition. However, beyond these moments, the students are culturally ambiguous. This led David Ehrenstein to conclude about the media offerings of this period that "White notions of Black life provide the ruling assumption that their comedy relies on."[32] Such neutrality may be for some an inroad to equalizing Black representations and garnering a respectful treatment that may be little different from, say, the opening credits of a *Square Pegs*. Consequently, Beatts's decision to include a scene where the cast washes a car becomes even more meaningful in that her choices *literally and visually* washed over difference.

What the opening credits montage did unwittingly reveal was that the series itself had not settled on a theme and therefore was left directionless. Through the stories, we eventually learn that one character is a nontraditional-aged student / divorcée, another is a less than stellar student, one is id-driven, and another is an adventure seeker. The opening reveals little about the cast's personalities or dispositions and may even confuse the audience. The nontraditional student is seen as the most playful and youthful, jumping rope not with peers but with girls. The less than stellar student is the one struggling to carry an armful of books. The id-driven character is depicted as the most chivalrous. The one who is most traveled and adventuresome is portrayed as clumsy and out of place. Rather than functioning as a stereotype buster, the opening exposes the work that still needed to be done in order to meaningfully situate the series.

Allen's Re-vision

By contrast, one of the most immediately recognizable changes that Allen made to the series when she took over in season two was to introduce a new opening cred- its montage. The renowned Queen of Soul, Aretha Franklin, was brought in to sing the theme, thereby asserting an uncompromising Blackness. Franklin's presence as a soul singer connoted pride and "r-e-s-p-e-c-t" for Blackness, delivering what Stu Gardner proclaimed a "soulful funk with a danceable feel to it," a dynamic version "oriented for kids ages 12 to 65."[33] The even younger, hip hop generation Grammy Award winners Boyz II Men would sing the theme song for *A Different World*'s final season. The theme song was not the only element to be wholly remade. The new opening was marked by the use of what looks like a single, horizontal, and continuous series of shots traveling through various adjacent spaces and rooms. The camera's eye and the viewer's eye hold the same point of view, and as the

Figure 2.2   *A Different World* cast under Debbie Allen and Susan Fales. Courtesy of PhotoFest.

vista slowly travels rightward, the audience peers through an absent fourth wall observing the activity in each room, a rarely offered vantage point.

As a striking and dynamic example of cinematography and editing for its time, Allen's montage succeeds in accomplishing three important goals. It signals to the audience the main characters and their personalities, employs the use of Black cultural signifiers, and resists the trend in popular culture to represent Blackness as Other. First, the opening credits not only identify for viewers who the core cast and supporting characters are, but it also adequately foreshadows their unique personalities. Shot two draws our attention to Whitley's vanity and shallowness. Fully dressed and standing alone, she is applying makeup in front of a long vertical mirror while affectionately admiring herself. Allen's decision to set Whitley apart from a group also spotlighted the character as one of the series' most notable stars. Dwayne Wayne's personality is evidenced in the opening credits as two of his most defining traits, his dedication to both his studies and pursuing women, are played out on-screen. As Dwayne is diligently studying, he becomes distracted by three attractive women and is soon locked in a passionate embrace with one. As a sidekick to the brilliant and smooth Dwayne Wayne, Ron is introduced as someone who continually and diligently tries to prove himself yet often falls short. It is fitting that pint-sized Ron is depicted as struggling to keep up and compete with a group of larger, more muscled football players.

Second, this new montage not only specifically situates the show as having a core cast of Black characters but also places it at a Black campus marked by Black cultural signifiers. In fact, from the very first shot, Allen works to mark the set-ting as educational, as it features a row of students intensely reading. As the cam-era pans across them, one student yawns, implying the group has been studying for quite a while. Shot three continues to reinforce the educational setting by fea-turing Jaleesa studying among more books. Of particular interest and importance in Allen's opening is the presence of a marching band. The marching band operates as a signifier of something far more specific—the importance of the Black band to Black college life—and is an "example of a robust vernacular American musical form that serves a social function and isn't aimed at commer-cial success."[34] Bands have long been a tradition at HBCUs, dazzling crowds dur-ing football-game halftime shows. As Ben Ratliff explains, "The joke about black-college football games in the South is that the crowd patterns are the reverse of the norm. The fans talk, flirt and eat during the first two quarters, then return to their seats to scrutinize the marching bands through their eight-minute shows at halftime."[35] Additionally, the inclusion of Mr. Gaines (Lou Myers), the campus cook in charge of "the Pit," in shot five is noteworthy.

In Beatts's montage, community is defined and represented outside of Hillman College in the local town. By contrast, Allen attempts to redefine com-munity by locating it on campus and through the presence of an individual who does not fit the typical campus populace—faculty or student. Rather, Mr. Gaines as the campus cook brings a distinctively southern flavor to both the food and conversations at Hillman. A military veteran, he does not appear to have availed himself of higher education. He is a different kind of educator who brings what faculty cannot, a folk wisdom and an experiential knowledge that cannot be accessed through book smarts. He is the students' reminder that there is a real world, a *different world*, outside of the protective, idyllic space of campus. The inclusion of Mr. Gaines as a star on the series communicates a diversity within Blackness, a type of diversity regarded as central and valuable.

The montage also introduces Black sororities and fraternities that have a strong presence on Black campuses and perform a valuable socializing function. According to recent research, membership in Black Greek organizations may facil-itate increased graduation rates for Black college students.[36] However, this scene goes well beyond reminding viewers that fraternities and sororities are an integral and vital part of the Black college experience. Rather, the members of the Kappa Lambda Nu fraternity are also shown, with help from the character Kim, engaged in the performative act of strolling. Like stepping, strolling is a form of artistic and expressive movement most often performed by Black Greek organizations in groups, only its pace is a bit slower, its style a bit smoother, and its feel less frenetic than stepping. Since they are always collectively performed, these art forms cele-brate community, unity, and solidarity within the Black college context. The montage also draws attention to another organization with a strong presence at both predominantly white institutions (PWIs) and Black colleges—the U.S. military.

While the ROTC is not a unique Black college tradition, the inclusion of Colonel Taylor and his soon-to-be officers, men and women alike, reminds viewers of Black patriotism and that America's military ranks are replete with Blacks.

The opening concludes with students coming to the end of their college careers and graduating. This scene exhibits a small, tightly knit group of students standing shoulder to shoulder looking earnest and dressed smartly in black business suits, noting even more seriously the time as they glance down at their watches. The function of looking at a wristwatch and recognizing (the expiration of) time presents various subtle meanings. In Spike Lee's *School Daze* the campus is implored, at the break of dawn, to "wake up," to become cognizant of and active in a host of sociopolitical issues as they pertain to the Black community. In the film, the screams of "wake up" are punctuated by the ringing of a gong signaling it is time to awaken. In the *A Different World* shot, the manner and aesthetic are conservative and businesslike; the group looks up above the camera as if gazing into their promising future. Such a scene is rare for Blackness on television.

Wrap-up

Creating opening credits that signaled the novelty and complexity of the show was an easy fix for Allen, yet something Beatts failed to accomplish. Finally, this new, pointedly defined, and never seen before direction for Black imagery worked to rewrite not only the emerging legacy of the series but also what had been (and continues to be) the trend in popular culture: representing Black students as supremely different and thus as Other (e.g., the films *Dangerous Minds* [1995] and *One Eight Seven* [1997]). Allen's characters were diverse and often atypical but not Othered. She was able to successfully paint Dwayne Wayne and Whitley, as well as the rest of the ensemble cast, as familiar yet culturally different, as complicated and yet comfortably predictable, and most importantly as Black college students with a shared history and racial identity, who struggled with the same issues as their non-Black counterparts.

Successful representations of Blackness are intimately connected to the ability to tap into a Black structure of feeling. Any cultural production must originate from the willingness and courage to engage with the complexity of Black life and subjectivity. Of considerable import are the creative starting points from which producers advance a text. Beatts started from the generic traditions of the situation comedy, a formulaic "go to" recipe circulated within the industry. As a result, the show's characters and narratives suffered from a lack of energy, depth, and believability. An opportunity to display Black diversity and culture was missed. *A Different World* necessitated a sensitivity and openness toward the experiences of Black college students and a respect for the cultural location in which the show took place. This is where Allen's vision began. While it is possible for producers and their creative teams to successfully write across racial and cultural lines, it is often the responsibility of Black showrunners to proffer Black imagery that runs counter to established industry canons. However, the influence of Black televisual image-makers like Allen is limited, as they do not hold complete autonomy in resolving the split image. Pressures from industry executives and the structural limitations of the televisual form continually present creative hurdles that obligate representational compromises, a dynamic that constitutes popular Black imagery as a site of continuous negotiation and redefinition.

NOTES

1. Horace Newcomb and Robert S. Alley, *The Producer's Medium: Conversations with Creators of American TV* (New York: Oxford University Press, 1983), 17.

2. David Marc, *Comic Visions: Television Comedy and American Culture,* 2nd ed. New York: Blackwell, 1997), 23.

3. Brett Mills, "What Happens When Your Home Is on Television," *Media/Culture Journal* 10, no. 4 (2007): 54.

4. Bryan Thompson, "'A Different World' Delights Audiences for 6 Years," *Recorder,* May 15, 1993, B1, http://proquest.umi.com.proxy.lib.umich.edu/pqdweb?did=49583071&sid= 1&Fmt=7&clientID=17822&RQT=309&VName=PQD (accessed July 20, 2006).

5. Jeremy Gerard, "Producers Carsey and Werner: What Have They Done for Us Lately?" *New York Times,* November 25, 1990, late-final edition, sec. 6, 55.

6. S. Reddicliffe, "The 1987 Fall Television Season," *Rolling Stone,* October 8, 1987, 32.

7. *A Different World,* DVD, Season One (1987; Thousand Oaks, CA: Ventura Distribution, 2005).

8. Elvis Mitchell, "A for Effort: But 'A Different World' and 'School Daze' Get Lower Grades for Achievement," *Rolling Stone,* April 21, 1988, 32–33.

9. See, for example, Beverly Daniel Tatum, *"Why Are All The Black Kids Sitting Together in the Cafeteria?" and Other Conversations About Race: A Psychologist Explains the Development of Racial Identity* (New York: Basic Books, 1997; rev. ed. 2003).

10. David Ehrenstein, "The Color of Laughter," *American Film,* September 1988, 8–11.

11. Eric Alterman, "Black Universities: In Demand and In Trouble," *New York Times,* November 5, 1989, http://query.nytimes.com/gst/fullpage.html?res=950DE2DD1F3DF936 A35752C1A96F948260.

12. Mitchell, "A for Effort."

13. R. Richard Laermer, "Sinbad the Stand-Up," *New York,* September 14, 1987, 34.

14. Brett Mills, *Television Sitcom* (London: BFI Publishing, 2005).

15. *A Different World,* DVD, Season One.

16. Carla Hall, "Back From a Different World; Director Debbie Allen, Making Each Step Count," *Washington Post,* May 8, 1993, final edition, B1.

17. Laura B. Randolph, "Debbie Allen on Power, Pain, Passion and Prime Time: Dancer/Director/Singer/Actress Looks for New Movie, Stage and TV Worlds to Conquer," *Ebony,* March 1991, 24–26, 28, 30–31.

18. Venita Ann Kelley, "Revealing the Universal Through the Specific in *A Different World*: An Interpretive Approach to a Television Depiction of African-American Culture and Communication Patterns" (PhD dissertation, University of Kansas, 1995), 158–160.

19. G. M. Sawyer, "Black Colleges and Community Development," *Journal of Black Studies* 6, no. 1 (September 1975): 79–99.

20. B. I. Perry Jr, "Black Colleges and Universities in Florida Past, Present, and Future," *Journal of Black Studies* 6, no. 1 (September 1975): 69–78.

21. David Swerdlick, "Different Strokes for Post–Civil Rights Folks on 'A Different World' DVD," *Creative Loafing*, February 22–28, 2006, 76, http://clclt.com/charlotte/different-strokes/Content?oid=2359362 (accessed May 29, 2006).

22. Emily Nussbaum, "Did 'Cosby' Do Better in College?" *New York Times*, September 21, 2003, http://query.nytimes.com/gst/fullpage.html?res=9800E2D6173AF932A1575AC0A9659 C8B63.

23. Cherie Saunders, "TCA Daily Blog: A Recap of Sessions Held at the 2006 Summer Television Critics Association Press Tour in Pasadena, CA," Television Critics Association, July 14, 2006, http://www.eurweb.com/story/eur27449.cfm (accessed July 15, 2006).

24. Ibid.

25. Margeaux Watson, "Class Reunion: The First Season of the 1990's Hit Series 'A Different World' Comes Out on DVD This Month, but What Has the Cast Been Up To Since They Graduated from Hillman College?" *Essence*, November 2005, 82.

26. David Marc, *Comic Visions: Television Comedy and American Culture* (Malden, MA: Wiley-Blackwell, 1997).

27. John Corner, *Critical Ideas in Television Studies* (New York: Oxford University Press, 1999).

28. Richard Stevenson, "Current Events in the World of Prime Time—TV Embraces Real-Life Issues as Way to Keep Shows up to Date," *San Francisco Chronicle*, June 9, 1990, Daily Datebook, C9.

29. F. McKissack, "The Problem with Black TV," *Progressive*, February 1997, 38–40.

30. James Greenberg, "Sitcom Writing: Riches Plus Respectability: As a Career, Writing Sitcoms Is Nothing to Make Fun Of," *New York Times*, August 5, 1990, H27.

31. Darnell Hunt, "Black Content, White Control," in *Channeling Blackness: Studies on Television and Race in America*, ed. D. Hunt (New York: Oxford University Press, 2005), 267–302.

32. Ehrenstein, "Color of Laughter."

33. "Black Stars Sing Theme Songs for Pop TV Shows," *Jet*, October 31, 1988, 30–33.

34. Ben Ratliff, "America's Music: Where the Game Is Just a Warm-Up for the Band," *New York Times*, September 8, 2007.

35. Ibid.

36. Ronald E. Severtis, "Greek-Letter Membership and College Graduation: Does Race Matter?" *Journal of Sociology and Social Welfare* 34, no. 3 (September 2007): 95–117.

3

A Black Cast Doesn't
Make a Black Show

CITY OF ANGELS AND THE PLAUSIBLE
DENIABILITY OF COLOR-BLINDNESS

KRISTEN J. WARNER

In a recent debate over the problematic characterization of Bonnie Bennett, the only Black female recurring character on the CW network series *The Vampire Diaries* (CW 2009), my challenger insisted that with all of the qualifiers I insisted she have, "maybe this is another hidden reason there are no minorities on television: everything becomes an issue and you just can't win." Indeed, the main qualifier I suggested that the series allow the character to possess—an innate sense of cultural difference—is difficult to grasp and maintain. However, I do not accept that just because race is difficult, it is impossible to represent in meaningful and complex ways. Characterization is one way to explore the possibility of meaningful representation. Yet characterization's most basic underpinning lies in casting the best actor for the part.

Casting, a vital practice in the Hollywood industry, determines the types of characterizations and representations that are allowed within media productions. Thus, rather than continue to focus solely on the actual televisual representations, I argue that studying casting practices enables media scholars to examine how representations are literally selected to be televised. An imperfect science further complicated by variables such as race, age, and gender, the casting process becomes a useful way to understand societal assumptions about people of color. Moreover, casting also shapes the nexus of labor directly impacted by casting decisions. The job of "character representation" involves not only actors and casting directors but also producers, writers, actors' and writers' guilds, and network/studio executives. Thus, exploring industrial casting processes not only enables scholars to understand race relations at a practical locus of specific interactions but can also shed light on broader social dynamics.

Expanding on the possibility of illuminating social dynamics through casting, one practice that serves the industry's sociopolitical needs is color-blind casting. On the surface, the link between color-blindness and casting practices may seem loose and perhaps even forced. However, I submit that this connection is anything but loose; in fact, we rarely consider how both practices contain similar ideologies and assumptions that depend upon social consensus. Both color-blindness and casting are founded upon un- (and in-) articulated assumptions about the irreducibility of physiology; that is, in both cases individuals (casting directors or just ordinary people) assume an equality of opportunity in others, regardless of physical appearance, allowing for a so-called leveling of the playing field, where everyone can then perform the same roles without any cultural specificity. Because we have been socialized into "not seeing race," when issues arise that are consciously or unconsciously informed by racism, color-blindness renders claims of discrimination and prejudice moot. More specifically, assuming "we are all the same" makes claims of racism appear as "oversensitivity" and the result of political correctness. Moreover, as Patricia J. Williams asserts, the failure to deal with the devastating effects of color-blindness can lead to a "self-congratulatory stance of preached universalism": "'We are the world! We are the children!' was the evocative, full-throated harmony of a few years ago. Yet nowhere has that been invoked more passionately than in the face of tidal waves of dissension, and even as 'the' children learn that 'we' children are not like 'those,' the benighted creatures on the other side of the pale."[1]

Williams's quote is powerful because it speaks to the double consciousness of people of color who, on the one hand, want to belong and desire to believe in the collective "we" but who, on the other hand, also recognize that the cost of joining is that their difference cannot be acknowledged and, what is more, that even to suggest that difference might be important would transform them into instigators of racial division. The paradox is clear: a message of universal goodwill renders people of color invisible.

In sum, practices of color-blindness and casting maintain a very idealistic but myopic view of the world based on normative (white) assumptions. Color-blind casting is therefore a viable lens for understanding the interdependence of cultural-racial politics and pop culture as related to television production. Thus, the purpose of this chapter is to discover through industry trade articles and personal interviews how media industry professionals rationalize the everyday decisions they make—particularly as they relate to casting. Reconstructing the discourses surrounding these industry professionals who are constantly negotiating and participating in a contradictory racial logic tied to economic as well as societal imperatives reveals the strategies and tactics of color-blindness that usually remain invisible. This assertion will be argued through the short-lived CBS series *City of Angels* (2000) and the interviews and reviews that emerged as a result of its untimely cancellation.

Color-blind casting, also known as blindcasting in the industry, is an old theater practice that has recently been recirculated in contemporary discourses surrounding prime-time television. After years of stalemate between the television industry and minority watchdog groups like the NAACP, the tipping point arose in 1999 when the networks unveiled their fall television lineup. Realizing that not one of the twenty-six new programs had minority leads, the media and the watchdog groups exploited the networks' failure, gaining a groundswell of support to browbeat the industry into becoming more diverse. As part of the final negotiations, television network executives created new positions called "executives of diversity." These individuals were charged with "coloring" the televisual landscape. Diversity executives' jobs typically involved setting up meetings with television producers and encouraging them to add more minorities to their programs.

With minority actors placed in shows that featured predominately white casts, the next step for the watchdog groups was to encourage the studios to give actors of color leading (or at least supporting) roles on the major network shows.[2] Blindcasting became a useful tool because it allowed industrial practitioners like showrunners and television writers to avoid explicitly writing race into the script while remaining confident that there could be "equal opportunity" for actors of diverse backgrounds. Yet this much-touted practice of equality is patently paradoxical. That is, rather than pursuing diversity by hiring minority writers and/or showrunners to create culturally specific roles for people of color, the television industry preferred to make roles racially normative. While on the surface this may have seemed a laudable practice, again, the problem with blindcasting is that racial normativity is a euphemism for "whiteness." Thus, blindcasting forces minority actors to input their cultural difference and output a standardized form of whiteness.

As I learned in a number of interviews with media professionals specializing in casting, actors of color being allowed to audition for characters implicitly written to be white is a progressive step for the industry, given the ways it has faltered with regard to diversity. Vincent Brook offers the numbers and what they signify based on the Screen Actors Guild (SAG) report:

> Released in February 2000, the SAG study, which focused on African Americans, revealed that blacks actually accounted for 16.0 percent of characters over the monitoring period, compared to the group's 12.2 percent of the U.S. population. However, further analysis showed that "overrepresentation" was undermined by the shunting of African Americans to "ghetto" networks (the WB and UPN), "ghetto" genres (sitcoms rather than dramas), and "ghetto" scheduling (the less-viewed Monday and Friday nights). Another study, released by the San Francisco–based advocacy group Children Now, added an even more damaging aspect to the marginalization of minorities: even programming that *did* include people of color frequently did so in an "exclusionary manner"—in other words, depicting them disproportionately as vagrants, dopers, gangbangers, and sundry predatory criminals.[3]

As a result of the SAG report, the post-1999 boycott threat, and negotiations between networks and actors' guilds to increase the visibility and screen time of minorities, watchdog organizations, each serving its own group (Black, Latino,

Asian, Native American), began issuing "report cards" to the networks in terms of their performance on diversity. These report cards had little consequence except for publicly shaming the networks into devising strategies for diversity. Brook outlines the distribution of grades below:

> Under a memorandum of understanding between the coalition and the networks in 1999, the various groups (black, Latinos, Asian Pacific American, and Native American) were to meet individually with the networks twice a year (since 2005 it has dropped to once a year) to discuss diversity in hiring and screen images, and each group was to issue a report card on each network's performance at the end of the year. The reports assess not merely casting—"Actors: On-Air Prime-time Scripted Shows" ("On-Air Prime-time Reality Programming" was added as a category in 2004)—but also behind-the-scenes hiring and other issues—"Writers and Producers: Prime-time," "Directors: Prime-time," "Program Development," "Procurement," "Entertainment Executives," and "Network Commitment to Diversity Issues." The reports have not been glowing, especially for Asian Pacific Island Americans. "Overall" grades (an average of all the categories), which started off in the D or C- range for all the networks, have remained stuck in the C range since the mid-2000s, with only ABC finally moving up to a B− in 2008 (reports are issued at the end of each calendar year). Grades for Latinos have fared somewhat better, with ABC and Fox rating overall Bs as early as 2004, NBC and CBS joining them at that level in 2006, and ABC shooting up to an A- in 2006 and 2007, although retreating to a B+ in 2008. African Americans have remained, as they started, ahead of the field, despite a "stern warning" from the NAACP that much more needs to be done.[4]

Nevertheless, to gain a better understanding of the place of race within the televisual landscape, I met with an upper-level executive assigned to issues of diversity at one of the main American actors' guilds, the American Federation of Television and Radio Artists (AFTRA).[5] This representative had much to say about how much race relations in Hollywood had improved over the last two decades—to the point that minorities have a substantial presence on television. When the conversation shifted to the politics of color-blindness, the AFTRA executive championed it as a way to avoid positive and negative racist representations. In other words, he conflated cultural specificity with long-standing historical tropes being enacted. Ironically, writing characters not intentionally designed to accommodate actors of color usually means that falling into these tropes can occur more frequently and unconsciously.

Perhaps the largest point stressed during our meeting was his understanding of the guild's purpose. The one thing that he repeated to me was that the guild was not in the business of regulating content; rather, its sole business was in creating opportunities for its members' gainful employment. "Actors want to work—period" was how he began to delve into this subject. He continued: "All acting is fiction, which allows our members to try for roles that they might otherwise not fit for." These two statements are key in identifying how the guild positions itself: not only as an organization that encourages productions to hire its actors but also as the biggest believer in the Hollywood culture of production. Regardless of the kind or the substance of the work, actors are encouraged to find gainful employment and figure out how to make themselves fit those jobs— regardless of skin color, sexuality, age, or ableism. Thus, since the guilds are concerned about employment, other factors that affect televisual and film representation, such as content, may compromise the goal of diversification. Furthermore, many actors self-regulate to avoid being cast in specific racial roles. The AFTRA representative asserted that some actors opt not to racially identify themselves in order to audition for roles where they may "pass" without fear of being told they are the wrong race. And as much as the actors' guilds encourage their membership to racially identify, they also enable racial passing. Indeed, the guilds are complicit in this practice of smoothing over racial (and cultural) differences. Upon becoming a member of the organization, every actor fills out a guild information sheet that asks him or her to identify which ethnicities/nationalities he or she could portray, as well as which language skills he or she possesses.

While the AFTRA representative did not tell me the percentage of non-identifying respondents, the existence of these forms demonstrates how the guilds function as accomplices to these practices of ignoring racial details. It is these contradictions that drive home the fact that as long as the goal is to have television reflect America's diversity of bodies and not actually to be concerned with the cultural specificity of those bodies, color-blindness remains.

The underlying conclusion based on my interviews is that the strength of blindcasting and universality must never be understated. Its hegemonic pull on Hollywood and audiences consistently shapes form and content. Russell Robinson argues that in film, box office success is paramount, and, as fickle as audiences are, studios need as many guarantees as they can obtain. As a result: "These opportunities to play a lead tend to go to white actors because the industry executives believe actors of color lack the universal appeal to sustain an extensive project."[6] I would assert that the same rationale applies in television. With this prototypical casting standard, color-blind casting seems a viable, if not totally progressive, alternative because, again, it ensures that minority actors, at least in some instances, receive equal opportunities for minor roles. However, if, as previously mentioned, the roles are written for white actors but are cast cross-racially, they often do not allow for cultural specificity, relegating the minority actor to a normative white viewpoint. If Robinson's claims are valid, then how is this color-blind casting model specifically deployed in service to the Hollywood television industry? The answer, to borrow from Joseph Turow, is that these kinds of "diverse" casting initiatives emerge in times of crisis and public scandal.[7]

Indeed, it was crisis *and* public scandal that brought about the swift deployment of *City of Angels*.

Moving from a conceptual examination of color-blind casting to a concrete case study, I want to provide the context for *City of Angels'* televisual moment. The discourse surrounding this CBS dramatic series, which lasted a season and a half, illustrates the paralyzing paradoxes of diversity and color-blindness because, while it was not blindcast and while the cast was predominately Black, the overall tone of the series was based in a universal and non-racially-specific logic. That is to say, although the show featured one of the largest predominately Black casts in a broadcast network drama, the show itself was not about race.[8] As one writer said about the show, "There is very little to distinguish the show from any other pass-ably good hour-long series. Which seems to be what Bochco and company actually want—a show that could be played by white actors as easily as by blacks: a stan-dard liberal notion of pop-culture progress."[9] But how were the creators of this show able to at least attempt this feat? Crisis and public scandal at the networks.

In January 2000, CBS launched a promotion for its new midseason pickup *City of Angels*. This show was no ordinary television program; rather, it was considered "prestige" programming because of its showrunner team of Steven Bochco and Paris Barclay. Bochco, executive producer of some of television's most iconic shows such as *Hill Street Blues*, *L.A. Law*, and *NYPD Blue*, teamed up with Barclay, a successful African American television director (who directed several episodes of *Blue*), for *City*, a medical procedural focusing on an inner-city Los Angeles hospital in decay and the staff who try to save it. *City* was also dif-ferent because it was a drama with a predominately Black cast—a rare program-ming strategy. Indeed, the operating Hollywood logic at work with regard to casting dramas relies more upon integrated ensemble casts with white leads rather than predominately Black casts with white supporting characters. This logic is heavily supported and reinforced by conceptions of a (white) mass audi-ence who will not watch "Black"-cast programming. And yet there were larger problems that overrode the hegemonic Hollywood logic—namely the near-boycott of the broadcast networks by media watchdog groups like the NAACP mentioned earlier. Although Barclay asserts that Bochco was given the green light to produce the *City* pilot in March 1999, almost six months before coverage of the lack of minorities in the fall season emerged, the show still became an asset for CBS when the networks faced attack from these watchdog groups. *Entertainment Weekly* reporter Ken Tucker succinctly explains CBS's strategy: "CBS Television president Les Moonves says, 'We don't need an instant 20 share to be able to let [*City*] survive' in its uncompetitive 8 p.m. time slot. But they will need both white and minority viewers to thrive and create the kind of cross-cultural exchange *City* aims at."[10]

With *City* being the only drama series that featured a predominately Black cast that season, the stakes were high for the creative team not just in terms of

Figure 3.1 *City of Angels* cast. Courtesy of PhotoFest.

the longevity of the series but also in terms of the future of minority-led series on network television. In an interview months before *City* premiered, Barclay said: "The only thing that will really create more opportunities—and I hate to be cynical about it— is enormous success. You can't just appeal to people that this is the right thing to do, that there needs to be more diversity like there is in our culture. Until a show like *City of Angels* or something like that is so successful that it spawns thousands of imitators, the industry doesn't seem to respond, because dollars are really what they're primarily interested in."[11]

Moreover, and most pertinent to this chapter, the fear that white audiences would not tune in created additional pressure for the showrunners, namely Bochco, to sell the series as the newest iteration of a color-blind program. That is, Bochco had to reinforce that while the actors were not necessarily blindcast, race and race relations would not be a focus of the show. Bochco's rhetoric was imbued with the spirit of color-blindness in that when audiences viewed the characters, they were not supposed to notice their race; rather, the characters just "happened" to be Black. Bochco surmises his viewpoint fairly succinctly: "I've never seen it as a show that was race issue-driven. I think it would be really dull and strident to every week be doing racially significant episodes."[12] The claim that the show was not about race but about characters who happen to be of color working in a hospital was juxtaposed with appeals to City's diversity, largely spurred by Barclay. In a number of articles, Barclay points to City as an illustration of the possible opportunities for people of color both in front of and behind the camera—many times through exposing Hollywood logic. Barclay asserts: "Building a show that has strong, three-dimensional African-American roles . . . allows the actors—some of whom have only played junkies or hookers—to really stretch and show what they can do."[13]

Writer Anne Bergman sets up Barclay's next quote concerning the paradigm of many network executives: "Barclay disputes the excuses proffered by some network execs who claimed they'd tried to hire minorities, but the talent pool was too shallow. Barclay diplomatically suggests that perhaps these executives meant to say that they didn't take any initiative to look harder. 'They're used to doing things in the easiest way possible,' he says, 'and the easiest way possible is to hire the usual suspects. And if the usual suspects are producers and writers who are not African-American, or people of color, then they're not going to think about casting a wider net.'"[14] Barclay's statements are provocative and to a large degree indict the myopic viewpoints of many network executives and showrunners—Bochco excluded. Furthermore, both Barclay's and Bochco's statements illustrate the co-creators speaking to their respective bases as a means of encouraging a mass audience to watch City.

But when City premiered in January 2000, critics gave the show lukewarm reviews. Not only that, but the ratings were not as high as the showrunners and the network hoped for. Limping to the finish line, City finished its thirteen-episode run in April 2000. On the bubble in terms of whether it would be renewed or not, one thing was certain: the show would have to be revamped. In a move that surprised most industry insiders, CBS renewed City for thirteen episodes (as opposed to the more traditional twenty-two-episode order most series earn in their second season).[15] News writers hypothesized that the added pressure of minority watchdog groups forced the network's hand. Ken Parish Perkins describes CBS's position: "Part of the reason CBS kept the series, which aired in the midseason, was political. Angels is a predominantly black-cast series, and after the network's passionate pledges regarding diversity and leading the charge by offering a so-called black drama, the network would have opened itself to a lot of criticism had it pulled the plug."[16]

However, the network was far from powerless. While publicly CBS supported a second season of City, it undermined the show's potential for success through programming it against NBC's powerhouse Thursday night "Must See

TV" schedule.[17] This kind of challenge programming is usually geared toward successful shows that networks believe have a chance to usurp ratings—or shows that the network is trying to kill. In the case of *City*, the latter seemed to be more accurate. And then, in June 2000, Barclay announced he was leaving the show, citing "creative differences."[18]

Barclay's resignation came just as Bochco's re-visioning of the show emerged.[19] Filling Barclay's vacated executive producer position with veteran African American director Kevin Hooks was Bochco's first change. Aesthetic and content changes would follow: "We're in the midst of making changes, making adjustments, making improvements to the show . . . So everything's open to scrutiny. The scripts have to be better. The production has to be smarter. The visual concept has to be more engaging. There have to be some adjustments to our music."[20]

Changing the music behind the opening credits from a gospel-sounding song to a more contemporary R&B number sung by balladeer Brian McKnight was just one of the many differences between seasons one and two. Bochco also fired lead actress Vivica A. Fox, saying that she was too young to portray a chief of medicine. Thus *City* rebooted its show from scratch, with the exception of its still predominately Black cast and crew.[21] However, for Bochco and Hooks, this majority-Black cast and crew contained its own issues that needed to be overcome. In an interview, Bochco spoke about the difficulty of merging a racially integrated crew, saying, "I don't think any of us were prepared for how hard it was going to be to find a common language."[22] While the article continues with Bochco explaining how the various parts of the show, from the writing to the overall aesthetic were never in sync, the quote about not speaking the same language begs to be unpacked. I argue that for Bochco, the diversity represented by the cast and crew spurred a diverse set of ideas on what *City* should become in terms of content and style. At best, his comments betray the idea that his singular voice, and more specifically his *white* singular voice, should determine the tone and ideology of the show.

Furthermore, the issue of how to overcome the race issue in terms of content was also at the top of the agenda. According to news writer Eric Deggans, *City's* cast overdetermined the show's content. "From the beginning, the show faced questions other series never did: Were the white characters, including a lecherous city councilman and a clueless, arrogant white resident doctor, set up as cardboard villains? And if the only predominantly black drama on network television isn't going to focus on race issues or black culture, what's the point?"[23]

In response to Deggans's questions, Hooks posited: "Society deals with race in a clumsy way . . . so I'm not surprised (by *Angels's* problems). A show as important as this one . . . sets up tremendous expectations. We may have (tried) to please too many people by trying to do too many things."[24] For Hooks, *City's* uncertainty stemmed from a fundamental lack of knowledge when attempting to simultaneously deal with and *not* deal with race. Employing almost exclusively Black actors on a show that was not necessarily about race but about the inner workings of an inner-city hospital amounted to these producers creating a varia-tion of a Chinese wall. In a sense, by building a wall where Bochco appealed to the universal (white) viewer through color-blindness and Barclay (and later Hooks) appealed to Black viewers through claims of cultural specificity, they could be seen as trying to balance the paradox of their show as diverse (seeing color) and color-blind (not seeing color). Yet pleasing these two divergent forces may have been perceived as inauthentic and disingenuous. How could Bochco's position and Hooks's position coexist? More specifically, how can a show that in its second episode foregrounds white people's ignorance about the dry-skin condition colloquially called "ashiness" also claim that it is not a "Black" show?[25]

Trying to serve too many masters ultimately killed the series. At the time of its cancellation in November 2000, *City* averaged just 7.4 million viewers, 27 per-cent less than its lead-in, *48 Hours*.[26] The fallout was minimal, with a few news articles trying to predict *City*'s effect on minority-led dramas. The consensus was that over time and through trial and error, dramas with predominately Black casts would become standard. However, a drama with two lead actors of color would not reemerge for nearly ten years on the network televisual landscape. NBC's action-adventure drama *Undercovers* (2010), executive produced by J. J. Abrams, learned the lessons of *City*. First, the all-white production team stressed that the lead roles were both blindcast and just happened to have two Black actors (Gugu Mbatha-Raw and Boris Kodjoe). At the July 2010 Television Critics Association session for *Undercovers*, co-executive producer Josh Reims said: "When J.J. and I wrote the script originally, we decided we wanted to write it like the [1940 movie] *Philadelphia Story*, with Katherine [sic] Hepburn and Cary Grant . . . but they're dead so we didn't hire them," he joked. "[We said] Let's just see every possible incarnation of person [so we won't end up with] the same people we've seen on TV a million times . . . Boris and Gugu came in, and we sort of knew immediately, these are them. We didn't go out of our way to say we are hiring two black people to be the leads of our show, but we didn't ignore it either."[27]

Stressing a blindcasting model is a significant shift from the intentional racially specific employment in *City of Angels*. But the benefits of such a process, namely that the show cannot inherently be labeled a "Black" show, outweigh the benefits of cultural specificity from an industrial viewpoint. Reims's reluctance to showcase diversity in favor of displacing it into a color-blind, "best person for the job" logic is a strategic and savvy industry move. Reims continues, "We were not going to hire two black people because they were two black people. We don't consider we are revolutionizing TV, at the same time we realize it is a big deal."[28] Unlike Bochco and Barclay, Reims foregrounds the "organic" casting process that allowed these two to find their way to the project, displacing notions of Blackness and Black televisual representation, but also still takes credit for "revo-lutionizing" television by hiring these actors of color. Second, the production team tried to ensure that audiences understood this show was not about race;

it was about adventure. Thus, in selling this show to the public, the notion of color-blindness was invoked as a means of reproducing and denying the systemic racism living in Hollywood.

Unfortunately, despite all of the hype and excitement around the *Undercovers* series premiere, the show failed to gain an audience and was canceled in November 2010. According to press reports, the series reached an all-time low viewer rating the night before NBC made the decision.[29] Investigating the cancellation, journalist Nikki Finke interviewed an *Undercovers* insider who surmises what caused the show to fail: "Many things. Mostly, what was meant to be a throwback lark of a show felt trivial to people. It felt flimsy and not compelling, partially because it was designed as a stand alone, non serialized show. Perhaps the stories lacked deeper interest and urgency. We tried to embrace a familiarity of form, but the public obviously didn't want something so familiar. Unfortunately we never got an audience from the get-go; our abysmal recent rating wasn't even one point lower than our premiere number. We just should have done better. It is a bummer to be sure. NBC did the best they know how."[30]

The assessment has merit. As an occasional viewer of the series, I thought the story left much to be desired. However, I would argue that race also played a role in the cancellation of *Undercovers*. In the comments section of Finke's story, a respondent calling himself "Curtis Schoon" wrote: "The ugly truth is mainstream is reluctant to tune in to shows or films with black leads for whatever reasons and black audiences are increasingly less inclined to tune into shows conceived, produced, directed and written by people who can't capture the subtle nuances and 'feel' that makes it seem authentic."[31]

Thus, while *Undercovers* learned several lessons from *City*, the largest lesson of all—not serving two masters—was not one of them. Yet we can garner some lessons from these series and the industrial framework that structures them.

What the discourse around *City* and, later, *Undercovers* obscured is how Hollywood as an industrial producer of content simultaneously reinforces and downplays its systemic racism. It should go without saying that this process is more complex than simply attaching the label "racist" to Hollywood. As a microcosm of society-at-large, Hollywood has made progress in terms of racial equity, but the ways that this equity manifests ultimately create a number of new problems and glaring holes in how we negotiate race both in governmental policy and in everyday life.

From my interviews with AFTRA and SAG, I learned that color is not a contextual, culturally specific issue but rather more like a flavoring additive. Hiring actors of color may work to reflect the literal diversity of America's population, but it fails to translate into actual representations of cultural difference. Cultural difference is not at the forefront of these professionals' agendas. Understandably, the guilds already have a difficult time gaining employment for their minority members; to be concerned with content would only be more daunting. Besides, how would they be able to affect content? The scripts have been written by the time the guilds' members audition. Thus, those commissioning these scripts (and also scriptwriters) must be the conscientious ones in providing the opportunities for cultural difference. And with new data suggesting that while the share of television employment for minority writers between 2007 and 2009 increased from 9 percent to 10 percent, the long-standing underrepresentation makes the burden of cultural difference even more difficult to manifest on-screen.[32]

So, what does all this mean for the future of minority-led television dramas? Most likely, the issue centers on the amount of time it will take the industry to try again. Ten years lapsed between *City* and *Undercovers*, but not because the networks bar people of color from leading roles. Hollywood is a risk-averse industry and, as mentioned earlier, only in the most extreme cases will it take a chance on alternative models of representation. In a November 2010 article, Eric Deggans recounts how Boris Kodjoe, the lead actor of *Undercovers*, was asked six times to audition for the part in the now defunct series.[33] He explained that he turned down the auditions because he felt that the network would never hire a Black man to star in such a large vehicle. Kodjoe's point leads Deggans to the larger questions of his article and the questions of this chapter: "Why do network TV shows led solely by actors of color keep failing? How much of the situation is really about race? And what's the impact on viewers when people of color are mostly supporting characters, whatever the reason?"[34] Deggans never answers his questions, but I believe the answer lies in old, anecdotal myths surrounding what white mainstream viewers will and will not watch. More specifically, because networks are so invested in the conventional wisdom of mainstream audiences' disinterest in culturally specific programming that they rarely allow these shows to be developed, the vitality of the programs lies in their harmlessness. Therefore shows that attempt to cast African Americans as leads must ensure that their characters will not "act" Black or perform in a manner that will offend mainstream viewers' sensibilities. Yet in so doing, as Curtis Schoon remarked, these series continue to distance Black audiences because they "feel" disingenuous. As long as this paradoxical, color-blind logic governs casting decisions, this stalemate will continue.

NOTES

1. Patricia J. Williams, *Seeing a Color-Blind Future: The Paradox of Race* (New York: Farrar, Straus and Giroux, 1997), 5.

2. The discourse surrounding the NAACP's strong encouragement for more minorities on television is discussed in Herman Gray's *Cultural Moves* (Berkeley: University of California Press, 2005), 81, as well as "TV's Great Black Hope—Special Report: Race on TV," *Entertainment Weekly*, June 20, 2008, 29–33.

3. Vincent Brook, "Convergent Ethnicity and the Neo-platoon Show: Recombining Difference in the Postnetwork Era," *Television and New Media* 10 (2009): 340.

4. Ibid. Brook gathered his report card information from the Asian Pacific American Media Coalition at www.advancingequality.org and the National Hispanic Media Coalition at

www.nhmc.org. The websites do not publish their criteria for report card grades. Thus, it is unclear how they specifically determine the grades.

5. AFTRA executive, personal interview by Kristen Warner, July 16, 2009. In the interest of preserving anonymity, I withheld my interviewees' names and titles.

6. Russell Robinson, "Casting and Caste-ing: Reconciling Artistic Freedom and Antidiscrimination Norms," *California Law Review*, 2007, 1.

7. Joseph Turow, *Media Industries* (New York: Longman, 1984), 161.

8. I would be remiss if I did not acknowledge the Showtime series *Soul Food* (2000–2004) and its place as one of the longest-running drama series with a predominately black cast. Premiering months before *City*, this series did prove that a show about black life could be successful. Yet that success would be relegated to a premium cable network.

9. Ken Tucker, "*City of Angels*: Television Review," *Entertainment Weekly*, January 21, 2000, http://www.ew.com/ew/article/0,275245,00.html?print (accessed October 17, 2010).

10. Ibid.

11. Anne Bergman, "Barclay Breaks Ground," *Daily Variety*, October 8, 1999, Special Section.

12. Eric Deggans, "'City of Angels' Finds Its Footing," *St. Petersburg Times*, October 12, 2000, http://www.sptimes.com/News/101200/Floridian/_City_of_Angels__find.shtml (accessed August 22, 2011).

13. Ibid.

14. Ibid.

15. Perhaps CBS executives thought that if the show gained the necessary ratings to succeed, they would order the additional nine episodes (called the "back 9") afterward.

16. Ken Parish Perkins, "*City of Angels* Flies Again," *Charleston* (WV) *Gazette*, October 12, 2000, Entertainment, C12.

17. Ibid.

18. Eric Mink, "Bochco Vows to Keep *Angels* Flying: Tweaking May Have Led Partner to Quit," *New York Daily News*, June 15, 2000, Television, 11.

19. According to an interview, after resigning from *City*, Barclay reached an agreement with Bochco and company not to speak about aspects of the production. Yet he does talk generically about how if he feels unable to influence a project, he will get frustrated and quit, which speaks to some of the underlying issues Barclay may have experienced working with Bochco and the network. Kevin S. Sandler, "Televising Difference: An Interview with Paris Barclay," in *Filming Difference: Actors, Directors, Producers, and Writers on Gender, Race, and Sexuality in Film*, ed. Daniel Bernardi (Austin: University of Texas Press, 2009), 334.

20. Mink, "Bochco Vows to Keep Angels Flying."

21. According to *Entertainment Weekly*'s Ken Tucker, more than 70 percent of the crew and half the writing staff were African American. Tucker, "*City of Angels*: Television Review."

22. Deggans, "'City of Angels' Finds Its Footing."

23. Ibid.

24. Ibid.

25. According to James Poniewozik, "In the second episode, a white resident panics when an African-American girl shows up with a gray efflorescence on her legs. A black pediatrician shows him the miracle cure: Vaseline. The girl has ash—a mundane dry-skin condition—and tells him, 'It's a black thing.'" Poniewozik's retelling of the story leaves out that the girl was diagnosed with a disorder that was dealt with earlier in the episode. This scene is the tag of that storyline. James Poniewozik and Jeanne McDowell, "Television: *City of Angels*," *Time*, January 24, 2000, http://www.time.com/time/magazine/article/0,9171,995903-3,00.html (accessed October 19, 2010).

26. Sandra P. Angulo, "'City' Bickers," *Entertainment Weekly*, December 14, 2000, http://www.ew.com/ew/article/0,,91594,00.html (accessed October 19, 2010).

27. Diane Haithman, "TCA: 'Undercovers' Producers Reluctant Trailblazers for Casting Two Black Leads," *Deadline Hollywood*, July 30, 2010, http://www.deadline.com/2010/07/tca-under-covers-producers-reluctant-trailblazers-for-casting-two-black-leads (accessed October 19, 2010).

28. Ibid.

29. Nellie Andreeva, "NBC Cancels New Drama 'Undercovers,'" *Deadline Hollywood*, November 5, 2010, http://www.deadline.com/2010/11/nbc-cancels-new-drama-undercovers (accessed December 11, 2010).

30. Nikki Finke, "Uncovering Why 'Undercovers' Went Wrong," *Deadline Hollywood*, November 5, 2010, http://www.deadline.com/2010/11/uncovering-why-undercovers-went-wrong (accessed December 11, 2010).

31. Ibid.

32. Writers Guild of America (WGA), "Recession and Regression: The 2011 Hollywood Writers Report," August 15, 2011, http://www.wga.org/uploadedFiles/who_we_are/hwr11execsum.pdf.

33. Eric Deggans, "It's Still Pretty Pale at the Top," *Charlotte* (NC) *Observer*, November 17, 2010, http://www.charlotteobserver.com/2010/11/17/1843217/its-still-pretty-pale-at-the-top.html (accessed December 11, 2010).

34. Ibid.

4 Blacks in the Future

BRAVING THE FRONTIER
OF THE WEB SERIES

CHRISTINE ACHAM

Television's synergy with the Web initially seemed inconceivable to network executives. With the rise of Internet use, newspaper and magazine articles announced the impending death of television. While that was clearly hyperbole, network executives, though often anonymously, expressed their fears that Web content would siphon off viewership and thus advertising dollars generated by television programming. Fears may have been quelled with the evidence of the success of television shows first made available streaming on network websites and then for paid download through digital servers such as iTunes. For example, in December 2005, NBC saw a rise in the ratings of the then-struggling *The Office* when the show became available on iTunes. The show also became the number-one downloaded TV program on iTunes.[1] Soon thereafter, in the summer of 2006, NBC unveiled a series of *The Office* webisodes on NBC.com. The original content webisodes successfully engaged viewers during the summer hiatus while pushing the products of advertising sponsors such as FedEx and Toyota.

Networks and advertisers followed the *Office* model with different levels of success. When revenue was not quickly visible, many studios pulled out of webisode production.[2] However, far from indicating the death of the webisode, production of these short-form series has continued and flourished as "hundreds of titles, numbering thousands of short episodes: dramas, comedies, Webisodes accompanying television series, cartoons, talk shows, reality shows, news-magazines, [and] documentaries, a cheaper and quicker parallel universe to television and film."[3] Webisodes are sponsored by individual advertisers, produced by mainstream production companies for network websites, and made by independent producers. Webisode production has particular relevance for Black viewers as the sites that host Black-themed webisodes have become loci for segments of the Black community who not only identify with the stories but also connect with other viewers through the Internet sites. Additionally, Black talent has turned to this short form in force due to the continuing lack of diverse representation on mainstream network television.

In recent years, the landscape of network television has seen some significant changes, especially in terms of African American representation. In mid-September 2006, both the Warner Bros. Television Network (the WB) and the United Paramount Network (UPN) closed their doors. The upstart networks were known for producing African American situation comedies. The WB showcased programs such as the *Parent 'Hood* (1995–1999), *The Wayans Bros.* (1995–1999), *The Jamie Foxx Show* (1996–2001), and *The Steve Harvey Show* (1996–2002). When the WB shifted away from African American–themed programming to shows catering to a teen demographic like *Felicity* (1998–2002), *Dawson's Creek* (1998–2003), and *One Tree Hill* (2003 to present on the CW), UPN became the hub for African American–cast shows and attracted a significant African American audience with *The Parkers* (1999–2004), *Girlfriends* (2000–2006; 2006–2008 CW), *One on One* (2001–2006), *Eve* (2003–2006), *All of Us* (2003–2006; 2006–2007 CW), and *Everybody Hates Chris* (2005–2006; 2006–2009 CW). When the WB and UPN folded and the CW Television Network premiered in the 2006–2007 television season, many consistent viewers of the Black-themed shows of UPN wondered what would happen to their programs. Many did not make the transition. *All of Us* was canceled in 2007, *Girlfriends* in 2008, and *Everybody Hates Chris* in 2009. The one African American sitcom created on the CW, *The Game,* ran from 2006 to 2009. In 2011, the cable network Black Entertainment Television (BET) picked up the show.[4] Currently the CW runs no African American programs.

The major networks suffer from a similar lack of programming. African American characters make up parts of ensemble casts. For example, African American writer and director Shonda Rhimes produces both *Grey's Anatomy* (2005–present) and its spin-off *Private Practice* (2007–present) on ABC. Both shows have Black characters in significant roles. In 2010, J. J. Abrams's spy drama series *Undercovers* premiered on NBC. It was the first action drama to have two African American actors in the starring roles. But the show lasted less than a full season, and only thirteen episodes were produced. Clearly a dearth of African American representation still exists on network television and African American dramas are a nonentity.

Even with this lack of representation, Black talent remains and creative individuals consistently seek an outlet to tell their stories. More recently African American producers, writers, and actors, many of whom were involved in the production of the aforementioned programs, have sought new avenues for expression and taken their skills to the Internet, producing a variety of Web series. African American webisodes from both amateur and professional producers have thrived, and at the beginning of 2011, over 125 series appeared online.

This chapter presents an overview of the state of webisodes as it pertains to African American production. Using information garnered from interviews with producers of Web series, it explores the challenges and rewards of working within this new medium. It will also offer a close analysis of two of these series in order to determine whether these webisodes are able to expand upon or nuance current network offerings and representations. Overall, through an analysis of the structure, content, and context of these Web series, this chapter assesses the power of the webisode as a tool for the expression of Black voices, as empowerment for Black creative forces, and as a potential site for creating Black community.

Contextualizing the Rise of the Black Webisode

In the 1980s and 1990s, major networks capitalized on the success of *The Cosby Show* (1984–1992) and *A Different World* (1987–1993) along with other Black comedies. Networks produced shows such as *Family Matters* (ABC, 1989–1997; CBS, 1997–1998), *The Fresh Prince of Bel-Air* (NBC, 1990–1996), and *Hangin' with Mr. Cooper* (ABC, 1992–1997). These efforts, along with the presence of African American programming on Fox such as *In Living Color* (1990–1994), *Martin* (1992–1997), and *Living Single* (1993–1998) and the rise of the WB and UPN, brought many Black actors, writers, directors, and producers to the attention of Hollywood. However, with the loss of the WB and UPN in 2006 and the continued lack of Black-themed production on the major networks, much of the Black talent that was not picked up by the mainstream network television industry or by cable remained out of work. This group of professionals, along with producers located across the United States, turned to webisode production.

The webisode is a generally inexpensive form of narrative production with the capacity for both niche and worldwide audiences. While there are no formal written rules for the webisode, dramas generally run at approximately ten minutes, while comedies have a run time of less than six minutes. Soap operas can have a longer format of approximately twelve to fifteen minutes. Some episodes complete an entire story arc, while others are serialized. Some Web series run for several seasons, while others are encapsulated in one series. These Web series vary widely in terms of subject matter, genre, and target audiences. So while African American narratives are absent from network television, they are flourishing on the Web.

Although the racial demographics of the United States continue to change drastically, whiteness continues to be the color of network television. On the Web, however, a completely different racial landscape is evident. The fact that an individual can buy an inexpensive camera, or lease one, and editing can be completed on a personal computer increases access to creative narrative production tools that eschew network television and cable. These producers tackle stories that are representative of various demographics within the Black community.

In terms of Black content, webisodes come in a variety of genres: soap operas, dramas, dramedies, comedies, and documentaries, which, in turn, deal with various groups within the Black community such as women, men, LGBTQ, young adults, single mothers, the wealthy, and the working class. *Drama Queenz,* for example, follows the lives of three gay actors living in New York, and *Diary of a Single Mom* is a soap opera about three single mothers living in Los Angeles. *The New Twenties* is a drama about a group of college friends, now young professionals, navigating life ten years after graduation. *Who . . .* is a comedy about three friends who meet for lunch daily and gossip about topical issues such as "Who . . . Is Black (But Passing)?" "Who . . . Is a Hot Mess?" and "Who . . . Better Not Look at My Man?"

The Black community is often perceived as monolithic by mainstream America, and television programming rarely notes differences within the Black community. Webisodes, on the other hand, revel in the unique stories of these diverse communities. The ability to tell such a wide range of stories makes the Web an attractive site for Black talent. Webisode writer, director, producer of *Who . . .* , and Web channel owner Michael Ajakawe states: "There are professionals in Hollywood taking advantage of this low-cost form of entertainment that you can broadcast worldwide. In the past if you were a frustrated writer you would make a short film or even an independent film. Well, today frustrated artists are putting their money into Web series and showing people what they are made of . . . Webisode producers are covering every aspect of Black life online. African Americans are no longer begging the networks to produce their shows and their ideas."[5]

The ability to work outside of the context and constraints of Hollywood, the power to tell a variety of stories, and the ease of access to the means of production and, even more significantly, to the means of distribution are ongoing themes in the conversations of Web producers who have clearly dealt with the racially static industry. Writer, director, and producer of *The New Twenties* Tracy Taylor shares Ajakawe's sentiments and asserts: "Black producers are able to get their stories out on the Web, and they don't have to wait for a green light from anyone. And these days, becoming a Web producer isn't hard at all. It's something that can be done inexpensively and quickly, so if you have an idea and access to a camera, you can do a Web series. There's space for everyone on the Web."[6]

Writer and producer of *Drama Queenz* Dane Joseph questions the state of Black television and again notes the importance of the Web: "It's alarming to me that we have such prominent Black voices like Oprah and Tyler Perry at the forefront of the media landscape, and yet there are very few movies and television shows either featuring African Americans and other minorities or produced by minorities . . . Many Black producers have decided to produce the indie route. It's not always ideal, but at least there's something to kind of fill the diversity void in pop entertainment."[7]

Challenging Network Narratives/Creating Black Community

An analysis of the span of Black webisodes reveals that with access to production and distribution comes the ability to address underserved audiences within the

Black community. While network television is at its core concerned with profitability, Web series producers have additional objectives for their shows that lead to some fruitful outcomes for Web audiences. Black Web series provide a community location for these niche audiences, spread across the Internet. Audiences can log on to these sites at their leisure to catch up with familiar Black characters dealing with everyday issues or simply laugh at inside jokes or vernacular that is particular to various Black audiences. They can also comment on what they have seen and engage with what other viewers have to say about their shows. Some of these Web series also address social issues and try to provide solutions to problems that impact the Black community. A close analysis of these series allows for a better understanding of how these narratives work dually at creating Black community while providing a space for Black expression.

Drama Queenz: Out of the Closet and onto the Web

The web series *Drama Queenz*, which premiered in 2008, features an ongoing narrative about a community practically ignored by mainstream television, Black gay men. *Noah's Arc* (2005–2006), which ran for two seasons on the cable channel LOGO, deals with the lives of gay Black and Latino men.[8] But fictional images of Black gay men have appeared only sporadically on network television and often in a derisive manner such as the questionable "Men on Film" skits of *In Living Color*. *Drama Queenz* tells the story of three Black gay roommates living in Queens, searching for love and the perfect, or simply any, part in a theatrical production in New York City. The roommates and friends are Jeremiah (Dane Joseph), Davis (Kristen-Alexzander Griffith), and Preston (Troy Valjean Rucker). According to Joseph, who is also the writer and producer, the Web series is an opportunity to finally tell his story: "My audience is mostly gay Black men, honestly, but I love them and they seem to mostly love the show. That's what's so great about webisodes. We can target niche audiences that are under-served, and therefore they truly appreciate programming that speaks to them."[9]

With Jeremiah's narration, the audience gets a firsthand glimpse into the mind of the protagonist and witnesses the careers, lives, and loves of these three friends. Unlike on network television, these three men are far from one-dimensional and thus, sadly, groundbreaking. While the show describes itself as a comedy, I argue that it is more of a dramedy. Jeremiah spends his days going from audition to audition and questions his chances to make it as he faces rejection time and again. He has trust issues and thus has an on-again, off-again relationship with a musical accompanist, Donovan (Fred Ross). He also deals with living in a cramped apartment with his two friends, who more often than not are also trying out for the same roles.

Preston works at a local restaurant to support his acting aspirations but spends more time gossiping with his friends than actually serving customers. Davis is the most serious of the three characters. He is involved with a man who

Figure 4.1   *Drama Queenz* main cast. Courtesy of Dane Joseph.

is on the "down low," living a heterosexual life with a girlfriend. The storylines reveal how through their close relationship, the friends support each other in all of their trials and successes.

Viewers access the show through the *Drama Queenz* website, and webisodes are posted by the production company on YouTube. The viewer commentary that accompanied the first episode indicates amazement at the presence of such characters and topics on the Web. ROA1988 stated, for example, "What NetWork does this come on??? Is it on DVD???" As the episodes evolve, viewers express how important this show is for Black gay men. *Cedcjazz* says, "wow i like this. i can't wait to see the rest of the episodes. we need more things like this showing us in many diversified ways. keep up the good work and god bless you guys. you got my support."

There is also the unique familiarity with the characters that viewing audiences embrace and respond to as if they were personal friends. For example, episode six, "Simple Little Things," finds all of the characters avoiding the love interests in their lives. Jeremiah discovers that Donovan is the accompanist at his audition and questions if he should skip it. Donovan pursues Jeremiah to reconcile. Preston's ex-boyfriend Trevor shows up at the restaurant where he works with the new man he is dating. Davis deals with his feelings for Diego, his "straight friend," who now wants to be his workout partner. Mixedgreens55 responds on YouTube: "Yay Donovan. That took courage shuga. Sometimes it's really hard to get out of your own way. I'm so glad they both said sorry and I LOVE them together. Bit worried about Davis though. Diego is gorgeous and sweet but dangerous. Umm, hmm. Trevor is all kinds of lovely but he's obviously not the man Preston wants to be with. Preston, be brave sugar. Take a chance on a love that you want, not just what's available and unlikely to get you hurt. If your heart's not in it, what is the point?"

The involvement with these characters indicates what an important role *Drama Queenz* plays in the lives of its viewing audience, who have created a community around the series, and suggests what a multiplicity of shows that target minority audiences could potentially do by giving a sense of affirmation through representation. The producers see the importance of *Drama Queenz* as a program that addresses Black gay men and understand that there is a duty to not only provide entertainment but also address social issues that impact their community. On October 11, 2010, the producers posted a video message to the viewers as a part of the Trevor Project and in response to the rash of suicides in the LGBTQ community due to bullying. Dane Joseph discusses their decision and the importance of using webisodes as a tool for direct action: "I believe that it's necessary. We know that people watch and we hope that if we even inspire one person, even save one life, that it's all worth it. With production costs being so low, there's no valid excuse to not try to inflict a positive change wherever possible."[10]

Public-Purpose Media and *Diary of A Single Mom*

Perhaps the show that most clearly blends this combination of creating community and addressing social issues is the Web soap opera *Diary of a Single Mom*. Produced and directed by African American writer, actor, and director Robert Townsend, the Web series is currently in its third season. Written by Cheryl L. West, *Diary of a Single Mom* examines the struggles and successes of three single mothers who live in an apartment building in Los Angeles.

The series begins as Ocean Jackson (Monica Calhoun) moves with her two children to a triplex (eventually her niece moves in), becomes manager of the building, and gets to know her neighbors, a Latina, Lupe (Valery Ortiz), and her two children and Peggy (Janice Lynde), a white widow who is bringing up her grandson and financially taking care of herself for the first time. The challenges that the women face include Ocean's pursuit of her GED, Peggy's search for a job, Lupe's quest for love, and the women's realization that pulling together as a small community will provide them with a support system.

The men of *Diary* include Lou Bailey (Richard Roundtree) who runs the local community center, Bo (Billy Dee Williams), Ocean's uncle, and Mike (Leon), Lupe's ex-boyfriend and father of one of her children, as well as a potential love interest for Ocean. As the series develops, the women deal with such issues as Internet predators, domestic abuse, breast cancer, alcoholism, and prescription pill addiction as well as the day-to-day struggles of living on a limited budget and the stress that this adds to a family.

Figure 4.2   *Diary of a Single Mom.* Courtesy of One Economy/V Studio LA.

As with *Drama Queenz*, the space left for responses by viewers is important. The majority of the comments are very positive, and many suggest the connection that people feel to the characters. Consistently single mothers say how thankful they are for a show that expresses their feelings or describes their circumstances. For example, after the first episode, a woman identified as *jpsidej* stated, "I really enjoy the show. I am a single mom myself and I directly relate to Ocean. It gives me strength to be better and to do right by my children!" In another webisode, Ocean struggles to get her GED, which she finally accomplishes. *Kathyaa* comments with a personal story: "I was a single teen mother, who dropped out of high school when I got pregnant. I got my GED and, eventually, finished college. Some people think a GED is not as good as a high school diploma, but I've been able to do everything a high school graduate can do. Later, I taught adult education to prep people for the GED test. Don't let anything hold you back!"

Other comments show the feeling of community that *Diary* has established for the viewers. *Singlemom75* reveals, "This show is superb, I look forward to new episodes every Tuesday. I don't feel alone when I see this show. Thank You." In the very next comment *Tonya Roberts* says: "[F]inally something I can relate to! My son is only 2 years old but his daddy and I separated 3 months after he was born. I've felt so isolated and misunderstood . . . this show gives me a sense of familiarity and that some of the struggles I got going on, I'm not alone in!"

In a continuing show of solidarity, viewers often not only react to the episodes but also converse with each other about their feelings. One exchange is of particular interest. *Redbutta* says: "DOSM have truly helped me to see outside my closed circle of life and embrace the potential within me as a young Black female. Ocean, Lupe, and Peggy represent the possibilities that are unleashed through the bound of sisterhood. I am definitely telling everyone I know about the series." *Msdeejay* responds: "Hello redbutta, I tell all my friends and family about this show and how the bonds of sisterhood get each of them through what ever they are dealing with God Bless you Robert."

On the lighter side, as with *Drama Queenz* the viewers respond as if they are at home talking back to the television and give Ocean advice. In an episode in which Ocean deals with the danger of an abusive ex-husband, *Shareesa* said, "Ocean girl, you betta give him all the fight you got. It's time to do a 'Madea/Karate Kid/Bruce Lee/Set It Off' on him. Don't go down without a fight. And you better believe he is going to get his, God will see to that." This type of very personal and active viewer commentary may have to do with *Diary*'s position on the Internet.

The series is located on the Public Internet Channel (pic.tv), which advertises itself as "a public-purpose network of writers, producers and directors bringing you videos, series, blogs and tools to enhance our world."[11] Here viewers can access a variety of Web series for free. pic.tv is a subsidiary of One Economy Corporation, which, along with Robert Townsend, is one of the producers of *Diary of A Single Mom*. Founded in 2000, One Economy Corporation is a nonprofit organization whose multifaceted programs bring technology to low-income and underserved communities by establishing affordable broadband connections, training on the use of technology, and "provid[ing] public-purpose media properties that offer a wealth of information on education, jobs, health care and other vital issues. Our mission is to ensure that every person, regardless of income and location, can maximize the power of technology to improve the quality of his or her life and enter the economic mainstream."[12]

As an Internet channel, pic.tv creates a form of social synergy with its programming. Unlike websites, social networks, or e-mail servers that use Web mining (scanning for the user's website searches in order to produce banner advertisements that specifically target a consumer), *Diary of a Single Mom* is implanted on a page that has what pic.tv calls a "Make It Easy Toolbox" located on the side of the player. This interactive toolbox provides helpful information based on the topic of the webisode screened.

For example, in the webisode "Running on Empty," the three women deal with potential eviction from their apartments when the new building owner demands an increase in rent. Ocean holds a meeting with her two friends to discuss information on tenants' rights and apartment leases that she explicitly says she obtained from the website The Beehive. The "Make It Easy Toolbox" works in tandem with the episode and provides links to information on what one should know as a renter, tenants' rights in your state, and the HUD website, as well as a link to the actual website The Beehive, a One Economy Corporation website.

Former CEO of One Economy Corporation Rey Ramsey described their relationship with *Diary of a Single Mom* as follows: "This is what we mean by 'public-purpose media'—programs like 'Diary of a Single Mom' that engage, inform and inspire action . . . The Public Internet Channel and 'Diary of a Single Mom' represent the potential that exists to deliver resources and information when traditional entertainment combines with the Internet."[13]

Connecting the Web series to a nonprofit activates a synergy of support for community through the narrative and literal community resources. Says creator Robert Townsend: "Having been raised by a single mom myself, I know first-hand the kind of struggles these women encounter . . I'm especially proud to bring a show of this caliber to the Public Internet Channel, which allows viewers to be entertained by the program while providing access to critical resources. In today's economy—where we have an unemployment rate twice as high for female-headed households as it is for married women—this is more important than ever."[14]

As an industry veteran whose film *Hollywood Shuffle* (1987) illustrated the struggles over African American representation, Townsend is well aware of the limitations of the mainstream industry. His relationship with One Economy Corporation ensures a level of autonomy over the narrative without concerns about advertisers' needs or network ratings. Yet with the popularity of the show, repurposing it for the television platform and a potential alternate reach to audiences is a possibility for Townsend, who has indicated interest if the right situation arises.

This particular scenario is debated on the *Diary of a Single Mom* Web page. Many avid fans cannot believe that the show is not on television and have shared numerous suggestions from starting campaigns to petitioning BET, TV One, and Oprah's network, OWN. Others urge that it remain on the Internet to secure its integrity. *Janmarie* stated it best: "I am grateful for this series . . . not particularly invested in seeing it on a network where it may be diffused, diluted or destroyed to make it palatable, in the name of profit, for the 'mainstream.'" Web series producers must make critical decisions. Can the webisode remain an art form unto itself and serve that niche Internet audience? Or is it a form born out of industry frustration and created with the goal of repurposing for the more mainstream formats of television or film?

Black Webtopia?

Web series provide a space for Black people to see everyday stories about life's complications or joys or culturally specific vignettes. Due to their wide range of characters, these narratives show us the diversity of Black life in terms of class, gender, and sexuality—opportunities that white audiences get every day on television. While Black people are certainly not absent on network television, consistent Black narratives are. So in a sense, the Web has proven to be a type of utopia for Black talent, Black stories, and Black viewers. Web festivals and conferences have been set up to draw Web producers together. For example, the Los Angeles Web Fest began in 2010. The festival, which is an annual event, includes a series of screenings, panels, and workshops. As its organizer, Michael Ajakawe, suggests, "We need to have something that brings us together outside of the Web to talk mingle, brainstorm and find a way to help each other with our projects."[15] Web producers share their experiences and offer production and script advice, as working in this new form requires a level of short-form specialization.

So is there a downside? The key obstacles of the webisode lie in the arenas of reach and financial viability. Will watching a webisode ever have the viewing potential of network television? In their feedback on the Web series, viewers will often comment on the ease of watching an episode on their lunch or a break from work. The format works in this sense, small doses of entertainment for a fast-paced multimedia world in which appointment television is less enticing. Yet without the space for advertising, viewers often come upon these webisodes or Web channels by chance, and word of mouth goes only so far. On the other hand, audiences cannot avoid the advertising for a new series as the fall season of network television approaches. Even with the worldwide accessibility of the webisode, network television's ability to reach the everyday viewer is necessarily greater. More practically, Web series producers note that not everyone is willing to watch their entertainment on computers. As Tracy Taylor of *The New Twenties* puts it: "Not everyone wants to watch TV on the Web . . . A lot of people want their entertainment to come through their flat-screen TV. So you take the chance of missing out on a large portion of potential viewers because they just don't like the format."[16]

Secondly, finances play such a key role in the longevity of a webisode. Without the support of advertisers, for example, Web series producers have sought alternate avenues. The majority locate ways of raising the money themselves, producing on a minimal budget. Joseph of *Drama Queenz* reports: "We produce on a shoestring budget out of pocket. We keep costs very low. The actors and crew work basically for free. We are fortunate enough to get some donations, but by and large we just hope we somehow find the means to keep it all going."[17]

Ajakawe has established a pay-per-view system with *Who . . that*, while generating some revenue, limits viewership to those willing to pay even the small amount requested per show. Production costs on *The New 20s* were high, as the series was shot with the goal of repurposing it for television. Although the aesthetics are impeccable, the series, which premiered at the New York Television Festival, ran for just one season.

Some Black Web series producers definitely see the webisode as the route to traditional television or film. There is a product in hand that can be shown to various networks, as well as evidence of established viewership. Other producers are committed to the format and their audiences. They see television's history with minorities as a sign that they should stay with the format that allows them the freedom of expression with no fear of whether or not their ideas will be given the green light by a random executive. For these producers and their audiences, webisodes provide a Black webtopia.

NOTES

1. Daisy Whitney, "'The Office,' 'Heroes' Power Online NBC Play; Work Force: Digital Spinoffs, Deleted Scenes Find Younger Audiences Catching Dunder-Mifflin Sagas via Web, Mobile, iPods," *Advertising Age*, March 5, 2007, 7.

2. Brooks Barnes, "Sony's Bet on Sticking with Web Shows," *New York Times*, August 23, 2010, 1.

3. Mike Hale, "A Parallel Universe to TV and Movies: Series on the Web," *New York Times*, November 14, 2010, 20.

4. [Editor's note: See Nghana Lewis's critique of *The Game* and its privileging of Black women's narratives in this volume.]

5. Personal interview with Michael Ajakawe, December 11, 2010.

6. Personal interview with Tracy Taylor, December 12, 2010.

7. Personal interview with Dane Joseph, December 15, 2010.

8. [Editor's note: See Mark Cunningham's chapter on *Noah's Arc* in this volume.]

9. Personal interview with Dane Joseph, December 15, 2010

10. Ibid.

11. "About," Public Internet Channel, http://pictv (accessed December 12, 2010).

12. "One Economy Fact Sheet," One Economy Corporation, http://www.one-economy.com/about (accessed June 1, 2012).

13. "Robert Townsend's V-Studio and One Economy Launch 'Diary of a Single Mom,'" *Today's Drum*, http://todaysdrum.com/5366/robert-townsends-v-studio-and-one-economy-launch-diary-of-a-single-mom (accessed December 12, 2010).

14. Ibid.

15. Personal interview with Michael Ajakawe, December 11, 2010.

16. Personal interview with Tracy Taylor, December 12, 2010.

17. Personal interview with Dane Joseph, December 15, 2010.

PART II
BLACKNESS ON DEMAND

5 "Regular Television Put to Shame by Negro Production"

PICTURING A BLACK WORLD

ON *BLACK JOURNAL*

DEVORAH HEITNER

In the first episode of *Black Journal*, before the opening credits, comedian Godfrey Cambridge appears dressed in overalls and a painter's cap with a paint roller in hand and methodically paints the television frame. To the viewer, it appears that his or her television is being painted black from the inside—a potent visual symbol from the first national Black public affairs program. Initially, though, the symbol emphasizes a visual challenge to the absence of Black faces on television—a show that "looks" Black, because of the visibility of its Black hosts and reporters, but where whites still have significant editorial control. Reviewers, who mostly praised the premiere episode of *Black Journal*, tended to see the production as Black produced and something of a novelty. For example, Frank Getlein titled his review "Regular Television Put to Shame by Negro Production," demonstrating, among other things, how deeply taken for granted, how "regular," the whiteness of television was to many in 1968.

Studying *Black Journal* today offers a window into the sometimes surprising collisions and intersections of Black Power and media. It gives us a sense of what was possible in this moment in the history of educational television (before there was a "public broadcasting system"—PBS) and when foundations and corporate sponsors seemed eager to respond to social crisis with dollars. The early history of the show illustrates the challenges of finding Black self-determination in a white- owned and -controlled medium. Yet the innovation of *Black Journal*, which was a surprise to NET, was that Black staff members were unafraid to bite the hands that fed them. They were in a position to demand aesthetically and politically radical content that often critiqued the other programming on public television and the rest of the dial as well as the broader situation of Blacks in America. Engaging what Catherine Squires defines as a "counterpublic strategy," *Black Journal* challenged and provoked white viewers and gratified Black audiences by offering a Black perspective on Black culture and politics.[1]

After the screen is painted black on the first episode, host Lou House appears on-screen and declares, "It is our aim in the next hour and in the coming months to report and review the events, the dreams, the dilemmas of Black America and Black Americans."[2] Although the style and approach of the show would evolve and the balance of editorial power would soon shift, the categories of content in this first episode—stories on Black communities in the United States, updates on Black activism, coverage of events in Africa, reports on Black politics both mainstream and radical and on Black economic initiatives, and critiques of Black absence from mainstream media—typified the program in its first several years. *Black Journal* was an hour-long newsmagazine with arts coverage, hard news reporting, and interpretive commentary by hosts and guests. Early episodes were structured as a mix of in-studio discussions—often featuring House framed by dramatic black-and-white images from the stories he was reporting—alternating with short- and long-form documentaries shot in the field. The cinematography and editing of these documentaries resembled experimental and documentary cinema more than they resembled other contemporary news programs, though the program's format was similar in some ways to *60 Minutes*, which premiered the same year.

Black Journal, like the many local Black public affairs programs that premiered the same year, originated from the sense of crisis brought about by several years of "long hot summers" and Martin Luther King Jr.'s assassination, which undermined any fantasy that the United States was moving toward racial consensus. The Kerner Commission pointed the finger at media's culpability for exacerbating rioting and ignoring Black perspectives. After King's assassination, an experienced white producer at National Educational Television in New York, Al Perlmutter, was working on a series about the urban uprisings.[3] Aware of the lack of Black voices in public television and shaken by the assassination of King, he asked the organization's program director to start a Black program using the funds from the riot series. *Black Journal*'s initial budget of at least five hundred thousand dollars per season, though small for television, was considerably larger than those of local Black public affairs programs such as Boston's *Say Brother*, San Francisco's *Vibrations for a New People*, or Detroit's *Colored People's Time* produced by educational stations around the country.

After getting the go-ahead from NET's administration, Al Perlmutter became the executive producer of *Black Journal*, and he brought on eleven Black and eight white staff members to make the program. Almost immediately, Perlmutter felt some pushback about being a white executive producer for a Black program when he sent a crew to Harlem to investigate the New Breed clothing line. The proprietor there, clearly savvy about how media is made, refused to talk with *Black Journal* unless the sequence was shot, produced, and edited by African Americans. Kent Garrett was promoted to associate producer to produce that segment and has gone on to a distinguished career in media making, as have virtually all of the other Black staff members from the early years of *Black Journal*.

Black Journal on Strike

After just three episodes, the Black staff met and agreed to strike to demand full editorial control. "NET has deceived the Black Community by advertising the program series as being 'by, for and of' the black community," said the strikers to the *New York Times*. Despite appearances, they had "no editorial control over the program's content or production." Staff member St. Clair Bourne said to the *New York Times*, "We, not only as black professionals but mainly because we are black people, feel that NET has been hypocritical." The network's staffing decisions represented not "tokenism" but "frontism" in that the visibility of the Black on-air staff was used, in the *Times* writer's words, to perpetuate "the idea that Negroes controlled the program," though in fact, white NET employees produced the majority of the segments.[4]

Embarrassed, NET soon offered terms, hoping to settle the dispute promptly.[5] NET claimed that it had intended "all along" for the show to have a Black executive producer but was "unable to find anyone qualified."[6] Eventually William Greaves, who had already appeared as a co-host on the program, was hired for the position, replacing Perlmutter. Greaves, an accomplished and well-regarded experimental filmmaker and theater artist, was, at forty-two, somewhat older than most "young Turks" on the staff at the time.[7] Acknowledging how unusual it was for Black media workers to take action against a powerful media entity, *Variety* reported about the strike: "Even if the series is cancelled and the group dispersed, 'Black Journal' has clearly signaled the end of a time when integrationist Negroes accepted the token generosities of white liberals with murmurs of gratitude. Because if NET public service initiative put the show on the air, it took the independent action of black staff members to make 'Black Journal' black."[8]

In 2010, Kent Garrett recalled that one of the most revolutionary things about the strike was that the staff went to the press with their story. "We knew we had them in the corner," he recalls, as they had been claiming the show was "by, for, and about" Black people. The tenor of the times made the striking staffers feel "almost invincible," he said: "You didn't care about losing your job; there is a bigger principle involved. You're young, you're talented, you feel that if they're not going to meet your demands, you're not going to do the show."[9] Other activists of color in the broadcast industry around the country successfully used similar tactics in the years that followed.[10]

The transfer of power on *Black Journal* was immediately signaled visually and verbally on the broadcast. At the beginning of *Black Journal*'s fifth episode, which aired in October 1968, host Lou House tells the story of the walkout and subsequent change in control in an understated way. Greaves appears in the studio with him, demonstrating that the program is now under Black direction. The new opening theme featured a red globe with images from the program inside a black space in the shape of the African continent, signifying *Black Journal*'s connection to a Black world. *"Black Journal* surprised itself by making headlines," said House of the strike. He smiled as he announced that the show was now truly "by, for and of Black people, and that's where it's at." Speaking with *Variety* after the strike, staff members reported that the show immediately gained "credibility in the black community" due to the strike.

Documenting a Black World: Capturing Black Reality

The installation of Greaves as executive producer seemed to forecast a radical departure from the "rationalist" style of PBS: "Journalistic objectivity is one of the biggest lies in Western culture," he said.[11] Greaves told his staff: "Always try to make films about Black people with the interior voice. Don't be like white people and just say, 'This is what so and so say.' Try to get *the Black people* to say it." *Black Journal's* staff under Greaves, who was at the helm through the twenty-fifth episode at the end of 1969, did "get the Black people to say it" and empha-sized an experimental style with documentaries, often shot partially in a cinema verité style with less voice-over and more discussion with the film's subjects, whether they were Black cops in Harlem or sharecroppers in the Mississippi Delta. These first two years of *Black Journal* emphasized the geographic and ideo-logical diversity of the Black world and Black liberation while also highlighting the importance of unity and connection.

While our historic misremembering of this critical moment in Black libera-tion history tends to emphasize an adversarial, Martin versus Malcolm or civil

Figure 5.1   William Greaves and *Black Journal* staff. Courtesy of William and Louise Greaves.

rights versus Black Power contest, an examination of *Black Journal* reminds us that this was a chorus of voices, not a contest, and that adherents to a broad spectrum of Black political thought found common ground or at least fruitful dialogue. In January 1969, *Black Journal* brought together an impressive group of Black public figures, including Kathleen Cleaver, Ron Karenga, and Andrew Young, to offer their retrospective views of 1968 and to predict what 1969 might bring. In response to the press release, Memphis-based white critic Larry Williams nervously predicted of this episode, "I'm sure the remarks will be occasionally bitter and even threatening."

Williams probably quaked when watching Kathleen Cleaver say: "There's a world of difference between twenty million unarmed people and twenty million people armed to the hilt . . . That's power." While some of her colleagues disagree on tactics, they engage with the Black Panther Party positions as she explains them, and she listens to their points of view as well. Each of the guests had proposals and promises for Black America; they spoke to one another with respect, even as they disagreed. *Black Journal* created a forum that brought prominent and ideologically opposed individuals into the same room—not an everyday occurrence. From a cultural nationalist perspective, Ron Karenga of the organization U.S. (United Slaves) points out the problems of alliances with white groups: "We can only do that [build alliances] with people of color as opposed to the colorless—we cannot make alliance when they have all the power. The white people are slick enough to understand that people are not going for nonviolence anymore." In contrast to Cleaver and Karenga, Andrew Young says he can imagine 1969 as a year when Black people, poor people and white people "of goodwill" can get together. Cleaver, with her brisk Black Panther rhetoric, distinctive Afro, and yellow miniskirt suit, is both aurally and visually striking in this room full of men, and she becomes the focal point of the conversation, though all get to air their perspectives in a wide-ranging conversation.

The forum offers no easy answers to these differences in strategy, but it does remind us that these leaders sat down together—and that *Black Journal* gave them a space to do it, implicitly encouraging such a dialogue. Furthermore, this was not a media circus to entertain, titillate, terrify, or reassure white folks but a serious grappling with varied strategies for Black liberation. *Black Journal*, along with some of the local Black public affairs programs, gave voice to a mix of Black liberation ideologies, representing a Black political spectrum that was far more diverse than mainstream television news' obsession with binaristic liberal and conservative points of view. Furthermore, once the program was under Black editorial control, one never saw white "experts" discussing Black issues on the program, a sight all too common on both public and commercial broadcasts in this era.

In a striking departure from public television's practice of having white professors and government officials speak as "experts" on Black conditions or on "race relations," in one 1969 episode we hear from a national panel of Black high school organizers working toward school reform and adding an African American Studies component to high school curricula. Using TV as a metaphor for some white teachers' cluelessness about the life experiences of urban Black students, one high school organizer from Chicago says: "Most white teachers come from the *Leave it to Beaver* suburbs." He describes how "the school curriculum is imposed on the students—we want to have a say in why we learn . . . Everything we learn is from the system." Another young man quietly points out the similarities between schools and prisons, a prescient observation in 1968, long before the critique of a school-to prison-pipeline for Black kids was in wide circulation.

While the student activists' analysis is the explicit reason for their presence on the show, their performance and representation of the "new Black look" as an alternative image of Black youth put their appearance in implicit contrast with the few other Black images on television.[12] On *Black Journal*, the new Black look is a constant reminder of changing times and new ideas, whether it is House in his dashiki or Kathleen Cleaver in her Afro. In his striking green dashiki and wire-rimmed glasses, the young man speaking about the "system" looks poised beyond his years, reminding us how mature and astute young activists can be. A young woman on the panel sports a generous Afro and wears a gray and white minidress, again communicating both by her words and her appearance that these students are part of a new generation of Black young people. She asks urgently, "How can a white teacher communicate with me if he hasn't gone through what I've gone through?" Her question demands an answer, and the program, by not offering resolution, implicitly encourages viewers to act in their own communities. Each of these young people models both intelligence and the height of Black fashion to a national audience eager to consider questions of Black identity in curricula and in personal aesthetics. By positioning these young, intelligent, and outspoken students as experts on school reform and bringing young people from across the country to be on the program, *Black Journal* advanced the national discussion on school reform while also highlighting the possibilities of a national Black program. Significantly, the program also offered role models for its youth audience, not an image of victimized youth such as had come out of the news documentation of the southern movement, but of youth in a position of strength, expertise, and beauty at a time when Black youth were either maligned or ignored by mass media.[13]

Black Journal was frequently pedagogical—for Blacks and whites. Unlike the local Black public affairs programs, which sometimes had a more "enclave approach" (though they too were educational for non-Black viewers), *Black Journal* always was aware that because it was the national Black program on educational television, white viewers and critics were watching. So the program, while explicitly addressing itself to Black people, also offered history lessons and made political connections explicit for everyone.[14] The program implied that Black viewers should consider themselves part of a national and international

Black community, assert themselves politically and culturally, know and take pride in their history, and seek out and demand alternative sources of news. By situating the topics it explored as common to Black people in many regions and nations, the program proposed that Black viewers should consider themselves part of an emerging Black world wherein all regions of Black America as well as Africa and the Black Diaspora were vitally relevant.

On the home front, the program's national inclusiveness was most pointed when it covered the American South. Whenever House spoke of southern Black people, he used the words *we* and *us*, as in "We are having trouble with voter registration in the South." Early episodes focused on business development, health care, and educational initiatives in the South, from basic literacy initiatives to the student activism at Duke University that led to the formation of Malcolm X University. One story features an innovative fishermen's collective that shares a boat among a number of poor Black fishermen who had previously been unable to purchase their boats and had to work for white, boat-owning fishermen.

While covering dynamic new initiatives in the South, *Black Journal* also insisted on giving airtime to the brutality and privation that many African Americans continued to face even after the southern civil rights movement, along with a focus on the ingenuity of various individuals and organizations in addressing southern injustices. In one episode, the privations of tenant farmers and their families in the Mississippi Delta and their brutal effects on the health and life chances of poor sharecropping families are exposed. Through interviews and in wide images that situate the people in harsh landscapes reminiscent of the Dust Bowl photographs taken by Dorothea Lange and Walker Evans, we see people literally starving before our eyes. A scene features a long conversation with a woman with thirteen children whose husband makes sixty-five dollars in a "good month" tending a local farmer's cattle. Another segment focuses on the continued challenge of Black disenfranchisement in the South even after the Voting Rights Act, including scare tactics, turning elected posts into "appointed" posts, and "redistricting to dilute our vote." Images of clothes drying on the line in front of shacks demonstrate that people are living in desperate conditions, conditions that *Black Journal* explicitly compares to the third world. The next scene shows Representative Robert Clark, who, in 1967, became the first African American elected to the Mississippi State Legislature since the Reconstruction era. The scene features Clark in his office helping people whose food assistance has been inexplicably cut. House angrily narrates: "The outrageous violation of our rights is an everyday occurrence in the Delta, and Representative Clark spends much of his time dealing with the criminal and discriminatory practices of most state agencies."

Far from the disinterested voice-over of an "objective narrator," House's voice bristles with anger as he describes the situation, emphasizing the first-person plural. At a time when other media tended to separate the southern civil rights struggle from the experiences of northern and urban Blacks, emphasizing dichotomies such as rural versus urban and southern versus northern, *Black Journal* purposely sought to resist those divisions, framing the national civil rights struggle as one struggle of unified African American people—despite acknowledged differences in priorities and approaches.

Black Journal also continually defined and redefined its commitment to a "Black world" as including not merely the United States but also Africa and the Caribbean. At the beginning of its second season, House enthusiastically introduced an "exclusive" film of the 1969 Pan African Cultural Festival. *Black Journal* began to produce African coverage, bringing Black Americans into dialogue with African liberation struggles. By August 1970, the program had attained the resources to open a bureau in Addis Ababa—an extraordinarily ambitious move that defined the show as cutting-edge and peerless and underscored the importance of Africa to African American thinking and politics.[15] Reflecting in 2010 on the program's emphasis on African coverage when other media were all but ignoring Africa, Wali Siddiq (formerly Lou House) said resolutely: "We wanted to do more on Africa. We should do more on Africa. There should be more done on Africa. Africa is your whole soul land."[16]

In an episode on apartheid, *Black Journal* hosted a number of South African intellectuals and artists living in the United States. It also showed a film made by South Africans in 1965, which was smuggled out of Africa, and offered its own commentary on the footage. In August 1970, *Black Journal* opened with a direct interrogation by William Greaves of audience members' ideas and/or lack of knowledge about Africa: "One thinks of Africa and thinks of . . . what? Rhythms . . . Black people in the jungle dancing, naked and perhaps scarred with body marks." Setting aside "such clichés, such Western myths about Africa," he announced, *Black Journal* had "examined the current situation in Kenya and Tanzania" for its viewers.

Following this opening, Tony Batten, who ran the newly created African bureau, interviews the brother of President Jomo Kenyatta, James Muigai, as well as President Julius K. Nyerere of Tanzania, individuals not frequently seen on U.S. television. In a long and heady discussion, Nyerere theorizes about socialism and capitalism, explains how a communal society in agrarian Tanzania offers an indigenous base for socialism, and discusses the need for manpower to modernize his country, directly soliciting African American engineers, doctors, and architects to consider how they could contribute to Tanzania's emergence. The episode also offers an interview with a field commander from the Mozambique Liberation Front who speaks of the challenging conditions faced by decolonizing forces in Mozambique. The content of the discussion, especially with Nyerere, was undoubtedly long-winded for some viewers. However, by refusing to simplify the complex issues of decolonizing nations, minds, and economies, it demonstrates the respect that *Black Journal* had for its audience. Furthermore, one gets the sense that the African leaders interviewed saw *Black Journal* as a vital opportunity to reach out to African Americans.

In the next episode, the program made more explicit connections between *Black Journal*'s American viewers and Black Africans—connections that *Black Journal*'s audience eagerly sought as well. David Sibeko, head of missions from the Pan Africanist Congress, offers a message for *Black Journal*'s viewers, saying it moves him that his "brothers" are wearing their hair "natural." While in the previous episode Nyerere had effectively invited skilled African Americans and Black Europeans to join the struggle for modernization in Tanzania, Sibeko asks for and acknowledges a more symbolic form of connection and support, suggesting that Black Americans were doing their part by decolonizing their minds—two vital messages to Black Americans about Africa's role in their lives. Reports such as *Black Journal*'s segments on African nations provided a much needed and much appreciated context for redefining Blackness in art, culture, and politics to American audiences.

When *Black Journal* premiered in June 1968, educational television was a prominent example of what *Black Journal*ist and historian Lerone Bennett designated as "white-oriented media," and the context for public television's emergence seemed to offer little hope for substantive change.[17] As educational television (ETV) was consolidating forces and funding to become what we now recognize as public television,[18] the public broadcasting system, (created from the previously loosely connected ETV stations around the country), provided a new space for Black programming, in part to counter charges of "elitism" that were being used by conservatives to argue against public television's government funding. Yet educational television had an overwhelmingly white staff and an overwhelmingly white audience—so *Black Journal* emerged within a great chasm.

Black Journal had to deal with a special kind of censorship, as some educational stations did not want to air the program and NET could not impose programming on stations. Ultimately, Alabama ETV lost its broadcast license because of the station's repeated refusal to air Black programs. *Black Journal* was one of the key points of contention. Alabama ETV was reluctant to show *Black Journal* (or *Soul!* or *Sesame Street*), ostensibly because its leaders theoretically objected to the language in specific episodes. A representative of Alabama ETV claimed to the FCC that *Black Journal* contained "lewd vulgar obscene profane and repulsive materials." In a rare victory for antiracist broadcast reformers, in a case similar to the better-known WLBT case, Alabama ETV lost its broadcast license in 1973.[19]

In 1970, after Greaves left, NET hired Tony Brown from *Colored People's Time* in Detroit as the executive producer. While Brown brought a vital energy to the program right away when he took the helm, the changes he made were not without their detractors. Critics argued that the new format sacrificed the shows' usual acute and clear assertions. "He is trying for a slicker and faster-moving fusion of assorted reports and occasional bridges of song," stated the *New York Times* in a review of the show.

Black Journal's status as the premiere Black public affairs program continued to erode in 1973, when *Black Perspective on the News*, which had started out as a local program in Philadelphia, surpassed it in national public television distribution. Many more stations chose to air *Black Perspective*, in part because Tony Brown had become a controversial figure in public television. One industry memo noted that "many members of the black communications community" felt that Brown arbitrarily kept "all viewpoints but his own from *Black Journal*."[20] Yet Brown also had ardent supporters and was able to rally them to continue to keep the pressure on public broadcasting for several more years.

The Black perspective of shows like *Black Journal* had begun to seem too radical to PBS decision makers by the mid-1970s. Many Black public affairs programs were canceled in this period; some of their replacements (when they were replaced) were more "interracial" in their address. In the first half of the 1970s, a number of articles in the Black press made the argument that Black viewers' taxes paid for PBS and that these vital programs should not be cut. One 1974 article in *Black Enterprise* characterized the Corporation for Public Broadcasting as "a tax-supported institution operated as a white-male-dominated plantation with a shocking lack of concern and sensitivity about racial matters."[21] Despite such protests—and despite *Black Journal's* support from the FCC's first African American commissioner, Benjamin Hooks, and sponsorship of two hundred

Figure 5.2   *Black Journal:* Percy Sutton, Adam Wade, and Tony Brown. Courtesy of PhotoFest.

thousand dollars from the Pepsi Corporation—PBS elected not to continue airing *Black Journal* in 1976. The show migrated to commercial television in 1977 as *Tony Brown's Journal* with funding from Pepsi-Cola that allowed Brown to offer the program free in syndication.[22] Eventually, the program returned to public television but remained, in both title and focus, *Tony Brown's Journal*.

Looking back at *Black Journal* offers a conspicuous reminder of the ways innovative Black media makers did the work of redefining the meaning of integration toward pluralism and recognition of Black politics, arts, and culture. In its early years especially, *Black Journal* called attention to the diversity and the common interest of Black people in all regions of the United States and the world. By asserting themselves with the strike, the staff "ended an era of thanks for tokenism" for good and provided an example of the possibilities of this kind of action. With its innovations in content and style, *Black Journal* offered a Black interpretation of Black experiences and envisioned a Black world documenting Black life, liberation, and struggle throughout the United States and the world. In all of these efforts, *Black Journal* considerably exceeded its mandate from NET—ultimately doing much more than simply painting the television screen Black.

NOTES

1. Catherine Squires, "Rethinking the Black Public Sphere: An Alternative Vocabulary for Multiple Public Spheres," *Communication Theory* 12, no. 4 (November 2002): 446–468.

2. House is now known as Wali Siddiq.

3. NET was an influential New York–based producing organization that sent programs to most educational stations around the country. The programs were literally sent through the mail in this era. They did not have technology to do a live feed to most other cities.

4. Robert E. Dallo, "11 Negro Staff Members Quit N.E.T.'s 'Black Journal' Program," *New York Times*, August 23, 1968.

5. George De Pue, "NET 'Black Journal' Ended Era of 'Thanks for Tokenism,' Producers Say," *Variety*, September 18, 1968

6. Ibid.

7. Charles Hobson, interview with author, August 14, 2004.

8. Ibid.

9. Kent Garrett, interview with author, September 3, 2010.

10. See, for example, Chon Noriega, *Shot in America: Television, the State and the Rise of Chicano Cinema* (Minneapolis: University of Minnesota Press, 2000).

11. George De Pue, "NET 'Black Journal' Ended Era of 'Thanks for Tokenism,' Producers Say," *Variety*, September 18, 1968.

12. See Maxine Leeds Craig, *Ain't I a Beauty Queen? Black Women, Beauty, and the Politics of Race* (Oxford University Press, 2002).

13. [Editor's note: The connections between what *Black Journal* does and what Bill Cosby attempts to do in his 1970s children's program *Fat Albert and the Cosby Kids* strike home here. See TreaAndrea Russworm's chapter on *Fat Albert* and play in this volume.]

14. Squires ("Rethinking the Black Public Sphere") proposes that Black publics use the enclave as a strategy of speaking primarily within Black communities when conditions are

too threatening to employ a counterpublic strategy of speaking both to Black and other publics.

15. Lawrence Laurent, "'Black Journal' in Ethiopia," *Washington Post*, August 1, 1970.

16. Wali Siddiq, interview with author, August 4, 2010.

17. Lerone Bennett, "Media White," in *The Challenge of Blackness* (Chicago: Johnson Publishing, 1972).

18. For accounts of this history, see Laurie Ouellette, *Viewers Like You? How Public TV Failed the People* (New York: Columbia University Press, 2002) and James Day, *The Vanishing Vision: The Inside Story of Public Television* (Berkeley: University of California Press, 1995).

19. [Editor's note: See Steven D. Classen, *Watching Jim Crow: The Struggles over Mississippi TV, 1955–1969* (Durham: Duke University Press, 2004), for more on the WLBT case.]

20. Bill Duke to John W. Macy, personal memorandum, NPBA, March 24, 1972.

21. James D. Williams, "Blacks and Public TV," *Black Enterprise*, January 1974, 31–33.

22. "Hooks, FCC Commissioner: Keep *Black Journal* on the Air," *New York Amsterdam News*, January 20, 1973; Gerald Fraser, "'Black Journal' Is Syndicated," *New York Times*, November 10, 1977.

"HEY, HEY, HEY!"

BILL COSBY'S *FAT ALBERT* AS
PSYCHODYNAMIC POSTMODERN PLAY

TREAANDREA M. RUSSWORM

Origins

Although the cartoon series *Fat Albert and the Cosby Kids* (CBS, 1972–1984) averaged only nine new episodes a year during its twelve-year run (compared to a
more standard production cycle of twenty-five to sixty new episodes a year for
other cartoons), the show remained a highly popular option for young viewers
on late Saturday mornings. By the time of the series' network premiere in 1972,
the cartoon's animated African American stars—Weird Harold, Dumb Donald,
Fat Albert, Rudy, Mushmouth, Bucky, Russell, and Bill—were familiar and
recognizable to American audiences as originating from Bill Cosby's boyhood
community of North Philadelphia. By then, Cosby had turned the characters into
urban folklore since he had spent the better part of the 1960s perfecting their personalities and mannerisms, describing their rites of passage rituals, and mytholo-
gizing their games and play activities as he performed them live and onstage,
often before sold-out audiences. During the 1960s and 1970s, Cosby cultivated the
strategic and marketable public persona of an authentic, humorous purveyor and
translator of ghetto life who also had the acumen, the philanthropic ambitions,
and (eventually) the credentials of an educator. *Fat Albert* became a cartoon, then,
precisely because of Cosby's ability to change his image from urban folklorist to
public educator.

As a cartoon backed by a major network, *Fat Albert* was atypical for any number
of reasons: it appeared to star animated Black children; it was a Filmation cartoon,
but it included live-action segments of Cosby commenting on the boys' adventures;
and it made heavy use of stock and recycled imagery, giving it a predictable and
consistent visual style. From Cosby's perspective, there was at least some concern
that the typical Saturday morning lineup of *Casper the Friendly Ghost*, *The Hardy Boys*,
Scooby-Doo, *The Archie Comedy Hour*, and *The Flintstones* did little to reflect the ethnic, racial, and economic diversity of American youth television audiences during
the 1970s. Educational programs like *Sesame Street*, *The Electric Company*, and especially *Fat Albert* could, according to Cosby, "establish in the minds of millions of

television viewers and educators that Black children are not by nature stupid or lazy; they are not hoodlums, they are not junkies. They are you. They are me ... Their problems are universal."[1] Additionally, *Fat Albert* was a remarkable programming initiative at the time because, as Cosby hoped, "for the first time Black children [would] have the opportunity to see themselves" in a televised cartoon.[2]

But what can be said of the cartoon's most unlikely of title characters—an obese Black boy who lives in the ghetto and plays with his friends, many of them caricatures, in a junkyard? In 1976, Cosby, who wrote his doctoral thesis on *Fat Albert* because he thought the show should be seen as a viable educational model and curricular supplement, offered these thoughts about the character for whom he provided the voice: "Fat Albert is two things: He is a modern super hero and he is a teacher. He is a sympathetic hero that children, especially Black children, can empathize with as he struggles with value conflicts and the peer group problems that confront children today."[3] Although Cosby might have been talking about Fat Albert as a guise for himself as superhero and teacher, I am particularly struck by the notion of Fat Albert as a superhero—for all children and, as Cosby notes, particularly for Black children. What kind of "superhero" is Fat Albert, and is that even the right word? What is gained by that visual motif of excess that Fat Albert symbolizes, especially as it is contrasted with the pronounced economic deficit of the animated neighborhood in which he lives?

Scholarly considerations of Bill Cosby's significant role in American television history have mostly been concerned with analyses of *The Cosby Show* (NBC, 1984–1992), his signature genre-saving sitcom. In this regard, Sut Jhally, Linda F. Fuller, Janet Staiger, Herman Gray, Michael Real, and other scholars of television and media have contributed close analyses and reception-based research on *The Cosby's Show*'s global cultural significance, including its complicity in projecting Reagan-era politics and bifurcating racial ideals.[4] In part to destabilize the centrality of *The Cosby Show* in written accounts of Cosby's career, this chapter will argue that although critically overlooked in televisual and African American cultural criticism, *Fat Albert* demonstrates that Cosby's formulaic recipe of caricature, hyperbole, and psychologically sensitive humor began much earlier than *The Cosby Show* and well before *Little Bill* (Nick Jr., 1999–2004), his most recent cartoon. More than a decade before *The Cosby Show*, *Fat Albert* animated the rich symbolic imagery of psychological possibility and Blackness at play in the guise of educational programming. Situating Cosby's first cartoon within the larger public discourses about Black emotional health, particularly the concerns about the mental well-being of Black children before and after the years of the civil rights movement, helps show how Cosby's creation of Fat Albert and the "gang" was committed to the serious business of challenging popular constructions that imagined the interior life of Black children as hollow and psychically unanimated.

Theories of play and subjectivity are central to my research on Cosby's career during the 1960s and 1970s. I examine Cosby's long-forgotten cartoon by culturally historicizing it and briefly considering other kinds of popular narratives about Black childhood that were commonplace during the time. These perspectives, I argue, are instructive in thematic, plot, and structural analyses of the sixty episodes that appeared between 1972 and 1981 during the network run of the cartoon and also in viewing the fifty episodes that were produced in 1984 to run in syndication with the original episodes.[5] With the protracted history of the series in mind, but especially the first two seasons, the cartoon is examined here using the language of psychoanalysis.

I find psychoanalytic principles essential for understanding *Fat Albert* not only because a good deal of the popular culture of the 1960s and 1970s widely appropriated psychological concepts as a way of understanding racism and the inevitability of change, but also because Cosby has spent his entire career integrating commonsense psychological rhetoric into his many entertainment endeavors. Cosby's stories and humor depend on central themes of psychoanalysis—the conflict between good and bad objects, the desire for appropriate "mirroring," and the healing potential of fantasy and playing make-believe.[6] While I argue that we cannot fully understand Cosby's televisual contributions without bringing psychology and psychoanalysis to African American cultural studies traditions, this chapter's methodological orientation makes clear that there were many other influences on the show that warrant consideration beside the psychological ones. In this vein, the psychodynamic significance of *Fat Albert* is complicated by the postmodernist attributes of image, sound, and animation techniques that "haunt" the psychic life of Fat Albert and the Cosby kids throughout the production history of the series.

Narrating Black Childhood

While the ambition to introduce a refashioned view of the moral fabric of Black youth to Black and non-Black audiences may have been unique for children's programming in the early 1970s, such goals were not new concerns for the larger stage of civil-rights-era America. What we can rightly think about as a civil-rights-era psychological culture (a culture that emphasized an explicit rhetoric of healing) persisted for quite some time in American cultural life. Black children became a fixture in that system of national fantasy about humanitarian concern. As Anne Cheng has intimated, "the politics of race has always spoken in the language of psychology," and we need not look very far to discern the applicability of this statement to the long years of the civil rights campaign.[7] Not only was there the Supreme Court's decision in *Brown v. Board of Education* (1954) that identified a concern over the "hearts and minds" of Black children as one major reason to desegregate the school system, but there was also a high concentration of research produced during the civil rights era by sociologists, social psychologists, and psychologists that took to analyzing varying accounts of the intimate logic of an imagined Black mind to a receptive American public.

From the 1930s on, but especially during the 1950s and later during a new peak in the 1970s, these discourses privileged inquires about the nature of Black self-esteem. It is here that we can situate Kenneth and Mamie Clark's work with Black children that sought to establish the causal relationship between segregation and Black self-esteem, demonstrating the likelihood that Black children could suffer from confidence and self-worth complexes as a result of systemic racism. In a similar vein, social psychological works from Abram Kardiner and Lionel Ovesey's *The Mark of Oppression* to Gunnar Myrdal's *American Dilemma* understood social and economic oppression as the *causes* of depleted and seething Black psyches. Such concerns were expressed in psychosocial literature that ranged from the infamous Moynihan Report to Clark's *Prejudice and Your Child* and *Dark Ghetto*.[8] These analyses insist that the psychological costs of racism were unjustly taxing Black people, especially children, since they were thought to be even more psychically vulnerable. In this way, the inequities of segregated and inferior schooling quickly became synonymous with Black childhood. The innocence, wonder, ability, and esteem of Black childhood and important activities governed by fantasy, play, and joy were often defined through a prism of lack, as evinced in the conclusion of Clark's famous doll studies.

Civil-rights-era American visual culture further reinforced the dominant impression of Black youth experiences, particularly in urban environments, as tragically endangered and devoid of playful spontaneity. This is a visual cultural archive that ranges from *The Quiet One* (1948), a documentary about an emotionally scarred Black boy who is in residence at the infamous Wiltwyck School for Boys, to *A Hero Ain't Nothing but a Sandwich* (1978), a film adaptation of a novel about a Black boy who becomes a junkie. The cinematic span includes lesser-known contributions like *A Bright Road* (1953), starring Harry Belafonte and Dorothy Dandridge as school workers who are called to action to intervene on behalf of one promising but emotionally neglected Black student. On television during this time of national concern over Black interiority, Bill Cosby contributes a few other works. For instance, in Cosby's 1972 television drama *To All My Friends on Shore*, the central narrative premise is that the poor financial health of a Black family bears a causal relationship to the chronic illnesses and compromised future of their young son. The 1968 television documentary *Black History: Lost, Stolen or Strayed*, hosted and narrated by Cosby, broadcasts several long segments that underscore the national need to comprehend and address the dynamics of the emotional and self-esteem predicament of Black youth.

In *Black History: Lost, Stolen or Strayed*, as was the norm in the public discourse on the issue of Black interiority, psychological experts offer analyses of Black life. One crystallizing moment occurs in an early segment as a psychiatrist examines the drawings of Black children and, in comparing them to the drawings of white children, concludes that the images drawn by Black children are—disturbingly— missing faces. According to the psychiatrist, this represents a fundamentally flawed and lost sense of self. As the critically acclaimed program draws to a close, Bill Cosby appears on camera to meditate on the overt esteem-building activities of preschool-aged Black children when they are encouraged to repeat, in a chant, that they are "Black and beautiful." Cosby comments: "This is kind of like brainwashing . . . or is it? I mean, can you blame us for overcompensating, I mean, when you take the way Black history got lost, stolen, or strayed. When you think about the kids drawing themselves without faces!" Cosby's on-screen outrage over Black children drawing themselves without faces is not so unlike Kenneth Clark's objection to Black children valorizing white dolls. In neither example is there consideration of the possibility of a fantasy life that could involve a less obvious, less literal, engagement with Clark's dolls. Both responses assume a de facto pathology instead of imagining an active fantasy life that might make productive, creative use of Clark's dolls and of these much-maligned faceless drawings.[9]

Animating Blackness at Play

Fat Albert and the Cosby Kids participated in this culture of concern by emphasizing something that was rarely, if ever, associated with Black children in the mass cultural archive: the restorative potential of play. As object relations theorist D. W. Winnicott discovered: "on the basis of playing is built the whole of man's experiential existence."[10] One of the things play does is help the self experiment with moments of grandeur possibility wherein the individual can feel omnipotent, as magically existing everywhere at once, as imminently capable and as creatively, symbiotically, connected to other powerful beings (such as mother, caretaker, an idealized figure, a powerful institution). Playing allows for productive boundary transgression, an expansion of the self, when it takes place in a neutral zone that Winnicott thought of as an intermediate territory, a "potential space," that is an alternate reality, neither entirely internally nor entirely externally experienced.

The healthiest of individuals, Winnicott thought, maintained a meaningful sense of creativity that flourished only as a positive consequence of playing; both children and adults would constantly need to have such experiences to cultivate and maintain any satisfying sense of oneself.[11] In the potential space where playing occurs, "without hallucinating" the child or adult experiments with "dream potential and lives with this sample in a chosen setting of fragments from external reality."[12] When engaged in this intermediate realm of living, then, the self is creatively blending fact and fiction, reality and fantasy, combining objects that represent other people with objects that represent the self in a protective zone that freely permits ambiguity, indeterminacy, and possibilities of being that register beyond objective reality. As Winnicott would conclude, true psychotherapeutic healing and progress could never happen for individuals who could not make playing an integral part of therapy and of life experience in general.

Bill Cosby's stand-up routines (which provided the basis for the character sketches of Fat Albert and the gang) and his revisionist, autobiographical reclamation of Black childhood as a playful and creative experience cannot be dismissed as insignificant in light of the many ways in which psychoanalytic thought, as we get to know it through Winnicott but also from many other analysts and philosophers, argues that the ability to make good, productive use of play and fantasy is essential to how individuals come to value or devalue life. It is important, then, to note the ways in which Cosby's stand-up performances used physical autobiographical humor, distinct voice acting, and character-specific sound effects to introduce fresh examples of Blackness at play to civil-rights-era audiences. In introducing his child-self at play while acting onstage as an adult comedian, Cosby was reclaiming two "potential spaces" at once for the purposes of staging his brand of civil-rights-era psychology. On the cartoon, in addition to the simulation of Blackness at play, Cosby was also no doubt playing as an adult as he performed his routine and improvised during the live-action segments of the program. These different levels of playing are always at work in the series and are compounded by the production's unique elements of televisual style.[13]

Under Cosby's projective, fantastical reenactment of the memory of Black boys at play, Fat Albert emerges in the initial episodes of the cartoon as that lost but now found Black interior sense of omnipotence. The physical space of the junkyard becomes a Winnicottian transitional potential space, and the members of the Junkyard Gang are remastered as indeterminate possibilities of an expansive self with little psychic limitation. It is not surprising, from a psychoanalytic perspective, that Cosby remembers his childhood friend Albert as so large or that Fat Albert is drawn in the cartoon as obese beyond belief, with his belly bulging over his pants and bouncing along far in front of him as he walks. Apparently, the most accessible way to imagine Black omnipotence (a combination of agency and reach, hope and potential) for children is to do so visually. Hence, the psychic "largeness" of the character is translated (both in Cosby's onstage simulation of play and in the show's drawing and scripting of it) as girth, as physical largeness and visceral spread. The exaggeration of the character's physical size, aside from signaling psychological expansion, also works to remind us that playing (though it takes place in the neither here/nor there psychic zone of experience) is necessarily a *bodily* experience. Just as the physical fact of Fat Albert and his arrival in scenes is often punctuated by that rumbling "Hey, Hey, Hey" that commands attention, he often seems to be everywhere in the neighborhood and is almost always a catalyst of conflict resolution, moral encoding, and problem-solving for the boys on-screen and especially for the imagined community of Black children viewing audiences.

During the early run of the series, Fat Albert's body and personality are complimented by the equally symbolic nature of the Junkyard Gang. The members of the gang, like Albert, are all proxies for a boundless self (Cosby) that work together to create meaning in ways that cannot be imagined or represented literally. The re-creation of the North Philadelphia ghetto as a playspace blurs the boundaries of fact and fiction from the start, and the characters that occupy it are

Figure 6.1   *Fat Albert and the Cosby Kids* (1976). Courtesy of PhotoFest.

a part of a psychically mobile domain that relies on caricature and contradiction, contrasts and symmetry. In this vein, we may also think of the members of the Junkyard Gang (who at times seem to be caricatures or neo-minstrelesque stereotypes) more rigorously.

In the third episode of the series, "The Stranger," for example, an outsider to the group, Betty (a young girl who wants to get to know the boys better), provides a contrapuntal analysis of the boys' personalities that is supposed to be effusive flattery. I argue, however, that the bit of dialogue draws our attention to the ways in which the stereotyped constructions of who the boys appear to be (both visually and audibly) is actually of a much more complicated, contested nature and demonstrates postmodern play and self-reconstitution at work. Accordingly, Betty interprets the stereotypical "cool man," Rudy, "as adventuresome, dashing, darling"; the typical "nerd," Weird Harold, becomes "intellectual, aloof, distinguished"; the "fat kid," Albert, is "mighty, powerful, magnificent, a monument of a man"; the "bucktoothed" Bucky is "that noble brow"; the inarticulate "buffoon," Mushmouth, is read as "rakish, debonair." When examined in isolation, each boy seems a gross stereotype that Betty's generous viewpoint cannot convincingly challenge.

When examined together, however, the boys represent an essence of postmodern fragmentation in ways that may be trans-therapeutic. For example, many of the gang's playspace activities, such as playing the dozens (which includes ruthlessly deriding each other), help establish important lines of difference in the junkyard, where self-knowledge is generated through a process of "othering" and "un-other-ing." Ridiculing Albert for being fat or Dumb Donald for being dumb or Rudy for having "no class!" keeps the self and others in a comfortable, if productively destructive, tension. In this way, the gang offers weekly lessons in the Hegelian and Winnicottian paradoxes of the "Me/Not-me" processes of self-actualization. Evident in this mobilization of stock character types are postmodern and psycho-analytic theories of self-multiplicity that imagine a single subjectivity can contain and maintain an active tension of many competing, inconsistent self-identities.

Play and Postmodern Style

Fat Albert's psychosocial and thematic conceits often rely on the use of post-modern devices of storytelling.[14] As Martin Coles and Christine Hall discuss in thinking about children's culture more broadly construed, "playfulness, parody, pastiche, and irony, as well as doubling, intertexuality and other metafictive devices" are often inherent in the creation, reception, and interpretation of post-modern children's culture.[15] *Fat Albert*'s highly ludic nature and model of play as psychic transformation are most evident in moments when the gang plays games like "buck buck," when they play fantasy-based games like football that sends them imaginatively soaring over cars, and when they use the objects of the street scene, particularly junk, as tools of play. The very basis of the "Junkyard Band" and the way the boys perform catchy songs using the magical junk (transitional objects) of urban waste hinges on a belief that fantasy, creativity, and subjectivity are intertwined. Cosby's playful tendency to make exaggeration a norm in reimaging Black boyhood is evident when his reenactments treat the mundane as fantastical, such as when Bill visits the dentist or when he gets his tonsils out and looks forward to the hyperbolic psychic experience of eating "all the ice cream in the world."

Similarly, *Fat Albert*'s "boundary breaking" persists in the frequent collapse of distinctions between high and low culture. In this regard, the boys often take turns adapting literary source material such as *Moby-Dick* and the tales of King Arthur just as often as they reenact scenes from *The Brown Hornet*, a fictionalized cartoon (starring an animated Cosby as a costumed figure that they watch on television in the clubhouse). The blurring of high and low is further evident in the musical interludes performed by the band that repeat the content from the previous fifteen minutes, creating a collage that blends disparate forms of art and culture. Children's culture tends to be well suited for experimenting with bound-ary transgression since fictional narratives designed for children are normatively fantastical and compositional. In their introduction to *Postmodern Picturebooks*, Lawrence Sipe and Sylvia Pantaleo note that "the blurring between story and real life," "playfulness, parody, and intertexuality," the use of "constructed artifice," and "metafictive, self-referential qualities" are all hallmarks of attempts to represent visually and reorder the world for children in less literal ways.[16] *Fat Albert* was animated using a good deal of static stills of storyboard drawings that depict the background of the city and the junkyard. Panning the camera over those still images creates a sense of motion, but at times this cost-saving animating technique makes entire segments of the cartoon appear like something closer to a postmodern picturebook than animation.

As a specifically televisual production, though, *Fat Albert* is both thematically and stylistically postmodern. In *Television Culture*, John Fiske argues that postmodern television "emphasizes the fragmentary nature of images, their resistance to sense, the way that images are more imperative than the real and have displaced it in our experience."[17] More than anything else, the image in postmodern television culture should be thought of as spectacle. In postmodern television shows like Hulk Hogan's *Rock 'n' Wrestling* (CBS, 1985–1986), Fiske sees a Bakhtinian example of "grotesque realism" in the representations of "beefcake" and hyper-masculine men. *Rock 'n' Wrestling* makes for an apt model of comparison to *Fat Albert* since both programs were animated series for children that were also both a part of CBS's Saturday lineup. In analyzing the postmodernist investments of *Rock 'n' Wrestling's* visual spectacles of masculinity that were, like Fat Albert (the character), often drawn and animated as a kind of Bakhtinian bodily excess, Fiske writes: "The excessiveness of this strength, in alliance with its ugliness, opens a space for oppositional and contradictory readings of masculinity: the grotesqueness of the bodies may embody the ugliness of patriarchy, an ugliness that is tempered with contradictory elements of attraction. There is a sense, too, in which this grotesqueness liberates the male viewer from the tyranny of the unattainably perfect male body."[18]

While I do not argue that the postmodernist play in *Fat Albert* and the psychological spectacle of Fat Albert's body consistently achieve Rabelaisian carnival, certainly inflections of this kind of disorder are very much a part of Cosby's televisual ghetto that at times does include Bakhtinian laughter, excessiveness, and bad taste—despite its packaging as innocuous educational programming.[19]

These moments of postmodern spectacle in television are eventually about consumerism, insists Fiske, and such moments can be found in shows that serve explicit market purposes and are intended for repeated viewing. Moreover, Fiske notes the postmodern tendency to recycle imagery, arguing that this can produce "free-floating signifiers whose only signification is that they are free, outside the control of normal sense and sense-making."[20] In light of *Fat Albert's* broadcast origins and the network's view of it as profitable as a series of reruns with borrowed material, the cartoon and its postmodernist attributes are examples of how television functions in late capitalism. Formally, in the case of *Fat Albert*, I am struck by how the show's use of recycled images, shaded character silhouettes, stock footage, and outlines of whole environments does not always make sense.

The *Fort! Da!* of Form and Walking in *Fat Albert*

Two features of *Fat Albert*'s visual style create motifs that fall outside the scope of "normal sense and sense-making." These two features are the repetition of walking and the frequent use of static black outlines and silhouettes of the characters. Every episode contains the same set of three or four shots of the gang walking (close, medium, and long shots that are placed in front of "mattes" of varying backgrounds of the junkyard and city). Likewise, nearly every episode contains a moment when black outlines or silhouettes of the characters are used instead of the colorful and fully cel-shaded character modules. This budget-conscious mechanism of rotoscoping and partially shading instead of coloring the characters carries additional symbolic meaning when viewed in the context of what the show is saying about identity, psychology, and playful nonliteral meaning.

The use of stock footage of the characters walking in exactly the same way in each episode conveys a sense of generalization, of nonspecificity about their destination and whereabouts as they move through time and space. In *The Practice of Everyday Life*, Michel de Certeau theorizes city walking as "a spatial acting-out of the place"—walking in an urban environment has the potential to distort a sense of the here and the now and map out new, unintended possibilities.[21] In the same way that Charlie Chaplin used his cane in creative and nontraditional ways, the habitual walker also challenges the "constructed order" of the city, makes discrete choices about which routes to take, and thus "increases the number of possibilities" of subjectivity.[22] The repetition of the stock group shuffle walk in *Fat Albert*, with its two-dimensional nonparticularity, expresses an equivocal illusion of mobility. Each time the gang walks through the city, then, this consequence of low-budget style conveys a highly metaphorical "long poem of walking" that has the potential to manipulate space and organization. Walking in this way compromises a sense of structure and creates what de Certeau describes, excitedly, as revisionary "shadows and ambiguities" of meaning.[23]

The repetition of walking combines with the second nonsensical element of postmodern style, the use of inky black silhouettes as substitutes for the main characters, to further express the difficulty in locating a literal space (or singular subjectivity) for the transgressive activity of Blackness at play. For instance, when they appear on television as shadowy outlines, the boys are not fully articulated renditions. Instead, they are physically indeterminate, unidentifiable as specific subjects. There is an interchangeability to this practice of outlining too, since sometimes the city appears as an outline in the background while the characters are fully shaded and vice versa. The result is that the city also becomes a much less specific, dreamlike spatial zone. Perhaps ironically, Fat Albert and the Cosby kids use the exercise of nonparticularized walking to exit and reenter the space of the junkyard, to manipulate and distort the (storyboard) city around them, and to further experiment with who they are (and are not). These two formal features of Filmation's style work together in unique ways in *Fat Albert* to create a visual style that matches the psychological persuasion of the project as a whole. Consistent with how play and fantasy are thought to work in the minds of children, these two formal features of the cartoon work together to condense and displace meaning, making the many long, repetitive walking-through-the-city segments look more and more like a colorful, portentous dream.

The cartoon's dreamlike walking and shadowy imagery create the illusion of being present and not present, representable and not representable, at the same time. In the classic Freudian children's game *fort! da!* (translated as "gone" and "there"), Freud analyzed the peek-a-boo-like play activities of children who wished away an object only to squeal in glee upon its return.[24] Like Freud, other analysts have interpreted such play as experimenting with the reality of the other by articulating the fretful fear that another/object is distinct (and can disappear) while longing to maintain control over its presence. The cartoon's form simulates and illustrates its own game of *fort! da!* as the members of the gang appear to be both "gone" and "there" against the backdrop of familiar storyboards. The visual cue of walking literally "disappears" the gang when they walk as shadowy cutouts and "returns" them to here and there with the practice of habitual walking. On the one hand, these aspects of style conflate the "law of being and the law of place" and turn it into a repetitive game of shadows and shapes.[25] On the other hand, the recycled imagery of walking and the shadowy otherness of the silhouettes create a complicated cycle of condensation, displacement, and projection around the hope/fear of what Black boys and the urban city represented during the 1970s and 1980s.

The Moving Body and "Unpresentable" Boyhood

Returning to the symbolic meaning of Fat Albert's body and to a concluding analysis of its relevancy to psychoanalytic and postmodern perspectives, I have selected the fifth episode of the first season, "Moving," to closely examine here because it is characteristic of how these dual influences persist throughout the span of the series, often in ways that communicate conflicting messages to viewing audiences. Specifically, three things happen in the episode that warrant attention. First, the boys unsuccessfully tamper with Albert's bodily and symbolic expansiveness by gorging him and intentionally making him even fatter—to disastrous, dehumanizing consequence. Second, after contaminating and mishandling their symbol of grandiosity externalized, the Cosby kids lose their treasured object as Albert informs them that he and his family are moving. After momentarily mourning the significance of his departure, the boys are rewarded with Albert's return. The structural pattern of the main story (specifically, Albert going away and returning) very well elucidates my assertions regarding the Winnicottian and Freudian affinities of the series and the formal repetition of the "gone" and "there" pattern/game. Thirdly, though, as the boys break into a gleeful song to celebrate the return of Fat Albert's unmoving body, the nonsensicality of the song's imagery and lyrics undermine any cohesive understanding of what has just happened.

As I have argued, Cosby's creation of Fat Albert depends heavily on a conflation of psychological wholeness and physicality. In this episode, much time is devoted to making Albert uncontainably obese so that the character may literally crush the members of a rival, menacing gang that has challenged the Cosby kids to a game of "buck buck." In an attempt to win the game, where a team loses if they cannot withstand the bodily weight of the other team, Albert's friends load him up with good and bad junk—bananas, sandwiches, "grits, bacon, and hot cornbread," along with an excessive amount of candy and sugary treats. This ritual of fattening up their important friend culminates with the gang parading Albert through city streets on their own sagging shoulders in order to preserve him for the competition. In this context, a part of the reason the gang needs Albert is the intrusion of people and objects who reside outside of their clubhouse, junkyard, and intermediate playspaces. The boys depend on Albert's heft as a symbolic buffer during times like these when rival gangs and "streetwise" characters threaten their safety and innocence. Such figures as the rival gang are ready signifiers for the assumed external toxicity of the ghetto. In Cosby's universe, only male bonding, fantasy, play, and externalized grandiosity can combat the influence of drugs, crime, and malfeasance of others. Most of the time Fat Albert represents a hopeful wish that the external signs of intrusion and contamination can be destroyed through the creative potential of their physically transgressive activities.

It is the mishandling of Albert's bodily excess, however, that suggests how faint the line between play and the uncanny (or even abjection) can be. After being overstuffed, Albert grips his body in agony, gesticulating and baring his teeth, painfully constipated by all of the junk in their environment. With Albert's grotesque and unavailable body, the mise-en-scène of the "buck buck" game represents the Cosby kids' bodies in extreme discombobulation—with legs, arms, feet, heads all hopelessly inseparable not only from each other but also from the other gang and their signification of abject urban waywardness. Despite his function as heroic psychic possibility, in moments like these, Albert's body is not so far from dehumanization and despair. As Rudy complains when Fat Albert cannot perform: "I always thought Albert was really cool, but he turned out to be a big turkey."

Discontinuity, distantiation, and disbelief are further emphasized in the coordination of image and sound during the episode's musical performance. Typically the music, along with new and repeated shots in these segments, reinforces the events of the main story.[26] Notably, however, in the case of this song ("Friends") the lyrics and added animations narrate events that did not happen in the main story. The song the gang performs emphasizes change and connecting with old friends. The words are clear about the movement to new places ("a brand-new neighborhood") and the creation of new community ("new friends, new friends"). Yet the new shots (of Albert talking with his father, getting hit with a baseball bat, crying, departing on a van, and circling the block in order to move in next door) never appeared in the main story of the episode and emphasize Albert's mourning, abstract danger, and implausibility of real movement.

Before the musical performance, Albert tells the boys that his family has only moved around the block. The image track of the song refutes this "reality" as it shows a moving van drive Albert around a city block and immediately return him to the row house he has just left. The next shot of the truck unloading cargo at the house next door signals that there has been a slight change in address, just not to the location specified by Albert in the narrative. The metaphor of leaving and returning in this case does more than replay the Freudian *fort! da!* game of Blackness that the series consistently animates. In this case, being driven around the block and returned to the exact location, despite the conflicting narration, elicits an eerie feeling of being forcibly suspended in the here and now (and by implication nowhere else) and evokes a more literal instantiation of bodily confinement. By contrast, the agency of the de Certeauian mode of walking that characterizes the boys' usual travel is replaced by the transportation of Albert to a place none of the characters can confirm as consistent with their understanding of how and where his body has traveled. After these contradictory narratives of bodily movement, the episode ends (with a sound bridge of the song still playing) rather distractingly. In a mimesis of cowboys on horses, the final frames depict Fat Albert and the boys reunited and running through the street riding broomsticks. Since this action is animated using blocky black silhouettes of the characters, though, the strange relationship between story and song, dialogue and image, produces a general impression of distantiation that is reinforced in the outlines of the characters that makes them appear less like cowboys and more like little witches prancing through the ghetto.

By the time of the cartoon's expiration twelve long years after its debut, what could Black audiences glean from watching *Fat Albert*?[27] As Cosby had hoped, there is indeed something of a superhero here. So too is the show's titular character a psychological paradox who comes packaged in a complicating costume of plot, theme, sound, and image. In writing about the postmodern condition, Jean-François Lyotard surmises that a postmodern work puts "forward the unpresentable in presentation itself" and "denies itself the solace of good forms" in a way that ultimately undermines any "nostalgia of the whole and the one."[28] *Fat Albert*, by participating in dominant discourses on psychology and extending Cosby's metanarrative about psychically whole Black youthful existence, insists that his vision of Black interiority is indeed presentable, communicative, and universal. While the themes and psychology of *Fat Albert* construct a corrective grand narrative of Blackness, the inadvertently postmodern animated form challenges the intelligibility of that new set of governing ideals.

In the end, Bill Cosby's televisual projects of the 1960s and 1970s, particularly the ones that reintroduce Black childhood, are modest enterprises that really address only one small slice of a social concern (in this case, that broader concern has to do with affect and psychology). One problem with this artistic approach is that in addressing issues pertaining to behavior and affect, the work obscures a focus on systemic issues, just as *The Cosby Show* has been criticized for doing. Yet if we reconsider a show like *Fat Albert*, at least partly on its own limited terms, we may begin to discern how, in the rhetoric of healing produced by civil-rights-era popular culture, Cosby's class-specific humor tried to open up the crushed metaphorical space of Black boyhood and redefine it as psychologically fluid, inquisitive, and creative. Both the cartoon and Cosby's stand-up routines necessarily simulate Fat Albert, Bill, and the Junkyard Gang as both real and as unreal, as autobiography and authentic but also as exaggeration and the stuff of mythological proportion. The inspiration for the cartoon was to make Blackness, fantasy, and feeling presentable even as the resulting show questioned the presentability of such abstractions.

NOTES

1. William Henry Cosby Jr., "An Integration of the Visual Media via *Fat Albert and the Cosby Kids* into the Elementary School Curriculum as a Teaching Aid and Vehicle to Achieve Increased Learning" (PhD dissertation, University of Massachusetts, 1976), 67.

2. Ibid., 67.

3. Ibid., 64.

4. Sut Jhally and Justin Lewis, *Enlightened Racism: The Cosby Show, Audiences, and the Myth of the American Dream* (Boulder, CO: Westview Press, 1992); Linda Fuller, *The Cosby Show: Audiences, Impact, and Implications* (Westport, CT: Greenwood Press, 1992); Janet Staiger, *Blockbuster TV: Must-See Sitcoms in the Network Era* (New York: New York University Press, 2000), 141–159; Herman Gray, *Watching Race: Television and the Struggle for "Blackness"* (Minneapolis: University of Minnesota Press, 1995), 79–84; Michael Real, *Super Media: A Cultural Studies Approach* (Newbury Park, CA: Sage Publications, 1989), 106–131.

5. The title changes are as follows: *Hey, Hey, Hey, It's Fat Albert* (pilot, 1969); *Fat Albert and the Cosby Kids* (1972–1973, 22 episodes; 1975–1976, 14 episodes); *The New Fat Albert Show* (1979–1981, 24 episodes); and *The Adventures of Fat Albert and the Cosby Kids* (1984–1985; 50 episodes).

6. I think there is ample evidence to indicate that Cosby has been quite intentional in mobilizing the rhetoric of psychology not only in his comedy and television shows from *Fat Albert* to *The Cosby Show* but also in his recent books and public speeches. For example, Cosby has co-written books like *Come on People* with *The Cosby Show* psychological adviser (and Harvard professor of psychiatry) Alvin Poussaint as an attempt to combine psychological research with folk wisdom for Black readers, especially parents. Similarly, Cosby discusses the sociological and psychological merit of *Fat Albert* at length in his dissertation. He also explains that the team of educational and psychological experts who served on the advisory board for the cartoon reviewed scripts of the show in order to assess the emotional impact each episode was likely to make on its young viewing audiences. As the board was comprised of experts with research backgrounds in psychology (Dr. Seymour Feshbach), education (several, including Dr. Gordon L. Berry), social welfare (Dr. Nathan Cohen), and children's mental health issues (Dr. James O. Simmons), it is apparent that most were aware of the popular

discourses on race and psychology during the time. It is certainly plausible that several were familiar enough with some of the Freudian and Winnicottian analytic concepts I discuss. I am less concerned, however, with establishing that there was an intentional use of psychoanalysis in the making of *Fat Albert* than I am with exploring how the show is a part of a cultural milieu that tended to appropriate, irrespective of intentionally, discourses of psychology to narrate stories about racial difference.

7. Anne Cheng, *The Melancholy of Race: Psychoanalysis, Assimilation, and Hidden Grief* (New York; Oxford: Oxford University Press, 2001), 28.

8. Kenneth Clark, *Prejudice and Your Child*, 2nd ed. (Boston: Beacon Press, 1963); Kenneth Clark, *Dark Ghetto: Dilemmas of Social Power* (New York: Harper & Row, 1965); Gunnar Myrdal, *An American Dilemma: The Negro Problem and Modern Democracy*, 20th ed. (New York: Harper & Row, 1962); Abram Kardiner and Lionel Ovesey, *The Mark of Oppression: Explorations in the Personality of the American Negro* (Cleveland: World Publishing Company, 1951). Also see Herbert Foster, *Ribbin,' Jivin,' and Playin' the Dozens: The Unrecognized Dilemma of Inner-City Schools* (Cambridge, MA: Ballinger, 1974).

9. Cosby's direct participation in this conversation with a clinician does offer some insight into whether or not he was aware of psychological discourses and research during the time. Further, the *Fat Albert* episode "The Stranger" intertextually relates to this moment in the documentary. During the song performance, the gang's faces are drawn without definition, turning them into faceless, indistinguishable blobs. The message of the song is that "everybody's different," and the visualization of facelessness is used to make a point about how unremarkable life would feel without distinct Black identities, thus addressing the indeterminacy of being that seems to horrify Cosby in the documentary segment. Over the course of his career, Cosby tells stories of deliberately playful Black children who are able to escape what he sees those faces connoting.

10. D. W. Winnicott, *Playing and Reality* (London: Routledge, 1991), 64.

11. Ibid., 54.

12. Ibid., 51.

13. It is important to note here that Cosby is modeling his nostalgic memory of play, an effort that should not be thought of as purely factual or pure fantasy. He is modeling his fantasy of himself at play and playing while doing it. He is always wishing a return to that magical space of Black boyhood at play.

14. Here, as others do, I am making a distinct between "postmodern" style (postmodernism), which theorists often read as inspiring artistic, literary, philosophical, and architectural production, and "postmodernity," the time period that comprises late capitalism.

15. Martin Coles and Christine Hall, "Breaking the Line: New Literacies, Postmodernism and the Teaching of Printed Texts," *Reading: Literacy and Language* 35, no. 3 (2001): 112.

16. Lawrence Sipe and Sylvia Pantaleo, eds., *Postmodern Picturebooks: Play, Parody, and Self-Referentiality* (New York: Routledge, 2008). Also see David Lewis, *Reading Contemporary Picturebooks: Picturing Text* (London: Routledge Falmer, 2001), 94–98.

17. John Fiske, *Television Culture* (London and New York: Methuen, 1987), 254.

18. Ibid., 247.

19. Formally on *Fat Albert*, "excessive laughter" is achieved in layers of overdetermination by the use of a laugh track, voice-acting laughter of the gang, and Cosby's live-action laughing. Bakhtinian "excessiveness . . . particularly of the body and the bodily functions" is the psychic conceit of *Fat Albert*'s psychology of Black omnipotence and of the titular character, but it also describes the waste, productive and otherwise, that surrounds the boys in the simulation of the ghetto. Bakhtinian "bad taste and offensiveness, and . . . degradation" function in *Fat Albert* as jokes and humor, especially when these veer playfully toward the lower end of respectability. The humor is contrasted with the high cultural references with which the

boys are always negotiating their relationships. Also see Fiske, *Television Culture*, 241, as he summarizes Bakhtin in his discussion of postmodern television.

20. Ibid., 250.

21. Michel de Certeau, *The Practice of Everyday Life* (Berkeley: University of California Press, 1984), 98.

22. Ibid.

23. Ibid., 101–102.

24. Sigmund Freud, *Beyond the Pleasure Principle*, trans. James Strachey (New York and London: Norton, 1961), 12–17.

25. de Certeau, *Practice of Everyday Life*, 110.

26. Interestingly, Richard Delvy and Ed Fournier, adults, perform all music. The music always has a light, "jingle" quality to it, though both artists had backgrounds in folk rock and surf music.

27. I offer an interpretative-based analysis of the show instead of a reception-based analysis partly because there is not currently a reliable way to vet exactly what civil rights audiences thought about *Fat Albert*. Today, bulletin boards and fan Web pages exist wherein contemporary viewers have expressed nostalgic attachment to Cosby's characters. But the kind of work Jhally and Lewis have accomplished in *Enlightened Racism* or Linda Fuller offers in her survey of reception in *The Cosby Show: Audiences, Impact, and Implications* still remains to be done for other Cosby televisual ventures. If these other studies are to be instructive in thinking about *Fat Albert*, though, we can remain convinced that audiences were likely to have ideologically conservative responses. There also would have been some conflicting, unpredictable reactions to the cartoon's content among children and older viewers alike.

28. Jean-François Lyotard, *The Postmodern Condition: A Report on Knowledge* (Minneapolis: University of Minnesota Press, 1984), 81–82.

7   *Gimme a Break!* and the Limits of the Modern Mammy

JENNIFER FULLER

Picture this: a comedy about an overweight Black woman who lives with and takes care of a white family. Joking all the way, she cooks, cleans, helps the father of the family, and comforts the children. Then at one point, we see the father holding his gun and pointing toward the door. The Black woman enters and jumps up and down, screaming, "Massa! Massa! Massa! Please don't shoot!" It is easy to imagine these scenes in a 1930s film about the antebellum South. But they are actually from the first episode of a 1980s sitcom. *Gimme a Break!* (NBC, 1981–1987) was highly controversial, and considering the above racial dynamics, it is easy to see why.

Little difference seems to exist between this housekeeper Nell (Nell Carter) and Hollywood's historic mammies. However, Nell's hysterical response to seeing her boss hold the gun isn't supposed to read as an actual expression of fear; it is mockery. It reiterates that even though she takes care of him, she's not subservient to him. Moments like these attempted to distance her from the very stereotypes that she resembles. *Gimme a Break* strove to present a character that in all respects seems like a mammy but is not one.[1] This tension, resulting from the social and industrial context that informed the show, shaped Nell's character. While it may be correct to classify her as a mammy, that designation only tells part of the story.

Scholarship on stereotypes is important for identifying racist representations that permeate society. It helps us to also understand the social contexts in which these images are created and circulated. Looking at the history of these images helps us to understand the tenacity of stereotypes. For example, the stereotype of a Black maid who is incredibly invested in the happiness of her employers is seductive and tenacious. While we see it clearly in the 1889 creation of the Aunt Jemima brand, it is also revisited in the 2011 film *The Help*.[2] But it is important that we don't see stereotypes as static and that we consider how stereotypes change over time. Those that persist, like the mammy, are reconstructed to fit the needs and the limitations of the social context and of the particular text in which they appear.

Analyses of television and the mammy stereotype usually discuss the title character of *The Beulah Show* (1950–1952). But scholars have identified several other Black women on television as mammies, including Nell Harper of *Gimme a Break*. However, they don't closely examine her or the show. This is partly because references to Nell are usually part of a broad analysis of Black stereotypes, and there isn't room for a closer look. But it is also possible that the scant attention paid to this character is because it seems "obvious" that she is a mammy. One only needs to point out that Nell is an overweight Black woman who cares for a white family, and the case is closed. This practice validates television scholar Sasha Torres's argument that in media scholarship, "as a mode of reading, the exclusive attention to stereotypes tends to flatten its textual objects to such an extent it almost always under-reads their complexities."[3]

This chapter argues that while Nell is indeed a mammy figure, a simple categorization of her as such is not sufficient.[4] Using discursive and textual analysis, I examine how Nell's role as a caretaker in a white household was shaped by the social and industrial demands and constraints of the 1980s. In its effort to capitalize on the success of other interracial domestic sitcoms while addressing criticisms that Nell was stereotypical, *Gimme a Break*'s producers changed the character over time, from frumpy housekeeper to quasi-homemaker to glamorous professional woman. Ultimately, these strategies failed to divorce Nell from the mammy stereotype. However, they demonstrate how Nell's character was a continually changing product of negotiation.

Nell and Negotiation

Nell Harper's main purpose was to help a widower, crusty police chief Carl Kanisky (Dolph Sweet), raise his three daughters. However, she was often shown cooking and cleaning in the home as well. Promotional photographs and print ads publicizing the premiere showed her serving coffee to Carl and suggested that Nell was the Kaniskys' maid. However, in the first episode, as Nell and Carl argue about how harshly he has punished the oldest daughter for shoplifting, Nell's "true" role in the household is revealed.

> NELL: Haven't you ever done anything that was crazy?
> CARL: Yeah. Hiring you.
> NELL: First of all, you did not hire me. I volunteered.

This retort was meant to establish that Nell was not a paid domestic (hired) but a surrogate mother of sorts (a volunteer). *Gimme a Break*'s premise was that Nell was fulfilling her friend Margaret Kanisky's dying request to help Carl raise their daughters. In the premiere and several other episodes, the series reminded the audience that Nell was not a career domestic but a struggling nightclub singer who gave up her career to keep her promise to care for a family that she loved.

Figure 7.1   Nell Carter and Dolph Sweet in *Gimme a Break*. Courtesy of PhotoFest.

Nell was always a controversial character. An exchange between *TV Guide* columnist Robert Mackenzie and National Black Media Coalition chairman Pluria W. Marshall illustrates the racial dimensions of competing readings of Nell's character. Mackenzie's review of *Gimme a Break* delights in aspects of the show that other critics would find stereotypical and concludes that the show is racially progressive: "Nell is Black, built like a medicine ball, and emphasizes her lines by tossing her enormous torso from side to side . . . Nell is the pivot character here, and has most of the topper lines, which she gives a certain ethnic twist . . . Anyway, I guess it's a sign that we have all loosened up on a touchy matter that a Black person can be cast as a household domestic."[5]

Mackenzie's pleasure in Nell's overweight physicality and sassy Blackness, and his assertion that making her a maid was a fresh and funny take on racial representations, are consistent with how the network promoted the show. But in a letter to the editor, Marshall compared Mackenzie's review to *The Beulah Show*: "*Gimme a Break* puts Blacks in the happy (?) days of separate but equal, Jim Crow and knowing our place—as medicine-ball maids."[6]

Several scholars and critics have argued that *Gimme a Break* was a throwback to pre-civil-rights representations of Blacks. In general, these criticisms suggest that Nell was an anachronism. By this, I mean that this criticism saw Nell as the same old mammy, transported intact to the 1980s. As one scholar put it, Nell was "Mammy dressed in . . . '80s clothes."[7] Another called her "the classic, the oldest stereotype in the history of America: Black 'mammy' to 'massa's three little children.'"[8] Like Marshall, Jannette L. Dates, co-editor of *Split Image: African-American Images in the Media*, saw Nell as the reincarnation of Beulah.[9] Nell was a mammy, but she wasn't an anachronism. Created and re-created for a 1980s sitcom, Nell's character was the product of ongoing negotiations with criticism of her stereotypical qualities. The show responded to criticism by making her role in the household ambiguous, making Nell more "professional" over time, and at times, openly wrangling with criticism.

Media scholars have used the concept of negotiation to analyze contradictory meanings in media texts. As Christine Gledhill writes: "Meaning is neither imposed, nor passively imbibed, but arises out of a struggle or negotiation between competing frames of reference, motivation and experience."[10] This concept is based on Antonio Gramsci's formulation of power as a temporary cultural "leadership" that results from constant struggles and concessions between opposing groups.[11] Therefore, the concept of negotiation helps us to understand why a television text like *Gimme a Break*, which was meant to draw a mainstream audience, would contain elements that reinforce dominant ideologies (like patriarchy and white supremacy) alongside elements that resist those same ideologies.

The image of the doting and sometimes irritable mammy who governed plantation households was invented near the end of the U.S. Civil War and flourished at the turn of the twentieth century, when segregation was under construction. The myth of the plantation mammy was part of white southerners' nostalgia for antebellum racial order and domesticity. It defused allegations that white men took sexual advantage of Black women during slavery.[12] The mammy myth was attached to Black domestics through the civil rights era and beyond. According to Patricia Hill Collins, the mammy stereotype masked the exploitation of Black women's labor and the structural inequities that limited them to domestic jobs by suggesting that they loved to care for white families and were naturally suited for the work. Collins also argues that the mammy stereotype creates the expectation that ideal Black women (no matter their profession) will be helpful and deferential to whites.[13]

Nell fits the mammy stereotype in that although she is defiant and stubborn, she has sacrificed her own goals in order to shore up white domesticity. However,

Gimme a Break attempted to earnestly depict a self-sacrificing big Black female care-taker of white children who was *not* a mammy. Although the series was successful enough to last six seasons, persistent criticism and repeated revisions of Nell's char-acter demonstrate that this construction was untenable. Its contradictions perhaps could have been resolved by marrying Nell and Carl, but a series about a Black-white couple would likely have been regarded as impossible in the early 1980s.[14] Therefore, by insisting that Nell was neither a maid nor a housewife (and therefore Carl's partner), *Gimme a Break* created a fantastical character: an unmarried house-wife with surrogate children, an unpaid domestic who has the run of the house, or both. Fantastical characters are not unusual in television programs. The trouble was that this particular character resembled the mammy stereotype—a fantasy about Black women's role in racial hierarchy and white domesticity.

Racial Difference and Humor

Nell looks less anachronistic when *Gimme a Break* is situated within its industrial context. Nell was often compared to Beulah, but it is important to consider other television programs that shaped *Gimme a Break* and its reception. Few sitcoms have been built around Black actresses, and before the 1990s, it was exceedingly rare. The first such program to follow *The Beulah Show* was *Julia* (NBC, 1968–1971), about Julia Baker (Diahann Carroll), a widowed nurse with a young son. Just as the racial politics of the early 1950s helped carry the popular Beulah character from radio to television, the focus on integrating television in the 1960s helped shape the portrayal of Julia as an assimilated, educated woman who lived among whites. In the early 1970s, the influence of Black cultural politics that insisted on the uniqueness of African-American culture intersected with televi-sion's shift regarding working-class urban environments. The result was a rise in Black-cast sitcoms based on working-class settings and Black vernacular culture. Big, bossy Black women figured prominently in several of these shows. For example, *That's My Mama* (ABC, 1974–1975) focused on the goings-on among young working-class men in a barbershop, but the barbershop was a family business in a home presided over by an influential big Black mother (Theresa Merritt). The teen comedy *What's Happening!!* (ABC, 1976–1979) also included a large, formidable mother (Mabel King), as well as a big, wise-cracking waitress (Shirley Hemphill) at the teen hangout.

The 1970s also saw the return of Black domestics to TV. However, they upended the fantasy of the dutiful, faithful Black servant. Florence Johnston (in *The Jeffersons*, CBS, 1975–1985), Benson (in *Soap*, ABC, 1977–1981), and Florida Evans (in *Maude*, CBS, 1972–78) were formidable and politically aware. Not only were they autonomous from their employers, these domestics often criticized them. This spate of wisecracking domestics overlapped with a mode of Black televisual representation that became popular in the late 1970s, the Black star–white environment show. *Gimme a Break* was one of several sitcoms in which Black characters livened up their predominantly white environments. This included shows such as *The Jeffersons*, *Benson* (ABC, 1979–1986, a *Soap* spin-off), and *Webster* (ABC, 1983–1987). The most prominent of these shows was *Diff'rent Strokes* (NBC/CBS, 1979–1986), a sitcom about an interracial family formed when a widowed white millionaire adopted his deceased Black house-keeper's sons. The show's success hinged on Gary Coleman's performance as the precocious Arnold Jackson who, along with his streetwise brother, brought Black style into the upper-crust household. *Diff'rent Strokes* was an instant hit, and NBC was eager to duplicate the formula with *Gimme a Break*.[15] Both shows had wid-owed white fathers of teen daughters, and in both a woman's death introduced sassy Blackness into a previously square white household. Nell introduced Blackness to the white suburban household through her history as a nightclub singer (and her occasional gospel and R&B performances on the show) and through her speech, especially in the form of saucy comebacks.

"That's Not a Typical Maid": Nell's Ambiguous Role

A *Los Angeles Times* column lambasting the clichéd and stereotypical aspects of the season's new shows took aim at *Gimme a Break*'s racial politics: "Tony-winning Black performer, Nell Carter, stars . . . as the maid to a white police [chief]. Look at the bright side. She could have been his slave."[16] Many television critics shared the view that Carter's talent was wasted on a racially regressive role.[17] Carter responded to this kind of criticism at length:

> Some [reviews] were really cruel, said it was an Aunt Jemima character. A lotta people seemed to pick on that show to say how Blacks weren't work-ing except to play maids. And in interviews, at press conferences, the whole first year that was always the opening question: "How do you feel about play-ing a *maid*?" I swear to God, I am so *sick* of that one question I don't know what to do. There is more to *Gimme a Break* than playing a maid. It's comical! She cleans the fishbowl, the fish *die*—I mean, that's not a typical maid. If you have a maid like that you should *fire* her . . . Even if she is a maid, I think it's wrong—especially for Blacks—to get mad about that. How dare you or anyone else put down a *maid*! Aren't they *people*?[18]

Indeed, those who advocated for "positive" Black representations would likely criticize Nell's occupation because it was a stereotypical role. Carter expressed this elsewhere, saying "So Blacks don't want to be represented as having menial jobs . . . I think anyone, Black or white, who looks down on a person because she's a maid or a waitress is a real butt-face."[19] But contrary to Carter's responses, what was likely more troubling than the domestic occupation *itself* was Nell's resemblance to the mammy stereotype. For example, Black actress Madge Sinclair, who was playing a nurse in *Trapper John, M.D.* (CBS, 1979–1986), didn't object to Carter taking the role, because she knew acting jobs for Blacks were limited. However, Sinclair laughed at a description of Nell's character: "A Jemima! . . . That's *the one stereotype*, the one maid who makes everyone comfortable. And she doesn't exist. None of the producers and writers have a lady like that at home."[20] In other words, they may have Black maids, but they didn't have *mammies*. It is the mammy mythology, that is, Nell's perceived selfless commitment to white domesticity, that makes *Gimme a Break* so controversial.

It is significant that Carter says Nell is a maid, since the show denies this from the first episode and moves further away from this characterization in the second season. Although Carter's responses to critics demanded more respect for maids, *Gimme a Break* increasingly confounded the issue of whether Nell was actually a maid at all. By the second season, Nell was shown less often doing housework. But from the beginning, even though she did household chores, she didn't follow traditional employer-domestic protocol and broke with the usual portrayals of TV servants. Nell worked in the Kanisky home, but it was also a place of leisure for her: it was her home as well. Nell didn't just cook for the Kaniskys, she ate with them. She played and relaxed with them. She entertained guests in the living room. In contrast, on *The Jeffersons*, Florence's spaces were the kitchen and her unseen bedroom. She was usually shown on her way between those rooms, or comically intruding on living room conversations by poking her head through the kitchen shutters. When Florence relaxed in the living room, it was a display of impudence.

Gimme a Break also made Nell's role in the Kanisky home ambiguous by making Nell glamorous. In the first season, Nell wore frumpy dresses suited for a maid's labor and pay. But starting in the second season, she wore fashionable hairstyles, heavier makeup, and showy jewelry. Her manicured nails and stylish outfits were more suitable for a professional career than cleaning house. The second season also brought a change in the opening title sequence. Now, "starring Nell Carter" appeared over a shot of Nell in a black sequined gown, strutting down the staircase and striking fashion poses. Although Nell slept (and presumably dressed) downstairs, this shot suggests that the house is actually hers and references the iconic image of the glamorous star on the staircase. This image runs counter to the mammy stereotype and more closely aligns Nell with Carter, whose weight-loss attempts and glamorous lifestyle were now part of her celebrity image.[21]

Redefining Nell

Prominent Black publications virtually ignored Carter and *Gimme a Break*. *Ebony* and sister publication *Jet*, a weekly entertainment magazine, rely heavily on celebrity interviews, and women's magazine *Essence* routinely profiles celebrities. During the series' run, *Ebony* interviewed Black actors from other Black star–white environment shows, including two cover stories on Gary Coleman, and lavished attention on the cast of *The Cosby Show* (NBC, 1984–1992). But neither *Ebony* nor *Jet* devoted an article to Carter. They gave token acknowledgments of her role in *Gimme a Break*: Carter was included in a 1982 *Ebony* story that briefly discussed (but didn't interview) Black women who were succeeding in the entertainment industry despite the odds against them,[22] and a publicity photo of Carter appeared on a 1985 cover of *Jet* for a story summarizing Black characters in the upcoming television season.

A 1984 profile in *Essence* was the only article on Carter in major Black magazines during *Gimme a Break*'s six-season run. Instead of giving the expected effusive account of a celebrity's career and lifestyle, the article labored to frame Carter as someone its readers should admire. By focusing on Carter's struggles with obesity, diabetes, heart disease, and a "nervous breakdown," the article tried to recuperate Carter *and* Nell by praising Carter as a strong woman struggling against illness and criticism. In fact, the first quote from Carter is "I react to my diabetes the way I react to criticism of me and the show . . . Both are things I've learned to accept; I'm not afraid anymore."[23] The article, which was written by a fellow Black actress, chastised Black viewers for criticizing Carter instead of mobilizing against television executives and implored readers to support the show.

> There's little doubt that many of us would feel better if in addition to Nell, we had a Black actress starring as a newscaster or lawyer in a weekly series. But it is clear that change in the media will occur only when we become the power brokers behind the images or when we, as viewers, begin to influence the current power brokers through massive-letter-writing campaigns.
>
> "We Blacks complain all the time," Nell declares, "but we don't call or write in because we're so conditioned to thinking that our votes don't count. But they do. Instead of writing letters demanding that images be upgraded, many Black people still criticize me personally. I'm called a Mammy and everything else. Why can't anyone say, 'Look, there's a Black gal that's got her own show!'"[24]

The author, Bever-Leigh Banfield, acknowledged that Nell's character was lacking, but by talking about it in relation to the limitations of the television industry, she suggested that the character wasn't necessarily bad in and of itself. Banfield and Carter asked Black audiences to be more sympathetic to the struggles faced by Black talent.

According to the article, Carter now had more creative control but needed letters of support from Black audiences. The assertion that Carter was fighting the television industry behind the scenes was a significant shift from Carter's earlier dismissals of criticism about *Gimme a Break*'s racial politics. Banfield clearly wanted readers to change their minds about Carter. And rethinking

Carter required rethinking Nell. Banfield urged readers to reconsider the show: "After all, Nell [Carter] has created an extraordinary character—a maid who is not only a real thinker, but also one who dictates to a police chief and usually saves the day through her unique approach to life. Perhaps we need to become an active audience, supporting talent that tries its best with what it has to work with."[25] The author wanted readers to see Nell's role as a product of negotiation and wanted them to make negotiated readings of Carter, Nell, and *Gimme a Break*.

The *Essence* profile ran in the middle of the third season, when the series was clearly working to recuperate Nell's image. The episode "Flashback" (season three, episode fourteen) depicted the events that led Nell to agree to take care of the Kanisky girls. Showing Nell's initial reluctance and the emotional bonds that led her to take on the task dramatizes the show's usually implicit claim that Nell is not a domestic servant. The episode "Nell's Friend" (season three, episode eight), in which Nell has to justify her position in a white household to a professional Black woman, seems to be a direct response to Black criticism of the show.

The episode introduces to the cast Nell's childhood friend and rival, Adelaide "Addy" Wilson (Telma Hopkins), a college professor who has just moved to town. Addy comes to the Kanisky home unannounced, and Nell is out. While Addy waits for Nell, she talks to the girls. Her PhD and Phi Beta Kappa pin awe the bookish daughter, Julie. Addy proudly tells her: "I'm just one of the many modern Black women who are out there making it. It took us a long time, but thank God we finally put to rest that old stereotype of the Black woman as nothing but an Aunt Jemima." On cue, Nell comes in, carrying a laundry basket and wearing a red bandana knotted at the forehead. She calls out, "I'm home!" The audience roars in response. The point here is that Nell *isn't* a mammy, she's just *mistaken* for one. But the reference to Aunt Jemima and Nell's red kerchief make explicit the racial stereotype that the series has been closely skirting. "Nell's Friend" is an exercise in negotiation: it attempts to expose, recuperate, and then alter the stereotypical aspects of Nell's character.

Nell's attempt to mask her unhappiness about the reunion becomes increasingly difficult as Addy tells the girls embarrassing stories about her. Fed up, Nell takes Addy into the kitchen, where they argue. Addy tells her condescendingly: "After all the disappointments, I'm glad you finally found your niche in life as a maid in a white household." The audience boos. The insult here is not just Addy's condescension but calling Nell a "maid." Embarrassed, but with conviction, Nell tells Addy that she and the Kaniskys love each other: "This family needs me and that's all that matters, lady." Addy tells her: "There's nothing wrong with being a *maid*, but Nell, I hope you haven't forgotten that there's a whole new world out there, just waiting out there for the modern Black woman." Nell throws open the back door, announces, "World! Here comes a modern Black woman!" and tosses Addy out of the house. The audience cheers Nell's ejection of the smug "modern Black woman" from *Gimme a Break*, but Nell immediately vows to go to night school to get her high school diploma.

Nell's night school plans are thwarted when she learns that Addy is her teacher. She walks out of class, and Addy later shows up at the Kanisky home demanding an apology. They have another argument, during which Nell defiantly hurls from her bookshelf the important books she's read. Nell's intellectual side is revealed here, as is her Black consciousness. One of the authors she lists is Alex Haley, author of *Roots*. The fight reaches its crescendo when Nell says, "Telling me I'm a failure as a modern Black woman. I was a *happy* Black woman until you brought your *modern* Black butt in the house!" The audience responds with extended applause. Indeed, this is a powerful scene for Carter, and there is pleasure in watching Nell defend herself. But the scene is also about *Gimme a Break* defending Nell against critics. Therefore, the "modern Black woman" must be defeated, since she has dared to intrude on Nell's pleasure (and perhaps the audience's) by questioning her role.

During the reconciliation that follows, Addy admits that she has always been jealous of Nell and, despite her accomplishments, envies the friendship and fun Nell has with the Kaniskys. She tells her, "I can see why you stay in this house." The resolution affirms Nell's role in the Kanisky household as one based on love, not money, but it doesn't erase Addy's critique of that role. Furthermore, it suggests that Nell hasn't been fully content with her life and starts her on a path that leads to college, employment outside of the Kanisky home, and eventually becoming a professional ("modern") Black woman herself. But in order to justify Nell's role, and therefore the show's premise, "Nell's Friend" first has to reverse the series' obfuscation of Nell's domestic labor. In a rare moment for the series, Nell is called a "maid," and while she recoils, she doesn't blatantly deny it. Addy doesn't see Nell in a glamorous light. She first sees Nell wearing a scarf and hair curlers while doing the laundry. When she returns to the Kanisky home, Nell is wearing an apron (over a stylish outfit) and slippers while she serves dinner. Unlike in other episodes, Nell isn't eating with the Kaniskys. Addy sees Nell *working for* the Kaniskys, not *living with* them. And perhaps like Nell's critics, Addy has gotten the wrong idea. But just as Addy's "misunderstanding" still leads Nell to change her life, *Gimme a Break* was clearly absorbing some criticisms and changing Nell's role.

"Nell's Friend" emphasizes Nell's *choice* to raise the Kanisky girls as a remedy to the "Aunt Jemima" accusation. But this assertion is not a departure from the mammy stereotype. For example, iconic film mammies also chose their roles; this was powerful evidence of their loyalty to white women and children. For example, in *Gone with the Wind* (1939), although most ex-slaves "abandon" the plantation after the Civil War, Mammy stays with her former owners until her death, despite her freedom and their years of penury. And in *Imitation of Life*

(1934), when Bea Pullman makes a fortune by packaging her maid Delilah Johnson's pancake recipe, Delilah agrees to a small percentage of the profits and continues to work in Bea's home. By insisting that Nell "volunteered," *Gimme a Break* actually aligns Nell more with this representation than with the defiant, unambiguously paid Black domestics elsewhere on television.

Professional, yet Obsolete

In *Gimme a Break's* last three seasons, behind-the-scenes events and new expectations for Black televisual representations overlapped with and fostered Nell's shift from "maid" to professional woman. The production staff had to work around the fact that Dolph Sweet was seriously ill with cancer, as well as the maturation of the actresses who portrayed the Kanisky girls.[26] In the fourth season, the series foregrounded the character Joey (Nell's white foster son), expanded the roles of minor characters Officer Simpson and Grandpa Kanisky, and featured more high-concept plotlines. *Gimme a Break* was struggling in the ratings at this point; new characters and high concepts are commonly used to reinvigorate flagging shows. This especially seemed to be the case with Joey's expanded role, as he was a favorite among young female viewers.[27] The narrative changes diminished Nell's role as an intermediary between Carl and his teen daughters. Instead, more stories emerged about Nell's relationships with other Black people: her family, friends, and boyfriends.

Sweet died in May 1985. The producers incorporated this into the narrative by setting the fifth season after Carl's death. The show lost a key part of its premise: the antagonistic relationship between Nell and Carl. By the end of the fifth season, the family unit bore little resemblance to its first-season makeup. With only one Kanisky daughter who wasn't an adult, Nell had a richer life outside of the Kaniskys' home and wasn't easily "mistaken" for a maid. But Nell's increasing independence from the Kaniskys was countered by the emphasis on her relationship to Joey. Because Joey was young, Nell's treatment of him, including cradling his blond head to her bosom, evoked the mammy stereotype even more powerfully than her relationship with the Kanisky girls. Indeed, Joey called her "Aunt Nell," a term that may have been meant to stress familial bonds but also evoked the practice of calling Black nannies "Aunt."

Another cause for changes in Nell's relationships and career goals in *Gimme a Break's* fifth and sixth seasons was *The Cosby Show*, which began during *Gimme a Break's* fourth season. The mainstream success of *The Cosby Show's* depiction of an upper-middle class Black family headed by a highly educated professional couple expanded possibilities for Black television characters. It led to Black-cast shows like *227* (NBC, 1985–1990), which was set in a Black working- and middle-class neighborhood. This outmoded Black star–white environment shows like *Gimme a Break. The Cosby Show's* ratings helped to make NBC the top network for the first time in decades. This success stripped *Gimme a Break's* importance to

Figure 7.2   The new Nell. Courtesy of PhotoFest.

what had been a struggling network lineup. Before the sixth season, network executives told Gimme a Break's producers to radically change the show, or it would be canceled.[28] In season six, Nell and Addy moved to New York, where Nell worked in the publishing industry. They were joined by Joey, Grandpa Kanisky, and a new foster son for Nell, Joey's younger brother. The Kanisky sisters were reduced to minor characters. The show now focused on Addy and Nell creating a new life in the city, a shift that was indicative of the success of women-centered sitcoms such as 227 and The Golden Girls (1985–1992), both of which initially shared a lineup with Gimme a Break, and CBS's Kate & Allie (1984–1989). But as Nell was becoming more professional, independent, and cosmopolitan, the show was also losing viewers. The same forces that allowed Nell to change dramatically also left the show unmoored. The show's radical changes didn't cultivate a large audience, and *Gimme a Break* was canceled.

Conclusion

Carter's only *Jet* cover read, "Nell Carter: Blacks Make Gains in New TV Season." But in fact, Carter is not quoted in the accompanying article.[29] A misleading headline isn't unusual for *Jet*, which has a sensational, tabloid style. However, whether or not it was intentional, putting Carter on the cover and attributing this statement to her puts her at the border between older, more conciliatory images of Blacks and the more robust post–*Cosby Show* characters. The story includes a note that Carter will have a boyfriend during several episodes. Considering that Black critics often clamor for portrayals of Blacks in loving, heterosexual relationships, this announcement is meant to signal racially progressive changes at *Gimme a Break*.[30] But amid discussions of programs such as *The Cosby Show* and *227*, which revolved around relationships between Black families and friends, this bit of optimism about *Gimme a Break* also made the show seem even more obsolete. Nell was accused of being shockingly out-of-date when *Gimme a Break* began, and although the series made major changes, it couldn't keep pace with the new expectations brought on by *The Cosby Show*. Therefore, Nell was passé when the series ended, as well.

Gimme a Break's circulation within the context of television nostalgia illustrates how Nell's character continues to be contentious. Based on conversations with Black college students during the show's run, Dates claims "many Black viewers were, at best, ill-at-ease with their feelings toward the series, for they viewed Nell Carter as very talented, but misguided. In fact, many middle-class African Americans made it a point to never watch the series."[31] This account is reminiscent of Sut Jhally and Justin Lewis's finding that while Black interviewees embraced *The Cosby Show*, they exhibited "ambivalence" about Black-cast shows that they deemed stereotypical, and framed their enjoyment of said shows as a "guilty pleasure."[32] Considering this, it is likely that Dates's students enjoyed *Gimme a Break* more than they admitted. On the other hand, *Gimme a Break* has not been embraced as a part of Black popular culture and nostalgia the way that *Diff'rent Strokes* and *The Jeffersons* have, despite the fact that these shows were also criticized as "stereotypical." Although this ambivalence remains, it has become more muted since Carter's death in 2003.

In 2006, Black-interest cable channel TV One aired a *Gimme a Break* marathon in anticipation of the DVD release of the series' first season. TV One attempted to bring *Gimme a Break* into the Black television canon by promoting it as one of the longest-running shows "in African-American television history." Several episodes chosen for the marathon featured Carter singing. Others were promoted for their "before they were stars" guest appearances of Black celebrities such as Whitney Houston and Danny Glover. Instead of simply heralding the marathon, TV One addressed possible misgivings about the show: "Controversial in its day for the 'stereotypical' set-up of a wise-cracking and over-weight Black housekeeper who takes care of a white family, the show neverthe-less endured six seasons on the strength of Carter's powerful persona, strong comic timing and musical chops."[33] This acknowledgment of *Gimme a Break*'s troublesome racial politics and the focus on Carter's skillful performance echo the *Essence* article's attempts to cultivate negotiated readings of Nell and the show twenty years earlier.

Nell was a contradictory and shifting character whose role as a Black woman taking care of a white household constantly had to be legitimated. In response to criticism, the show changed and obscured aspects of Nell's character that made her seem like a maid. However, by portraying her relationship to the Kaniskys as motivated by love instead of money, and by depicting her as a mother of white children, *Gimme a Break* made Nell seem *more* like a mammy. Evidence of the show's attention to changing Nell's occupation more drastically than her relationship to whites can be found in the fact that years of changing Nell's character ended with her as its version of a "modern Black woman," an editorial assistant at a publishing house who was a single mother—to two white children. Coming to the rescue of white femininity and continuing to care for white chil-dren despite advancements in career and education, the character Nell was a negotiation between the maid, the mammy, and the "modern Black woman." Caught between these constructions, Nell was a mythical motherlike figure. And that is precisely what the mammy stereotype is: a fantasy of a Black surrogate mother.

Gimme a Break's very premise fastened Nell to the mammy image; it was con-siderably easier to make changes that made her seem less like a maid than it was to make her seem less like a mammy. It is important to identify and track stereo-types. However, without nuanced analysis of these representations, we risk the essentializing move of suggesting that stereotypes exist outside of history. Closer analysis of the negotiations between racist and antiracist discourses in the creation of media images allows us to see not only the tenacity of stereotypes but also their limits.

NOTES

1. I will refer to the show as *Gimme a Break* without the exclamation point.

2. I cannot fully address the film *The Help* (or the book on which it is based) and the con-siderable debates around it here, although I do want to point out that its depiction of 1960s Black maids also demonstrates negotiation with contemporary racial politics. The film resists some of the historic constructions of Black maids: they are not docile, and they have lives outside of the white homes they work in. However, the film also adheres to aspects of regressive racial politics, including reveling in the fantasy of the Black servant's overwhelm-ing love for the white child she is paid to care for.

3. Sasha Torres, "Television and Race," in *A Companion to Television*, ed. Janet Wasko (Malden, MA: Blackwell Publishing, 2005), 403.

4. Elsewhere, for example, I have examined how Nell's overt sexuality complicates the stereotype of the asexual mammy. See Jennifer Fuller, "The 'Black Sex Goddess' in the Living Room: Making Interracial Sex 'Laughable' on *Gimme a Break*," *Feminist Media Studies* 11, no. 3 (2011): 265–281.

5. Robert Mackenzie, review of *Gimme a Break*, *TV Guide*, January 9, 1982, 23.

6. Pluria W. Marshall, letter, *TV Guide*, January 30, 1982, A4.

7. Shawna V. Hudson, "Re-creational Television: the Paradox of Change and Continuity Within Stereotypical Iconography," *Sociological Inquiry* 68, no. 2 (1998): 245.

8. Melbourne Cummings, "The Changing Image of the Black Family on Television," *Journal of Popular Culture* 22, no. 2 (1988): 81.

9. Jannette L. Dates and William Barlow, eds., *Split Image: African Americans in the Mass Media*, 2nd ed. (Washington, DC: Howard University Press, 1993), 298.

10. Christine Gledhill, "Pleasurable Negotiations," in *Female Spectators: Looking at Film and Television*, ed. E. Deidre Pribram (New York: Verso, 1988), 68.

11. Stuart Hall, "Gramsci's Relevance for the Study of Race and Ethnicity," in *Stuart Hall: Critical Dialogues in Cultural Studies*, ed. David Morley and Kuan-Hsing Chen (New York: Routledge, 1996), 432.

12. Grace Elizabeth Hale, *Making Whiteness: The Culture of Segregation in the South, 1890–1940* (New York: Pantheon, 1998), 85–119.

13. Patricia Hill Collins, *Black Feminist Thought* (New York: Routledge, 1991), 71.

14. The Willises, a Black-white couple, were secondary characters on *The Jeffersons*, and interracial couples appeared on episodes of other sitcoms. But consistent, Black-white primary romantic pairings wouldn't appear on television until the late eighties and early nineties in shows such as *The Days and Nights of Molly Dodd* (1987–1991), and finally as the central couple in Fox's *True Colors* (1990–1992).

15. *E! True Hollywood Story: Gimme a Break*, E! Channel, April 27, 2003.

16. Howard Rosenberg, "Gimme That Old-time Television," *Los Angeles Times*, October 23, 1981, J15.

17. John J. O'Connor, "TV: 2 NBC Comedies Have Premieres," *New York Times*, October 29, 1981, C28; Tom Shales, "Please! 'Gimme a Break!'" *Washington Post*, October 29, 1981, B1, B8; Harry F. Waters, "Hello Mayhem, Goodbye Sex," *Newsweek*, October 12, 1981, 61–62.

18. Tom Noles, "There Was a Time When I Didn't Like Nell," *TV Guide*, August 21, 1982, 22.

19. Suzanne Adelson, "Feasting on TV Stardom and a New Marriage, Nell Carter Celebrates Life in, Well, Fat City," *People Weekly*, June 17, 1982, 102.

20. Judy Flander, "Blacks on Television Still Fight Stereotypes," *Washington Star*, July 14, 1981, B5.

21. Adelson, "Feasting."

22. "Black Women in Entertainment," *Ebony*, August 1982, 102–104, 108.

23. Bever-Leigh Banfield, "Feeling Fit and Fabulous," *Essence*, January 1984, 72.

24. Ibid.

25. Ibid.

26. *E! True Hollywood Story*.

27. Ibid.

28. Ibid.

29. "Nell Carter: Blacks Make Gains in New TV Season," *Jet*, October 14, 1985, 60–63.

30. Ibid.

31. Dates and Barlow, *Split Image*, 299.

32. Sut Jhally and Justin Lewis, *Enlightened Racism: The Cosby Show, Audiences, and the Myth of the American Dream* (Boulder, CO: Westview Press, 1992), 118–119.

33. *Gimme a Break! Online*, http://www.sitcomsonline.com/gimmeabreak.html (last accessed December 5, 2008).

8

Down in the Treme . . . Buck Jumping and Having Fun?

THE IMPACT OF DEPICTIONS OF POST-KATRINA NEW ORLEANS ON VIEWERS' PERCEPTIONS OF THE CITY

KIM M. LEDUFF

Five years after Hurricane Katrina devastated New Orleans, Louisiana, life remained not normal *still* for many residents of the city. And while mainstream news organizations remembered the fifth anniversary of the hurricane with extensive coverage, it was the work of filmmaker Spike Lee and television program creators David Simon and Eric Overmyer that perhaps created the greatest buzz about the fifth anniversary of Katrina in 2010. Spike Lee's first documentary, *When the Levees Broke,* was released in 2006. It documented what happened in New Orleans through the voices of local residents, politicians, and experts during and immediately after the storm. In 2010, Lee revisited the city with the release of *If God Is Willing and da Creek Don't Rise,* which was originally intended to chronicle a story of triumph for New Orleans residents who were resilient in the wake of Katrina. But during the process of filming the documentary, the Gulf Coast was ravaged by the British Petroleum (BP) oil spill. Both documentaries aired on cable network HBO, and in 2010, the network began airing Simon and Overmyer's creation, *Treme.* This series has been described as "being set in New Orleans three months after Hurricane Katrina. The story is told through the eyes of the musicians, chefs, and Mardi Gras Indians you'll only find in New Orleans, and locals are heavily involved in the production."[1] The show explores the challenges and triumphs of everyday citizens as they recover from one of the greatest disasters in American history. Though the storylines are fictional, they reflect the reality of the city and its residents post-Katrina. The cast is made up of a combination of nationally known actors and local celebrities. The city of New Orleans serves as the backdrop. Most of the show is shot in the actual city, but some scenes have been created to reflect the state of the city in the months following Katrina.

While a great deal has been written about Lee's work and some beginning scholarship on *Treme* has appeared, the impetus behind this study comes from discussions with New Orleans natives in response to the release of these productions. I am a New Orleans native, and I was struck by residents' concern that the reality of New Orleans post-Katrina be reflected accurately not only in Spike Lee's documentaries but even in the fictional account of the city on *Treme*. I was curious to find if this was a common reaction amongst New Orleanians. I also hoped to investigate how viewers from other parts of the country might perceive post-Katrina New Orleans based on these specific media portrayals.

Thus, the purpose of this analysis is to examine how both local and national viewers might make sense of the state of New Orleans five years after the storm, if they compare and contrast Spike Lee's nonfictional documentaries with the fictional account of Katrina on HBO's series *Treme*. In order to gauge audience reactions, reader posts on NOLA.com and HBO.com have been examined.[2] NOLA.com is the website for the *Times-Picayune*, the New Orleans daily newspaper. Staff writer Dave Walker offers a breakdown of each episode of *Treme* on the site and provides a space for audience commentary. HBO has a "Talk" section on its website where viewers can post topics related to specific programs, soliciting responses from fellow viewers. According to Hangwoo Lee, "There is a higher chance for the users of the Internet to make contact with others who have different political perspective, cultural taste, and national background than in other communication conduits."[3] In these settings, local and national viewers have the opportunity to ask questions and exchange thoughts, ideas, and opinions about real life in post-Katrina New Orleans in response to what they view in both the documentaries and the fictional portrayal in the *Treme* series.

What Is Important About New Orleans?

The message in Lee's as well as Simon and Overmyer's work must not be lost. They all saw that through the power of mass media, they could offer voice to the voiceless. They saw that they could give the people of New Orleans a national stage upon which to share their grievances. Kevin Foster, Tifani Blakes, and Jenny McKay remind us that "in such an era when assaults on humanity are so easily forgotten, documentaries such as *When the Levees Broke* play an important role . . . The documentary debuts one day. But then, and much more important, it quickly becomes available for purchase . . . This access provides the means for voicing and sharing alternative perceptions, experiences and realities that counter sensationalized, repetitive, racist and otherwise inaccurate portrayals of people and events."[4] In an interview on NPR, Lolis Eric Elie, a local writer for the show *Treme*, explained just how important *Treme* is to the city: "To have people like David Simon and Eric Overmyer come here and go to the heart of a community that is emblematically black and is also, in local terms, often considered an area of high crime and high blight is a hell of a statement about what is really important about New Orleans."[5]

New Orleans residents recognize how the devastation of Hurricane Katrina impacted their lifestyle, culture, and economy. But of greater concern to many residents is how New Orleans is perceived by the rest of the United States and the world in the wake of Katrina. In *If God Is Willing and da Creek Don't Rise*, author and professor Douglas Brinkley explains what he identifies as "an inferiority complex" with which many New Orleans natives grapple. He says, "The one thing that unites everybody is the feeling that they are spending their whole life telling everybody how great things are, but secretly they know they're not."[6] For good or for evil, these new narratives have created opportunities for national audiences to gain insight into the "ugly truth" about pre- and post-Katrina New Orleans.

Based on posts from viewers on both NOLA.com and HBO.com, it is clear that a dialogue is taking place between New Orleanians and those from other parts of the country. The conversation is complex and multifaceted, but perhaps one local's comment on NOLA.com best explains why the story of New Orleans after Katrina continues to resonate:

> MANDEVILLEDAT: Katrina was a very group storm. We were all hurt by it. Katrina was a very individual storm. No one pain is what we all experienced. I was blessed that my home's damage was minimal compared to others. Making a show about the recovery is very challenging. I appreciate that the writers are trying to reflect post storm realities. No show, book or song will show everyone. But I am very happy they are trying to keep us in the public mind rather than thinking, Saints won the Super Bowl. The city must now be all better. We need to reminding people that this was (we pray) a once-in-a-generation storm. We will rebuild. We will remember the pain.

While Lee's documentaries and the show *Treme* were created for a national audience, without question, current residents and those displaced by the storm have a heightened interest in media of this nature. Katrina was an actual event, but not everyone involved was privy to viewing it firsthand. This was especially true for New Orleans residents who were either caught in the flooded city or near the Gulf Coast without power or access to news coverage in the hours and days following the storm. Once residents returned to the city, many depended on news coverage and documentaries to see what was happening and to get a more informed grasp on the politics behind many of the decisions made during and after the storm. For viewers with a working knowledge of the city, its people and culture factor into conceptions of what is even believable in the generated media.

Even though *Treme* is labeled as fictional programming, popular media coverage of the production upon release also suggested major concern on behalf of New Orleans residents that the depictions of the city, people, and events be as realistic as possible. Elie notes, "You have to be careful about the use of the word 'based.' The show really is contemporary historical fiction."[7] New Orleanians and those closely tied to the city want to make sure that their story is told accurately so that people understand what they have experienced and continue to deal with from day to day. New Orleans resident Mary Howell (featured in Spike Lee's *If God Is Willing and da Creek Don't Rise* and the basis for a character on *Treme*) explained: "This is not just telling our story to us. But for non-natives, I think it's hard to convey the trauma of a whole community while attempting to show our resiliency. People may think, 'they can't be all that traumatized if they're still laughing and having fun and playing music.'"[8] Research into social reality construction demonstrates that individuals who deem the television they watch as more realistic are more likely to be influenced by its content.[9] And that is precisely the concern.

The Conversations

These productions have sparked conversations in an environment that is not hindered by geographic, physical, or emotional borders. According to Katelyn McKenna and John Bargh, essentially four main differences exist between communication over the Internet and in real life. First, it is possible to be anonymous on the Internet; second, physical distance does not matter on the Internet; third, physical appearance and visual cues are not present on the Internet; and finally, time becomes immaterial.[10] As a result, viewers appear to be willing to post beliefs, opinions, and feelings about Katrina that they might not be willing to share face-to-face. These posts sometimes include information that might be considered inflammatory, especially in regard to sensitive topics such as race. In looking at blogs, Melissa Wall noted, "On blogs audiences are often invited to contribute information, comments . . . and co-create content." She found that the comments are often personal, very opinionated, and typically one-sided. She explains that "this provides a sort of virtual town hall but one that can be and often is anonymous."[11]

So how does the juxtaposition of two documentaries and a fictional depiction of post-Katrina New Orleans play out in the minds of viewers? How might audiences make interpretations, especially when the people and places incorporated in both genres of media often overlap? First it is important to understand how they overlap: 1) The actual city of New Orleans is the backdrop in the documentaries and the HBO series. 2) The series incorporates a combination of real and fictional locales within the city. For example, Treme is a real neighborhood in New Orleans, though the depiction in the show by the same name is fictional. 3) Many of the fictional characters on *Treme* are based on real live New Orleanians. 4) Some actual New Orleanians play fictional characters on *Treme*, and some play their real-world selves on the fictional show. 5) Some of the storylines in the fictional program parallel real events that took place during and after Katrina. 6) Some individuals have roles in the documentaries and *Treme*.

Perceived realism has to do with how realistic audiences deem media content to be. Michael Shapiro and T. Makana Chock note, "Some researchers have explored perceived reality as a filter that may enhance critical viewing." They found in their research that "understanding judgments about perceived reality requires understanding judgments about typicality. How do people decide what is typical? Direct and indirect experience has some influence. But the results indicate it has more to do with expectations about what is typical in a particular situation if it did happen."[12] Atrocities occurred as a result of Katrina that many people cannot or refuse to believe could happen in the United States, but they indeed happened during and after Katrina. All of these things have the potential to influence viewers' perceived reality. Investigators have long recognized that perceived reality of media presentation may influence mental processes, attitudes, beliefs and behaviors.[13] Rick Busselle and Bradley Greenberg identify six arguably different conceptual dimensions of perceived realism:

1. Magic Window: the extent to which television allows one to observe on-going life in another place or inside the set itself.
2. Social Realism: the extent to which television content, whether real or fictitious, is similar to life in the real world.
3. Plausibility: the extent to which something observed on TV could exist in the real world.
4. Probability: the likelihood of something observed on TV existing in the real world or the frequency with which it occurs.
5. Identity: the extent to which viewers incorporate television content into their real lives or involve themselves with content elements.
6. Utility: how much information or events observed on television are useful to the viewer in real life.[14]

In order to better understand how perceived realism may affect viewers of *Treme* and Spike Lee's documentaries, I will use these dimensions as a lens through which to decode various elements of the documentaries and the TV program and discuss how these elements might connote meaning for viewers.

Viewing New Orleans Through the Magic Window

Treme and Spike Lee's documentaries serve as the magic window, allowing viewers to peer into the city and residents' lives after Katrina. It is important to begin this analysis by looking at the city of New Orleans when Katrina occurred. All three media contain real images of the city, although creators of *Treme* explain that they re-created some destruction and embellished already bad conditions at times to reflect the scene in the three months after Katrina. Lee simply uses file footage to remind the viewer of the dire situation during and immediately after Katrina. Lee and Simon and Overmyer chose different genres of programming— but all saw the need to shine attention on the hurricane-ravaged city. And though they took different approaches, the goal appears to be very much the same. The magic window allows audiences access to cultural elements of the city with which they may have little or no experience.

On NOLA.com only a few responses addressed the reality of the city as depicted in the documentary or the TV series, but many responses indicated New Orleanians' desire for viewers to be exposed to the realities of New Orleans post-Katrina. One viewer expressed mixed feelings:

PARADEGIRL: How strange is it that I'd like for them to get things right, but don't want them to tell such a real and terrible story. I want it to feel real, but not too real . . . I think *Treme* is telling our story as well as it can be told.

On HBO.com, viewers were asked about their expectations of *Treme*. Most had high hopes that the show would shine a light on the problems that still exist in the city. One viewer posted the same response on both sites:

ALISTER: I expect *Treme* to continue to raise awareness about the plight of New Orleans and to inspire people to rise up and make the best of things even when all hope is lost, to bring a human story to the many headlines about Katrina and New Orleans that were lost in the media numbing news about the recession and to continue to deliver the best damned show I've ever seen with the best soul-filled music I've heard ever! Hang on New Orleans and *Treme*—we love you!

The real images of an entire city underwater in Spike Lee's documentaries are difficult to watch. And much like the early news coverage of Katrina, many of the images are of African American residents, who are seen on rooftops pleading for help, wading through water, and suffering in the heat outside the convention center. But Lee allows for a restoration of dignity by telling their stories in interviews and allowing audiences to hear their voices rather than just seeing horrific and stereotypical images.

Based on the responses on NOLA.com, it was clear that race-based perspectives are a major issue for many New Orleanians. Multiple posts suggested the race of the viewer because of complaints about the lack of representation of one racial group or another. The following posts in response to an announcement that Lee was producing a sequel to *When the Levees Broke* indicates racial polarization amongst locals in the city:

6PLAYER6: Why would it amaze you that these no good haters hate. Rush and Palin have enough money to make or loan them to make a documentary the way that they want it to be told but Rush and Palin as we know don't really give a care about New Orleans to do it. So all that they can do is hate on the ones who do care. We all know the hate is because Spike Lee is BLACK. One of Spikes best friends is Terence Blanchard who has been doing the music scores of spike Lee for many years and many movies. So, yes he has a reason to care and tell the story from the eyes and thoughts of the people that he knows the best. So ReThuglicans you can call FOX to come down and tell the lies for you because Spike won't do. Ya herd me?

TYGERBATE: @ 6player6 . . . Spoken like a true racist . . . this is typical Spike Lee propaganda not documentary it's like saying the movies Michael Moore makes are documentaries, sure they are. Plaquemines Parish was destroyed, St Bernard Parish was destroyed, Lakeview was destroyed, Pontcharain Park was destroyed, the Mississippi Gulf Coast was destroyed but all we hear about is the 9th Ward, I know there are many minorities who live in the areas I named why are they forgotten by the media? That is the true racism.

6PLAYER6: You would know a TRUE RACIST because you are one yourself. Because he did not tell the story the way that you wanted him to he is racist? What a FOOL you are you load of cat litter. Why don't you make one and then tell it from your point of view? Call up FOX, you may get some help from them, oh that's right, too many Blacks live in New Orleans for them to care. My bad.

In *Treme*, audiences meet and come to know the cast of characters—including African American musicians and Mardi Gras Indians—over the course of the first season. Audiences come to know the characters before they experience Katrina (through flashback) and are able to create an emotional bond with the characters that in turn allows them to see that it wasn't laziness that left them stranded in the flooded city—it was lack of financial resources, lack of assistance from the government, and an infrastructure broken long before Katrina ever hit. In the posts on both NOLA.com and HBO.com, viewers explain that the show gives them insight that they might not have had otherwise:

KIRAHT: As someone not from NOLA, nor even in the vicinity, the show gives insight and as observed from previous episode I get to be a tourist without being on the obnoxious bus with my camera. It makes me long to visit and get the peak behind the curtain.

Emotion and Construction of Social Reality for Viewers

While it is without question that Katrina evokes emotion for those who lived through it, the story also has the capacity to evoke emotion in national audiences as a tragedy. Two very similar stories incorporated in the documentaries and in *Treme* examine a deeper level of understanding for viewers who have experienced Katrina firsthand and those who have not. It is the story of an adult child having to help an elderly parent make decisions about living arrangements. Helping elderly parents make choices of this nature is an issue that many people encounter at some point in life. However, in this case, the devastation of Katrina forces them to grapple with the issue more poignantly.

In *When the Levees Broke*, musician Terrence Blanchard is seen taking his mother, Wilhelmina Blanchard, on a tour of her home for the first time post-Katrina.[15] She lives in Pontchartrain Park, a predominately Black middle-class

Figure 8.1   Terence Blanchard in *When the Levees Broke.* Courtesy of PhotoFest.

neighborhood in New Orleans. The interior of her home is unrecognizable and covered with mold and dried sludge. As Blanchard carefully guides his elderly mother through her home, her emotions are raw. At times she is simply over-whelmed when she sees the home she's lived in most of her life destroyed.

In *If God Is Willing and da Creek Don't Rise*, audiences are returned to Wilhelmina Blanchard's home. But this time, she shares with them her newly renovated kitchen. She quips that she doesn't like the granite countertops and that it has too many cabinets. But her son explains that he wanted her to have a real kitchen, whereupon she quickly responds that her old kitchen was a real kitchen. Blanchard notes that when speaking to one of the contractors who worked in his mother's neighborhood (made up of mostly older residents), he was told that 99 percent of people asked that their homes be rebuilt exactly as they were before. This is not surprising in a city like New Orleans where families often have generational ties to the place. Many were living in homes and neigh-borhoods where their families resided for decades prior to Katrina.

In *Treme* one of the main characters, Albert Lambreaux (Clarke Peters), an older African American man, decides to return and rebuild his home and business in the Treme post-Katrina. He decides it is important to make an effort to bring his community back and wants to be at the forefront of the effort. His son, Delmond Lambreaux (Rob Brown), a musician in Houston, Texas, doesn't under-stand his father's desire to return to New Orleans and appears to resent having to go back and assist his father in the rebuilding process. In the first season of *Treme*, the elder Lambreaux faces a number of challenges in his effort to rebuild.

Figure 8.2   *Treme*'s Albert Lambreaux (Clarke Peters). Courtesy of PhotoFest.

He is forced to live in desolate conditions, has his tools stolen while working on a house, and faces doubt from his family and friends about his desire to rebuild. But he remains steadfast in his decision to come back and rebuild what was.

Audiences responded to the characters on the HBO website. A few of them noted the emotional response to the father/son relationship depicted on *Treme*:

> V. SCHRAMPF: Being in New Orleans, just as a regular visitor who loves the city and melange of cultures there dearly, is an experience of both beauty and heartbreak . . . As for my thoughts on this season, the relationship between Delmond and his daddy has become my favorite one. Delmond in particular I can relate to as someone who moved far away from home, and gradually felt an increasing need to embrace the identity of the place he came from.
>
> R. PANZAR: Albert (Lambreaux) still has a sense of humor. It just takes a pretty woman to bring it out of him. Their father/son relationship rings very true to me. Reminds me of my own family.

The story of these musicians helping elderly parents after Katrina was a dilemma that many residents dealt with post-Katrina. But it is a story that many Americans can relate to as they make decisions about life and living arrangements with their aging parents. At the same time, the parents in both the fiction and the documentaries appear to not want to create difficulty for their children and have a strong desire to restore their lives, homes, and neighborhoods to "the way things used to be." In watching these relationships and the combination of frustration and mutual consideration the characters exhibit, audiences can better understand the struggles New Orleanians face as similar to what most people face as part of their social reality. Katrina not only brought about new and different situations to deal with, it forced some residents to deal with issues that are a regular part of life but under more difficult and unfortunate terms. Both of these depictions have the potential to play on viewers' emotions and, in the process, help audiences better understand the impact of Katrina on families.

Truth Can Be Stranger than Fiction

When it comes to plausibility (the belief that something is possible in the real world), Spike Lee addresses a number of realities about Katrina in the documentaries that many people may find difficult to comprehend. In *If God Is Willing and da Creek Don't Rise*, Lee incorporates the stories of two families who lost family members in senseless acts of police brutality after Katrina. Both stories made national headlines when officers were tried and convicted.

The Danziger case involved two brothers, Lance and Ronald Madison, who were attempting to get help by crossing the Danziger Bridge when the city flooded. The police stopped and accused them of being armed, beat Lance, and shot and killed Ronald, who was mentally challenged. In a separate case, police shot Henry Glover, then set fire to his vehicle with his body inside in an effort to destroy the evidence. When the remains of the car and his body were found, his skull was mysteriously missing. In both cases, the victims were Black males. Civil rights attorney Mary Howell (who is white) addressed the real-world police brutality after Katrina in *If God in Willing and da Creek Don't Rise*: "The most recent developments in the Danziger case have been pretty astonishing to people who live here. And even those of us who have been involved in the police department for thirty years. I would say it's been pretty shocking developments. At this point five police officers and one citizen have come in and pled guilty to bills of information. They are charging them with federal criminal charges related to the shooting and cover-up of shootings . . . It sounds like bad fiction or something."

In *Treme*, the character Toni Bernette (Melissa Leo) is a civil rights attorney. Her character is based on the real-life Howell. In the opening episode, Toni enters a diner and sits at a table with police officers, only to be cursed by one officer who is annoyed because of her investigation of him for improper conduct post-Katrina. She spends most of the first season helping another main character, LaDonna Batiste-Williams (Khandi Alexander), an African American woman, search for her brother who was jailed during Katrina and nowhere to be found afterward. Throughout the first season, his family searches for him. Toward the end, Toni finds and helps the family identify his body. It is clear that something sinister led to his death.

According to an article in *Gambit*, "Toni's storylines parallel Howell's practice to a certain extent, but Howell says the character's quest to find an Orleans

Parish prisoner lost in the system is a composite. 'The criminal justice system had collapsed,' Howell says of post-Katrina New Orleans. 'Thousands of people, literally, were spread out all over the state. No one could locate them; families couldn't find their loved ones. There were some amazing lawyers post-Katrina, mainly criminal defense lawyers, from all around the state, who really stepped up.'"[16] This storyline might come across as just another crime drama in its presentation on *Treme*. And the version of the story on *Treme* is fictional. But the truthful accounts of police brutality incorporated in Spike Lee's documentaries are disturbing and serve as painful reminders of the grave injustices that many innocent African American residents faced in the days following the storm.

Audience commentary suggests that these stories make the program more believable and strike a chord with both local and national viewers. A New Orleans resident commented on HBO.com:

> JAN CLEMENTS: We've been through so much here, it means a lot to us. It's kind of beyond glib criticisms that I see on this thread. Give our people some respect, we've been through so much, and I think it's the least people can do is to let us have our story told, and told properly. If you don't like it, go watch something else, please, respectfully. If it soothes the post-traumatic stress of even a few people and most likely thousands, then it's more that just a series. It's therapy, and it's art. It's intelligent, and it's beautiful. It's sad and it's funny. And the music touches the heart and soul of every single New Orleanian. I heard somebody say it was unrealistic to have so much local music in every scene. Guess what? That stuff is real, we're really into our music, it is who we are, it is our culture, our heritage, our city, our identity, our pride. I'm sure that *Treme* haters can find something else to watch on HBO. Please don't insult our dignity and our pain.

Identity in The Wake of Crisis

Perhaps one of the most memorable New Orleanians introduced to viewers in Spike Lee's *When the Levees Broke* was Phyllis Montana-LeBlanc. Montana-LeBlanc is a Black female and a former resident of a predominately Black area of the city known as New Orleans East. Through a mixture of four-letter words and satirical description, Montana-LeBlanc explained the challenges she and her family faced trying to get out of New Orleans shortly after Katrina and her struggle to come home again. Her appearance was so successful that she later published the book *Not Just the Levees Broke*.

Montana-LeBlanc was also given a part on *Treme*. She plays a fictional character, Desiree, the girlfriend of the main character, Antoine Batiste (played by actor and New Orleans native Wendell Pierce). In an interview on NPR's *All Things Considered*, Montana-LeBlanc explained her role: "It's easy. The lines that

Figure 8.3   Phyllis Montana-LeBlanc. Courtesy of PhotoFest.

I'm reading. The episodes that I'm doing is, like, stuff that I might say to my husband every other day or so. My boyfriend is a musician, so I'm giving him hell. So I'm Phyllis, I'm Desiree, but I'm Phyllis."[17] Montana-LeBlanc's role in the documentary served as an inspiration to some viewers, based on posts. On NOLA.com one respondent explained:

> KATRINASCARS: I probably have nothing in common with Phyllis Montana Leblanc, other than a shared pain of Katrina. I applaud her no holds barred honesty that is her poetry. I wish I could bare my soul as she does to rid myself from the absolute horror that was Katrina. I cried as I watched last night. Thank you, Phyllis, for honestly revisiting the emotions that are difficult and real for so many. Yes, life has gone on, but for so many of us, forever changed who we are.

Including Montana-LeBlanc in the first documentary, one of the more outspoken and eccentric people he met in the process of shooting, allows Lee to offer a candid account of her experiences. She has the potential to have the greatest impact on audiences because she is "just a regular person." Her rise to the national scene has not prompted her to change her appearance, her manner of speech, or the way she interacts with others. As she says, "she's Phyllis." She has achieved local celebrity status in New Orleans, and many residents felt that she did a great job representing regular, everyday folks and their true feelings about being dejected and rejected when they were labeled "refugees."

As a local resident, she also has a voice and joins in the discussions on NOLA.com. She responds as herself and as her character:

PHYLLISMONTANALEBLANC: I'm doing my best to make my city a proud place to live, thrive, and succeed. I am taking a tragic time in my life and turning it into something positive. I am still an advocate for my city and people of New Orleans. You will continue to see me and hear me defend New Orleans. "Antoine is sooooo lucky I don't know where he left the rest of that money! I tell you that much! LOL . . . "BUCK JUMPING AND HAVING FUN" WHEW!!!

Not all responses to the inclusion of Montana-LeBlanc were positive. In one thread, a respondent was especially critical of Montana-LeBlanc. So much so that the original post was removed. But she used the online forum to respond:

PHYLLISMONTANALEBLANC: @saintssand: Your are either drunk or stupid, or both. I'm rich in helping New Orleanians to move forward and grow stronger. Pity has never been in my bloodline. My riches come from God's Blessings in spreading love, peace and togetherness. I was told a long time ago that God takes care of fools and children. Don't ever worry, you're covered . . . you fall under both categories. I would say that you are annoying, but that would mean that you actually matter to me and my efforts to continue standing by, with and for my city of New Orleans. Real New Orleanians know who we are . . . Peace. One Love. Mrs. Phyllis Montana-LeBlanc. Boh Brothers. 7–12's. Pile Driving Crane Operator. Deal with it.

Other viewers used the forum to offer their support and praise:

RANGERUSARMY: Keep pushing, speaking and inspiring Phyllis Montana-Leblanc. I used to see you around in New Orleans East all the time. You are truly genuine all the time (not to mention funny). Most people who haven't talked to you or met you in person are really missing out on a gem. God bless and much success to you. Hope to see you around soon.

Montana-LeBlanc is not the only New Orleanian crossing the boundaries of reality and fiction. A number of local musicians from New Orleans have been incorporated into the *Treme* storyline as well, including Kermit Ruffins, Deacon John, Dr. John, John Boutte, and Allen Toussaint. Jacques Morial (son of former New Orleans mayor Ernest "Dutch" Morial and brother of former New Orleans mayor Marc Morial) had an important role in *If God Is Willing and da Creek Don't Rise* and played himself in a small role on *Treme*. Audiences appear to make the connection and see similarities between the fictional and nonfictional characters. In the process, they learn more about the reality of life for people in post-Katrina

New Orleans and recognize that *Treme* is indeed more than just fiction. Viewers on NOLA.com recognized that many who were featured in Lee's documentaries made the cross-over to the fictional show:

> ASWEPE J.: I have something positive to say. throughout the series I've loved seeing the real life people from New Orleans as introduced by Spike Lee's *When the Levees Broke*.
>
> RAINY KINCAID: I'm excited about Phyllis Montana LeBlanc's role. She was one of the people who spoke out about her experience on Spike Lee's *"When the Levees Broke."* She was the person on that film who touched me the most. She was so brave and authentic in sharing her story. When I saw that she'll be playing *Treme* character Antoine Batise's (Wendell Pierce) girlfriend, I was so excited for her and for us, the audience. I don't know if her part of the series is big or small, but I'm rootin' for her :-)

They Survived; but Could I?

Two of the dimensions identified by Busselle and Greenburg will be taken into account together. They identify probability (the frequency with which something may occur in the real world) and utility (usefulness of information to real-world scenarios) as affecting perceived reality of programming for viewers.[18] How probable is it that one might experience a catastrophe like Katrina in his or her lifetime? Hopefully, not very likely. Katrina is often referred to as a "once in a lifetime" type of event. It is not the event so much as the circumstances surrounding it that make it a viable topic for a documentary or fictional program. In viewing these types of shows, viewers who have never experienced such a disaster likely ponder what they would do in such a situation. In light of all the natural and man-made disasters around the world in recent years (the tsunami in Thailand, the earthquakes in Haiti and China, the fires and landslides in California, the BP oil spill on the Gulf Coast, flooding in Australia), viewers may be reminded that each of us is essentially only one disaster away from having our lives changed forever.

So how might *When the Levees Broke, If God Is Willing and da Creek Don't Rise*, and *Treme* be useful to audiences? Whether a viewer is from New Orleans or not, it is important to think about the primary messages that Lee as well as Simon and Overmyer attempted to share with viewers. They tell a story about how one city dealt with disaster. By watching documentaries and fictional programs about people who are resilient in the wake of catastrophe, audiences can learn what they as individuals have the potential to endure and even overcome. It may also help them feel a little less defeated about daily struggles at work or at home when they see that people who lost their loved ones, their culture, and lifestyle as they knew it still manage to function and persevere. Responses on both HBO.com and

NOLA.com indicate that the productions helped audiences think about life and the potential to overcome:

DEBIKAT7: As an American citizen, I have watched If God Is Willing and Da Creek Don't Rise for the fourth time! I can't remember any other time in my life being so angry at the establishment for the neglect that they have shown New Orleans and the rest of Louisiana! To effect the simple pleasure of every day life, whether at work, home or play, you have lost it all! Discrimination of the poor people is appalling! Are the poor now excluded from equality? To be taken away from the only way of life that they know, away from an area that they call home. I have ideas that could have been used with projects to empower the people, not defeat them! The war is not in New Orleans or even Louisiana and I feel you are fighting the biggest battle that has been fought on American soil. New Orleans, don't surrender until their promises have been kept! I feel as though I should apologize for the bureaucrats in Washington! Good luck on your fight! It makes me wonder why more Americans aren't as angry as I am!

For those who survived Katrina and continue to live in the city, perhaps there is some validation in seeing their stories told through a cast of real and fictional characters. Interestingly, even some people who do not watch the series responded on NOLA.com:

LIZA G. MAY: First I'll say, I haven't watched it. Why should I ? I live here, lived here before during and after The Thing. I hope it does well. I hope its nuanced and multui-layered and whatever else they call good TV. But just the thought of re-living those early dark days is enough to make me tense up, I don't cry every day and more, in my car when I'm alone. I'm still driving past broken things and abandoned houses every day. For me, and this is only for me, it's too soon. I hope they do a great job with *Treme*. I hope people everywhere else watch it and learn something and learn to love New Orleans. I think it's great that folks come to this site and talk about New Orleans.

For those who do watch, they may hear the voices of friends and neighbors telling the reality of what happened in one of Spike Lee's documentaries. They may identify with characters that remind them of themselves or their loved ones and be able to relate to how situations are resolved in the fictional stories on *Treme*. They can see a local musician or activist playing a small role on *Treme* and feel glad for that individual receiving national attention after losing a home or almost losing a career. They may also recognize that promotion of New Orleans musicians is good for the city's image and may encourage tourism—the city's most lucrative industry. Perhaps being able to identify with the people and stories, whether fictional or real, allows current and former residents of New Orleans to feel less alone and more normal in knowing that they are not isolated in the struggles they face even five years after the disaster. Finally, seeing "their own" representing the city fulfills their desire for accuracy in representation. This was evident in commentary from both sites:

(NOLA.com)

NOLALOU: Maybe you didn't experience anything shown in *Treme'* so far, but I can relate to almost all of the characters and stories. I'm not sure what exactly you're complaining about. I find most of what I've seen to be pretty accurate, with some minor exceptions.

(HBO.com)

T. COLEMAN-WILLIAMS: *TREME* CAN'T CHANGE MY LIFE BECAUSE I LIVED THROUGH THESE STORIES BEING TOLD. KATRINA CHANGED MY LIFE AND THIS ENTIRE CITY. *TREME* BRINGS BACK MEMORIES OF THE TIME RIGHT AFTER THE STORM WHEN I WAS AT MY LOWEST AND MOST DEPRESSED POINT. I LOVE THIS CITY AND I APPRECIATE THIS SHOW FOR SHOW- ING OUR STRUGGLE. IT COMES CLOSE, BUT CANNOT ACCU- RATELY PORTRAY WHAT IT FELT LIKE. IT DOES A REALLY GOOD JOB, THOUGH.

As Foster, Blakes, and McKay describe, "Because we live in an age when television media 'news cycles' dictate collective memories of events (no matter how monumental and catastrophic those events may be), documentary films that capture and bear witness to unvarnished realities of devastation, triumph, or even everyday life take on special importance."[19] Fictional programs have that power as well. Shapiro and Chock argue: "Since ancient times fictional stories have been expected to have an effect."[20]

In the June 2010 feature story about *Treme*, *Gambit* news magazine reported, "From both local and national reviews it seems that creator David Simon's vision of post-Katrina New Orleans life has proved—at last—that it's possible to capture the city accurately on film . . . Treme started in an obvious place: reality."[21] Prior to Katrina, New Orleans and its residents had a reputation: they party (Mardi Gras is the biggest free show on earth); they let the good times roll! (Laissez les bon temps rouler!); and they eat well (jambalaya, crawfish pie, filé gumbo). But the new face of post-Katrina New Orleans as portrayed in these fictional and nonfic- tional depictions suggests something a bit different. They persevere; they over- come; and they triumph in the face of the storm. And with the help of people like Spike Lee, David Simon, and Eric Overmyer, they refuse to be "the city that care forgot."

NOTES

1. "New Orleans Locals Put Their Stamp on HBO's 'Treme,'" *All Things Considered*, National Public Radio, April 8, 2010.

2. Posts will be reported here exactly as they were on the sites with no grammar or spelling corrections.

3. Hangwoo Lee, "Implosion, Virtuality, and Interaction in an Internet Discussion Group," *Information, Communication & Society* 8, no. 1 (2005): 47–63.

4. Kevin Foster, Tifani Blakes, and Jenny McKay, "Documenting Tragedy and Resilience: The Importance of Spike Lee's *When the Levees Broke*," *Urban Education* 43, no. 4 (2008): 489.

5. "New Orleans Locals Put Their Stamp on HBO's 'Treme.'"

6. Spike Lee, *If God Is Willing and da Creek Don't Rise*, HBO, 2010.

7. "A City of Treme Characters," *Gambit* (New Orleans, LA), June 14, 2010, 2.

8. Ibid., 6.

9. Rick Busselle and Bradley Greenberg, "The Nature of Television Realism Judgments: A Reevaluation of Their Conceptualization," *Mass Communication & Society* 3, nos. 2–3 (2000): 249.

10. K. McKenna and J. Bargh, "Plan 9 from Cyberspace: The Implications of the Internet for Personality and Social Psychology," in *Living in the Information Age*, ed. Erik P. Bucy, 2nd ed. (Southbank, Vic., Australia: Wadsworth, 2005), 193–203.

11. Melissa Wall, "Blogs of War: Weblogs as News," *Journalism* 6, no. 2 (2005): 153–172; 161, 163 quoted.

12. Michael Shapiro and T. Makana Chock, "Psychological Processes in Perceiving Reality," *Media Psychology* 5, no. 2 (2003): 164, 187.

13. Ibid., 163.

14. Busselle and Greenberg, "Nature of Television Realism Judgments," 257.

15. Blanchard created the soundtrack for both of Lee's documentaries as well as for much of his fictional work.

16. "City of Treme Characters," 5–6.

17. "New Orleans Locals Put Their Stamp on HBO's Treme."

18. Busselle and Greenberg, "Nature of Television Realism Judgments," 257.

19. Foster, Blakes, and McKay, "Documenting Tragedy and Resilience," 489.

20. Shapiro and Chock, "Psychological Processes," 167.

21. "City of Treme Characters," 1.

PART III

NEW JACK BLACK

9 Keepin' It Reality Television

RACQUEL GATES

Introduction: Keepin' It *Real . . . Housewives of Atlanta*

On November 4, 2008, CNN anchor Anderson Cooper appeared on *The Ellen DeGeneres Show* via satellite. One of the more memorable moments of the interview came when Cooper expressed shock that DeGeneres was unfamiliar with the hit Bravo television show *The Real Housewives of Atlanta*. "You mean you don't know about NeNe?" he demanded incredulously, referring to cast member NeNe Leakes—the most outspoken and self-proclaimed "realest" of the Housewives. Cooper's segment, along with his admission that Leakes was his favorite of the cast, brought even more attention to the already widely debated show, the first of Bravo's *Housewives* series to feature a predominantly African American cast.[1]

The Real Housewives of Atlanta profiles the lives, experiences, and interactions of a group of wealthy women living in Atlanta, Georgia. The show built on the success of Bravo's previous two offerings, *The Real Housewives of Orange County* (2006–) and *The Real Housewives of New York* (2008–).[2] Having developed an enthusiastic following over the course of its first season, *Atlanta* opened its second season with a record-breaking 2.7 million viewers, beating out viewership for any other *Housewives* premiere by over 1 million viewers. As the first primarily nonwhite offering in the *Housewives* franchise, the show presented race as a significant characteristic from the outset. In the premiere episode, the words *African American* or *Black* are mentioned no less than three times in the first thirty seconds, all before the opening credits. The background music common to all of the *Housewives* shows was given a pronounced drumbeat for the Atlanta edition, adding a tinge of hip hop flavor to various scenes.

The success of the show, however, was tempered by mixed responses from various groups. The aforementioned NeNe Leakes garnered the largest amount of press and the greatest variety of responses due to her gregarious behavior and habit of "telling it like it is." Not everyone was impressed by her larger-than-life personality. One viewer complained, "It was like a herd of cattle wearing wigs and lipstick passed through my living room."[3] Another viewer disgustedly commented, "This show needs subtitles. I don't think anyone speaks English. Must get out my Detroit Ghetto Translation Guide. Holy shit, what a mess of ugly, gross bimbos."[4]

The criticism of Leakes and her cast mates overwhelmingly converged on the women's femininity, speech patterns, and mannerisms: sites where preconceived notions of "upper class," "successful," and "housewife" (historically underscored by an implicit vision of whiteness) did not match the image that the Black *Atlanta* housewives projected. The elements that marked them as "different" and thus a symbol of the racial diversity that Bravo sought to achieve also signaled their deviation from the norm established by the white housewives from the Orange County and New York series.[5] From the very first episode, *Atlanta* involved a clash of realities that was based on the specificities of racialized, gendered difference.

The same traits that many cited as flaws, however, took on radically different interpretations depending on who was doing the watching. As I noted in the opening paragraph, CNN journalist Anderson Cooper equated these qualities with a kind of "authenticity" that he found refreshing. Bravo executive Andy Cohen defined Leakes's behavior as "camp." An openly gay man, Cohen explained the relationship between Bravo's gay male viewers and the Housewives: "Gays love these shows for the same reason gays love drag queens. They're an exaggerated portrayal of women, what gay guys want women to be in their twisted fantasy lives."[6] Far from viewing the Housewives as "negative" representations, Cohen celebrated the unique perspective that the women brought to everyday issues and struggles.

The Real Housewives of Atlanta illuminates certain questions inherent to racial representation and reality television. Yet this chapter is not interested in qualitative evaluations of *The Real Housewives of Atlanta* or any other reality television program. Though there are certainly many convincing arguments for and against the utility of reality-based narratives in service to progressive representations of race in the media, that project, I fear, runs the risk of continuing to group media into categories of "positive" or "negative." Instead, this chapter offers an overarching view of how reality television resituates discourses of racial representation within the specificities of its generic conventions. In particular, I argue that reality television thrives on the tensions that result from the multiple versions of "reality" that circulate inside and outside of the programs. These realities emanate from the shows' narratives, the types of individuals cast to participate, and audiences' own lived experiences as racialized and gendered persons. Programs that revolve around competition such as *Flavor of Love* (competing for a man), *The Apprentice* (competing for a job), and *Survivor* (competing for one million dollars) feature more pressing kinds of struggles between conflicting realities and the power to have one's own version of reality recognized as the definitive "reality." I question, how do reality-based narratives involving African Americans fit into a larger history of racial representation in media history? How does reality television present, manage, and reinforce dissonant versions of "reality," particularly those based on the historical and social experience of race? Finally, how might shifting the lens of analysis uncover resistant interpretations of seemingly "negative" representations and texts?

Regarding this last point, I fully acknowledge the tension that accompanies the alternative or negotiated readings of these shows. Admittedly, arguing for a subversive reading of a controversial television program such as *Flavor of Love* is a difficult task, given the show's reliance on racial and gender stereotypes. As cultural theorists such as Paul du Gay, Stuart Hall, and others remind us, consumers do not invent meaning in a vacuum. Thus, we should not jettison critical analysis in favor of an exclusive focus on alternative readings, disengaging consumption from matters of production in the process.[7]

Rather than suggest that the readings offered in this chapter should replace other interpretations, my analyses rest on an understanding of these texts as intrinsically polysemic, laden with meanings and significance that are activated by a variety of factors. For example, intertextual knowledge of Flavor Flav's rap career adds another dimension to his performance on the show *Flavor of Love*: those viewers already familiar with Flav's controversial music and troubled history with drugs and law enforcement are primed to read his casting as a satirical commentary on the "Prince Charming" conceit around which most dating shows (such as *The Bachelor*) revolve. Thus, my readings of programs like *Flavor of Love*, *Survivor*, and *The Apprentice* do not cast aside considerations of production and regulation in the meaning-making process but rather highlight interpretative strategies that have yet to be privileged.

Criticism of African American Representations in Reality Television

One criticism made of reality television is that it promotes "negative" images of African Americans more effectively than television programs such as the sitcom or drama because, unlike these fictional offerings, reality TV masks itself as documentary, which straightforwardly presents, rather than *represents*, people and situations. The problem, critics argue, is the claim that what appears on the screen is an accurate depiction of real people with no intrusion by scripts, producers, or any of the other elements of fictionalized representation. Without the acknowledgment that these representations are constructed fictions, such images run the risk of being interpreted as truthful and accurate reflections of essentialized racial identities.

Though this argument highlights an important issue in reality television's handling of race, it is also predicated on two faulty assumptions. First, it takes for granted the fact that reality television characters always perform their identities according to their preconceived roles. Second, it presumes that audiences straightforwardly accept the dominant version of "reality" that the programs carefully assemble and present to them. Instead, the strategy of casting participants from diverse backgrounds in order to create an interesting program carries with it opportunities for moments that do not adhere to the expected norms or conventions concerning performance of racial identities, and that cannot be wholly controlled by the very sophisticated production methods that these shows employ.

Rather than seamlessly performing their prescribed roles, reality show participants regularly act in ways that reflect their own backgrounds and lived realities. As Laurie Ouellette and Susan Murray note in the introduction to their book, *Reality TV: Remaking Television Culture*, "Reality TV promises its audience revelatory insight into the lives of others as it withholds and subverts full access to it. What results is an unstable text that encourages viewers to test out their own notions of the real, the ordinary, and the intimate against the representation before them."[8] With viewers ever more savvy about how reality shows are produced to convey "reality," we should assume that audiences for shows like *Flavor of Love* and *The Apprentice* are well aware that the portrayals they see are manipulated in various ways by the processes of production. Furthermore, as Stuart Hall has theorized, both white and Black audiences participate in "negotiated readings" of texts, evaluating the mainstream version of reality in relation to their own lived experiences and against the realities of the form itself.[9]

Citizenship, Race, and Respectability: From *Survivor* to *The Apprentice*

Much of the appeal of reality television results from the way that the programs act out essential conflicts of human existence on the small screen. Moments when these conflicts wade into the murky waters of race-based experience and social membership, however, prove particularly fascinating. For example, on the fourteenth season of the show, *Survivor: Fiji* (2007), African American contestant Andria "Dreamz" Herd quickly became the show's villain when he reneged on a promise made between himself and another contestant, Yau-Man Chan.[10] The public vitriol that erupted in response to Dreamz's action was surprising given *Survivor*'s history of contestants who lie and backstab their way to the win. Ostensibly, the criticism of Dreamz by his fellow contestants as well as the viewing public—most of which concentrated on issues of his integrity—erupted from a sense of indignation at his betrayal of a promise made to Yau-Man, a player well-liked for his intelligence, fairness, and kindness. Closer inspection, however, suggests that Dreamz's decision to go back on his promise constituted a kind of rejection of normative codes of social behavior, one that pushed him to the margins of acceptability and that completed the marginalization already at work because of his race and class.

The demonization of Dreamz hinted at a larger truth about the relationship between race and the rules that govern citizenship both in the constructed environments of reality television and in the world more broadly. As an African American man who had grown up in poverty and had been homeless for a portion of his adult life, Dreamz's self-appointed moniker was an optimistic declaration of the positive direction in which he hoped his life would continue. At the same time, his background quickly became an impediment to his ability to accurately read social cues and navigate interpersonal dynamics—skills crucial to the game of *Survivor*. If, as Laurie Ouellette and James Hay argue, *Survivor*

Figure 9.1   Andria "Dre" Herd (2007). Courtesy of PhotoFest.

"enacts (weekly and seasonally reenacts) the *birth* of government and the rein-vention of new liberal citizen players," then Dreamz's controversial decision to break his promise to Yau-Man marked him as an unfit member of the vision of society constituted on *Survivor*.[11]

If we understand *Survivor* as a reality television society in which good citizens are rewarded with cash prizes and bad citizens are voted off, then Dreamz's deci-sion marks the point where his own lived reality clashed with *Survivor's* concept of proper citizenship. *Survivor* presented a scenario where Dreamz had to choose between greed and integrity. By choosing the former, Dreamz broke the rules of citizenship governing *Survivor's* social dynamics. Dreamz, on the other hand, saw

Figure 9.2   *Survivor: Fiji* cast (2007). Courtesy of PhotoFest.

the situation as one of self-interest versus self-sacrifice. Yau-Man, with an impressive education and profession, could literally *afford* to give up a brand-new car and gamble away a chance at a million dollars.[12] For Dreamz, his past experience with poverty made such a risk unthinkable. Furthermore, by implying that Dreamz should sacrifice potential material comfort in favor of honoring a promise to someone he had only known for a few weeks, *Survivor* implied that Dreamz's real-life concerns were secondary to his responsibilities to "play fairly." Dreamz's "betrayal," therefore, signified a conscious decision to operate in accordance with his own reality as an individual who did not have the privilege to take material comforts for granted. By condemning Dreamz's action, his fellow contestants (along with *Survivor* host Jeff Probst and countless fans of the show) essentially denied the version of reality that dictated his choice.

Similar conflicts between race and iterations of citizenship abound on reality television, particularly as far as African American men are concerned. On a program such as *The Real World*, vaguely defined "house rules" dictate cast members' right to remain in the homes provided by producers (and thus the right to continue participating in the show). Second-season cast member David Edwards was evicted from the house for pulling a blanket off of another cast member who was partially dressed, and seventh-season cast mate Stephen Williams was asked to leave after slapping a female roommate.[13] Notably, in each case, the decision to evict the men was spurred by complaints from the other roommates, indicating that the group dynamics of the cast mates are crucial in defining what constitutes "citizenship" in the house.

Figure 9.3   *The Apprentice* with Randal Pinkett. Courtesy of PhotoFest.

A particularly significant clash between race and citizenship played itself out on the fourth season of *The Apprentice*. On December 15, 2005, Randal Pinkett became the first African American winner of Donald Trump's popular reality show, where contestants compete in a number of business-oriented challenges to win the ultimate prize: a job working for the real estate magnate. *The Apprentice* had been under scrutiny as far as racial representation was concerned ever since the casting of controversial contestant Omarosa Manigault-Stallworth on the show's first season. Critics claimed that even though Manigault-Stallworth possessed an impressive professional background, she was chosen primarily for her brash, troublemaking demeanor. They argued that this demonstrated the extent to which Trump and *Apprentice* producers were more interested in selecting contestants based on their skill at approximating racial stereotypes than on their résumés.[14]

Thus it was with high hopes that audiences tuned in to view Pinkett—Rhodes scholar, Academic All-American, holder of both an MBA and a PhD—as he sailed from challenge to challenge, avoiding elimination up until the final episode, where he was named the winner. The festivities were cut short almost as soon as they began, however. In an unprecedented twist, Trump interrupted Pinkett's celebration by asking the newly appointed Apprentice if he believed that Rebecca Jarvis, the twenty-three-year-old runner-up (and a Caucasian woman), should also be named a winner. Pinkett, whose amicability and kindness had been noted throughout the season, surprised Trump, his fellow contestants, and viewers by firmly asserting his desire to share neither his prize nor his title with Jarvis. He stated, "Mr. Trump, I firmly believe that this is *The Apprentice*, that there is one, and only one, Apprentice."

Pinkett's answer ignited a firestorm on Internet message boards, where people blasted him for what they viewed as selfishness and poor sportsmanship. The public's sudden about-face regarding Pinkett's character was a direct consequence of the abrupt collision between Pinkett's reality as an African American man and the reality constructed by *The Apprentice* (and ultimately accepted by most viewers). Pinkett's reality, which he would be forced to articulate in countless interviews after his win, was grounded in a desire to have his hard work and efforts recognized by being awarded the title of "Apprentice." In an interview with *Black Enterprise* magazine, Pinkett expressed the significance of being recognized for his lifetime of hard work: "Nothing has been handed to me. I've put in a lot of hours working and a lot of hours studying and a lot of hours persevering. And it will take just as much, if not more, to get me to the next level."[15] In an interview with the *Black Collegian*, he put the matter more succinctly: "Do you share? Do you deliver a message that excellence should be rewarded or not recognized?"[16] Though many may have assessed Pinkett's words as selfishness (and indeed, a repeated sentiment was that it would not have cost Pinkett anything to endorse Jarvis's hire), such an interpretation in no way acknowledged the significance of minority achievement in predominantly white spaces given the history of structuralized racial oppression in this country. As journalist Jacob Clifton wrote in his online recap of the episode, "'Sharing' = 'marginalizing' when you're talking *firsts*."[17]

The version of reality presented by *The Apprentice* ignored the significance of Pinkett's achievement as the first African American Apprentice. Instead, the show had carefully crafted a persona around Pinkett that was meant to neutralize his racial identity. Pinkett's respectability thus became the primary marker of his status as an ideal citizen within the predominantly white world of *The Apprentice*. While Dreamz's personal history (and the choices he made based upon it) was a hindrance to his citizenship on *Survivor*, Pinkett's real-life experiences worked in the opposite way. Repeatedly highlighting his prestigious education and his overall niceness—perhaps as a remedy for the controversial Omarosa Manigault-Stallworth of the first season—*The Apprentice* equated Pinkett's identity as a model minority with his identity as a model citizen. This undoubtedly accounted for his widespread fan base among *Apprentice* viewers across racial lines, but such a representational strategy also fixed Pinkett into a particular trope of Blackness that relied completely on respectability, and thus also framed him as "safe" and nonthreatening.[18] This portrayal, coupled with his reputation as a good "team player" (a trait immensely valued within the world of *The Apprentice*), worked to characterize Pinkett as what Patricia Hill Collins calls "the Black buddy": "he [is] friendly and deferential; he [is] loyal both to dominant societal values such as law and order as well as to individuals who seemingly uphold them."[19] Pinkett's refusal to share his win with Jarvis, therefore, directly contradicted this previous characterization.

The controversy and Internet buzz surrounding Pinkett's "decision" effectively created a reality that had little to do with actual events. First, it presented Pinkett as the decision maker in the situation, conveniently ignoring the actual scenario in which Trump wielded the power and pretended to place the fate of one minority contestant (Jarvis) in the hands of another (Pinkett). The implication that Pinkett had *denied* Jarvis a job radically rewrote the reality that both candidates—minorities because of their race and gender, respectively—were competing against each other for a prize that only Trump had the power to bestow. By framing Pinkett's statements within this framework rather than in the reward rubric that he continually asserted, the argument shied away from what might have been a fruitful consideration of how privilege still operates in American society to marginalize both racial and gender minorities.

Furthermore, Trump's conduct during the segment—in which he patronizingly told "Randal" to come back and sit down as he was in the midst of embracing his family—suggested an effort to put Pinkett "in his place" as a racialized subject. In their book, *Better Living Through Reality TV: Television and Post-welfare Citizenship*, authors Laurie Ouellette and James Hay argue that *The Apprentice* "is not only a vehicle for displaying Trump's business ventures and brands, but a lab for teaching/producing/inventing an ideal corporate citizen."[20]

Devon Carbado connects the concept of citizenship to racial performance, arguing that racialization is a process enforced by governing institutions by which individuals become citizens.[21] Examined within this perspective of citizenship, it becomes clear that Trump's actions worked to racially socialize Pinkett into an "ideal citizen" within the controlled world of *The Apprentice*.[22] Pinkett's assertion of his *own* version of reality, however, challenged the seamlessness with which the show attempted to sell a particular type of "appropriate" racial performance.

Pinkett's action and the unsympathetic, disproportionate responses that it generated reveal the limitations of respectability and "positive" representation as a strategy for increasing racial awareness in reality television, and by extension in the media at large. Though Pinkett embodied the self-made man and espoused the kind of bootstraps mentality that neoliberals love to propose as a solution to racial inequality, his decision to momentarily (and it only took a moment) privilege his race- and gender-based reality served as justification for harsh mischaracterizations and public scrutiny. Rather than rescue him from the limiting media tropes of Black men, his impeccable résumé and upright conduct simply locked him into *another* stereotype (the "safe" sidekick) that proved problematic when his actions did not perfectly align with this image.

Flavor of Love: Modern-Day Minstrelsy or Social Satire?

If Pinkett's unquestioned respectability and good citizenship were not enough to secure a favorable characterization in the world of reality television, one might assume that a Viking-hat-wearing ex–crack addict like rapper Flavor Flav would certainly fare no better. Yet I argue that by eschewing the veneer of respectability, Flavor Flav and the popular dating show *Flavor of Love* activate a particular satirical reading approach that may operate, in the words of Stuart Hall, as a cultural strategy that "changes the dispositions and the configurations of cultural power."[23] And furthermore, taking up the "modern-day minstrel" charge that has been so hatefully directed at the show and its star might, in fact, reveal a subversive system of social critique that lurks beneath the guise of apolitical buffoonery.

"Perhaps not since 1915's racist epic *The Birth of a Nation* have we been depicted as offensively as we are on VH1's *Flavor of Love*," declared journalist Debra Dickerson in the November 2006 issue of *Essence* magazine.[24] Earlier that year, VH1 premiered *Flavor of Love*, a dating show in which twenty women vied for the affection of Flavor Flav, the former "hype man" from the highly political rap group Public Enemy. Over the course of ten episodes, women competed in a number of challenges, completing tasks such as frying chicken and hosting Flav on a date in a hot tub. Prizes bestowed throughout the season included a romantic dinner at Red Lobster and the ultimate gift—a gold "grill" awarded to the winner as a symbol of Flav's commitment.[25]

Though critics intended the label of "modern-day minstrelsy" as an insult to the show and Flavor Flav, the comparison is apt for more complicated reasons and helps contextualize much of the condemnation of *Flavor of Love*. Mel Watkins and Arthur Knight have argued that African American participation in Blackface minstrelsy both on stage and on celluloid were marked by a complicated set of meanings among performers and audiences. Watkins argues that the negative critique of African American minstrel performers by African American critics is deeply connected to politics of uplift and respectability during times of racial inequality. Writing about the tendency of middle-class African Americans to disparage Black folks culture seen as "low," he notes that these criticisms had less to do with the formal qualities of the performances themselves and more to do with how they were assumed to operate in larger discussions of race in society.

In suggesting that *Flavor of Love* might best be read as a satire of white dating shows, I do not mean to gloss over the very real issues of the historically problematic representation of African Americans in the media. Instead, I want to suggest that the show, while indulging in the clownish behavior of Flavor Flav on the one hand (and thus deserving the intense scrutiny it has received), also adopts a tone that criticizes the way that race and gender roles are prescribed to viewers through "serious" shows like *Who Wants to Marry a Multi-Millionaire?* (2000), *Average Joe* (2003–2005), *Farmer Wants a Wife* (2008), and *The Bachelor* (2002–), among others.

Rachel Dubrofsky and Antoine Hardy note that *Flavor of Love* "self-consciously acknowledges its appropriation of 'The Bachelor'" and the inherent racial differences between the two series in the very first episode in which Flav announces, "I know many of you have seen that show 'The Bachelor,' but Flavor is the Blackchelor!"[26] In fact, even the negative criticism of *Flavor of Love* hints at some of the more promising aspects of the show as a parody of mainstream dating shows like *The Bachelor* before moving on to condemn it. Teresa Wiltz of the *Washington Post* questions whether "the difference between racial satire and perpetuating racial stereotypes [is] too fine a line to tread."[27] Lola Ogunnaike of the *New York Times* calls the show "a ghetto-fabulous spoof of the dating show 'The Bachelor.'"[28]

Viewed as a parody, *Flavor of Love* calls attention to the constructed nature of media representations, particularly within the reality television genre. The show demonstrated its parodic tone in a number of ways. For instance, it used humorous sound effects to emphasize contestants' statements and actions, such as the bicycle bell sound that accompanied Schatar "Hottie" Taylor to emphasize her affected pretensions of upper-class sensibilities. In addition, the show created a distance between the real and performative identities of the participants through the use of a ritualistic naming ceremony. On the first episode, Flav gives each of the contestants nicknames by which they will be known for the duration of the show. These names—"Hoopz," "Smiley," and "New York," among others—single out specific aspects of the participants' identities but also call attention to the fabricated personae that the women adopt and act out on the show. The distance created between person and persona also applies to Flavor Flav himself. Like the

Figure 9.4   Flava Flav in *Flavor of Love*. Courtesy of PhotoFest.

female contestants, he calls attention to the fact that he is performing within a fictionalized context. Dubrofsky and Hardy argue that Flav's repeated distinction between his "real" self, William Drayton, and the public persona of "Flavor Flav" reveals the "performative aspect of Flavor's presentation."[29]

Returning to the "modern-day minstrel" charge, it is possible to view this dissonance between William Drayton and Flavor Flav as part of a larger tradition within Black folk culture. Arthur Knight argues that African American minstrel performers used Blackface as a way of differentiating between the performers themselves and the characters that they played. In film, he maintains, scenes that show the transition from African American to African American in Blackface foreground "a diegetic shift from 'natural' character to 'made-up' performer."[30] In the case of Flavor of Love, scenes such as the one mentioned above force viewers to acknowledge the ways in which performers, producers, and spectators are all complicit in the process of creating legible racialized tropes. Embracing these manufactured identities, even the "negative" ones, can strike a preliminary blow against the power of mainstream culture to construct normativity via the invisible markers of whiteness and maleness.

This emphasis on performativity also supports the argument that Flavor of Love ridicules the version of romantic love and normative gender roles that is routinely sold by mainstream media, especially other reality dating TV shows like The Bachelor. Placed within a Black cultural tradition, Flavor of Love could be said to be engaging in what Henry Louis Gates Jr. calls "motivated Signifyin(g)," in which a text directly critiques another via parody.[31] If interpreted as a "motivated Signification" on The Bachelor, some of Flavor of Love's "failures" can instead be seen as critiques. For instance, many might view Flav's distribution of oversized clocks on chains (resembling his own clock necklace) as a shoddy derivation of The Bachelor's rose ceremony. Flavor of Love's unique spin, however, renders the entire ritual silly and strange, refusing to adhere to The Bachelor's pretense that women should, in fact, degrade themselves for a material token of one man's affection. Similarly, the gift of a gold grill rather than an engagement ring to the eventual winner calls into question whether or not women should view a marriage proposal as a "reward" for successfully backstabbing and clawing their way into a man's heart over the course of a few weeks. By turning each major convention of The Bachelor on its head, Flavor of Love effectively presents the absurdity in not only the shows themselves but also the social norms that govern how romantic relationships are presented via these programs.

Another major "failure" in Flavor of Love is the inability of both contestants and Flav himself to meet standards of appropriate gender performance. Numerous critics commented on Flav's unconventional looks, such as Lola Ogunnaike, who noted that he "bears more than a passing resemblance to a California Raisin character."[32] As far as the female contestants were concerned, they quickly became known for their own outrageous—sometimes violent—antics.

As DeWayne Wickham noted in *USA Today*, "The competition among them is anything but ladylike."[33] These critics do not, however, interrogate the race, gender, and class norms that constitute the foundations of their condemnations. Why, for instance, should it be acceptable for women to engage in a game show where every aspect of their bodies and personalities is placed before the judgment of one man as well as the viewing audience, as long as they behave in ways deemed appropriately "ladylike?"[34]

Flavor of Love offers an example of women who have not bought into (or do not have access to) the Cinderella myth that other dating shows try so hard to market to audiences. Unlike some of their counterparts on other shows, contestants on *Flavor of Love* prioritize a number of other concerns besides simply finding a man. "Serious," for example, presented Flav with a calendar featuring modeling photos of herself. "Krazy" "accidentally" played her demo CD on the house's stereo system. And numerous other contestants over the course of *Flavor of Love*'s three seasons used the pursuit of Flav as a convenient forum from which to launch careers. It is this rejection of "appropriate" dating show behavior that constitutes their appeal. Jonathan Gray argues that *Flavor of Love* contestant "New York" "became a quick fan favorite for her continued refusal to behave in appropriate *Bachelor* contestant style" and compares her to other "unruly women" on television such as Mae West and Roseanne Arnold.[35] Gray's assertion supports a reading that positions *Flavor of Love* as commentary rather than failure. Thus, *Flavor of Love* offers a representation of women who refuse the fairy tale that is marketed to young women in everything from children's books to Disney films and provides viewers with an alternative narrative to the princess who waits patiently for her prince to arrive.

The potential for "unruly" women to subvert the conventions of race and gender manifests in the large number of reality television shows that attempt to contain these disruptive figures. One need only glance at the landscape of reality television to see how preoccupied the genre is with reconditioning African Americans into a version of Blackness that is acceptable by mainstream standards. Take, for instance, Danielle, the eventual winner of the sixth cycle of *America's Next Top Model*. As scholar Amy Adele Hasinoff astutely notes, much of the season focused on getting rid of Danielle's identifiably Black, country accent before she was awarded the title. According to Hasinoff, Danielle's voice signified "a particular regional racialized class position that the judges deem[ed] unmarketable."[36] Likewise, African American contestants on *Model* are routinely given long, straight weaves in order to make their look more "high fashion." Black men do not escape these racialized makeovers, either. *From G's to Gents* (2008–2009), for example, promoted its goal to transform self-proclaimed "gangstas" into old-fashioned gentlemen.[37]

Notably, following the controversy of the depictions of African American women on *Flavor of Love*, VH1 premiered *Flavor of Love Girls: Charm School* in 2007, which substituted a cash prize of fifty thousand dollars in place of a man as the reward for which the women competed. Shedding their nicknames in a symbolic ritual and participating in challenges where they raised money for charity and participated in forensic debates, *Charm School* positioned itself as a remedy for the "damage" done to Black women's images by *Flavor of Love*. At the same time, the constant emphasis on "fixing" the way that the women spoke, dressed, and behaved seemed to suggest that the program was more interested in moderating their "errant" performance of femininity.

Keepin' It Real(ity) Television

The examples discussed in this chapter suggest the possibilities of reality television beyond a traditional analysis of representation. Admittedly, what I propose— subversive reading strategies, reclamation of problematic images—is a tall order given the history of racial representation in the media. It is, in fact, a *privilege* to be able to ignore the ways that racialized images have operated throughout history, one that African Americans have not traditionally been able to afford. And yet, if reality television participants such as NeNe Leakes, Dreamz, Randal Pinkett, and countless others can choose to privilege their version of reality over those of the institutions that attempt to control them, then we as viewers can similarly *choose* to read their realities as dominant. Thus, we can choose to interpret *Flavor Flav* as satire; we can choose to embrace unruly women who lapse into the territory of "ghetto." And finally, we can choose to substitute our own interpretations of images in place of what we fear others see when they look at the television.

NOTES

1. Cooper's praise of *Housewives* was juxtaposed against the backdrop of the presidential election. By the end of the day on November 4, 2008, Barack Obama would become the first African American in history to be elected president of the United States, having ridden a wave of popularity partly based on his carefully worded rhetoric surrounding racial politics in the country.

2. The success of the Atlanta season spawned another ethnic *Housewives* series, this one set in New Jersey and featuring women of Italian heritage.

3. Myrna C, comment on *Real Housewives of Atlanta*, *Television Without Pity* message boards, comment posted on July 31, 2008, http://forums.televisionwithoutpity.com/index.php?showtopic=3173865&st=30, (accessed December 9, 2010).

4. Biscuitsngravy, comment on *Real Housewives of Atlanta*, *Television Without Pity* message boards, comment posted on October 8, 2008, http://forums.televisionwithoutpity.com/index.php?showtopic=3173865&st=225, (accessed December 9, 2010).

5. Hortense Spillers reminds us "we must observe those undeniable contrasts and differences so decisive that the African-American female's historic claim to the territory of womanhood and 'femininity' still tends to rest too solidly on the subtle and shifting calibrations of a liberal ideology." Hortense Spillers, "Mama's Baby, Papa's Maybe: An American Grammar Book," *Diacritics* 17, no. 2 (Summer 1987): 77.

6. Jason Lamphier, "Andy Knows Best," *Advocate*, October 2009, http://www.advocate.com/printArticle.aspx?id=98180.

7. Paul du Gay, Stuart Hall, Linda Janes, Hugh Mackay, and Keith Negus, *Doing Cultural Studies: The Story of the Sony Walkman* (London: Sage/Open University, 1997), 102–109.

8. Susan Murray and Laurie Ouellette, "Introduction," in *Reality TV: Remaking Television Culture*, ed. Susan Murray and Laurie Ouellette (New York: New York University Press, 2009), 8.

9. Stuart Hall, "Encoding, Decoding" in *The Cultural Studies Reader*, ed. Simon During (New York: Routledge, 1999), 516.

10. Chan won an expensive car in one of the challenges. He offered the car to Dreamz in exchange for the immunity idol that Dreamz was expected to win in the next challenge. Dreamz agreed, accepted the car, and went on to win the next immunity idol as predicted. He then decided, however, to keep both the car and immunity for himself, thus going back on his agreement with Yau-Man and sealing the fate of his fellow contestant, who was subsequently eliminated in the next vote.

11. Laurie Ouellette and James Hay, *Better Living Through Reality TV* (Malden, MA: Blackwell, 2008), 186.

12. Chan has bachelor's and master's degrees in science and is the chief technology officer for the College of Chemistry at the University of California, Berkeley.

13. Edwards was a cast member on *The Real World: Los Angeles* (1993); Williams participated in *The Real World: Seattle* (1998).

14. Although Manigault-Stallworth is best known for her outrageous behavior on *The Apprentice*, she also possesses a master's degree in mass communications from Howard University and held a number of administrative positions in the White House during the Clinton administration prior to her television debut.

15. Sakina P. Spruell, "Back Talk with Randal Pinkett," *Black Enterprise*, March 2006, 124.

16. Hildee Weiss, "The Newest Apprentice: Dr. Randal Pinkett," *Black Collegian*, February 2006, 70–72.

17. Jacob Clifton, "Lesson Thirteen: People Aren't Metaphors," *Television Without Pity*, December 20, 2005, http://www.televisionwithoutpity.com/show/the_apprentice/season_finale.php?page=33.

18. For more in-depth discussions of Black respectability, see Sut Jhally and Justin Lewis's *Enlightened Racism: The Cosby Show, Audiences, and the Myth of the American Dream* (Boulder, CO: Westview Press, 1992) and Herman Gray's *Watching Race: Television and the Struggle for Blackness* (Minneapolis: University of Minnesota Press, 1995).

19. Patricia Hill Collins, *Black Sexual Politics: African Americans, Gender, and the New Racism* (New York: Routledge, 2004), 167.

20. Ouellette and Hay, *Better Living Through Reality TV*, 188.

21. Carbado claims, "Racial naturalization is what produces and renders intelligible race-based American identities." Devon Carbado, "Racial Naturalization," *American Quarterly* 57, no. 3 (September 2005): 646.

22. Later, on the February 16, 2006, episode of *Your World with Neil Cavuto*, Trump claimed that if Pinkett had chosen to share his prize with Jarvis, he might have considered it evidence of Pinkett's faulty decision-making abilities and given the win solely to Jarvis instead. Whether Trump was telling the truth or merely trying to add yet another level of drama to the controversial finale, his insistence on maintaining a kind of puppet master persona supports the argument that the finale was ultimately about his demonstration of power over the contestants, and particularly Pinkett.

23. Stuart Hall, "What Is This 'Black' in Black Popular Culture?" in *Black Popular Culture*, ed. Gina Dent (Seattle: Bay Press, 1992), 24.

24. Debra Dickerson, "Slaves to the Clock," *Essence*, November 2006, 154.

25. A grill is a piece of molded metal jewelry that is worn over the teeth as decoration. The grill that the winner receives matches the one that Flav wears.

26. Rachel Dubrofsky and Antoine Hardy, "Performing Race in *Flavor of Love* and *The Bachelor*," *Critical Studies in Media Communication* 25, no. 4 (October 2008): 376.

27. Teresa Wiltz, "Love Him, Or Leave Him? Flavor Flav's Popular Show Sets Off Passionate Debate on Comedy and Race," *Washington Post*, November 2, 2006, http://www.washingtonpost.com/wp-dyn/content/article/2006/11/01/AR2006 110103414.html.

28. Lola Ogunnaike, "A Ladies' Man Everyone Fights Over," *New York Times*, October 1, 2006, http://www.nytimes.com/2006/10/01/fashion/01flav.html.

29. Dubrofsky and Hardy, "Performing Race," 383.

30. Arthur Knight, *Disintegrating the Musical: Black Performance and American Musical Film* (Durham: Duke University Press, 2002), 50.

31. Gates distinguishes between "motivated Signifyin(g)," which he likens to parody, and "unmotivated Signifyin(g)," which he compares to pastiche. Henry Louis Gates Jr., *The Signifyin(g) Monkey: A Theory of African-American Literary Criticism* (New York: Oxford University Press, 1998), xxvi.

32. Ogunnaike, "Ladies' Man."

33. DeWayne Wickham, "A Bitter 'Flavor': Reality Show Should Make Us All Cringe," *USA Today*, September 4, 2006, http://www.usatoday.com/news/opinion/columnist/wickham/ 2006-09-04-flavor-love-wickham_x.htm.

34. *Flavor of Love* is not the only program to receive harsh criticism for its portrayal of Black women. *Bad Girls Clubs* (Oxygen, 2006–) has received its fare share of criticism for basing its premise around casting women with acknowledged anger and behavioral issues.

35. Jonathan Gray, "Cinderella Burps: Gender, Performativity, and the Dating Show," in *Reality TV: Remaking Television Culture*, ed. Susan Murray and Laurie Ouellette (New York: New York University Press, 2009), 270.

36. Amy Adele Hasinoff, "Fashioning Race for the Free Market on 'America's Next Top Model,'" *Critical Studies in Media Communication* 25, no. 3 (August 2008): 339.

37. Greg Braxton, "From an Oscar to a Felix: Jamie Foxx Finds Himself in a New Reality with His 'From G's to Gents' on MTV," *Los Angeles Times*, July 15, 2008, http://articles .latimes.com/2008/jul/15/entertainment/et-foxx15.

10   Prioritized

THE HIP HOP (RE)CONSTRUCTION
OF BLACK WOMANHOOD IN
GIRLFRIENDS AND *THE GAME*

NGHANA LEWIS

Why is it important that a Black woman created, wrote for, and co-produced[1] two highly-regarded television situation comedies that engaged a variety of Black women's health issues while at the same time these issues were being reduced, simplified, or altogether ignored in mainstream American hip hop? Mara Brock Akil tacitly responded to this question when asked why four episodes of the third season of *Girlfriends* (2000–2008), the situation comedy she created and co-produced for UPN, addressed the HIV/AIDS crisis among Black women in America. "I have things I want to say," explained Brock Akil, "about bridging television's gap between entertainment and education. I'm doing a show about women—African-American women—and I feel that a lot of times our issues don't get national attention. Prioritized."[2]

Over their eight- and three-season runs respectively, neither *Girlfriends* (2006–2009) nor *The Game* (2010–; also created and co-produced by Brock Akil), secured large mainstream followings. Both shows were, however, well received among Black audiences, especially Black adults and the subgroup of women eighteen to thirty-four. According to Nielsen Media, both were consistently ranked among the top ten African American TV programs during their series runs.[3] The prioritization of Black women's health issues in *Girlfriends* and *The Game* and the popularity of these programs with Black viewing audiences invite inquiry into Brock Akil's creative vision and market capital throughout the first decade of the twenty-first century. During this period, HIV/AIDS became the leading cause of death among Black women ages twenty-five to thirty-four, and new rates of HIV/AIDS infection were second highest among Black women (behind only gay Black men). The same period gave way to the virtual disappearance of female MCs in mainstream hip hop while simultaneously the representation of Black women's bodies, Black female sexuality, and Black womanhood as mere spectacles accelerated hip hop's global expansion and influence. The appeal of *Girlfriends* and *The Game* to Black viewers and the challenges these programs experienced gaining mainstream audiences tell us something about the possibilities and limitations of pop cultural investments in narrative constructions of Black womanhood at the turn of the twenty-first century.

This chapter argues that among the enduring legacies of *Girlfriends* and *The Game* are their positioning and location of Black women's experiences within rounded narratives of identity, sexuality, health, and authority. These negotiations serve not so much to countervail as to complicate the reduced projections of Black female subjectivity and sexuality in mainstream hip hop. Given the undeniable influence of hip hop culture on Brock Akil's creative vision and the role of the hip hop generation in keeping *Girlfriends* and *The Game* on the air both during their series runs and in syndication, this conundrum is especially perplexing. For Brock Akil and other Black women born after the civil rights and Black Power movements of the 1950s and 1960s, these negotiations set in motion what Molefi K. Asante Jr. describes as a search for a "deeper, more encompassing understanding" of Black womanhood "in a context outside" the corporate monopoly of mainstream hip hop.[4] They attribute a "broad range of abilities, ideals, and ideas" to Black women and acknowledge shifts in public discourse on race, gender, class, and sexuality brought about by the women's movement, antipoverty campaign, and gay rights movement—historical forces that, as Asante rightly points out, mainstream hip hop "has either failed or refused to prioritize."[5]

As early as 1987, when the initial spate of scholarship giving rise to hip hop studies was published, critics projected that the failure to prioritize these and other issues reflective of the social contexts and economic conditions that fostered hip hop's emergence would deepen the "elision of women" in hip hop's growing commercial image.[6] The following decade produced several classic hip hop recordings by female MCs including Salt-n-Pepa's *Very Necessary* (1993), Da Brat's *Funkdafied* (1994), Lil' Kim's *Hard Core* (1996), Foxy Brown's *Ill Na Na* (1996), Missy Elliott's *Supa Dupa Fly* (1997), Lauryn Hill's *The Miseducation of Lauryn Hill* (1998), and Eve's *Let There Be Eve . . . Ruff Ryders' First Lady* (1999), all of which were certified platinum or multi-platinum. But as veteran MCs Trina, Missy Elliott, Yo-Yo, Rah Digga, MC Lyte, and Eve make clear in the recent BET documentary *My Mic Sounds Nice: A Truth About Women in Hip Hop* (2010), at about the same time that female MCs were demonstrating their appeal, influence, and staying power with the masses, profit motives caused many industry producers to cut female hip hop artists, viewing them as too "high maintenance" in comparison with their male counterparts. In addition, the 2000s marked a shift in the production goals of the music industry: pushing units, rather than grooming artists and making quality music, became sacrosanct.

What T. Denean Sharpley-Whiting refers to as the "'playa-pimp-ho-bitch' gearshift of hip hop culture"[7] captures the synergy between the ethos of American patriarchal capitalism and the stock images of available, appropriative Black female sexuality.[8] In foreshadowing the impact that this trafficking would have on Black women's hip hop presence, few of hip hop's earliest critics could have fathomed, let alone predicted, the roles that misogyny, homophobia, sexism, and materialism—staples of commercial hip hop—would play in the spread of HIV/AIDS among Black women.[9]

It is important to remember that over the same period that commercial hip hop evolved from what Tricia Rose germinally described as a form of oppositional "Black cultural expression that prioritizes Black voices from the margins of urban America" to what Rose now calls a "breeding ground for the most explicitly exploitative and increasingly one-dimensional narratives of Black ghetto life,"[10] HIV/AIDS among people of African descent reached pandemic proportions. Brock Akil's channeling and critique of mainstream hip hop situate her among a sizeable body of Black media producers such as Nelson George, Larry Williams, Eunetta Boone, Saladin K. Patterson, Patrik-Ian Polk, Yvette Lee Bowser, Kriss Turner, Jay-Z, Sean Combs, Salim Akil, Will Smith, Jada Pinkett Smith, Queen Latifah, Jamie Foxx, Lee Daniels, Tyler Perry, Shonda Rhimes, and Antoine Fuqua—all of whom are strategically using popular culture to foster public discourse and critical thought about HIV/AIDS and other pressing issues confronting Black people today. Through themes, tensions, and imagery, Brock Akil's mediation of the HIV/AIDS crisis specifically summons for critique other neglected issues in Black women's health including sexual and domestic violence, mental illness, abandonment, homophobia, and substance abuse. The (re)construction of Black women's stories in *Girlfriends* and *The Game* can thus be said to have advanced—or attempted to advance—conversations about the representation of Black womanhood in mainstream hip hop by breaking the silence around HIV/AIDS and related health matters confronting Black women in the new millennium.

"Safe" Sex and Sisterly Redemption

The narrative structures of *Girlfriends* and *The Game* center on four Black women who live in Los Angeles, California, and one white and two Black women who live in San Diego, California. These women's experiences in their professional careers, with family members, with one another, and with men catalyze the comedy and drama that drive plot developments. These developments form an array of images, issues, and themes that underscore widespread understandings of HIV/AIDS as a biomedical phenomenon in light of modes of HIV transmission. Yet both *Girlfriends* and *The Game* move beyond clinical points of the disease to address the complex array of social, sexual, and moral codes that construct HIV/AIDS as a cultural phenomenon. Recurring locations and character-driven humor provide for repetition and reinforcement of personal attitudes, social dynamics, and structural conditions that account for the prevalence, scope, and impact of HIV/AIDS among Black women, specifically.

The perils of economic dependency and the importance of self-reliance and economic self-sufficiency are overarching themes in both *Girlfriends* and *The Game*, but none of the female leads in these series lives in poverty. Consistent with her vision of creating prime-time television that would "accurately portray the urbane omen of color she was familiar with,"[11] Brock Akil writes characters with access to resources and information about HIV/AIDS and thus sets up for repeated debunking the myth that only poor Black women are vulnerable to HIV/AIDS infection. Storylines work in tandem with casting to compel understandings of what scientists call "the ecological pathways to disproportionate infection"[12] among Black women by balancing consideration of characters' individual lifestyles and the effects of their lifestyle choices on the collective. The implications of this narrative structuring for sustaining discursive thinking about HIV/AIDS cannot be missed, because sex and its consequences are indispensible conflict-creating agents in both series.

Of course, not every reference to sex is relevant to HIV/AIDS; nor does every relevant reference fall under the index of deliberate HIV/AIDS discourse. Nonetheless, analysis of the structural frameworks that occasion these references reveals patterns in story setup and conflict, creating story arcs within and across the two series that read like veritable reference guides to Black women's health in the age of hip hop and HIV/AIDS. The repetition of themes related to HIV and sex pushes the HIV/AIDS dialectic further by underscoring what Anita L. Allen calls the public implications of private sex acts.

"Sex is private. But we are clearly accountable for sex. First," explains Allen, "we are accountable to our intimate partners for our sex lives." She continues: "Accountability for sex is not just about who or who else a person may have slept with. It is also about the frequency, sincerity, variety, competence, and safety of sex. In addition to intimate partners, we are also, secondarily, accountable to our families and friends for sex. This is obviously true for children and teenagers whom parents want to shelter from premature and unhealthy sex. But it can also be true of adults whose parents, extended families, or wider kinship groups assert a 'say' over the choices they make about their sex lives."[13]

Girlfriends and *The Game* drive these axioms home through first-season story arcs that "make real and believable" what Brock Akil characterizes as the capacity of all human beings to allow selfish decision making around sex acts to imperil the sanctity of their most cherished relationships.[14] Those familiar with the sequence of events in *Girlfriends* recall that Joan (Tracee Ellis Ross) returns from Jamaica to find Toni (Jill Marie Jones) and Sean (Dondre T. Whitfield) half-clad on her sofa. Toni's actions are motivated by a desire to retaliate against Joan for having inadvertently revealed to Greg (Chuma Hunter-Gault), Toni's one and only true love, that Toni had not only been unfaithful but also that her partner in the infidelity—not Greg—infected her with chlamydia.

Figure 10.1   *Girlfriends* cast (2000). Courtesy of PhotoFest.

The scene that closes season one of *Girlfriends* sets up at least two critical lines of narration in season two that reinforce the personal-collective sex accountability dyad about which Allen writes. First, Toni confronts the consequences of her infidelity to Greg when he reunites with her only to set her up to catch him in the act with an unidentified woman. The scene recalls the emotional impact of the randomness of Toni's affair with Clay (Phil Morris) on Greg, as well as the physical risks to which the affair subjects both Toni and Greg. Toni assumes that because Clay is a doctor, he is a "safe" sex partner. Second, Toni confronts the consequences of her betrayal of Joan, when Joan, determining to "learn to say no," and "save herself," terminates her friendship with Toni.

Blocking in the breakup scene from the episode "Buh-Bye" works in tandem with dialogue to walk the two women through the series of manipulations, exploitations, and denigrations to which viewing audiences already know Toni has subjected Joan. Initially lying on the floor, Toni assumes a symbolic position of reckoning. As she rises, she looks Joan in the eye and listens as Joan elaborates the pain of Toni's actions—first, in attempting to sleep with Sean, and second, in discussing Sean's battle with sex addiction with Joan's boss. Importantly, Toni shadows Joan's movement. As Joan walks through every room, she collects belongings and mementos of Toni and packs them in a box, invoking the proverbial sentiment that reconciliation between the two can occur only after Toni walks in Joan's shoes. Toni must not only feel Joan's pain but also accept responsibility for having caused that pain by a single, selfish sex act. It is no coincidence, therefore, that the scene from the concluding arc episode, "Trick or Truth?," brings closure to the conflict and provides for their friendship's renewal. The dramatic effect of Toni rising a second time from a symbolically prostrate position and finally accepting responsibility for her betrayal of Joan is heightened by their physical location in a church and the casting of Donnie McClurkin to sing his gospel song "We Fall Down" (1998). With the soundtrack for the face-to-face encounter, the women speak:

> TONI: Joan.
> JOAN: Yes, Toni.
> TONI: I am sorry I hurt you. I'm sorry I blamed you for Greg. For every-
> thing. I did it. I made all the mistakes. I know that.

The volume of the gospel song's refrain "for a saint is just a sinner who fell down and got up" is neither lowered nor muted in this moment. Toni's apology is synchronized with the choir's singing, casting her as the symbolic wayward sister who literally finds salvation in the forgiving arms of Joan, Lynn (Persia White), and Maya (Golden Brooks), all of whom embrace Toni at the scene's end.

The whole of Toni's dilemma, framed on one end by a risky sex act and on the other end by sisterly redemption, extends the personal-collective sex accountability thematic to a realization of the prominence with which infectious disease, and thus, by extension, risk of exposure to HIV/AIDS, factors into the narrative equation. An analogous theme drives the story arc in season one of *The Game* that culminates with Derwin (Pooch Hall) sleeping with Drew (Sidora, cast as herself). In the cliffhanger episode, Melanie (Tia Mowry Hardrict) discovers the infidelity and breaks off her engagement to Derwin. She declares, as she walks out on him, that she hopes he didn't wear a condom with that "Skank [Drew]," because he deserves "whatever [he] get[s]" ("Diary of a Mad Black Woman, Redux"). However, whereas the fallout from Toni's affair immediately sensitizes her to the personal risks associated with selfish sex acts, the fallout from Derwin's indiscretion cuts to the core of Melanie's emotional and mental foundations, making her more vulnerable to high-risk sexual behavior.

Initially evidenced by her one-night stand with Trey Wiggs (Chaz Lamar Shephard) the night after she and Derwin break up, the psychosomatic effects of Derwin's infidelity on Melanie crest when she attempts to seduce Malik (Hosea Chanchez) after she thinks Derwin has betrayed her again. "Come on, Malik," she tells him. "Just do this for me, OK. I just want to feel better" ("Fool Me Twice . . . I'm the Damn Fool"). Tasha's (Wendy Raquel Robinson) introduction into the scene at this moment is significant because it compels Melanie to question the logic of her actions. "You done lost yourself, Melanie," Tasha tells her. "You done lost yourself in this world. It's time you called your parents." The directive nudges Melanie out of a self-destructive state of mind and into a more self-reflective space. Although it does not solve immediate problems extending from her lack of financial resources, Tasha's advice has the effect of restoring Melanie's sense of accountability to herself and to others besides Derwin with whom she has intimate relationships.

What is revealed in Toni's and Melanie's negotiation of the public implications of private sex acts is two women struggling to ground themselves, to come to terms with who they are, what they want, what they will tolerate from others, and what others are willing to tolerate from them. Their related identity crises offer a definition of Black womanhood as a condition of becoming, rather than of already being. These definitions are indispensible to an understanding of the larger aesthetic principles underlying Brock Akil's critique of mainstream hip hop and her systematic reconstruction of Black womanhood for twenty-first-century viewing audiences.

Of "Shades of Gray" and (Sister) Circles

> TEE-TEE: All I'm saying is, you gotta find a greater meaning. I mean, what's your rhyme about?
>
> MALIK: Losing the game.
>
> TEE-TEE: No, see, it's bigger than that. See, the game is a metaphor for a bigger loss. Think about it: it's not about losing the game; it's about losing your daddy.
>
> MALIK: I didn't lose him. I just don't know where he is.
>
> TEE-TEE: Then explore that. ("The Iceman Cometh," season one, *The Game*)

Malik Wright, a.k.a. "Forty Million," is the son of Tasha Mack, the "elder" among *The Game*'s three female leads.[15] A running theme in the growth of Tasha's character during season one is the balance she must strike between mothering Malik and managing his career as the Sabers' superstar starting quarterback.[16] Among the events that make up Tasha's backstory and complicate this balancing act are Malik's father's abandonment of Tasha when he learns that she is pregnant at sixteen; Tasha giving birth to Malik and becoming a teenage mother; Tasha cultivating Malik's athletic talents; and Tasha negotiating Malik's $40 million contract once he is drafted into the pros. While the last two of these developments make clear Tasha's seriousness and skill as a businesswoman, the first two impute vulnerable dimensions to her character that are introduced in season one and fleshed with detailed specificity in seasons two and three.[17]

Tasha's character flaws are mediated through a range of hip hop significations, as exhibited in the dialogue above between Malik and Tee-Tee. The dialogue is excerpted from a scene where Malik is putting together rhymes for Tee-Tee to critique. The deeper meaning that Tee-Tee drives Malik to discover compels reflecting on his upbringing without a father, but it also mandates audience consideration of the economic and emotional tolls of single parenting on Tasha. While Malik's method of rhyming invokes mainstream, masculinist hip hop, his lyrical content contemplates the multiple capacities and dimensions of subjectivity that shape Tasha's experiences as a Black woman. The effect works doubly to model and advance a hip hop feminist aesthetic, the larger value system underlying the construction of Black womanhood in both *Girlfriends* and *The Game.*

In her classic collection of personal essays *When Chickenheads Come Home to Roost,* Joan Morgan outlined fundamental elements of hip hop feminism in reflecting on how she came to understand the kind of discordant harmony that exists between the social conditions and power dynamics that shaped the lives of her mother's generation of Black women and cultural forces molding the experiences of her generation of Black women. "As a child of the post–Civil Rights, post-feminist, post-soul hip-hop generation," she begins, "my struggle songs consisted of the same notes [as my mother's] but they were infused with distinctly different rhythms." Whereas the process of self-definition for her mother's generation involved shedding "the restrictive costumes of domestic, mother, and wife," for Morgan's generation, the process involves being "willing to take an honest look at ourselves—and then tell the truth about it. Much of what we'll see will be fly as hell"; "a lot," she admits bluntly, "will be painful and trifling." For hip hop generation Black women, "love no longer presents itself wrapped in the romance of basement blue lights, lifetime commitments, or the sweet harmonies of The Stylistics and The Chi-Lites. Love for us, is raw like sushi, served up on sex platters." Thus, "more than any other generation before us," Morgan reasons, Black women need "a feminism committed to 'keeping it real.'"[18]

In a 2004 interview, Brock Akil echoes Morgan's sentiments in describing precisely what about Black women's lives she sought to introduce to television as a creator-writer-producer. She explains, "I thought that what I could add were all of our shades of gray and our complexities. I didn't see a lot of vulnerabilities in (the depictions of Black women on television). A lot of times, I think we are represented as very fearless, tough women. The word 'sassy' gets used a lot." To appeal to audiences in a "more real and tangible way," therefore, Brock Akil set about combating the stereotype that "Black women are either the sister-girl or the asexual judge with no life. I can be fearless at work, but I can also be stupid over a guy. I can be all those things at once. I wanted to show how fashionable we are. The fashion and the femininity, I really wanted to talk about that."[19] In a nutshell, Brock Akil concludes, she wanted to see the multifaceted existences of Black women "validated."[20]

Among all of the episodes in *Girlfriends'* eight-season run, "The Pact" offers the most visually detailed and densely narrated representation of HIV/AIDS infection among Black women. In it, Kimberly Elise appears as Reesie Jackson, a classmate of Joan, Lynn, and Toni, with whom Joan had a falling-out in college because, according to Joan, Reesie stole and eventually married Joan's boyfriend, Brian. A series of flashbacks, filtered through Joan's and Reesie's points of view, recall a scene wherein Brian arrives in Joan's dormitory room with two tickets to an MC Hammer concert. He discovers that Joan is unable to attend the concert because of a prescheduled study group. Joan's recollection of the scene casts Reesie as a provocatively clad predator who captures her prey—Brian—by using Joan's ticket to accompany him to the concert. Reesie's recollection depicts Joan as a bookworm, annoyed both by Brian's invitation and presence, and content to cast him off on Reesie. The naming of the year of Joan and Reesie's falling-out—1991— situates its terms within larger developments shaping Black expressive culture at the time, including the resuscitation and mass marketing of Black Power rhetoric fueled by the commercial and critical success of hip hop artists Public Enemy.[21] The naming of the year also locates the consequences of the falling-out between Joan and Reesie in an historical period that is paradoxically distinguished, on one hand, by increased rates of HIV/AIDS diagnoses among Black women and, on the other hand, the underreporting of this phenomenon in mainstream media outlets as well as a dearth of public discourse regarding its root causes.

Reesie's subsequent entry onto the scene initially purposes an occasion for Joan to indict Reesie in person, to hold her accountable for Joan's besieged status as a thirty-something, unmarried Black woman—despite Joan's considerable professional success. "If it weren't for you," Joan argues, "I would be the one that was married, I would be the one with two kids, and I would be living your happy life." Joan's begrudged socioeconomic plight is among *Girlfriends'* core themes and underscores much of the drama—and comedy—framing Joan's characterization and, thus, driving plot development both within and across individual episodes. Almost immediately after this indictment, however, we learn that the conflict between Reesie and Joan that opens "The Pact" is designed not to reinforce the controlling narrative of Joan's characterization but rather to bring Reesie's story into sharp focus.

The focal shift is bluntly perfected through a discordant antiphony that highlights the naivety of Joan's assumptions about marriage in general and Reesie's marriage to Brian specifically:

REESIE: You want my happy life!

JOAN: Yes!

REESIE: You want Brian!

JOAN: Yes!

REESIE: Then you can have him. And you can have the AIDS he gave me, too!

After Reesie's announcement, a mise-en-scène reflective of Brock Akil's envisioned prioritization and validation of Black women's complex identities and issues takes shape. In piecemeal fashion, Lynn, Toni, and Joan approach Reesie, bearing items intended to comfort (and humor) her—a blanket, an apple, and a heating pad—as they settle into symbolically supportive spaces that encircle Reesie, who sits on the sofa. Maya's initial location outside the circle, with arms akimbo and legs stiffly spread apart, visually represents the hesitation, and often outright rejection, with which HIV/AIDS-infected people are met when their status is revealed. Maya's discomfort when Reesie states that she has full-blown AIDS and is not "simply" HIV-positive is apparent, yet her steady movement toward the sofa facilitates the audience's observation of her transition from a symbolically guarded (and, perhaps, even reactionary) position to a location from which she, like Joan, Toni, and Lynn, can listen—and learn—as Reesie details the plight of a Black woman living with HIV/AIDS.

Plain expository dialogue among the women strips Reesie's testimony down to its clinical basics at the same time that it fosters analysis of the cultural dynamics that instance and impact the management of her status:

LYNN: Do you know how Brian got it?
REESIE: From another man.
JOAN: Oh my God. He couldn't use a condom?
REESIE: No, because if he put a condom in his pocket, then he'd be admit-ting to himself that he was going out to have sex with men, and that would make him gay, which, according to him, he's not.

In a moment rare for situation comedy, let alone Black entertainment television, the concept of MSM is explicitly voiced and explicated. But because it is integrated into Reesie's larger discourse on living with AIDS, it does not control her narrative. Rather, the articulations work to clarify without stigmatizing the sexual practice and to bring the narrative arc of "The Pact" full circle. We are invited to infer that Brian's struggles with his sexual identity preceded his relationship with Reesie and, thus, likely overlapped with his relationship with Joan. In this moment of reconciling the cultural contexts informing Reesie's, Joan's, and Brian's interrelated back stories with their respective present conditions, the imprint of Brock Akil's hip hop feminism becomes markedly clear. The moment emboldens Reesie to acknowledge to Joan—and, perhaps, for the first time to herself—that she did, in fact, steal Brian. "You've been right all along," she confesses, "I stole him. He was fine. Karma's a bitch, huh?" she quietly quips. "Don't say that," Joan insists, "don't even think that." The scene closes on a less somber note when Toni makes a joke about Reesie having ashy feet. Importantly, however, the chords of truth-telling, reckoning, and healing that the sister-circle gives rise to reverberate beyond the scene, setting the tone for sustained, informed discourse both among Black women *and* about Black women and HIV/AIDS.

Brock Akil's Hip Hop Feminism: Predecessors and Prospects

In a 2004 article for *Essence* magazine titled "Quitting Hip-Hop," Michaela Angela Davis, founding editor of *Vibe* magazine and former editor in chief of *Honey*, declared: "If there is not a shift in how the hip hop industry portrays women, then our 20 year relationship is officially O-V-E-R." At the heart of Davis's contention with the culture on which she built her career as one of hip hop's foremost fashion stylists and journalist was the danger she observed in a male-dominated industry that tended to "view women as moneymakers (as in the kind you shake). Few of us," she lamented, "are in a position to be decision makers."[22] This chapter has argued that throughout the 2000s, Mara Brock Akil provided the goods for Davis and other hip hop generation artists, critics, and consumers seeking diverse, salient popular cultural representations of Black womanhood. These representations are ones that mainstream hip hop has not been able, or willing, to offer for several decades. Beyond providing for the development of rounded characters, these narratives produced textual space for exploring the particular health challenges confronting the masses of Black women to and for whom Joan, Maya, Toni, Lynn, Tasha, Melanie, and Kelly speak in the twenty-first century. Foremost among these challenges is HIV/AIDS.

To be sure, *Girlfriends* and *The Game* were preceded by a number of Black television moments that addressed disease and the racial, gender, sexual, and cultural mores that contribute to Black-white health disparities in America. Many of us can probably remember exactly what we were doing on November 7, 1991, when regularly scheduled broadcasts were interrupted for Earvin "Magic" Johnson to announce his retirement from the NBA because he was HIV-positive. How many remember that nearly a year to the date earlier, *A Different World* aired "Time Keeps on Slippin'" (1990), which acknowledged the growing problem of HIV/AIDS at historically Black colleges and universities by putting "a condom" in the 1990 Hillman time capsule?[23] A few months later, in "Monet Is the Root of All Evil" (1991), the series again acknowledged the epidemic by exploring the crisis in interpretation and generational conflict created when a hip hop artist's painting of a crack-addicted mother, cast in the image of the Madonna and nursing her baby, is displayed in the Hillman Art Gallery. The very next episode marked the climax in the series' first HIV/AIDS story arc by letting Josie, a minor character adeptly acted by Tisha Campbell-Martin, take center stage to reveal her HIV-positive status. Memorably, Whoopi Goldberg (guest-starring as a Hillman professor who encourages Josie to disclose her status), warns students who initially shun Josie in a calm, steady tenor: "AIDS is not a moral judgment."

The layering and gynocentric points of view that shaped *A Different World*'s HIV/AIDS storylines are part of the larger creative re-visioning that Debbie Allen and Susan Fales brought to the series, after its first season.[24] On multiple levels, *A Different World* achieved what even *The Cosby Show* was unable to accomplish, by entertaining, engaging, and enlightening the masses through narratives that centered the specific social, political, and cultural plights of upwardly mobile, high-achieving hip hop generation Black youth. It is of little surprise, therefore, that Brock Akil cites *A Different World* as one of her influences.[25]

It provided a blueprint for Black situation comedy that arguably remained unmatched in prime-time television until *Girlfriends'* 2000 debut.

The pathway that Brock Akil charted with *Girlfriends* and *The Game* parallels those charted by female MCs of the 1990s in that both point to the adeptness and creativity with which hip hop generation Black women artists made their marks on the media industry. The eerie echoing sounded in the rationales hip hop executives gave for declining to bankroll female MCs beyond the 90s, the rationale CW executives gave for not giving *Girlfriends* a proper closing, and the method used to bring *The Game's* series run to an end on that network points to larger issues of racism, sexism, and patriarchal capitalism in the media with which, bell hooks and many other Black feminist theorists remind us, Black women have always struggled. However, the global influence that hip hop has enjoyed for over three decades adds a distinctive layer of complexity to these struggles for Black women artists who not only identify with hip hop but also draw upon hip hop for creative inspiration.

If, as W.J.T. Mitchell observes, "hypervisibility—being remarked, noticed, stared at—can only be understood if it is placed in some relation to its dialectical twin: invisibility,"[26] then situating and sustaining HIV/AIDS and other Black women's health issues as focal points of rounded representations require vigilant attention to the array of forces that control Black women's presence and absence in hip hop and other mainstream media outlets. Among the best examples of this

Figure 10.2   *The Game* cast (2006–2007). Courtesy of PhotoFest.

type of vigilance are the very efforts undertaken by fans of *The* Game to return this series to network airwaves.

In a November 2009 interview on *The Monique Show*, the cast of *The Game* related that Black Entertainment Television was in discussions with CBS, the parent company of *Girlfriends* and *The Game*, to purchase the series and bring the entire cast back for a fourth season. In reviewing the sequence of events leading up to these talks, the cast cited the influence of fans that systematically logged complaints about the cancellation of the show in 2008 and launched "bring *The Game* back" blogging sites soon afterward. They cited as well the tremendous impact that syndicated broadcasts on BET had on expanding the series' already substantial fan base. Significantly, a common sentiment among bloggers, reviewers, and posters was that *The Game*'s return was a good thing, and an even better thing would be for *Girlfriends* to return, too. As one blogger succinctly put it: "they are bringing back the game. I liked that show. I just wish another show, girlfriends, could be back on air. But I will take what I can get. Thank you BET."

Placing *Girlfriends* and *The* Game side by side, as this chapter has done, renders more easily visible how clearly each elaborates Brock Akil's vision of Black womanhood in the twenty-first century. *Girlfriends* and *The Game* remind us that representations of Black female sexuality and subjectivity in mainstream hip hop carry weight beyond the contexts of their lyrical and visual expressions. This weight bears substantially on current conditions of Black women's health as well as the conditions we can expect future hip hop generations to inherit and endure. Will their future be one in which the risk of HIV/AIDS is no longer real for roughly one-third of Black women and girls throughout the world? Stay tuned.

NOTES

1. Mara Brock Akil co-produced *Girlfriends* and *The Game* with Kelsey Grammer (best known for his role as Frasier Crane on *Cheers* [1982–1993] and *Frasier* [1993–2004]) and CBS Paramount Network Television.

2. Chael Needle, "Girlfriends for Life: Mara Brock Akil, Creator of UPN's *Girlfriends*, Shares with A&U's Chael Needle the Inside Scoop on the Show's HIV Story lines and the State of Sexual Health on TV," *The Media Project*, 2003, http://www.themediaproject.com/news/itn/040103.htm. Originally published in *A&U: America's AIDS Magazine.*

3. Viewership for *Girlfriends* averaged 4 million for the series' first, second, and third seasons; seasons four through six averaged 3.5 million, and season seven averaged 2 million. Season eight, which did not run in full, also averaged 2 million. The first season of *The Game* had an average of 2.3 million viewers; that average increased slightly to 2.35 million in season two. In the final season of *The Game* on CW, viewership dropped to 1.75 million. *The Hollywood Reporter*, http://www.hollywoodreporter.com/hr/content_ display/television/features/e3ifbf dd1 bcb53266ad8d9a71cad261604f?pn=2; *ABC Medianet*, http://abcmedianet.com/web/dnr/dispDNR.aspx?id=052808_06. Also see Nielsen Media ratings, "Top 10 African-American TV Rankings, April 20–April 26, 2009," http://blog.nielsen.com/nielsenwire/ media_entertainment/top-10-african-american-tv-rankings-april-20-april-26-2009.

4. M. K. Asante Jr., *It's Bigger than Hip Hop: The Rise of the Post-Hip-Hop Generation* (New York: St. Martin's Press, 2008), 7.

5. Ibid.

6. Nancy Guevara, "Women Writin' Rappin' Breakin,'" in *Droppin' Science: Critical Essays on Rap Music and Hip Hop Culture*, ed. William Eric Perkins (Philadelphia: Temple University Press, 1996), 49.

7. Tracy Denean Sharpley-Whiting, *Pimps Up, Ho's Down: Hip Hop's Hold on Young Black Women* (New York: New York University Press, 2007), 13.

8. Nghana Lewis, "You Sell Your Soul Like You Sell a Piece of Ass: Rhythms of Black Female Sexuality and Subjectivity in MeShell Ndegeocello's *Cookie: The Anthropological Mixtape*," *Black Music Research Journal* 26, no. 1 (Spring 2006): 113.

9. Notable exceptions are the observations of the late Sherley Anne Williams, who, in 1992, presciently wrote: "The sexuality promoted in such lyrics as 'Do Me Baby,' 'Try Me,' and 'Push It, Baby' is a particularly pernicious ethic to push in this age of AIDS." "Two Words on Music," in *Black Popular Culture*, ed. Gina Dent (Seattle: Bay Press, 1992), 168.

10. Tricia Rose, *Black Noise: Rap Music and Black Culture in Contemporary America* (Middletown, CT: Wesleyan University Press, 1994), 2; Tricia Rose, *The Hip Hop Wars: What We Talk About When We Talk About Hip Hop—And Why It Matters* (New York: Basic, 2008), 3.

11. Tatiana Siegel, "Girlfriends' 100th Episode," *Hollywood Reporter*, November 8, 2004, http://www.hollywoodreporter.com/hr/search/article_display.jsp?vnu_content_id=1000 708463.

12. Sandra Lane, Robert Rubenstein, Robert Keefe, Noah Webster, Donald Cibula, Alan Rosenthal, and Jesse Dowdell, "Structural Violence and Racial Disparity in HIV Transmission," *Journal of Health Care for the Poor and Underserved* 15, no. 3 (August 2004): 320.

13. Anita Allen, *Why Privacy Isn't Everything: Feminist Reflections on Personal Accountability* (Lanham, MD: Rowman & Littlefield, 2003), 142.

14. Mara Brock Akil, "We All Fall Down: A Closer Look at 'Trick or Truth?'" Special Feature, Disc 1, *Girlfriends* (CBS Studios 2006).

15. At forty-something, Tasha's age is the source of much comic relief in the series given Melanie's and Kelly's relative youth. Her racial rhetoric obscures the fact that she is too young to have participated in any of the social movements of the 1960s; thus, like Melanie and Kelly, Tasha is a product of the hip hop generation.

16. The Sabers are a fictional San Diego–based professional football team at the center of *The Game*.

17. Two episodes from season three are worth mentioning here: "Punk Ass Chauncey," in which Malik meets his biological father, and "The Third Legacy," in which Tasha vocalizes and comes to terms with the anger she's harbored toward Malik's father for not staying with her and supporting her during her pregnancy.

18. Joan Morgan, *When Chickenheads Come Home to Roost: A Hip-Hop Feminist Breaks It Down* (New York: Simon & Schuster, 1999), 22, 20, 23, 61–62.

19. Allison Samuels, "Women on the Verge," *Newsweek*, June 12, 2010, http://www.newsweek.com/2010/06/12/women-on-the-verge.html.

20. Robin Givhan, "Echoes of TV's First Lady: Michelle Obama's Last True Cultural Antecedent Is Cosby's Claire Huxtable," *Washington Post*, June 19, 2009, C01.

21. Jeffrey Ogbar, *Hip-Hop Revolution: The Culture and Politics of Rap* (Kansas City: University of Kansas Press, 2007), 146–148.

22. Michaela Angela Davis, "Quitting Hip-Hop," *Essence* (2004), 155.

23. In 1991, when the episode originally aired, the Federal Communications Commission would not allow the condom to be displayed. In syndication, the condom is visible.

24. A respectful nod must be made here to the Fox Network Television series *Roc* (1991–1994), which starred the inimitable Charles S. Dutton and Ella Joyce. *Roc* became another early Black situation comedy to pointedly address the HIV/AIDS crisis in the Black community. In the touching series finale episode, "You Shouldn't Have to Lie" (1994), Joyce's character, Eleanor, learns that the daughter of a close friend is HIV-positive. [Editor's note: Robin Means Coleman and Andre Cavalcante explore *A Different World*'s transformation in this text.]

25. Tatiana Siegel, "Dialogue: Mara Brock Akil," *Hollywood Reporter*, November 8, 2004, http://www.hollywoodreporter.com/hr/search/article_display.jsp?vnu_content_id=1000708461.

26. W.J.T. Mitchell, "Seeing Disability," *Public Culture* 13, no. 3 (Fall 2001): 393.

11

Nigger, Coon, Boy, Punk, Homo, Faggot, Black Man

RECONSIDERING ESTABLISHED
INTERPRETATIONS OF MASCULINITY,
RACE, AND SEXUALITY THROUGH
NOAH'S ARC

MARK D. CUNNINGHAM

Black men loving Black men is the revolutionary act.
—Joseph Beam

At best, our knowledge about the lives and experiences of Black gay men is limited to a series of stereotypes, snap judgments, and ridicule. In terms of television media product, this aforementioned knowledge has been packaged mostly within the framework of comedy: a red-leather-clad Eddie Murphy talking about the most effective ways to shield his ass from the gay male gaze in the 1983 HBO stand-up performance *Delirious*; Damon Wayans and David Alan Grier's effeminate film critics Blaine Edwards and Antoine Merriweather on the 1990s television variety show *In Living Color*; fashionista panel members Miss J and Andre Leon Talley on Tyra Banks's *America's Next Top Model*, or real-life gay man Antoine Dodson, who became a flamboyant talk-show-circuit sensation after his humorously stereotypical diatribe admonishing his sister's would-be attacker became a hit on the Internet.

In fairness, some attempts to curtail the obviously offensive depictions of homosexual Black males of years past have been made. Yet even these efforts prove problematic, as more recent depictions find these men to be gay in name only and not fully developed characters. Examples such as those portrayed by Michael Boatman in the comedy *Spin City*, Vondie-Curtis Hall in the hospital drama *Chicago Hope*, and Taye Diggs in a guest-starring role on the award-winning *Will and Grace* as a love interest for the titular male character are all largely asexual, have no mates, and appear to function mainly as an attempt to silence any critics who might protest their omission otherwise. Even Black gay male characters with more complexity such as Mathew St. Patrick's amiable and conflicted police officer in HBO's *Six Feet Under*, Michael Kenneth Williams's malevolent urban gangster Omar Little in HBO's *The Wire*, and Nelsan Ellis's vampire-blood-dealing cook Lafayette Reynolds in HBO's *True Blood* are relegated to supporting character status and not always prominently featured in support of the narrative.

However, in the midst of less than innovative portrayals, filmmaker Marlon Riggs audaciously challenged the thinking about Black gay male culture with his controversial and groundbreaking documentary *Tongues Untied* (1989). Using poetic verse, music, and bold imagery, Riggs composes a striking chronicle of how the harshness and difficulties of reality shaped his ability to find a balance between his racial and sexual identities, and in so doing, deftly tells a story that is as much about the affirmation and celebration of self as it is about racism and homophobia. Scholar Jacquie Jones considers it to be "possibly the most powerful examination of Black sexual identity ever produced"; she also recognizes how the work valuably "integrates on all levels, structurally and thematically, and ultimately delineates the immediacy of situating the sexual at the core of self-definition by equalizing it with the political and social imperatives of Blackness."[1]

Unfortunately, this attempt to address the Black gay male experience was not achieved without contention. A portion of the documentary was funded by the National Endowment for the Arts and was broadcast on the public- and government-funded PBS network, and many conservative detractors were incensed that federal monies had been used to support media that featured nudity, coarse language, and homosexual intimacy. In fact, as a result of this firestorm, many PBS affiliates declined to show the documentary, which was featured on the network's series *P.O.V.*—a series that has long served as a showcase for independent nonfiction media.

Interestingly, Riggs opens the video with the staccato cadence of Black male voices chanting the words "brother to brother," which serves as a rallying call of sorts for the owners of those voices to freely love one another without apology or shame and despite narrow-minded and ignorant opposition. In the spirit of the African and African American tradition of call and response, writer/director Patrik-Ian Polk answered Riggs's appeal to revolutionize how we think about love and affection among Black gay men with the creation of his television series *Noah's Arc*.

Aired on the cable network Logo, a subsidiary of MTV targeted to lesbian, gay, bisexual, and transgender communities (LGBT), *Noah's Arc* focuses on the devoted friendship, relationship complexities, and professional lives of four African American gay men. Often compared with the television shows before it that featured a quartet of different personalities and sexual appetites such as *Living Single, Girlfriends, Sex and the City, Queer as Folk*, and even *The Golden Girls*, the show depicts Black gay male relationships in an uncensored and honest manner. However, despite being touted by Logo as the most popular show on the network, *Noah's Arc* was abruptly canceled after two seasons and only seventeen episodes, leaving storylines untied as a result. The network was heavily criticized for this decision (some viewers even suspended their cable service in protest), as it was one of the few shows to feature gay African American and Latino characters, two highly underrepresented groups in American media. Thus, in this chapter, I trace the journey of *Noah's Arc* from concept to cancellation for the purpose of showing how the show's subject matter provides for a more diverse and inclusive depiction of the Black community while also bringing attention to how culture and race continue to be relegated to the backseat within the industrial and narrative logics of television programming as a whole.

The Pursuit of Diversity and Difference

When Logo debuted on cable in the summer of 2005, it did so with little more than announcements featured in gay and lesbian publications such as *The Advocate* and *Out*. Many critics, namely other gay-themed network executives and programmers, considered this low-key approach to be an attempt on the part of Logo to diffuse any negative reactions that might arise against the newly formed network.[2] Whatever the reason for the ambiguity in marketing, the focus of the network was clear: programming would not be indicative of the hypersexual stereotypes that often plague the gay community. Brian Graden, then the president of Logo and MTV Networks, explained the reason for this choice, stating: "When you tell a story about gay rodeo or gay surfers it's not a story about sex nor does it need to be . . . So much connects us beyond sexuality." On a grander scale, he visualized Logo, as a "hybrid of the Sundance Channel . . . and a general entertainment network." In this amalgamation of the independent filmmaking spirit and broad popular culture output, Graden, who is gay, saw the network as an instrument that could be used to extricate some of the restrictive identifiers bandied about when assessing gay culture, commenting: "As much as labels have been assigned to us historically, we didn't want to do the same by pigeonholing . . . We caught onto it early that the gay and lesbian community is very, very diverse."[3]

Graden made good on his promise to generate an extensive roster of programs for Logo. In addition to featuring shows with established reputations on other networks such as *Buffy the Vampire Slayer*, *Queer as Folk*, and *The L Word*, and gay-themed theatrical releases like *Bound*, *Laurel Canyon*, and *D.E.B.S.*, he also greenlighted such varied telecasts as the variety program *The Big Gay Sketch Show*, the original comedy series *Exes & Ohs* (a show similar to *Noah's Arc* in premise except the characters are lesbian and white), the animated series *Rick & Steve: The Happiest Gay Couple in All the World*, and the hyperbolic reality competition series *RuPaul's Drag Race*. This move toward differentiated programming by Logo certainly applies to the focus of my analysis here.

At the nucleus of *Noah's Arc* is the complicated romantic and professional life of budding screenwriter Noah Nicholson (Darryl Stephens). Orbiting him are his three best friends, Alex Kirby (Rodney Chester), the mother hen of the group and an *O* magazine aficionado who runs an HIV and AIDS clinic; Ricky Davis (Christian Vincent), a very promiscuous clothing store entrepreneur who comes from money; and Chance Counter (Doug Spearman), a professor of economics at UCLA. In a symbolic suggestion of the familial nature of their friendship, the "arc" in the title not only represents the continuing storylines in Noah's screenplays and a play on the religious steadfastness of the central character but also reflects the first letter in each of his friend's names. Also significant is Wade Robinson (Jensen Atwood), an outwardly heterosexual man grappling with his sexual identity and his affections for the terminal romantic at the center of the show's narrative.

Noah's world was born while Polk watched several gay Black men enjoy themselves without pretense at a nightclub gathering during the annual Black Gay Pride celebration. He immediately saw the potential for a successful media project targeted to this niche market: "In that moment I was struck with the notion that no one's making programming about this group . . . So, I decided, standing in that club . . . that I was gonna do a show and it was going to be about four Black gay men, and I didn't know how I was going to do it or when but . . . I made up my mind that was what I was going to do."[4] With only one feature film in his repertoire, (the independently made comedy *Punks* [2000]), Polk raised the

Figure 11.1   *Noah's Arc* cast. Promotional frame grab.

money for production independently, made the pilot, and began to distribute it via the Internet and at gay film festivals and gay pride events during a twenty-two-city promotional tour sponsored by the Human Rights Campaign (HRC) and the Black AIDS Institute.[5] Having heard the buzz about the pilot generated from the screenings, the fledgling Logo approached Polk about giving *Noah's Arc* a home on its network.

First broadcast in October 2005, the show was the first scripted series for the network and garnered immediate popularity, receiving honors from *The Advocate* as one of its top ten television shows of 2005.[6] This highly unconventional show, thought of as such based on premise alone, was heralded as "pioneering" and championed for the very diversity that Graden had sought to infuse the network with in the first place. Many gay activists extended praise to the series for shedding "an insightful spotlight on the lifestyle of Black gay men— a way of life that has been a largely taboo subject in the Black community."[7] Author and journalist Keith Boykin astutely stated, "'Noah's Arc' is both a burden and a blessing. It's a burden because it's the first Black gay TV show, and it's carrying all the weight. But it's a blessing because it's showing the world that . . . not all gays are white."[8] Yet one could easily refute Boykin's assessment if Logo's past and current programming is an indication of the racial makeup of the gay population.

Despite an initial claim of wanting to portray the diversity that is truly indicative of the gay community, Logo's programming remains overwhelmingly white. Longer-running and more short-lived shows feature all or mostly white casts.[9] Even the adoption of television programs from other major television and cable networks suggests a transference of the same less than racially diverse programming strategies utilized by those networks to the decision making at Logo. In fact, with the exception of the current new program featuring RuPaul (which, in addition to the program mentioned previously, now includes another reality competition titled *RuPaul's Drag U*) and reruns of *Noah's Arc*, Black faces appear in limited numbers on the network.

What does the advent of these Black gay male bodies on television suggest about the narrative direction of the industry as a whole? As discussed earlier, *Noah's Arc* is shaped by subject matter that stands on the periphery of mainstream visual entertainment. In addition, Polk has moved these unconventional characters out of their usual supporting status and made them the multidimensional chief focus of each storyline. This action is the basis for much of the innovation that distinguishes *Noah's Arc*, and that this occurred on cable television is no great surprise. Pointing to cable network HBO's track record with dramatic films and comedy series featuring the biting commentary of comedians such as Chris Rock, Christine Acham reveals that despite the limitations of accessibility, "cable perhaps holds the greatest potential as a Black site of resistance within the context of television . . . and . . . is a forum in which Blackness has not been erased."[10]

However, even though the situations Noah and his friends are involved in are dramatic, the show is still shrouded within the easier-to-take confines of comedy. In this case, the usually less restrained guidelines of cable television become more akin to network television sensibilities. If we can laugh at the acid-tongued quips, humorous observations, and exaggerated behaviors, the characters' sexuality becomes less threatening and it becomes easier to accept them as "leading men." Herman Gray explains that if commercial television is to address the cultural shifts of society and simultaneously make a profit, "it must, of necessity, frame its representations in appropriate and accessible social terms that express the shared assumptions, knowledge, experiences of viewers who are situated along different alliances of race, class and gender (and, increasingly, sexuality)."[11] Therefore, *Noah's Arc* might be a pioneer in terms of its narrative structure, but Polk is still confined by the public's (and network's) resistance to creative material surrounding Blackness, and even more so homosexual Blackness.

Noah's Arc, Season One

With *Noah's Arc*, Polk makes a bold step to move Black gay culture out of the confines of homophobia and into a more affirmative and humanizing space. Through the journey of Noah, Alex, Ricky, and Chance, Polk places his characters in circumstances that are not altogether different from those experienced by heterosexual individuals and couples. In the first season of the show, which consists of only nine episodes, Polk dismantles many of the stereotypical images and ideas that have proven to be the source of homophobic attitudes stifling Black gay men's relationship with Black people as a whole. He counters this animosity with portrayals that compel the audience to see beyond sexuality and even race and instead accept Noah and his friends as separate individuals with distinct motivations, inspirations, and belief systems. In so doing, the goal becomes to challenge these less than progressive notions and exchange them for, if not complete approval, something that at least resembles tolerance.

Set in Hollywood, *Noah's Arc* does not resemble the Black Los Angeles we know from films such as John Singleton's *Boyz n the Hood* (1991), The Hughes Brothers' *Menace II Society* (1993), or Ice Cube's *Friday* (1995). In contrast to these depictions and similar to the television show *Girlfriends*, the Los Angeles Polk presents consists of upscale apartments and houses, power lunches and meetings at Paramount Pictures, art galleries, dance clubs, and designer clothing stores.[12] When entering the "hood," as when the characters venture into the Crenshaw Swap Meet, hardly a menace to society is in sight. This subverts yet another stereotype by showing a South Central Los Angeles beyond the baleful existence created by hood movies and television news.

Within that existence, Polk offers viewers varying examples of Black gay masculinity: Noah and Alex represent the more effeminate members of the group; Chance falls somewhere in the middle, though what might be read as effeminate could possibly be assigned to his rigidity about convention, his middle-class values, and his higher level of education; while Ricky, all muscles and brawn, is arguably the most masculine of the four. Their partners are all very masculine, including Wade's borderline thuggish appeal complete with corn-rows, Trey's sinewy bodybuilder exterior, and Eddie's coding as man of the house. Only Ricky, remaining true to his assignation within the show's narrative as a sex addict, has multiple partners that are both manly and effeminate.

When thinking about gay men, the more hackneyed interpretation suggests that they are definitely *less than* in a number of ways: "Gay men are often per-ceived as being effeminate socially and passive sexually . . . The evidence . . . sug-gests that the process of socialization for some gay Black men begins in the home with non-gay family members as early role models . . . Most gay men have been subjected to the stereotype that they are not really men. As boys, they are pres-sured to live up to prescribed standards of masculinity."[13] While Polk does not disqualify the fact that effeminate gay Black men exist, as that characteristic is certainly descriptive of some of the main characters on the show, he also gives us men who definitely exhibit their (hetero) masculine sides.

As E. Patrick Johnson clarifies, "Unlike the motivations of Black heterosexual men, Black gay men's performance of heterosexuality has less to do with need or desire to repudiate the Other as much as it does with an attempt to expand the discourse of the heterosexual Other to include a Black gay subjectivity."[14] For every quip from Alex about some well-taken advice from Oprah Winfrey's self-titled magazine, Ricky tells one of his conquests that his posterior area is "exit only." This suggests that he maintains the masculine and dominant position during sexual relations. In another example, though Noah's particular style encompasses clothing complete with off-the-shoulder shirts, ruffles, and ornate accessories and hairstyles (including female-inspired Bantu knots, cornrows, and curly Afros), in contrast, the bulk of the characters wear clothes and hairstyles that are not what would be considered distinguishably "gay." In fact, when Noah asks Alex's partner, Trey (Gregory Keith), if he liked the glitter spray applied to his face, he responds, "I always thought that the great part about being a guy is we don't have to wear all that crap." But the line between enjoying glitter and makeup and not having "to wear all that crap" is a fine one.

Andrew Ross speaks of this connection in his discussion of hypermasculine street culture and drag performance culture, commenting: "Being fierce, in the ghetto street or in the nightclub version, is a theatrical response to the phenom-enal social pressure exerted upon Black males in the waning years of the twenti-eth century." Ross goes on to say that both cultures represent the ill-treatment and misrepresentation of Black masculinity. The emergence of the drag queen and the hypermasculinity that often permeates Black male behavior, particularly as it pertains to the gangster rapper, "ought to be linked (one could say, dialecti-cally) . . . as a dual symptom of the conditions that have made it commonplace to speak of young Black men as an endangered species in our society."[15] Therefore, heterosexual or gay, the issue at hand still revolves around the shortchanging of Black male culture in general in this society.

What makes the disavowal of Black gay male culture doubly worse is the rejection that comes from within and without. For example, in the episode "I'm with Stupid," we witness Chance and Eddie's failed attempt to convince the "old-fashioned, dyed in the wool, Baptist traditionalists" on the church board to let them have their wedding in the sanctuary. Citing the usual and arguably misinterpreted admonition in Leviticus 18:22, the board instead offers an alternative venue in the church, but Chance and Eddie respectfully decline what is less about goodwill and acceptance and more about the continuous denial of who they are as Black gay men and faithful members of the church. Unfortunately, differentiations like this and others among Black people create an "us vs. them" dynamic as opposed to the wholeness that suggests a community. That said, Johnson's assessment of Marlon Riggs's elegiac final film, *Black Is . . . Black Ain't*, applies here: "Black Americans cannot begin to ask the dominant culture to accept their differences as Others nor accept their humanity until Black Americans accept the differences that exist among themselves."[16]

In the first season of the show, Polk counters much of the labeling assigned to Black gay men by portraying his characters as well rounded and reflective of the diverse nature of a group often marginalized racially and culturally. With this foundation and the subsequent creation of a dedicated fan base, the show in its second season would examine other situations unique to the Black gay community while continuing to provide the entertainment and humor so deftly on display in the debut episodes.

Noah's Arc, Season Two

While the first season seemed to concentrate more on the task of setting the record straight, so to speak, about Black gay male identity and life (with moments and dialogue that were too obviously didactic), the second season opens with an earthquake to shake things up literally and figuratively—a decidedly more soap-opera-like move in its storytelling. The series begins to concentrate on two themes very important to the Black gay community: the first, AIDS/HIV.

Statistics from the Centers for Disease Control (CDC) state that by the end of 2007, Black people "accounted for almost half (46%) of people living with diagnosis of HIV infection in the 37 states and 5 US dependent areas with long-term, confidential, name-based HIV reporting."[17] Given the enduring connection this disease has with the gay community, it seems obvious that Polk would give attention to this still critical matter in the series. Throughout much of the first season, the show's narrative revolved around the creation of Alex's self-run HIV/AIDS clinic. After being fed up with bureaucratic nonsense standing in the way of truly preventing and treating victims of the disease, he creates the Black AIDS Institute.[18]

As opposed to discussing the impact of AIDS on the Black gay community in a way that is sensationalized like J. L. King's popular book, *On the Down Low: A Journey into the Lives of "Straight" Black Men Who Sleep with Men*, or depictions in films such as *Longtime Companion, In the Gloaming,* or *Angels in America,* Polk chooses to show just how far AIDS research has come. He demonstrates how people with HIV can lead fruitful and productive lives and pursue meaningful romantic relationships. This leads to the other central theme for the second season, hate crimes.

The episode "Baby Can I Hold You?" tackles the serious and alarming issue of gay bashing. Noah stops at a West Hollywood gas station and is the victim of an unprovoked attack by three men, one of whom punches him in the face. After Noah sprays them with Mace in an attempt to protect himself, they repeatedly kick him and break his ribs. This is hardly dramatic hyperbole. According to a 2008 report done by the Federal Bureau of Investigation, of the 1,617 incidents reported, 58.6 percent were the result of anti-male-homosexual bias and 25.7 percent were the result of homosexual bias in general.[19] Furthermore, not only is Noah falsely accused by the perpetrators' lawyers of soliciting sexual favors from those who attacked him, this hate crime is given the lesser charge of aggravated assault. The slow pace taken by local and federal governments to address these hate crimes "clearly conveys the message that lesbians and gay men do not deserve full legal protection and justice."[20]

Though Polk does not devote more than an episode's worth of attention to the issue, it is still important to mention that he points to the need for more legislation in the effort to protect the well-being and interests of the gay community. Arguably a flaw of the show is that this incident becomes seemingly a nonissue after the thirty-minute episode. Polk, instead, uses it ostensibly to set in motion the reconciliation of Noah and Wade. Despite the show's shortcomings in dealing with issues like this, Polk does inspire discussion and further analysis about violence against those in the gay community.

"What's the T, Girl?" Why *Noah's Arc* Lives On in Our Memories but Not on Our TV Screens

The end of the second season left viewers with little reason to believe that *Noah's Arc* would not return for a third season to answer questions and continue the adventures of Noah and his friends. At that juncture, the head of the network seemed very pleased with how audiences were receiving the show, commenting, "I get incredible feedback on 'Noah's Arc' . . . The No. 1 compliment is how likable the show is. It's our first breakout hit."[21] Initially, National Public Radio reported that representatives from Logo confirmed they were on board for the show's return.[22] Yet, despite these promises and votes of confidence, *Noah's Arc* shockingly did *not* return for its hoped-for third season.

Viewers were outraged, starting petitions, canceling cable subscriptions, writing a tremendous amount of letters to Logo, and bombarding message boards on numerous gay-themed blogs and websites. One blogger noted that when he typed "Noah's Arc canceled" on the search engine Google, fifty-five thousand hits surfaced, many of which included interviews with the cast expressing their confusion and consternation about the show's cancellation.[23] Truly, it did not make sense. If the show, as Graden had stated, was extremely popular and struck a chord with audiences, why cancel it?

Loyal fans of the show saw the cancellation as a move that was less about business and more about the further polarization of Black members of the gay community and racism. Along these lines, much in the same way the then blossoming Fox Network used Black-themed programs such as *In Living Color*, the sitcom *Living Single*, and the police drama *New York Undercover* to build its cachet only to dump them in favor of more mainstream fare as its popularity rose, blogger Jasmyne Cannick deduced: "This network came out of nowhere, and they used *Noah's Arc* to launch itself. And they try to deny it, and they hate when people say it, but the fact is for African-American gays and lesbians, that's the only reason why we watch Logo."[24] On the other hand, other critics, despite their skepticism, slightly dismissed the racism claims and saw the cancellation as a hazard of the entertainment business. In this vein, journalist Rod McCullom concluded, "I think they're [Logo] probably being more careful than they need to be because it's a Black gay audience, but I don't necessarily think that the audience or the complexion of the characters dictated [anything]."[25]

Admittedly, Logo was quite passive in its announcement of the cancellation, failing to issue a formal statement announcing such but leaving it to the actors of the series to hit their social network pages and blogs to be the bearers of bad and puzzling news. Christian Vincent, who plays Ricky, wrote on MySpace: "I have not written a blog in awhile. The first part goes out to all The Noah's Arc fans. The show will NOT be returning for a third season. I feel glad that we had two seasons which many shows do not even get. The show laid ground work for many other shows that may come after it. Noah's Arc opened a door which I realize from the fans was very liberating. Logo should have an announcement posted as of today."[26] Oddly, the announcement Vincent revealed did arrive, but in another manifestation altogether.

In another bizarre, head-scratching decision, Graden announced that *Noah's Arc* would next come to audiences in the form of a feature film, stating: "We're proud that our first flagship series will now be Logo's first original movie. Logo and the show's fans have been with Noah and his friends from the beginning and we're excited to see that Patrik-Ian Polk will be continuing their stories on the big screen."[27] Graden spoke also of the show's devoted fan base, saying that because of them, Logo was "thrilled to harness the power of film to let Patrik-Ian Polk continue the story he has so skillfully woven. Noah's Arc has so many dimensions and possibilities, so advancing to the feature film format is an exciting way to motivate our loyal fans and engage an even wider audience."[28]

Figure 11.2   The love of Noah and Wade. Promotional frame grab.

Read another way, Graden turned what could have potentially been a source of ire into a shrewd business move and a pacification of the show's largely Black viewership.

The series' creator appeared to have bought into this manufactured excitement as well, commenting, "I began this series as a straight-to-DVD project, and Logo gave us a home as its flagship scripted series. And now we're taking it to the big screen! Never in my wildest dreams could I have imagined this little independent show in movie theatres! Hats off to MTV Networks and Logo for believing in us enough to take Noah to that next level."[29] On one hand, it is difficult to place any blame Polk's way for "playing the game," but it is difficult not to read his seemingly well-orchestrated, pre-prepared proclamation and the fact that he did not appear to question Logo's decision—not publicly, anyway—as very different in spirit and activism than the visual manifesto he created with the series. Even those who claim to know him well find something awry in his statement.

Cannick flatly admits, "In the entire time I have known Patrik, I have never known him to use the word 'wildest' to describe anything."[30]

Detraction and doubt notwithstanding, Logo's promises were more than just lip service. *Noah's Arc: Jumping the Broom* was released in theaters in October of 2008. With the majority of the cast intact, the film ambiguously tied up the storylines from the last season of the aborted television series and opened with the arrival of the group to Wade's family vacation home on Martha's Vineyard for his and Noah's impending nuptials. Mostly well received in terms of the reviews posted on gay-themed Web pages, despite very little publicity and nine theaters being its widest release, the film did quite well. It earned $532,878 and nearly topped Clint Eastwood's drama/thriller *Changeling* (2008), starring Angelina Jolie, in respect to opening-weekend per-screen average (*Changeling* earned $32,000 per screen; *Noah's Arc: Jumping the Broom* earned $30,000 per screen). So what does this success, modest as it might be, mean to the future of Polk's one-of-a-kind series? As of this writing, it means absolutely nothing.

In the section of the network's website designated for frequently asked questions, someone posed the question, "What's the Deal with *Noah's Arc?*" Logo answered this way: "Honestly we're not sure yet. Scripted programming is very expensive. It's like the Gucci of TV shows and it takes a long time to make properly. We love *Noah's Arc*, we know you love *Noah's Arc* (trust—we hear you), and after *two seasons* and *a movie* we need to think carefully about what's next for Noah, so that's what we've been doing with Patrik-Ian Polk. There are a few ideas floating around but as soon as anything is definite you'll be the first to know."[31] This gives the impression that Logo is attempting to string fans along. However, there seems to be no real intention to bring new episodes of *Noah's Arc* back to television screens. As the network explained, scripted series are very expensive to produce, and Logo has a slew of relatively inexpensive reality-based series, acquired television shows, movies, and repeats of long-canceled series that by now must have paid for themselves to fill its slate of programming. This diminishes any urgent need for Logo to return to *Noah's Arc*.

Conclusion

In a June 1991 interview, Marlon Riggs discussed the impetus that gave him the courage to make the documentary *Tongues Untied*:

> I remember when I first decided to make that step in front of the camera, and in some ways by the time I made that decision, it was easy. But the process, the walking toward that moment was difficult. Because everything within me was saying no, no, no, don't do it! Find somebody else. Find somebody else who will talk about being HIV positive. Find somebody else who will talk about being an Uncle Tom. Find somebody else who will talk about

being called nigger and punk and faggot and so forth. Let them tell their story. Let them sort of take the heat if there's gonna be heat about this. Let them take the praise if there's gonna be praise about this. But you hold back. Because there's too much at risk here. Too much at risk personally. Too much at risk professionally. Let someone else do it. And yet every time I realized that I was thinking in that way, I also realized that I couldn't ask anybody to do that. That really was my responsibility.[32]

With these words, Riggs demonstrates the need to not succumb to fear, just as much as the need to not hide behind the insults, abuse, and homophobic attitudes that permeate this culture. The example set by him and many of his contemporaries, writers such as Essex Hemphill, Larry Duplechan, and Joseph Beam, has inspired a new set of champions, like novelists James Earl Hardy and the late E. Lynn Harris, journalist Keith Boykin, and former NBA basketball star and philanthropist John Amaechi, to continue challenging the negative perceptions associated with Black gay male culture. The success of *Noah's Arc* certainly puts Patrik-Ian Polk among those currently leading the way to assure this transition of thought.

To reiterate Boykin's earlier point, though the series was a welcome presence, much, indeed, rode on *Noah's Arc* because of what it might mean to the gay and male members of the Black community. Had it been shoddily produced or less than emblematic of the culture, the likelihood of seeing another production of its ilk would have been highly doubtful. But if the multiple and enthusiastic message board posts and newspaper articles (nearly all targeted to the Black gay community) indicate what the show has meant to the countless Black men who have gone without any significant and meaningful representation of themselves in entertainment, Polk has accomplished a gracious plenty in seventeen episodes.

Though the future of *Noah's Arc* on Logo or any other network is uncertain, the adventures of Noah, Alex, Ricky, Chance, and the rest exemplify how complex, unpredictable, and varied Black gay male culture is. If amateurish acting and the characters' predilection for talking in bumper stickers and public service announcements sometimes hamper the show, the beguiling nature and amiability of the characters trump any derision these flaws might instigate. That we can overlook the obviousness of sexuality when relating to these men testifies to the show's charm and, more importantly, proves that Polk has created a program that is less about controversy and more about humanity. In place of stereotypes and disapproval, we receive love, humor, pain, and sincerity. This is a narrative that speaks to all the tenets of what family is, including families that are constructed out of necessity as opposed to blood bonds. In this way, brevity aside, *Noah's Arc* has moved our society even closer to going about being who we truly are.

NOTES

1. Jacquie Jones, "The Construction of Black Sexuality," in *Black American Cinema*, ed. Manthia Diawara (New York: Routledge, 1993), 256.

2. Julie Salamon, "Logo, a New Gay Channel, Looks 'Beyond Sexuality,'" *New York Times*, June 28, 2005, http://www.nytimes.com/2005/06/28/arts/television/28Logo.html?_r=1& scp=1&sq=LOGO%20Network&st=cse.

3. Ibid.

4. Patrik-Ian Polk, "Interview," *Noah's Arc: The Complete Second Season*, DVD, dir. Patrik-Ian Polk, Mina Shum, Sheldon Larry, Laurie Lynd (MTV Networks/Paramount Pictures, 2007).

5. Greg Shapiro, "Interview with Noah's Arc Creator Patrik-Ian Polk," *AfterElton.com*, October 25, 2005, http://www.afterelton.com/archive/elton/TV/2005/10/polk.html.

6. Gust A. Yep and John P. Elia, "Queering/Quaring Blackness in *Noah's Arc*," in *Queer Popular Culture: Literature, Media, Film, and Television*, ed. Thomas Peele (New York: Palgrave/Macmillan, 2007), 28.

7. Greg Braxton, "'Noah's Arc' Quickly Becomes a Logo Hit," *Los Angeles Times*, October 4, 2006, http://articles.latimes.com/2006/oct/04/entertainment/et-arc4.

8. Ibid.

9. In terms of minority representation, a number of these shows do include Latino cast members, which raises the question of whether or not one minority is preferred over the other. Certainly, on first glance, many of the actors/personalities featured on these shows who are Latino could appear to be white. This raises another question about Logo's goal to be more diverse in their portrayals of gay culture. Still, in saying this, I do not want to give the impression that Latino gay culture is widely portrayed on the network either, because it is not.

10. Christine Acham, *Revolution Televised: Prime Time and the Struggle for Black Power* (Minneapolis: University of Minnesota Press, 2004), 176.

11. Herman Gray, *Watching Race: Television and the Struggle for "Blackness"* (Minneapolis: University of Minnesota Press, 1995), 58.

12. Given the exorbitant living costs in California, one wonders how the struggling Noah and the other less wealthy characters pay the rent.

It is worth noting that, just as some of the markers of the urban dramas and comedies mentioned in these pages are stereotypical in their portrayal of the Black community, the scenes in *Noah's Arc* set in nightclubs, art galleries, and upscale shopping districts could be considered as stereotypes of gay male culture.

13. William G. Hawkeswood, *One of the Children: Gay Black Men in Harlem*, ed. Alex W. Costley (Berkeley: University of California Press, 1996), 161–162.

14. E. Patrick Johnson, *Appropriating Blackness: Performance and the Politics of Authenticity* (Durham: Duke University Press, 2003), 77.

15. Andrew Ross, "The Gangsta and the Diva," in *Black Male: Representations of Masculinity in Contemporary American Art*, ed. Thelma Golden (New York: Whitney Museum of American Art/Abrams, 1994), 159–160.

16. Johnson, *Appropriating Blackness*, 19.

17. "HIV Among African Americans," *Centers for Disease Control and Prevention*, http://www.cdc.gov/hiv/topics/aa/index.htm.

18. Black AIDS Institute is an actual organization that has been instrumental in and dedicated to highlighting the importance of HIV/AIDS awareness in the Black community since 1999.

19. Federal Bureau of Investigation, "2008 Hate Crime Statistics," *U.S. Department of Justice*, http://www2.fbi.gov/ucr/hc2008/incidents.html.

20. Kevin T. Berrill and Gregory M. Herek, "Primary and Secondary Victimization in Anti-Gay Hate Crimes: Official Response and Public Policy," in *Hate Crimes: Confronting Violence Against Lesbians and Gay Men*, ed. Gregory M. Herek and Kevin T. Berrill (Newbury Park, CA: Sage Publications, 1992), 293.

21. Braxton, "'Noah's Arc.'"

22. "Actor Jensen Atwood on 'Noah's Arc,'" *NPR*, January 23, 2007, http://www.npr.org/templates/story/story.php?storyId = 6955377.

23. Donnell Russell, "LOGO Axes: Noah's Arc," *Yahoo Voices*, February 9, 2007, http://voices.yahoo.com/logo-axes-noahs-arc-189458.html.

24. Christie Keith, "What Does the Future Hold for *Noah's Arc*?" *AfterElton.com*, February 28, 2007, http://www.afterelton.com/archive/elton/TV/2007/2/noahsarc.html.

25. Ibid.

26. J. Brotherlove, "No Season 3 for *Noah's Arc*," *thebrotherlove.com*, January 24, 2007, http://www.thebrotherlove.com/mediumrare/no_season_3_for_noahs_arc.php.

27. Brian Juergens, "It's Official: The *Noah's Arc* Movie Is on the Way," *AfterElton.com*, February 14, 2008, http://www.afterelton.com/blog/brianjuergens/its-official-noahs-arc-movie-on-its-way.

28. Keith Boykin, "*Noah's Arc* Cancelled; Film Planned Instead," *keithboykin.com*, January 25, 2007, http://www.keithboykin.com.

29. Juergens, "It's Official."

30. Jasmyne Cannick, "More on the Cancellation of *Noah's Arc*," *jasmynecannick.com*, February 2007, http://jasmynecannick.typepad.com/jasmynecannickcom/2007/02/more_on_the_can.html.

31. "What's the Deal with *Noah's Arc*?" *LogoTV*, http://www.logotv.com/about/faq.jhtml.

32. Marlon Riggs, "P.O.V. Interview," *Tongues Untied*, DVD, dir. Marlon Riggs (San Francisco: Frameline, 1989).

12

Graphic Blackness/Anime Noir

AARON MCGRUDER'S *THE BOONDOCKS*
AND THE ADULT SWIM

DEBORAH ELIZABETH WHALEY

DR. MARTIN LUTHER KING JR: *I want young men and young women who are alive today to know and to see that these new privileges and opportunities did not come without somebody suffering and sacrificing for them.*
RESPONSE: *Whatever, NIGGA.*
—"The Return of the King," *The Boondocks*

Aaron McGruder's "The Return of the King" (2006) is one of many of the artist's controversial episodes, yet it stands out because of the criticism it received among mainstream media outlets and civil rights leaders.[1] It was the ninth episode to air from his series *The Boondocks*, which is an anime show that airs on the Cartoon Network's Adult Swim cable channel. McGruder presents the following scenario in "The Return of the King": What if Martin Luther King Jr. (MLK) did not die after his April 4, 1968, shooting and instead awoke after being in a coma for thirty-two years? How would he assess racial progress in the United States today, and how would the masses and the country's leaders perceive his politics? McGruder's answer to this question is that if MLK were alive today, America would see him as naïve at best, or as an unpatriotic traitor at worst. He asserts that Martin Luther King Jr.'s calm demeanor would transform to outrage given his perception of political apathy within African America in the twenty-first century. In McGruder's episode, nihilism among a portion of the Black masses provokes MLK to organize a quasi-political rally to galvanize them into political action.[2] Unbeknownst to King, his audience attends the rally not because they are interested in political transformation; rather, they attend the event because they believe they are there for a chance to win tickets to a rap concert.

McGruder's episode reveals an interception of MLK's dream for the masses of Black Americans. Instead of the dream, McGruder's King sees only a

Bakhtinian carnival of an irrepressible nightmare.[3] As MLK approaches a podium to speak to the group, he finds that the crowd's laughter, fighting, loud talking, and signifying on each other mute his relatively soft-spoken voice. After bearing witness to audience members who sucker punch and kick each other, inhale malt liquor, and dance to hip hop music in hoodies (men) or scanty outfits (women), MLK, as the show's voice-over says, "did what all great leaders do. He told them the truth." In an inflective mixture of religious oratory, hip hop intellectual bravado, and seething outrage, he berates the unruly audience by shouting:

MLK: Will you ignorant Niggas please shut the hell up?

CROWD: Huh? What? Did he just say what I think he said? (The room falls silent as the crowd freezes in their tracks).

MLK: Is this it? This is what I got all those ass whoopings for? I had a dream. It was a dream that little black boys and little black girls would drink from the river of prosperity, free from the thirst of oppression. But lo and behold, some four decades later, what have I found but a bunch of trifling, shiftless, good for nothing Niggas. And I know some of you don't want to hear me say that word. It is the ugliest word in the English language, but that is what I see right now: Niggas. And you don't want to be a Nigga. 'Cause Niggas are living contradictions. Niggas are full of unfulfilled ambitions. Niggas wax and wane; Niggas love to complain. Niggas love to hear themselves talk, but hate to explain. Niggas love being another man's judge and jury. Niggas procrastinate until it's time to worry. Niggas love to be late. Niggas hate to hurry . . . I've seen what's around the corner. I've seen what's over the horizon, and I promise, you Niggas have nothing to celebrate. And no, I won't get there with you. I'm going to Canada![4]

Outside of its die-hard fan base, the *Boondocks* series largely ran under the radar until television promotions began to air on several networks announcing the MLK episode. They provided brief snippets of the civil rights icon unable to relate to what McGruder illustrates as a post-9/11, hyperpatriotic, nearly apocalyptic "hip-hopscape." On the MLK holiday, which was the night the show was to air, McGruder appeared on the ABC television network show *Nightline* to defend his position on national politics, his perception of nihilism, and his illustration of their uneasy collide through his "Return of the King" episode. When questioned by *Nightline* news anchor Cynthia McFadden about his decision to arm MLK with what she refers to as the offense of the "N-Word," McGruder defiantly remarked, "Actually, we had him use the word NIGGA; we don't use the N-Word on our show. [King] is disappointed in the world and with his people. By the end of the show, he is driven to the point where he has to use it. The points are there, and they justify the language."[5]

In a follow-up story on *ABC News Online*, various cultural critics critiqued the comic artist, perceiving him as ahistoric and naïve about the consequences of his

MLK representation. William Jelani Cobb, a professor of history at Spelman College in Atlanta, told ABC, "I think Aaron McGruder did something with Martin's character without really thinking about or understanding who Martin Luther King was. To portray him as a depressed old man, calling people niggers . . . it was offensive. Martin was a philosopher." Another interviewee, Mark Chapman, a professor of African American studies at Fordham University, shared that *The Boondocks'* viewers "have no historical reference on which to base the meaning behind the [N]-word."[6] In response to such criticism, McGruder commented in a later interview: "This isn't the nigga show. Nigga, nigga, nigga, nigga, nigga, nigga. I just wish we would expand the dialogue and evolve past the same conversation that we've had over the past 30 years about race in our country . . . I just hope to expand the dialogue and hope the show will challenge people to think about things they wouldn't normally think about, or think about it in a very different way."[7]

Soon after the *Nightline* feature and the airing of "Return of the King," the Reverend Al Sharpton publicly denounced the episode in media outlets as grossly inappropriate and as a bad representation for young adults, especially because of McGruder's decision to have his MLK character gratuitously use the N-word. Sharpton asked for a public apology from Cartoon Network executives, a request that neither the network nor McGruder obliged. Instead, the network released the following statement: "We think Aaron McGruder came up with a thought-provoking way of not only showing Dr. King's bravery but also of reminding us of what he stood and fought for."[8] As one might expect, the media hype concerning the episode and ensuing protest led to an increase in ratings and in the show's visibility. In 2005, it ranked twelfth among the top fifty cable shows and maintains the distinction of being the highest-rated series premiere in the first five years of the Cartoon Network. In spite of Sharpton's protest, in 2006, McGruder won the prestigious Peabody Award for Broadcasting for his "Return of the King" episode.

Although scholarship exists on the print version of *The Boondocks*, including my own work published elsewhere, the anime series is only beginning to receive scholarly inquiry.[9] Television scholar Timothy Havens has addressed the global circulation of the show in conversation with Black television programming, including its treatment of female characters, while scholar Rex Krueger takes up the strip's adaption to animation, the "cultural borrowing" of Japanese culture, and intertextuality.[10] The work of this chapter is to theorize how what I name *AfroAnime* and *graphic Blackness* visualize narratives that merge Black cultural politics with the aesthetic of Japanese animation.[11] Within the field of sequential art, graphic novels refer to comics with explicit themes of violence, sexuality, and coarse language. McGruder's *The Boondocks* represents a similar viewing space where the image and narrative of AfroAnime convene with graphic Blackness to produce a version of Black cultural politics that critiques race relations, African

America, and repressive aspects of the nation-state. *The Boondocks* functions as a mixture of the visual and the political; parody, polemic, and prescription; Black, Euroethnic, and Asian; dangerous and redemptive. In so doing, McGruder's AfroAnime swims through the murky waters of representation to produce his version of a complicated and contradictory vision of contemporary Black cultural politics that pushes aesthetic and political boundaries.[12]

Because I Know You Don't Read the Newspaper: Aaron McGruder's Adult Swim

Aaron McGruder earned a degree in African-American studies from the University of Maryland. Since the beginning of his career as a cartoonist in 1998, he has used *The Boondocks* for political critique. The title of his 2000 book, *The Boondocks: Because I Know You Don't Read the Newspaper*, is a tongue-in-cheek statement that hints at his perception of his demographic.[13] His comic strip portrayed Black youth as a central source for fresh political outlooks and political mobilization. In October of 2001, for example, McGruder came under verbal assault by newspaper conglomerates for his comic strip because it questioned nebulous patriotism after the terrorist attacks on the World Trade Center and the Pentagon. On October 5, 2001, McGruder's comic strip featured one of the Black characters, Huey, telephoning the FBI to report a perceived connection between the September 11 terrorist attacks and the 1980s Reagan-Bush administration. *Boondocks'* Huey went so far as to suggest that Ronald Reagan and the CIA trained Osama bin Laden and that the current Bush administration covertly funded the Taliban. As a result, the *Boondocks* comic strip was pulled from many major newspapers.[14]

The *Dallas Morning News* isolated the comic strip from the comic section; Long Island's *Daily News* pulled it altogether for one week; and the *Daily News* in New York examined the strip each day for appropriateness before making the decision to print it. McGruder responded to the censorship by temporarily changing the name of *The Boondocks* to *The Adventures of Flagee and Ribbon*. The strip featured an animated flag and ribbon that would "pontificate" Monday through Friday on the wonderful state of the nation, the necessity of patriotism at all costs, and how vital it was to shield youth from the dirty truth of American race relations, international policy, war, and politics. In one strip, Ribbon asks, "Flagee, why do people do bad things to America?" To which Flagee responds, "Because they hate our freedoms Ribbon. They hate our right to privacy. They hate our right to free speech." The most consistent critique of McGruder's strip was that it presented a negative message about the U.S. government during a time of national mourning. A reader in the *Pittsburgh Post-Gazette* echoed this sentiment, writing in opposition to the strip's inclusion in the comic section. "If publishers are committed to Aaron McGruder's serial diatribe," wrote the reader, "why not move it to the editorial pages where people are invited to vent their bitter spleens?"[15]

In 2005, *The Boondocks* made the transition from print to anime. At the time, the comic strip ran in the daily funnies section in three hundred U.S. newspapers. In anime form, *The Boondocks* was intended to widen the distribution and expand the brand and market of McGruder's popular comic strip. However, in 2006, McGruder ceased creating *The Boondocks* for newspapers, telling media outlets that he felt he had done all he could with the strip. In the special edition DVD for his first season of *The Boondocks*, he offers additional explanations for this choice, addressing the relationship between art, audience, and reception. According to McGruder, younger adults (eighteen to thirty-four) are the target market for his Adult Swim series, and older adults who read the daily newspaper were the target market for his former comic strip. *Boondocks'* transition from print to television, he shares, represents his desire to reach those he believes should listen to and act upon contemporary problems in African America, i.e., the hip hop generation.

Aesthetics and character development are a significant element of his weaving of anime and Black cultural politics. In keeping with the genre and aesthetic of Japanese anime, McGruder's characters have large, expressive eyes, simple facial features that allow the eyes to become the central focus, and bodies that ebb and flow between rapid movement and momentary stasis.[16] His main protagonist in the series is the ten-year-old Huey, who takes his name from the Black Panther activist Huey Newton and reflects McGruder's self-avowed radical political consciousness. Huey often provides didactic answers to the vexing political problems McGruder presents to his audience. Huey's antagonist and

Figure 12.1   Samurai Huey illustrating graphic Blackness. Frame grab.

brother, the eight-year-old Riley, reflects the perniciousness of those problems and performs a wannabe gangsta mentality. Their caretaker, the elderly Granddad, is the mediator between the cultural and political poles that Huey and Riley represent. The show's peripheral characters include the multiracial DuBois family, the white sociopaths and "wiggers" Ed Wuncler III and Gin Rummy (voiced by the Black American actors Charlie Murphy and Samuel Jackson), clueless white secondary education teachers, and the self-hating Black Uncle Ruckus. They collectively present the moral, material, and ideological positions that the three main characters are challenged to negotiate in each week's episode.

The DuBoises, who take their name from W.E.B. DuBois, are McGruder's metaphor for racial integration and light-skin privilege. Ed and Gin are metonyms for the real-life former president George W. Bush (Ed) and former secretary of state Donald Rumsfeld (Gin); the partial masking of their identities through the lens of hip hop culture is intended to magnify their danger to McGruder's audience. Uncle Ruckus is a mimesis of white-supremacist, dominant-culture-identified ideology, as seen with his ascription to the superiority of whiteness and the inferiority of blackness. McGruder's supporting white characters embody the bilateral cultural blindness of neoliberalism, whereas his peripheral Black characters take the form of hip hop nihilists or neoconservative politicians, preachers, and popular icons. The setting in which their conflicts take place, Woodcrest, is a fictional suburb that exists as a geopolitical landscape of nation making and belonging that each character seeks to access or defy. The series works within a largely masculinist formation, with women of African descent seldom appearing as historical actors or innovators in his production of Black cultural politics. Yet the female actor Regina King voices both Huey and Riley, thus situating women's central role in the show's aesthetic production of anime behind the scenes. Taken together, McGruder's characters, setting, aesthetic, and subject matter create a simulacrum or unreal semblance of a nation unable to sustain its current political positions and rhetorical strategies that each player in *The Boondocks* invokes.

Four representative episodes serve as examples of Aaron McGruder's critique and his forging of a new, even if at times unreconcilable and problematic, Black cultural politics: "The S-Word" (2008), "The Story of Thugnificent" (2007), "The Story of Gangstalicious" (2005), and "The Garden Party" (2005).[17] All four episodes show the trappings of our current neoliberal and neoconservative moment. While "The Garden Party" directly addresses American jingoism and the war on terror, "The S-Word," "The Story of Thugnificent," and "The Story of Gangstalicious" are statements on the collision between inter- and intracultural conflict, economics, consumption, sexuality, and masculinity. The first episode asks viewers to consider the place of Black cultural politics as a metacritique on a national scale, whereas the latter episodes challenge spectators to reevaluate consumer practice, as well as the historical significance and rhetorical strategies of race, class, and sexualities in popular culture and in the public sphere. A consistent strand in all of the episodes is their anime production of the sublime terrain of postmodern narratives; that is, an intellectual ground that seeks to move spectators into alternative ways of seeing not easily captured in language alone, but artfully abetted by the addition of the moving anime image.

This Isn't the Nigga Show

"The S-Word," airing in season two, appears as a challenge to critics of McGruder who admonished him for his use of racial epithets in "Return of the King."[18] In the show, a white secondary education teacher, Mr. Petto, refers to eight-year-old Riley as a "Nigga" to get his attention during class. This show is a visual and narrative reenactment of an actual incident in 2006, when administrators at Valley High School in Louisville, Kentucky, suspended the white teacher Paul Dawson for berating a Black American student by telling him to sit down and calling him the N-word. In his defense, Dawson said that his suspension was misguided because he used the version of the N-word with an *a* at the end, and therefore, it was a term of affection and not a racial epithet meant to hurt or injure the student. The local news story went viral on the Internet after the posting of Paul Dawson's apology on the media channel YouTube, inciting bloggers and national news media to use Dawson as an example of white naïveté and thus heightening anxiety about the use of racialized language.[19]

In McGruder's satire of the Valley High School incident, Republican pundit Ann Coulter, characterized as a hate-spewing psychotic, Reverend Rollo Goodlove, and the insincere Riley appear on various news programs to argue over who has the right to use the N-word in the public sphere. They engage in the debate not in the name of social justice but rather in the name of each of them gaining monetary benefit from being on the media circuit to discuss the topic. This episode is more than an obvious move on McGruder's part to imply that characters such as these seek to keep the fires behind their names lit. In almost an exact replica of news coverage on the Valley High School event, the episode opens up dialogue about the current use of the N-word, and it questions the motives of the pupil, Dawson, and the news media:

> WHITE MALE NEWSCASTER 1: It's a derogatory racial remark that has divided people for many years.
>
> WHITE MALE NEWSCASTER 2 (Sitting next to Newscaster 1): And a J. Edgar Hoover Elementary teacher has now been suspended over calling a student the N-word. Stacey Rene investigates what happened and why.
>
> STACY RENE (Black female field reporter): And what did he say specifically to you?
>
> RILEY (Appearing unusually studious at a desk and wearing non-prescription reading glasses): He said, "Sit down Nigga."

STACY RENE: Riley Freeman is a third-grade student at Hoover Elementary
School, a basketball player, an avid reader, and one day hopes to spread
his philosophy through rap music. (The camera images the young Riley
writing at a desk and then voraciously reading a textbook.) He was in
class when he had a verbal exchange with his teacher, Joe Petto. But Mr.
Petto said it was Riley who used the N-word first.

MR. PETTO: (The camera cuts away to Petto.) So, I told him to take his seat,
and here comes this barrage of insults. I mean, some of the words I've
never even heard before, and I was just stunned. And, well, I just said,
"Sit down, NIGGA!"

The name of the school at which the incident takes place, J. Edgar Hoover
Elementary, invokes the history of government surveillance and censorship of
Black Americans and radical activists during the mid-1950s and 1960s civil rights
era.[20] It further signals an expansion of rights for the Federal Bureau of
Investigation at the expense of the civil liberties and rights of everyday
Americans. The school name and the responses of Riley and Petto point to the
reality that Black Americans live in a nation where city officials name schools
after J. Edgar Hoover and where educators, students, and the populace at large
remain unable to deal with the First Amendment conflicts mismanaged during
Hoover's reign. McGruder exposes the halfhearted apology of Mr. Petto and the
misleading, angelic representation of Riley to account for the multiple sides of a
complex story of injury, insult, and, as the show later reveals, *monetary gain*.

Toward the end of the "S-Word" episode, McGruder's Ann Coulter turns
from right-wing Republican pundit to a street-talking homegirl, who flaunts
her Black American boyfriend (Abdul) backstage at CNN's *Larry King Live*
show. Coulter and Reverend Goodlove embrace backstage and admit to Huey,
Riley, and Granddad that they often work together to help sell their respective
books or to provide publicity for their self-serving causes. A shocked Huey asks
Coulter, "So, are you really even a Republican?" to which Coulter replies, "Hell
no. You think I like going out there and saying this ridiculous shit?" The camera
switches to the talking head of Uncle Ruckus. While sitting in a recliner chair in
front of a wall where a Confederate flag hangs, Uncle Ruckus defiantly looks
into the camera. Ruckus says that he will fight to the death for white people's
right to use racial epithets and to speak about, speak to, and treat Black
Americans in any way they see fit. In one of the final frames of the episode,
McGruder introduces his version of the well-known actor and philanthropist Bill
Cosby. An overwrought Cosby, wearing a colorful sweater reminiscent of his
role in *The Cosby Show*, says that any Black person who uses the N-word is a
"Coon or a Sambo." As Cosby continues to speak, his words become increasingly
incomprehensible, and there is an aesthetic abstraction of his voice into sonic
noise by the episode's end.

The comments of Uncle (Tom) Ruckus constitute an obvious white suprema-cist sentiment via Blackface as well as the common white liberal excuse to use the word, that is, "Black people use the N-word, so why can't I?" However, the Cosby portrayal requires more intellectual probing. In its brevity, Cosby's appearance as the final frame of the episode signals the controversy of his 2004 NAACP Awards Ceremony speech where he blamed the Black working poor for their own disen-franchisement. In a subsequent 2006 speech commemorating the *Brown vs. the Board of Education* decision to desegregate schools in Topeka, Kansas, Cosby reit-erated his disappointment with the Black masses by noting, "*Brown vs. the Board of Education* is no longer the white person's problem . . . It can't speak English." The "it" Cosby mockingly and disparagingly refers to is, of course, the Black poor.[21]

White conservatives and a significant portion of his Black audience responded to Cosby's NAACP speech with praise for his rhetoric of accountabil-ity among the Black working poor in urban communities. However, Cosby's condescending diatribe did little to address the reality of our post-civil-rights moment—a moment that is more "present" than post; a moment where the Black underclass remains in an entanglement of social and economic problems that the 1960s did not end. Thus with his portrayal of the popular American icon, McGruder accomplishes two tasks at once. He aesthetically situates Cosby within the 1980s *Cosby Show* discourse of respectability and class ascension at the expense of the Black masses, a discourse resurrected in Cosby's 2006 NAACP speech. At the same time, his subtextual narrative has the potential to expose audiences to an important contradiction in Cosby's recent and historical rhetoric of race. Older audiences might recall that Cosby's earlier comedy routines in the 1960s and 1970s did employ controversial language, which he now, at least pub-licly, claims to deplore. The graphic artist (McGruder) therefore introduces to the audience a litany of historical terminology, that is, Coon, Sambo, and the N-word, and he reveals each term's historical and contemporary usage as social critique, social containment, and comedic device. Younger spectators thus face a challenge to link the history of *Brown vs. the Board of Education* to contemporary issues concerning education, class, and race that the "S-Word" episode grapples with via its extreme characterizations and narrative of political satire. The con-flict between neoliberals (Mr. Petto), neoconservatives (Coulter), and Black neoconservatives (Cosby and Reverend Goodlove) is not solved in "The S-Word." Rather, these positions raise questions about language, rights, and race. In so doing, the episode's AfroAnime *narrative* makes use of the postmodern turn by unveiling unequal power relations, the multiple referents of language (e.g., Nigga vs. Nigger), and the deceiving aspects of authority.

"The Garden Party": Necropolitics and the War on Terror

In the episode "The Garden Party," McGruder uses a pastoral background as the setting for Huey to announce troubling news to a group of wealthy socialites.

Wearing army fatigues and combat boots, Huey walks up to a podium and microphone and announces that "Jesus was Black, Ronald Reagan was a devil, and the government is lying about 9/11." Partygoers become frantic about this news and begin to riot; a woman passes out after she screams, "It can't be true!" McGruder's anime aesthetic derives from the use of what he names "black fu" (i.e., kung fu with a Black twist) among the rioting partygoers, one of whom is visually "marked" as being of Asian descent. Further, the lush landscape of a garden is typical of anime visual cues that make use of panoramic settings in conjunction with live-action sequences.

The mayhem ceases, however, when Huey awakes from his black fu nightmare to his grandfather's open-handed slap. The viewer thus learns that the opening moment is not real; it is a dream of the main protagonist. Granddad

Figure 12.2   *The Boondocks*. Courtesy of PhotoFest.

scolds Huey by exclaiming, "Uh, huh; you having that dream again about making white people riot." Huey responds while rubbing his eyes, "I was telling them the truth." Granddad responds to Huey with anger and frustration: "How many times have I told you that you better not even dream of telling white folks the truth? You better learn to lie like me. I'm going to find me a white man and lie to him right now." Granddad turns off the bedroom light and leaves the room, and a blue hue engulfs the shadow form of Huey, whose large eyes stare into the eye of the camera and therefore into the eyes of an imagined spectator. The frame then freezes, and Huey's eyes illustrate a mixture of anger and anguish.

Although the pastoral ideal in American art typically conjures an aesthetic presentation of nature, innocence, and the human subject's harmonious relationship to a budding garden of plenty, such lofty images implode in the AfroAnime mixture of "The Garden Party." McGruder's pastoral background leans closely to the arguments of cultural critics and Americanists Leo Marx, Henry Nash Smith, and Richard Slotkin about the powerful impact of the pastoral as myth. In particular, Slotkin maintains that images and narratives of the pastoral ideal of America as a vast garden allowed for the "legitimized violence [in the frontier] which recalled the desperate need" for Anglos to "believe in their own innocence."[22] Marx and Smith write separately that such myths of innocence as the pastoral aesthetic of the garden conveys can simultaneously elide the tragic dimensions of westward expansion, cultural imperialism, and bellicose actions in international relations. As Smith wrote in 1986 about the myth of the garden and American politics during the Reagan-Bush administration: "Does the resurgent American ethic of 'looking out for number one' in any way represent a carry-over of frontier individualism? Are we bellicose and moralistic in international relations partly because of habits of mind acquired during the conquest of North America?"[23] McGruder's choice to situate his truth of the tragic dimensions of state and international imperialism (as voiced by Huey) in a luxurious garden thus provides a visual and narrative collide between pastoral beauty as facade and the power behind the author's alleged "truth" concerning U.S. international defense policy.

McGruder's opening scene to the "Garden Party" foreshadows a later moment in the episode where Huey and Riley meet the sociopath Ed Wuncler III. Ed is the grandson of a wealthy investor and a recent discharge from service in the Iraq War. At a pivotal moment in the episode, Granddad says to Ed, "I hear you just got back from Iraq." Riley, wearing a fedora hat and a white and black suit that conjures an Italian gangster stereotype, approaches Ed and says with wide eyes, "For real, what was it like?" Ed answers, "What was it like? What am I suppose to say to that? That it was cool, that there were bitches. OK, there were bitches, but you know, a lot of them were covered up in those curtains that they be wearing. But I digress. It was war!" As Ed spins in a circle and extends his hands to replicate a machine gun, he yells, "In war, mutha fuckers be like shootin' pa-pow! Bombs be blowing up, and, you know, the shit scared me . . . I shit on myself a dozen of times while I was over there."

Ed's rant serves as McGruder's commentary on how the Bush-Cheney administration approached the Iraq War. Ed's discussion of war as analogous to school kids playing cops and robbers to help, as Ed later says, "bitches who wear curtains on their faces be free," exposes one of the irrational rationales for U.S. intervention in Iraq. It also underscores the immaturity of the decision maker and, at the least, the class dimension in initiating a war for which there is little personal consequence for the initiator. Indeed, Ed ends his tirade with his middle fingers pointing downward, indicating that he is screwing the nation and dismissing the consequences all at once, while he shouts at the partygoers, "What the fuck you all looking at? I don't give a fuck. I'm rich, bitch." Here, McGruder arms Ed Wuncler III with hip hop language and style to show the national repercussions of international policy that involves repressive ideologies and the violence of war. In so doing, his combination of national defense language with characters that perform gangsta rap mentalities exposes the real gangstas with capital and power.

Homeboys and Homonationalism: The Stories of Gangstalicious and Thugnificent

McGruder's characters Gangstalicious and Thugnificent represent the commodification of the rap music industry. Their narratives reveal how some young men may seek to make sense of their own masculinity and sexuality vis-à-vis the rap performers that they see as idols. McGruder's Gangstalicious is a gay Black male on "the down low"; he and his adversaries engage in hypermasculine identities and violence to mediate and nullify their "true" sexual selves. Comparatively, Thugnificent represents the gender performance and former gangsta facade of rapper Snoop Dog in the 1990s and the rags-to-riches story of rapper 50 Cent in the twenty-first century. Thugnificent is slightly feminine in appearance yet boasts a robust sexual life with women. Wearing ponytail Afro puffs—a style common among young Black American girls during their toddler years—and a wife-beater shirt (tank top), Thugnificent brags about his accumulation of money and his sexual conquests. As Thugnificent says in the episode that bears his name (i.e., "The Story of Thugnificent"): "There's more to life than what you're born into, there's also bitches." This ideology, he remarks, is a political movement that takes up where "activists like Malcolm X left off." "The Story of Thugnificent" and "The Story of Gangstalicious" present a narrow depiction of the complexity of hip hop, yet one that looms in the popular, dominant imagination—an image so powerful that it at times obfuscates more radical and progressive aspects of the hip hop movement. Though these episodes are essentialist in their portrayal of hip hop and rap musicians, McGruder reminds the viewer through the titles that they are an extreme refraction of hip hop, that is, partial fables from which one might learn—stories that are dangerously tantalizing (Gangsta*licious*) and significant (Thug*nificent*).

In "The Story of Gangstalicious," unknown assailants shoot Gangstalicious while, ironically, he is singing his hit song, "I Got Shot." The rapping of his lyrics during a performance turns to actual cries for help, something that the audience does not recognize as real since the lyrics to his song mimic the actual occurrence. Here, McGruder highlights the call-and-response aspects of rap and hip hop music, and he reveals the ramifications of the commodification of the rapper and his music:

GANGSTALICIOUS (Stumbling onstage after three unknown men "bum rush" the stage and shoot him multiple times before fleeing into the crowd): I got shot!

AUDIENCE (Enthusiastically responding and not realizing he is actually wounded): I got shot!

GANGSTALICIOUS (With a tonality of panic): No, I got shot for real!

AUDIENCE (With increased enthusiasm): I got shot for real!

GANGSTALICIOUS (This time moaning in a nearly inaudible murmur): No, I really, really got shot!

AUDIENCE (Screaming louder in a nearly inaudible chant): I really, really got shot!

The inability to distinguish between lyrics and material life on the part of the audience shows the blurring of reality between gangsta performance and gangsta life—both, suggests McGruder, are simulacrums of the real. Such a lure is the life that Gangstalicious presents, his audience consumes the rapper's music and his story voraciously. Thus, the commodity of Gangstalicious and his product (music) is divorced from the consequences of real-lived social relations skewed and abused while "playing" gangsta onstage.

A similar incident occurs in "The Story of Thugnificent" after the rapper records a hit song about Huey and Riley's grandfather, "Eff Granddad" (as in "fuck Granddad"), in retaliation for Granddad attempting to run the rich rapper out of their upper-middle-class neighborhood. The song's accompanying music video shows the rapper and his crew, Magtastic and Flownomenal, beating a Granddad look-alike. "Eff Granddad" captures the aesthetic of anime through its use of multiple perspectives and angles of Thugnificent, Magtastic, and Flownomenal stomping the Granddad look-alike, cross-cutting sequences where Granddad is spying on, running from, and hiding from Thugnificent and his crew, and duplicate backgrounds that magnify the quick, truncated action scenes. As the music video gains popularity on BET and MTV, a wave of attacks perpetuated by white middle-class youth against senior citizens occurs in Woodcrest and across the world, something for which the public holds Thugnificent responsible. In an interview on MTV, Thugnificent proclaims in his defense the following: "This is about what I'm going through. Thugnificent never said go out and beat old people!"

McGruder uses satire in this scene to combine the insidiousness of the Parents Music Resource Center (PMRC), known for its misguided censorship campaign against heavy metal and rap music in the 1990s, with the insidious notion of a wealthy rapper complaining about the hardship of his ousting from an upper-middle-class neighborhood by a Black senior citizen. Having Thugnificent's eviction campaign spearheaded by his Black neighbors (Granddad, Tom, and Uncle Ruckus) allows McGruder to highlight the shifting class status of rappers and the bankruptcy of their "keep it real" rhetoric, along with the equally problematic values of the Black middle class. Granddad, Tom, and Uncle Ruckus, like Cosby, walk a tightrope between racial uplift and Black neoconservative rhetoric. The latter group succumbs to PMRC's race- and class-inflected fantasy that music, rather than people, enacts crimes and violence, while the former group argues for a contradictory rhetoric, that their lyrics constitute "keeping it real," while at the same time arguing that their lyrics do not advocate behavior in real life.

Parodying the East Coast/West Coast feud between rappers in the mid-1990s, the episode "The Story of Gangstalicious" also uses the lyrics of the title character's recent hit song, "Thuggin' Love," to insinuate that Gangstalicious's feud with rival rappers is not only about acquiring capital and monopolizing the hip hop market but is also about "thug love." Here, "thug love" is a reference for same-sex desire masking as male/female romantic desire. McGruder's Riley, who is Gangstalicious's biggest fan, is obsessed with the process of Othering non-normative sexual identities. This stance allows him to tightly patrol and legitimate his own heterosexual identity during his prepubescent years, an identity that is dependent upon the type of hypermasculine performance that Gangstalicious shows to his fans.

In many episodes of The Boondocks, Riley engages in relentless dialogue about what he perceives as unmasculine performance, that is, behavior that is not violent, aggressive, or gangsta, as proof that "a Nigga is gay." When he is faced with his idol Gangstalicious's complex identity as being gangsta and gay, Riley (and perhaps McGruder's audience) faces a remix of gender, sexuality, and masculinity that calls into question the identities of maleness and Blackness that had hitherto seemed stable through monolithic constructions. For Riley, finding out that Gangstalicious is gay and not as wealthy and tough as his music videos portray is, as he says, "like going to heaven and finding God smoking crack."

"The Story of Gangstalicious" shows that aggression between males signifies competition in the elusively labeled "free marketplace" (in this case, the music industry) for the sustaining of a profit-bearing capitalist nation-state, as well as a desperate and violent attempt to deny same-sex attraction by enacting hegemonic masculinity. In so doing, Gangstalicious's suppression of same-sex sexual expression through the performance of gangsta rap mentalities constitutes a critique of homonationalism. McGruder illustrates that the sustaining of a nation-state is congruent with the patrolling and containing of sexualities and sexual identities into a mimesis of capitalist-inscribed heteronormativity (Thugnificent's "getting riches and bitches"), thereby creating homonormativity or homonationalism (Gangstalicious's suppression of "thug love").

As cultural critic Jasbir Puar argues, homonationalism consists of the national project of interpolating heterosexual and lesbian, gay, bisexual, and transgender (LGBT) communities into a national citizenship via a "you are with us or against us post 9/11 discourse." A U.S. national project therefore dangles the carrot of cultural citizenship to queer communities that it never intends on providing for fear of alienating a portion of its heterosexual constituency. Rights such as nationally recognized marriage or the dismantling of "don't ask, don't tell" are carefully deployed via amorphous necropolitics in order to garner support for the maintenance of, as the episode "The Garden Party" reveals, the national war on terror.[24]

Conclusion

The combination of Black cultural forms and the grammars of anime with McGruder's characters, premises, and depiction of nation cannot be divorced from the reality that culture is political and the deployment of politics occurs through cultural forms. *The Boondocks* constitutes a collision between the graphic Blackness of his cultural politics and his AfroAnime aesthetic, thereby rearticulating the conventions of anime as a whole. McGruder's third season continues his adult-themed narrative and anime aesthetic mixture. In a cluster of episodes in 2010 (e.g., "It's a Black President, Huey Freeman," and "The Fried Chicken Flu") he provides a trenchant critique of the centrist politics of the Obama presidential administration constituting remnants of the previous Republican administration.

His television series thus continues to engage contemporary social issues, and he places spectators in a position where they might contemplate his consistent, anime diegesis as a form of Black cultural politics. McGruder is unrelenting with his polemical writing of interracial race relations, nihilistic aspects within African America, and repressive aspects of the nation-state, including homonationalism, the U.S. war on terror, and how citizens are interpolated as arms of national enforcement. If, as McGruder muses, his younger audience members are not reading the newspaper for information on a daily basis, his AfroAnime satire is ever the more vital in serving as the medium through which they might find encouragement to raise their consciousness to a critical level.

NOTES

The author would like to thank Timothy Havens and Hye Jin Lee at the University of Iowa for their thoughtful comments on an earlier draft of this chapter.

1. "Return of the King," *The Boondocks*, Aaron McGruder (w), Rodney Barnes (w), Seung Eun-Kim, (dir), Aaron McGruder (prod) Season 1, Episode 9 (2006).

2. Cultural critic Cornell West employs the term *nihilism* to describe apathy among the Black American masses that stems from a chronic depression concerning their disenfranchisement and marginalization. He argues that nihilism constitutes unpredictable and self-destructive behavior. Cultural critic Steven Steinberg views West's arguments about nihilism as bearing the components of neoconservativism and class essentialism. West's arguments about nihilism and self-determination, argues Steinberg, underemphasize institutional racism. I employ the term gingerly and with unease. See Cornell West, "Nihilism in Black America," in *Race Matters* (Boston: Beacon Press, 1993), 15–32; Stephen Steinberg, "The Liberal Retreat from Race During the Post–Civil Rights Era," in *The House That Race Built,* ed. Wahneema Lubiano (New York: Vintage, 1998), 13–46.

3. On the carnivalesque, see Mikhail Bakhtin, *Rabelais and His World* (Bloomington: Indiana University Press, 1984).

4. McGruder integrates into the MLK speech lyrics from rapper Asheru's song "Niggas," which is based on the group The Last Poets' song "Niggas Are Scared of Revolution."

5. See ABC broadcast, "Pushing the Envelope: An Interview with Aaron McGruder" (host Cynthia McFadden), *Nightline*, January 16, 2006. See also Associated Press, "Sharpton Criticizes 'Boondocks' for Showing King Saying the N-Word," *USA Today*, January 25, 2006, http://www.usatoday.com/life/television/news/2006-01-25-sharpton-boondocks_x.htm.

6. Bryan Robinson, "The N-Word: The Most Popular Ugly Word Ever: Why Memory of the Racial Slur's Sinister Past Must Be Preserved," February 8, 2006, *ABC News Online*, http://abcnews.go.com/US/BlackHistory/story?id = 1543526&page = 1.

7. Ibid.

8. Associated Press, "Sharpton Criticizes 'Boondocks.'" Also DeWayne Wickham, "'Boondocks' Steps over Line in Its Treatment of King," *USA Today*, January 31, 2006.

9. See Deborah Elizabeth Whaley, "Black Expressive Art, Resistant Cultural Politics, and the (Re)Performance of Patriotism," *Trotter Review* 17, no. 1 (Autumn 2007): 14–16. For a brief treatment of the anime version of *The Boondocks* in comparison with comedian Dave Chapelle's *Chapelle's Show*, see Ted Gournelos's "Coda" to his book *Popular Culture and the Future of Politics: Cultural Studies and the Tao of South Park* (Lanham: Lexington Books, 2009), 223–246.

10. Tim Havens, "The Worldwide Circulation of Contemporary African American Television," in *Black Television Travels: Media Globalization and Contemporary Racial Discourse* (New York: New York University Press, forthcoming) and Rex Krueger, "Aaron McGruder's *The Boondocks* and Its Transition from Comic Strip to Animated Series," *Animation: An Interdisciplinary Journal* 5, no. 3 (2010): 313–329.

11. My term *graphic Blackness* is a mixture of the graphic novel narrative and the politics of visual representation. Indeed, the differences between Adult Swim's animated series and cartoons are parallel to the differences between comic books and the graphic novel. While the target for comic books is a youth market, graphic novels are lengthier comics targeted toward adults. The Cartoon Network features animated shows for young children during the day, but its Adult Swim segment begins its programming at 9 P.M.; its episodes contain content intended for an adult audience; it shows simulated nudity, and it contains coarse language, including the racial epithet *nigga*. *The Boondocks* airs at 11 P.M. because of its MA rating.

12. *Cultural politics* refers to the way organic intellectuals, community activists, and organizers, that is, cultural workers, intervene in processes of subjugation produced and upheld within cultural realms. On Black cultural politics, see Brian Alleyne, *Radicals Against Race: Black Activism and Cultural Politics* (Oxford: Oxford University Press, 1998); Bill Mullen,

Popular Fronts: Chicago and African-American Cultural Politics, 1935–46 (Urbana: University of Illinois Press, 1999); Michael Dawson, *Black Visions: The Roots of Contemporary African-American Political Ideologies* (Chicago: University of Chicago Press, 2001), Paul Gilroy, *"There Ain't No Black in the Union Jack": The Cultural Politics of Race and Nation* (Chicago: University of Chicago Press, 1993).

13. Aaron McGruder, *The Boondocks: Because I Know You Don't Read the Newspaper* (Riverside, NJ: Andrews McMeel, 2000). Although 85 percent of Americans read the daily or Sunday newspaper, 60 percent of readers who read the newspaper daily are over the age of twenty-five. Newspaper readership increases greatly based on age. See "Who's Reading the Newspaper," *American Demographics*, July 1, 2001, and the Newspaper Association of America annual report on newspaper readership, http://www.naa.org/info/facts08/readership-demographics.html.

14. Jayson Blair, "Some Comic Strips Take an Unpopular Look at U.S.," *New York Times*, October 22, 2001, sec. C, 9. Censorship of *The Boondocks* continued when McGruder retired *The Adventures of Flagee and Ribbon*. In a November 22, 2001, strip, Huey is pictured at a table on Thanksgiving reciting the prayer: "Ahem—in this time of war against Osama bin Laden and the oppressive Taliban regime, we are thankful that our leader isn't the spoiled son of a powerful politician from a wealthy oil family who is supported by religious fundamentalists, operates clandestine organizations, has no respect for the democratic electoral process, bombs innocents and uses war to deny people their civil liberties. Amen." The *Dallas Morning News* pulled this strip. See Eric Celeste, "What's Up, 'Docks? The Morning News Keeps the Evil Thoughts Away," *Dallas Observer*, December 6, 2001.

15. Author unknown, "Letters to the Editor: Move *The Boondocks*," *Pittsburgh Post-Gazette*, Sooner Edition, September 27, 2002, 43.

16. The exception to this aesthetic consists of characters meant to "look" like real celebrities and politicians.

17. "The S-Word," season 2, episode 11 (2008); "The Garden Party," season 1, episode 1 (2006); "The Story of Gangstalicious," season 1, episode 6 (2005); "The Story of Thugnificent," season 2, episode 5 (2007). All four episodes were written by Aaron McGruder and Rodney Barnes and directed by Seung Eun-Kim, and produced by Aaron McGruder.

18. McGruder reveals in an interview that the title of this episode was initially "The N-Word." See Evan Jacobs, "Aaron McGruder Sounds Off on *The Boondocks*," *MovieWeb*, October 9, 2007, http://www.movieweb.com/news/NEjjgmnphpICmm.

19. On the real-life occurrence, see Renee Murphy (reporter), "Teacher Calls Student the N-Word," Louisville, KY, ABC Channel 11 News broadcast, Tuesday, February 14, 2006.

20. For a historical account of this surveillance, see Ward Churchill and Jim Vander Wall, *Agents of Repression: The FBI's Secret Wars Against the Black Panther Party and the American Indian Movement* (Boston: South End Press, 1988).

21. On the Cosby speeches controversies, including Cosby's conservative cultural politics and public reaction, see Michael Eric Dyson, *Is Bill Cosby Right? Or Has the Black Middle Class Lost Its Mind?* (New York: Perseus Books Group, 2006).

22. These revisionist essays include Henry Nash Smith, "Symbol and Idea in *Virgin Land*," in *Ideology and Classic American Literature*, ed. Sacvan Bercovitch and Ira Jehlen (London: Cambridge University Press, 1986), and Leo Marx, "The Idea of 'Technology' and Postmodern Pessimism," in *Does Technology Drive History? The Dilemma of Technological Determinism*, ed. Merritt Rowe Smith and Leo Marx (Cambridge: MIT Press, 1999). See also Henry Nash Smith, *Virgin Land: The American West as Symbol and Myth* (Cambridge: Harvard University Press, 1950); Leo Marx, *Machine in the Garden: Technology and the Pastoral Ideal in America* (London: Oxford University Press, 1964). This quote is from one of Marx's and

Smith's contemporaries, Richard Slotkin. See Richard Slotkin, *Regeneration Through Violence* (Middletown: Wesleyan University Press, 1973), 565.

23. Smith, "Symbol and Idea in *Virgin Land*," 27–29.

24. *Necropolitics* refers to the figurative and literal death of genuine political discourse and action in the public sphere. The term especially aims to mark a connection between violence, death, and sovereignty, or, as Jasbir Puar reminds us, a way of describing systems of domination that are, drawing from Achille Mbembie, "embodied, sensory, and tactile" (112). On necropolitics and homonationalism see Jasbir Puar, *Terrorist Assemblages: Homonationalism in Queer Times* (Durham and London: Duke University Press, 2007).

PART IV

WORLDWIDE BLACKNESS

Resistance Televised

THE TV DA GENTE TELEVISION
NETWORK AND BRAZILIAN
RACIAL POLITICS

REIGHAN ALEXANDRA GILLAM

As activists and political leaders in Brazil call for increasing rights, recognition, and redress to address the multiple forms of marginalization that Afro-Brazilians have endured, media has become an increasingly important sphere through which different constituencies mobilize to advance a project of racial equality.[1] Among these groups enlisting available media resources was a group composed predominately of Afro-Brazilian media professionals who joined together to launch the TV da Gente (Our TV) television network, Brazil's first television station with the mission to produce racially diverse programming directed toward a Black viewing audience. They launched the network on November 20, 2005, Brazil's National Day of Black Consciousness, which celebrates and honors Afro-Brazilians and the life of Zumbi dos Palmares. Zumbi led a group of fugitive slaves and was captured and killed by the Portuguese on November 20, 1695. TV da Gente's launch on this day forged for its initiators a symbolic connection between historic and contemporary sources of critical Black resistance to hegemonic forces that sought to marginalize or erase the presence of Blackness within the country.

Scholars of television and communication have examined both Black- and majority-owned network television as a complex, complicated, and dynamic site of Black cultural politics in the United States.[2] This chapter expands upon these studies to examine the issue of racial representation within the Brazilian national and cultural context. It seeks to embed media production within narratives of race and nation as well as within both the mediated and material conditions of racial inequality in Brazil. The presence of televisual Blackness on mainstream networks was, and continues to be, limited in the amount of and portrayal of Afro-Brazilian characters, themes, and experiences. An ideology of racial democracy that deemphasized racial inequality in Brazil allowed the issues of Black representation to remain marginal and ignored within many areas of life, including television.

Projects of Black antiracism are mobilizing on all available fronts, including the mass media, to call attention to the ways in which minority groups, particularly Afro-Brazilians, are represented within the public sphere. I analyze the relationship between commercial media and social activism in Brazil by focusing on television as not only an object of activist critique but also the site for diverse media producers to enact a politics of representation to produce their own images. Although a short-lived television project, TV da Gente presents a case to understand media production as an activist project that calls attention to the ways in which Afro-Brazilians have been represented and, in turn, how Afro-Brazilians create visual images in order to represent themselves. I argue that media producers at TV da Gente constitute a set of new social actors in the struggle for racial equality in Brazil. They create images that challenge the aesthetic dimensions of racism.

Racial Democracy and Mediated Racism

Brazil has historically been characterized as a racial democracy where racial miscegenation between the African, Portuguese, and Native Indian populations is thought to have blurred the color line between discrete racial categories.[3] Gilberto Freyre has been credited as the main architect of the racial democracy ideology, setting forth its blueprint in his book *The Masters and the Slaves*, published in 1933. In this book, he argued that during the colonial period "a widely practiced miscegenation tended to modify the enormous social distance that otherwise would have been preserved between Big House and tropical forest, between Big House and slave hut."[4] Freyre advanced and popularized the idea that race mixture produced more democratic relations between the foundational groups of the Brazilian population, which informed the so-called absence of racial discrimination and racism between white Brazilians and those of color. This centralization of racial mixture within the national narrative of belonging casts racial mixture as part of every Brazilian's background and inheritance. A widely held belief in racial democracy has underwritten the state's and general public's inattention to racial inequality by denying the very existence of this inequality and the existence of discrete racial groups. Today, many Brazilians will dismiss attempts to point out racial discrimination with the assertion that everyone is mixed in the country.

A general silence around race and racial inequality sustains the idea of racial democracy within everyday Brazilian life and social interaction.[5] Anthropologist Robin Sheriff identifies the silence around racism as "cultural censorship" through which "the avoidance of open discussions on racism is directed toward the containment of racialized oppression."[6] A palpable silence about race pervades quotidian encounters between Brazilians of all colors through their avoidance of or refusal to voice experiences of racism, accuse others of racist actions, or draw attention to the unequal distribution of resources and opportunities along racial lines. This silence directs attention away from the empirical conditions of racial inequality within the country, leaving many Brazilians with the ability to maintain the belief that racism is less severe or nonexistent.

In contrast to this national ideology of racial democracy, scholars within a variety of disciplines have produced studies demonstrating consistent patterns of inequality along racial lines in Brazil. Some of the social indicators of racial discrimination include unequal compensation for work, discrimination in the labor force, increased attention from the police, residential segregation, low political representation, and a higher infant mortality rate.[7] Indeed, Afro-Brazilians experience decreased social opportunities for upward mobility and inequitable access to economic resources. Inequality and marginalization do have a color in Brazil, and it is Black. Yet the vast amounts of academic scholarship produced both within Brazil and internationally have done little to publicly puncture the veil of racial democracy that has become entrenched within Brazilian culture and daily life.

The mainstream media constitutes an area that activists and scholars have targeted as a space of racism and racial discrimination.[8] Afro-Brazilians are either conspicuously absent or marginally present within the visual images that circulate through the mediated public sphere. In a country that many say has the largest Black population outside of Africa, white Brazilians continuously dominate within mainstream media representations. For example, Xuxa, a blond Brazilian woman of German descent, has become nationally and internationally renowned for her popular children's television program. Her popularity promotes a white ideal of beauty, femininity, and success that invests whiteness with considerable power through mass mediation.[9] In 2001, Jacques D'Adesky analyzed the soap operas that aired on the TV Globo network from 1993 until 1997 and found that only 7.9 percent of the 830 actors and actresses that appeared were black or brown.[10] Carlos Hasenbalg and Nelson do Valle Silva note, "The number of white, blond, blue-eyed models appearing in [Brazilian] publications makes one think more of Sweden than Brazil."[11]

Not only is the absence of Afro-Brazilians indicative of televisual racism, but also the ways in which they are marginally present through limited and stereotypical roles evidence another form of exclusion on mainstream television. Within the soap operas (novelas), a popular staple of Brazilian prime-time television entertainment, Afro-Brazilians are consistently cast in the roles of service providers, such as cooks, maids, and chauffeurs. Of the several novelas offered nightly, one is generally set during the colonial period and includes several Afro-Brazilian actors cast as enslaved men and women. Other novelas present Afro-Brazilians as residents of favelas, the poor neighborhoods found in many of Brazil's major cities. Joel Zito Araújo conducted an extensive analysis of the role of Afro-Brazilians within the novelas on the Globo television network.[12] He found that when Afro-Brazilians interpret roles of middle-class professionals, they are rarely shown with a connection to other Afro-Brazilians as either family or friends, nor does the storyline include any racism that they may face or have encountered within their work or daily life. If Afro-Brazilians are present within a television show, they generally portray characters at the margins of society or upwardly mobile characters that lack depth.

Within their narratives, soap operas in Brazil will typically integrate relevant, timely, or contemporary social themes, such as electoral politics, disability, illness, sexuality, or poverty. Occasionally, they will attempt to represent the issue of racism as a social ill within Brazilian life. *Duas Caras* (Two Faces), a soap opera broadcast on TV Globo from October 2007 to May 2008, included the issue of racism within its storyline. This soap opera has been labeled the first to include an Afro-Brazilian hero, in the central role of Evilásio, played by Lazaro Ramos. The storyline focuses on Evilásio's election to a political position within the favela in which he resides, as well as his romance with and marriage to Júlia, the wealthy white daughter of a racist businessman. When dating, Evilásio encountered racism from Júlia's father, who hurled derogatory names at him and professed hatred for Black people. However, the father changed his attitude after Evilásio won the election. The novela attempts to represent the problem of racism within Brazil through the dialogue, relationships, and encounters of many of the characters, contributing to, and in some ways complicating, the public discussion of race relations.[13] However, mimicking past attempts to address racism within soap operas, *Duas Caras* presents racial mixture as a remedy for racism in Brazil, thus reinforcing the belief that miscegenation ameliorates social distance between Blacks and whites through the relationship of Evilásio and Júlia.[14]

Afro-Brazilian activists have organized to draw attention to the conditions of racial inequality in Brazilian society.[15] Through the Movimento Negro Unificado (Unified Black Movement) and a diversity of other organizations, they have held rallies, marches, and meetings to both raise consciousness about the nature of racism in Brazil and suggest ways to produce a more equitable environment.[16] An activist within the Black movement in Rio de Janeiro connects the racism within the mass media to the idea of racial democracy: "The mass communication media, principally television today, are fundamental instruments of this racial ideology, this ideology of racial discrimination—because you can see very well that all the concepts that work, all the images that are put forth, are stereotypical white images. And the negro, where is he in this question? When they show negros they are always *favelados*; they show them doing domestic service, clearly implying that the negro is incapable of doing anything else."[17] This Black movement activist draws a connection between the idea of racial democracy that implies racial equality and the contradictory images within the mass media that reveal the claims of racial democracy to be false. He articulates an understanding of racism in the media that is similar to Stuart's Hall's idea of inferential racism. Hall defines this as "those apparently naturalized representations of events and situations relating to race, whether 'factual' or 'fictional,' which have racist premises and propositions inscribed in them as a set of *unquestioned assumptions*."[18] The conspicuous absence or marginal presence of Afro-Brazilians remains largely unquestioned by the public and television industry and thus continues to support the idea of "the place" of Afro-Brazilians within public and everyday life.

Brazilian televisual images that continue to represent white middle-class interests and subject positions are made within television networks that hire few Afro-Brazilians as producers or writers. Herman Gray argues that the presence of a small but influential group of African American producers, writers, directors, and talent within the U.S. television industry helped create programs with more complex renderings of Black experiences, characters, stories, and themes.[19] In comparison, Afro-Brazilians employed by television networks commonly work within positions that have no control over or relation to the content of the programs or their storylines.[20] An Afro-Brazilian woman who worked for TV da Gente as a director referred to her experience working for a mainstream television talk show: "Until now I forgot that I was Black. I always worked with whites, always worked with other issues . . . My path didn't have many successful Blacks, and even fewer Black women. Television is very difficult."[21] Working in the mainstream Brazilian media, she did not encounter many Black professionals, specifically Black female media professionals. Few Afro-Brazilian students are enrolled within journalism or media production programs, leaving the pipeline to these professions inadequately populated to produce a critical mass of Afro-Brazilian media professionals. Afro-Brazilians have not had the same kinds of opportunities as African Americans to exercise creative control over the media images and narratives on mainstream network television.

The few Afro-Brazilian media professionals who do work within the mainstream media have considerable difficulty integrating their own ideas for content into the media vehicle. My interviews demonstrate that they experience censorship from their supervisors or do not have the space to propose content that discusses race and racism or represents Afro-Brazilians in different ways. One Black media worker for a mainstream magazine said that her editors would reject her ideas to write stories featuring Afro-Brazilians for placement within the general pages or fashion spreads. Her positioning attests to a systemic inability for Afro-Brazilians to incorporate Black issues or concerns in media products. Limited images of Afro-Brazilians continue to dominate due to the dearth of Afro-Brazilians who have control over mainstream media production, the racist conditions of working within the media for Afro-Brazilian media workers, and the cultural silence that surrounds issues of race and racism. These conditions prompted several Afro-Brazilian media workers to found their own television network to counter the kinds of Afro-Brazilian images that saturate the Brazilian public sphere.

From Racial Democracy to Racial Recognition

The relatively recent governmental support for programs to address racial inequality has spurred contemporary debates surrounding the appropriate measures to recognize racial distinctions and redress historically marginalized populations. TV da Gente emerged within this current process of transition as Brazil moves from racial democracy to the recognition of racism and racial inequality. The election of

Fernando Cardoso as president in 1995 was a political turning point for racial politics in Brazil. He openly acknowledged the existence of racism in Brazil and instituted governmental policies to combat the issue. The Brazilian government sponsored a delegation of antiracism activists in 2001 to the Third World Conference on Racism, Racial Discrimination, Xenophobia, and Related Intolerance in Durban, South Africa. Within this international context, the delegation was able to make demands for policies such as affirmative action to combat racial inequality in Brazil.[22] President Cardoso signed the National Program for Affirmative Action in May 2002, which "proposed federal administrative mechanisms to promote disadvantaged populations but did not set any quotas or goals."[23]

Elected in 2003, President Luiz Inácio "Lula" da Silva continued the momentum to enact policies and programs to address racial inequality. He signed Law 10.639, which requires elementary schools to include information about Afro-Brazilian and African history and culture within their curriculum. This law also designates November 20 a federal holiday celebrating Black consciousness and Zumbi dos Palmares. He created the Secretariat for Promoting Policies of Racial Inclusion (SEPPIR) and appointed Matilde Ribeiro, a Black woman and leader within the Workers Party, as its minister.

This governmental action has unleashed an unprecedented level of discussion within the academy, news media, and school classrooms about the appropriate ways to acknowledge racial difference and viable strategies to overcome racial inequality. The support from the state provides many Black movement activists with public platforms and monetary support to fund and promote initiatives surrounding race relations. TV da Gente participated within this dynamic movement for racial rights and recognition by attending to the televisual terrain of racial hegemony and, through its actions, pursuing strategies to fairly represent Afro-Brazilians and other Brazilians of color.

The TV da Gente Television Network

José de Paulo Neto, commonly known as Netinho, acquired the capital and assembled a team of media producers to carry out his vision of erecting a television network that would produce representations of Brazil's racially diverse population and represent Afro-Brazilians in different ways than mainstream media had done. Netinho is an Afro-Brazilian celebrity who rose to prominence singing pagode, a form of samba, with the musical group Negritude Júnior (Junior Blackness). He also had his own television programs on mainstream television networks, including *Dia de Princesa* (Princess for a Day), and continues to perform in Brazil. Netinho aimed for TV da Gente to remedy the racial imbalance on mainstream Brazilian television, stating: "Our country is marked by racial mixtures. But the actual model of TV does not represent the majority of Brazilians. We are trying to help our own people, given that nobody else seems to want to do it. This is where the real fight starts."[24]

Figure 13.1   TV da Gente logo. Frame grab.

The TV da Gente television network developed from resources both inside and outside of Brazil. Netinho acquired money to start the fledgling network from Angolan investors and obtained television programs produced on the Black Family Channel of the U.S. to be dubbed into Portuguese and distributed on TV da Gente.[25] He gathered together media professionals from around the city of São Paulo to create and produce a series of programs in Brazil.

The name TV da Gente does not explicitly refer to racial identity or Blackness in the way that the United States' Black Entertainment Television includes the label "Black" in its name, situating Black audiences and content as central to its representational mission.[26] The name TV da Gente has been translated to "Our TV" in international newspaper articles. It can also be translated as "TV of the People." This ambiguous title that does not explicitly refer to race would possibly enable the network to navigate the complicated racial terrain in Brazil, characterized by a shift from racial democracy to racial recognition.

TV da Gente opened to national attention and international coverage from the press in countries including the United States and England. Many of the international and domestic media framed the network as a response to televisual racism in Brazil and embedded it within contemporary actions for racial equality. However, the network also received accusations of racism within Brazil from various journalists and commentators. For example, journalist Flavio Porcella stated, "I think it's legitimate that a channel specialize in sports, politics, sex, religion and any other type of segmentation. I don't agree with a channel segmented for race, color, or religion. Therefore, this means racial discrimination for me." Porcella then asked, "If people are equal independent of color, why does a television channel show only people of one color?"[27] In Brazil, policies and programs enacted to target one segment of the population based on historical and contemporary exclusion can be met with the charge of racism or are thought to heighten the problems of racism, not remedy them. These allegations of racism can work to challenge the actions of antiracist organizations by casting them as harbingers of racism and racial inequality, rather than as catalysts for racial equality.

During one of my interviews with the executive producer of TV da Gente, Paula Moura,[28] she responded to these accusations of racism by saying that "the Brazilian media called us racist without looking in the mirror because all of the other networks are extremely racist and don't think that they are." Furthermore, Moura stated that TV da Gente's "objective was really to show Black people, because if Black people see themselves they will have more pride in themselves. Our greatest problem is self-esteem." The executive producer claimed that the other mainstream television networks neglected to include Afro-Brazilians within their programming in sufficient numbers as well as within meaningful and significant roles. The dearth of Black representations motivated her to become affiliated with TV da Gente in order to produce representations that affirmed Blackness for the Brazilian viewing population. She thought that the presence of Black people on television would provoke feelings of self-esteem and pride for many Afro-Brazilian television viewers.

I will focus on some of the programs locally produced by the TV da Gente media team in order to examine the ways in which they created a televisual presence for Afro-Brazilian subjects, concerns, and people. They came up with a variety of ideas for programming that followed mainstream television shows' formats but included Afro-Brazilians within the central positions of program production and conception, as well as program hosts and presenters. The network featured a children's program, a talk show, a news program, a sports program, a program about civil rights and civic action, a game show for schoolchildren, a samba show, and a hip hop show. These programs composed the local lineup of Brazilian television shows that were made in Portuguese and filmed around the city of São Paulo or within the TV da Gente studio.

The children's television program was called *Turminha da Hora* (Class Hour) and hosted by Cinthya Rachel, a former child star and current entertainer. The show featured various musical performances, and Rachel would introduce them to the viewing audience. The program also featured Afro-Brazilian journalist Oswaldo Faustino, who interpreted the character of Tio Bah (Uncle Bah). Tio Bah lived in a Bao Bao tree, one commonly found in East Africa with a distinctive shape of a wide trunk and several thinner branches sprouting upward out of it. This tree emblematized an African origin and its continued cultural significance for contemporary Afro-Brazilian creative expression. Tio Bah would tell allegorical stories to children, intended to communicate a particular lesson or illustrate positive values and behavior. The character of Tio Bah incorporated the idea of African orality through the act of instructing children by telling stories. This children's program valued a Black or multicultural aesthetic as an example for children's entertainment.

The network's game show featured students from two different schools in competition to give the most correct answers to questions regarding African and Afro-Brazilian history and culture. An Afro-Brazilian man and a Japanese woman hosted the show, which was called *Quem Sabe Clica!* (Who Knows Clicks!). The winning team would win a computer for their school. Some of the questions included:

> An engineer from the Brazilian state of Bahia, son of a slave, born in Bom Jardim, municipality of Santo Amaro (BA), on January 7, 1855. He planned major infrastructure works and buildings in the city of São Paulo. Today a street there is named after him. Answer: Teodoro Sampaio.

> This country was a colony of Belgium. It was freed in 1960, and among the heroes of independence was Patrice Lumumba. What's its name now? Answer: Zaire.

The questions' subject material ranged from Afro-Brazilian historical figures to Afro-Brazilian cultural products and festivals to African and African Diaspora history and culture. The questions were meant to test the knowledge of the students and educate them and the viewers about this particular subject matter neglected within many Brazilian school curriculums. The creators of the program intended for it to contribute to Law 10.639, the one requiring African and Afro-Brazilian history and culture within classroom lessons. By considering this law within their television programming content, the TV da Gente media producers extended this legislation into the area of the mass media, thus linking a political and representational commitment to Black visibility and equality.

Questão de Direitos (Question of Rights) was hosted by Dr. Hédio Silva, a Black civil rights lawyer and activist in the city of São Paulo. Through this program, the producers intended to inform viewers of their rights and showcase others taking civic action to improve their communities and neighborhoods. For example, Silva interviewed a disability rights activist who advocated for increased access to buildings and public facilities for disabled men and women. Silva's presence on the show provided an example to viewers of a successful lawyer and advocate who speaks out in support of programs and initiatives that support the Black community. The guests on the show were also examples of those who would take action to improve social conditions for all Brazilian citizens.

These programs were all created by the TV da Gente media production team and executed by the network workers. They chose to cast Afro-Brazilian personalities and leaders within the roles of hosts and presenters to privilege their position as central to programmatic control and authority. By including other groups as well, such as the Japanese female host of the game show, they wanted to signal that the network also aimed to showcase the ethnic diversity of Brazil and representationally account for the country's many different groups and people. Through their program production, they sought to fairly represent Afro-Brazilians, as well as other racial and ethnic populations in Brazil, in ways that mainstream television had not already done.

Conclusion

The TV da Gente television network ceased to produce and broadcast programs in the city of São Paulo in 2007 due to its inability to secure a consistent source of funding from advertisers. The network attracted so few viewers that the audience numbers could not be tracked through any formal means or institution. Of the many white and nonwhite Brazilians with whom I spoke and interacted, very few people had heard of the network and no one had watched the programs. This makes it difficult, if not impossible, to access the reception of the network and its creative content. Rather, TV da Gente presents a unique opportunity to examine the role of television and visual culture within movements for racial equality in Brazil. By creating a television network with the mission to racially diversify its content and presenters, the TV da Gente team developed a site for televisual resistance to the racist conditions of image circulation within the Brazilian public sphere. Their acts of program creation and dissemination mobilized the very medium of their marginalization to imagine, invent, and distribute oppositional images to those within the public sphere, thus creating a televisual presence that is meaningful and affirming of Black people, experiences, and culture.

The very act of creating and publicizing a television network with the intention to produce representations along racial lines runs against the grain of racial democracy, which promotes the belief that every Brazilian is mixed, making it impossible to delineate distinct racial groups. The producers' speaking candidly and openly about the dearth of Black racial representations on television and their desire to change this mediated landscape of whiteness also resists the silencing mechanisms of the racial democracy and the idea that racism is not a legitimate topic of conversation or argument. Although they were working to "break the silence" around racism in Brazil and pioneer viable strategies to overcome it, they did not avoid the criticism of racism by the press and public. These accusations of racism are emblematic of the continued hold that the idea of racial democracy has in Brazil and demonstrates that ideologies and national narratives do not easily fade away in the face of fervent opposition.

Although the Brazilian national narrative of racial democracy purports to include all citizens equally, business ownership and management remain largely in the hands of white Brazilians. Netinho's decision to invent, organize, and finance the TV da Gente television network draws attention to the critical need for Black business and industry ownership in order to create spaces in which people committed to racial equality can carry out their work. Given the small number of Black media producers and the friction they face working in many mainstream media organizations, these kinds of places can have an important role in providing equitable access to the means of representation and visual production. This network confronted the structural and institutional presence of racism within the television and media industry through its commitment to employ and support diverse media workers and their ideas.

By casting predominately Afro-Brazilian hosts and presenters and including content that referred to Black history and culture, TV da Gente distributed images that resisted and expanded past conscriptions of Afro-Brazilians as either invisible or as service workers, enslaved men and women, or other marginal roles. In this way, the media workers at TV da Gente extended the movement for racial equality in Brazil from the government and Black movement organizations to the arena of visual images and mass media by demanding to be seen in ways that they control. The media work and mission of the TV da Gente team created a new front in the fight for racial equality by targeting the aesthetics of power and domination to make visible what racial equality can look like.

NOTES

1. I refer to race not as a biological given but as a socially constructed category produced through historical and ideological processes.

2. See Christine Acham, *Revolution Televised: Prime Time and the Struggle for Black Power* (Minneapolis: University of Minnesota Press, 2004); Herman Gray, *Watching Race: Television and the Struggle for Blackness* (Minneapolis: University of Minnesota Press, 2004); Beretta E. Smith-Shomade, *Pimpin' Ain't Easy: Selling Black Entertainment Television* (New York: Routledge, 2007).

3. National narratives of racial mixture that include logics of exclusion are common to many nations within Latin America. For further analysis of such cases in different countries see, e.g., Viranjini Munasinghe, "Nationalism in Hybrid Spaces: The Production of Impurity out of Purity," *American Ethnologist* 29, no. 3 (2002): 663–692; Jean Muteba Rahier, "Mestizaje, Mulataje, Mestiçagem in Latin American Ideologies of National Identities," *Journal of Latin American Anthropology* 8, no. 1 (2003): 40–51; Ronald Stutzman, "El Mestizaje: An All-Inclusive Ideology of Exclusion," in *Cultural Transformations and Ethnicity in Modern Ecuador*, ed. Norman Whitten Jr. (Urbana: University of Illinois Press, 1981); Peter Wade, *Blackness and Race Mixture: The Dynamics of Racial Identity in Colombia* (Baltimore: Johns Hopkins University Press, 1993).

4. Gilberto Freyre, *The Masters and the Slaves: A Study of Development of Brazilian Civilization* (1933; New York: Alfred E. Knopf, 1944), 5.

5. Scholars have demonstrated that the Brazilian racial democracy is a complex social project maintained through a variety of social and cultural mechanisms. See Donna Goldstein, "'Interracial' Sex and Racial Democracy in Brazil: Twin Concepts?" *American Anthropologist* 101, no. 3 (1999): 563–578; Thomas Skidmore, "Race and Class in Brazil: Historical Perspectives," in *Race, Class, and Power in Brazil*, ed. Pierre-Michel Fontaine (Los Angeles: Center for Afro-American Studies, 1985), 11–24; Kia Lilly Caldwell, *Negras in Brazil: Re-Envisioning Black Women, Citizenship, and the Politics of Identity* (New Brunswick, NJ: Rutgers University Press, 2007).

6. Robin Sheriff, "Exposing Silence as Cultural Censorship: A Brazilian Case," *American Anthropologist* 102, no. 1 (2000): 121.

7. Peggy Lovell, "Development and the Persistence of Racial Inequality in Brazil, 1950–1991," *Journal of Developing Areas* 33, no. 3 (1999): 395–418; Carlos Hasenbalg, "Racial and Socioeconomic Inequalities in Brazil," in *Race, Class, and Power in Brazil*, ed. Pierre-Michel Fontaine (Los Angeles: Center for Afro-American Studies, UCLA, 1985); Nelson do Valle Silva, "Updating the Cost of Not Being White in Brazil," ibid., 25–55. Michael J. Mitchell and Charles H. Wood, "Ironies of Citizenship: Skin Color, Police Brutality, and the Challenge to Democracy in Brazil," *Social Forces* 77, no. 3 (1999): 1001–1020; Edward Telles, "Residential Segregation by Skin Color in Brazil," *American Sociological Review* 57, no. 2 (1992): 186–197; Ollie A. Johnson III, "Racial Representation and Brazilian Politics: Black Members of the National Congress, 1983–1999," *Journal of Interamerican Studies and World Affairs* 40, no. 4 (1998): 97–118.

8. Silvia Ramos, ed., *Mídia e racismo* (Rio de Janeiro: Pallas Editora e Distruidora, 2002); Michael Leslie, "The Representation of Blacks on Commercial Television in Brazil: Some Cultivation Effects," in *Black Brazil: Culture, Identity and Social Mobilization*, ed. Larry Crook and Randal Johnson (Los Angeles: UCLA Latin American Center Publications, University of California, 1999), pages 368–375; Muniz Sodré, *Claros e escuros: identidade, povo e mídia no Brasil* (Petropolis: Vozes, 1999).

9. Amelia Simpson, *Xuxa: The Mega-Marketing of Gender, Race, and Modernity* (Philadelphia: Temple University Press, 1993).

10. Jacques D'Adesky, *Pluralismo étnico e multiculturalismo: racismos e anti-racismos no Brasil* (Rio de Janeiro: Pallas, 2001).

11. Carlos Hasenbalg and Nelson do Valle Silva, "As imagens do negro na publicidade," in *Estrutura social, mobilidade e raça* (São Paulo: Edições Vértice, 1988), 200.

12. Joel Zito Araujo, *A negação do Brasil: o negro na telenovela brasileira* (São Paulo: Editora SENAC São Paulo, 2000).

13. Samantha Nogueira Joyce, "Race Matters: Race, Telenovela Representation, and Discourse in Contemporary Brazil" (PhD dissertation, University of Iowa, 2010).

14. Solange Martins Couceiro de Lima, "A personagem negra na telenovela brasileira: alguns momentos," *Revista USP* 48 (2000–2001): 88–99.

15. Michael Hanchard, *Orpheus and Power: The Movimento Negro of Rio de Janeiro and São Paulo, Brazil, 1945–1988* (Princeton: Princeton University Press, 1994).

16. Many activists within the Unified Black Movement think they cannot gain a following because of the people's failure to connect their condition of poverty with racial discrimination and a history of slavery. John Burdick notes that activists' insistence that their followers claim a Black (negro) identity as opposed to a mixed-race identity may also hinder their attempts at antiracist mobilization in "The Lost Constituency of Brazil's Black Consciousness Movements," *Latin American Perspectives* 98, no. 2 (1998): 136–55.

17. Robin Sheriff, *Dreaming Equality: Color, Race, and Racism in Urban Brazil* (New Brunswick: Rutgers University Press, 2001) 196.

18. Stuart Hall, "The Whites of Their Eyes: Racist Ideologies and the Media," in *The Media Reader* ed. Manuel Alvarado and John O. Thompson (London: British Film Institute, 1990), 13.

19. Herman Gray, "The Politics of Representation in Network Television," in *Channeling Blackness: Studies on Television and Race in America*, ed. Darnell M. Hunt (New York: Oxford University Press, 2005), 155–174.

20. Flávio Carrança and Rosane da Silva Borges, *Espelho infiel: o negro no jornalismo brasileiro* (Rio de Janeiro: Editora Selo Negro, 2004).

21. Personal interview with a director at TV da Gente on March 1, 2007.

22. Mala Htun, "From 'Racial Democracy' to Affirmative Action: Changing State Policy on Race in Brazil," *Latin American Research Review* 39, no. 1 (2004): 60–89.

23. Edward Telles, *Race in Another America: The Significance of Skin Color in Brazil* (Princeton: Princeton University Press, 2004), 73.

24. Tom Phillips, "Brazil's First Black Television Channel Tackles Legacy of 300 Years of Slavery," *Guardian*, November 21, 2005.

25. [Editor's note: This is yet another example of why discussions circulating around the viability of African-American televisual and filmic production to move beyond domestic markets are false. See work done on this subject by Timothy Havens in this volume and elsewhere.]

26. I would like to thank Joshua Roth for bringing this to my attention.

27. Ana Maria Brambilla, "Black TV Channel Ignites Ire in Brazil," *OhMyNews*, January 16, 2006.

28. This is a pseudonym to protect the identity of my research participants. The interview was conducted on March 28, 2007.

14   South African Soapies

A "RAINBOW NATION" REALIZED?

NSENGA K. BURTON

In the United States, daytime soap operas are often critiqued as escapist fantasies with narratives that provide leisure and pleasure for middle-class and stay-at-home mothers. The storylines typically involve forbidden sexual liaisons and business relationships, with physical and psychological behaviors that center on powerful families. One family unit usually represents "old money" while the other family represents "new money" or an upwardly mobile group with aspirations of power, status, and influence. The economic differences are usually the source of conflict between the families, around which all other social relationships develop. The temporal space expands and contracts to accommodate storylines, which are marked by repetition. It is the repetitive nature of the genre that allows viewers to stay connected to the characters and the storyline no matter when they decide to interact with the visual text.

South African soap operas have taken the dominant characteristics of U.S. soap operas and infused them with issues of social justice in their narrative constructs. While the narrative elements of the genre are very similar, specifically the centrality of families and the struggle over power and influence, South African soap operas, affectionately known as soapies, are decidedly different in how they incorporate issues of social justice into their narratives and the speed at which this occurs. Social issues that have been incorporated into the narratives include HIV/AIDS, sexual behavior, birth control, discrimination, inequality, homosexuality, social rejection, and exclusion. These issues are deconstructed through narratives that address struggles over language, power, and meaning.

The incorporation of issues of social justice is not necessarily due to a higher consciousness of writers, producers, and network executives. Instead, soap operas are part of the programming of the South African Broadcasting Corporation (SABC), a state-owned broadcaster with a public service mandate. SABC was previously the mouthpiece of the Nationalist Party, an apparatus of the state if you will, whose mission was to help maintain the system of apartheid in the country. The corporation was reimagined in 1993, one year before the historic elections marking the end of apartheid in South Africa and the election of former political prisoner and iconic activist Nelson Mandela as president of the country. A new board was voted into power, albeit under the old regime. With the election looming, the current board of the SABC and the African National Congress (ANC) agreed not to use SABC as a mouthpiece for either party.

As part of the "new" SABC, the mission was to use media, including entertainment programming, to promote Bishop Desmond Tutu's "Rainbow Nation"—a concept that envisioned people of all colors living peacefully together with equal access to aspirational devices. While SABC and its relationship to the ANC-controlled government has been heavily critiqued since those historic elections, the mission of using media to reimagine South Africa as a democratic society and as a tool for nation building has continued, particularly in the soap opera genre. Using the South African soap operas *Isidingo* and *Generations* (not to be confused with the now defunct U.S. soap opera of the same title), this chapter will explore how the "Rainbow Nation" mandate is reflected in the narratives of soapies and why the democratic potential of the genre trumps the relationship of SABC with the government.

South African Broadcasting

In order to understand the integral role of SABC in the lives of South Africans, and thus South African soap operas, it is important to examine the development history of the broadcaster and its use to reinforce dominant ideologies about race relations. SABC was established in 1936 as South Africa's national broadcaster. It was modeled along the lines of the British Broadcasting Corporation (BBC), except that it was to serve dominant white interests. The SABC was to conduct programming in English and Afrikaans (a Dutch and German mix) and advance the interests of the English and Afrikaners. The Broadcasting Act gave the governor-general the authority to appoint members of the SABC Board of Control with the stipulation that the board be comprised of nine members, roughly half English and half Afrikaans speakers.[1] This was before the rise of the Afrikaner Nationalist Party and the formal institutionalization of apartheid as the official policy of government and race relations in South Africa.[2] Even though the English and Afrikaners could not agree on how to best enact this mandate, they could agree that Black South Africans were to be shut out of broadcasting altogether.

In 1945, in cooperation with the Department of Native Affairs, SABC developed a separate radio channel specifically for Black South Africans. It was a single-channel service via wire and posted loudspeakers to compounds, hostels, and residences in some Black townships. The purpose of the channel was to entertain, educate, and exercise social control. The service was developed to "orient the emergent urban black labor force to the dominant ideology," although it was shut down shortly after it started. Nevertheless, it was revived again in 1952 under the name Radio Bantu.[3] Thus when the Nationalist Party rose to power in 1948, broadcasting was already fully within the control of the English and Afrikaners. This laid the foundation for SABC to become an ideological tool for the Nationalist Party.

Once de facto segregation had been established under apartheid, SABC's role was seen as the "defender of the apartheid state and propagator of its separate development policies." Furthermore, in 1960, a Broadcasting Amendment created an "equal but separate" structure for the administration of Black programs. For example, the government began subsidizing program production for Radio Bantu and placed it under a separate administrative structure with thirty-five white supervisors, mostly linguists and anthropologists, controlling output.[4] South African soap operas developed under the National Party's segregationist policies that outlined what could be shown on television. Interestingly, the rise of the National Party coincided with the invention and subsequent mass production of television. In South Africa, broadcasting's state-run status enabled television stations, like radio stations before, to be used as a tool for promoting principles of ethnicity and ethnic loyalty.

SABC and Soap Operas

The first South African soap operas arrived on television in the 1990s and were almost exclusively white.[5] They were created specifically for female audiences. The timeslots for the initial screening were late afternoon or early evening, but they were broadcast multiple times throughout the day, allowing housewives and working women to view them. Advertisements that aired during the soap opera were for products targeting women, including shampoo, retail chain stores, and time-specific commercials for Mother's Day or Christmas. The themes for soap operas centered on presumed "feminine interests" such as the family and romantic love.[6]

South African soap operas are narratively very similar to U.S. soap operas that originated during de facto segregation. Both present middle-class and wealthy whites as the standard with a focus on family and feminine interests. Tania Modleski's observation that soap operas were "visual, narrative art" specifically developed for women is more complicated when examined through a sociopolitical lens.[7] The absence of soap operas from earlier Nationalist Party television programming was likely due to the party's inability to fathom how a "woman-centered" genre could further the aims of its apartheid-era social and economic policies. White women were superior to all nonwhite races but were still considered subordinate and inferior to white men.

Even though soap operas have been critiqued by feminists as satisfying stereotypical representations of women,[8] one could also reason that the focus on housewives and the desires of white women had as much to do with promoting dominant ideologies about race as it did gender relations in the United States. While U.S. soap operas promote and transform national "ideologies" or mythologies, South African soap operas "metamorphise the political processes that are marking the country's transition from apartheid, becoming striking political documents in genres usually known for their apolitical insistence."[9]

Soap operas in general and in South Africa specifically have always been seen as a vehicle to model social relationships for viewers while serving as a tool for social control and, subsequently, social change.

Although soap operas were introduced as a genre to broadcasting after the fall of the Nationalist Party and before the rise of the ANC, in working through the transfer of power, the ANC and National Party agreed that SABC needed to be "reconstituted" as an independent broadcaster. This included a new board that had to "reflect society as a whole, taking into account its gender, geographic and social composition." The emergence of South African soap operas featuring multiracial casts coincided with this period. *Egoli: Place of Gold* debuted in 1992 and is South Africa's first soap opera. It aired on the Electronic Media Network (M-Net), a subscription television service established in 1986 by a consortium of newspapers. M-Net was controlled by Naspers, an Afrikaner company that granted its license "in perpetuity," enabling the mostly white cast of English and Afrikaans language to exist, long unfettered.[10]

Additionally, in 1993, the Independent Broadcasting Authority Act was introduced. This radical piece of legislation established an independent regulatory authority to ensure the development of three levels of broadcasting (public, private, and community), encourage ownership and control of broadcasting services by persons from historically disadvantaged groups, act as an antitrust watchdog, and recognize the importance of developing local South African program content. Most importantly for this chapter, it called for the "provision of a diverse range of sound and television broadcast services on national, regional, and local levels, 'which when viewed collectively, cater for all language and cultural groups.'"[11] With gender and racial equality identified as issues that needed to be addressed in SABC and in its programming, the landscape was ripe for the introduction and success of the soap opera genre.

Generations

In 1993, SABC 1 launched *Generations* in response to a mandate calling for the production of a soap opera that would "depict the needs, dreams and aspirations of Black South Africans" by portraying them as "prosperous living and working alongside white, coloured and Indian South Africans." It was a multicultural and multilingual production intended to "evoke and endorse 'multiracialism'" as a range of social ideals, in anticipation of South Africa's first democratic elections.[12] South Africa had yet to elect Nelson Mandela as president, so this initiative reflected a collective consciousness to work toward Tutu's concept—one further embraced and promoted during President Mandela's administration.

SABC 1 broadcasts in isiZulu, isiXhosa, Tshivenda, and isiNdebele (all Nguni languages) and English. There are two other free channels—SABC 2 and SABC 3—and a pay channel, SABC Africa. Each has a flagship soap opera, and *Generations* is SABC 1's flagship. It is not only the most-watched soap opera but also the most-watched program of any genre in South Africa, with five million viewers. It is also the longest-running soap opera, suggesting that it delivers audiences to broadcasters, the ultimate goal of soap operas, along with successfully implementing and satisfying the mandate of reflecting a free and democratic South Africa and its citizens. Initially, *Generations* had a multiracial cast, which was mandated for all soap operas on all three channels, including *Isidingo*, which will be discussed later. Interestingly, the mandate of *Generations* shifted to require an all-Black cast. So the initial multiracial cast was written out in order to appeal to a younger, Black demographic. *Generations* was given the mandate to "represent a (fictional) reality that would endorse a clear-cut aspirational model for young Black South Africans."[13]

Generations' move from a multicultural cast and setting to an all-Black cast and setting corresponded with the election of Thabo Mbeki, Mandela's successor. Mbeki moved away from Tutu and Mandela's "Rainbow Nation" vision to one of embracing one's "Africanness." Identity politics, specifically the "re-assertion of race," was seen as a particular feature of Mbeki's presidency.[14] His focus on an African identity and the need to foster a new view of Africa as a continent reflected the idea of an "African Renaissance," which was to counter the local, national, and international media's depiction of Africa as a troubled, tribal, and dispossessed continent. This more "Africanist" vision was in opposition to former president Mandela's policy of reconciliation between Blacks and whites that deemphasized race.

Generations began to reflect an aspirational model that represented social and economic pursuits of Blacks embodied in the Black Economic Empowerment

Figure 14.1   Nandipha (Hlubi Mboya) on *Isidingo*. Frame grab.

Act (BEE) of 2003, a strategy to address inequality within the South African economy.[15] This was achieved by ensuring that historically disadvantaged, low-income South African workers would have a meaningful stake in South Africa's economy through various programs and initiatives. The BEE was endorsed by the ANC and Mbeki, becoming a controversial government policy arguably tied to a specific political agenda. SABC's intent to redress the damage and injustices inflicted by apartheid and its legacies through the soap opera became more in line with the political party in power, specifically the ANC. This undermined the repurposing of SABC as an independent entity postapartheid. Yet in spite of the changes in presidential administrations, *Generations* still successfully incorporated issues of social justice and nation building in its narratives.

Generations centers around media companies located in Johannesburg, South Africa. Karabo Moroka (Connie Masilo-Ferguson) inherits a media company, becoming quite wealthy in the process. Constantly at odds with competitor Sibusiso Dlomo (Menzi Motlhalaphuti Ngubane) of Afri-Media, the character of Karabo is interesting in that early on in the serial, she is engaged to a white man. When questioned by her white girlfriend about being involved in an interracial relationship, she responds that they like to call it a "nonracial" relationship. The storyline reflects the changes postapartheid South Africa was experiencing regarding race relations, ideas about racial purity, and rules of dating. Within two years of the end of apartheid, the soap opera introduced this interracial relationship between Black and white South Africans. The storyline and dialogue attempted to promote an idea of how unimportant race is in a country just out of a system of racial separation and superiority with a president who had been imprisoned for fighting against this system.

Generations presented a multiracial cast of Black, white, colored, and Indian South Africans working and living next to each other. While real life was slow to reflect societal changes postapartheid, soap operas imagined a multiracial society where people were equal regardless of race. There was conflict between the characters, but they were able to work through their issues through dialogue and action. Tutu's "Rainbow Nation" was more than a vision on this soap opera—it was a fictional reality that played a critical role in helping to realize Tutu and Mandela's dream for the country. Over the years, Karabo has had a range of lovers of various races. Her choice of lovers rejects dominant ideologies of racial purity.

While *Generations* is progressive on issues of race, the same cannot be said necessarily of gender; this is indicative of how aligning storylines and characters with political agendas or ideological visions can be complicated. On *Generations*, women are empowered as business owners, but the businesses fail or suffer under their leadership—that is, until they partner with a man to bring stability. For example, Karabo inherits New Horizons, an advertising agency, from her father, Archie (Sello Maake). The company was profitable under Archie's leadership but loses its footing in the market once Karabo takes it over. She is unable to cope with the demands of running the company, bringing in her lover Tau Mogale (Rapulana Seiphemo) to take over. When Tau leaves (dies), Karabo is again unable to handle the job, so she joins forces with rival Afri-Media to form Ezweni Communications.

Ezweni Communications' main competition has been Mashaba Media, headed by a woman, Dineo Mashaba (Katlego Danke), who took control from her husband after he suffered a stroke. Under Dineo's leadership, Mashaba Media faces financial ruin. In one scene, she cries hysterically to her brother-in-law about her inability to run the business and how she has destroyed it beyond salvage. She literally begs him to help her save Mashaba Media, which he does. While grieving, Dineo, who is unable to manage Mashaba Media, somehow manages to have an affair with her stepson, getting pregnant in the process. The other female characters of *Generations* are generally employed as secretaries or in service to men in business settings.

Moreover, women are portrayed continuously as duplicitous, emotionally unstable, fiscally irresponsible, and extremely poor business managers. They inherit positions of social status from men instead of earning them. The attempt to show women in roles traditionally designated for men, like those of company owners and presidents, is undermined by their stereotypical depictions as weak-willed and unable to manage a business or their personal lives without a man in charge. While the IBA mandate includes redressing sexism in the soap opera genre, little has been done to remedy problematic representations of women. This could be a reflection of the overwhelmingly male government and current President Jacob Zuma's flippant attitude about women. When being tried for rape in 2006, he remarked that as a Zulu man, he was "duty-bound" to oblige the woman, who was wearing a short skirt.[16] Just as Mandela's "Rainbow Nation" and Mbeki's "Africanist" vision were a major part of the narrative elements of soapies, Zuma's sexist beliefs are also reflected in the soap opera genre.

Isidingo

Like *Generations*, *Isidingo* was created as part of the mandate to create a multi-cultural cast in a multicultural setting—representing an aspirational model informed by Tutu and Mandela's vision of a "Rainbow Nation." *Isidingo* is the flagship soap opera of SABC 3, an "English only" channel, and, unlike *Generations*, has adhered to its mandated multiracial cast and setting. The storyline of *Isidingo* revolves around two major families, the Haines family and the Matabanes. The soap opera takes place in Johannesburg and the mining town of Horizon Deep. While Johannesburg is an actual major city in South Africa, Horizon Deep is a fictional one—borrowing from Horizon View in Roodepoort, Gauteng, located just outside of Johannesburg. The characters speak in their Afrikaans, Zulu, or ixiHosa, and English subtitles are provided for English-speaking viewers. Conversely, if the characters speak in English, Afrikaans, Zulu, and ixiHosa subtitles are provided for non-English speaking viewers. Thus the dialogue of the soap opera is able to be interpreted and understood by many of the viewers, whose racial and cultural identities are reflected in the racial composition of the main characters, including Black, white, Indian, and colored South Africans.

Most of the action on the series revolves around a television studio, a bar/restaurant (now dance club), and a mine run by the Matabane family. One of the main characters, Nandipha Sithole (Hlubi Mboya), is a glamorous on-air personality for ON TV and the former daughter-in-law of Agnes Matabane (Keketso Semoko), a matriarch and business owner who brings a decidedly different ability to business operations. Matabane is strong-willed and challenges her husband's patriarchal demands that she run her business decisions by him, leaving him at one point during the marriage.

Nandipha was married to Agnes's son Parsons (Tshepo Maseko). Before marrying him, she was abducted and raped, which led to her contracting HIV. Shortly thereafter, the character developed full-blown AIDS and had to make the conscious decision to fight it. She started on a regimen of antivirals that helped her recover and learn to live with HIV/AIDS.

The writers of the show made a purposeful decision about this storyline due to the pandemic AIDS crisis that impacts South Africa. An estimated 5.6 million people were living with HIV and AIDS in South Africa in 2009, more than in any other country. It is estimated that in 2009, over 310,000 South Africans died of AIDS. Among those aged fifteen to forty-nine, 17.8 percent have AIDS. Almost one in three women aged twenty-five to twenty-nine, and over a quarter of men aged thirty to thirty-four, are living with HIV.[17] In spite of its prevalence, millions of people reject treatment or cover it up because of the stigma attached to the disease. Greig Coetzee, head writer for *Isidingo*, stated that making one of the most popular soap opera actresses on television HIV-positive was a conscious decision on the part of the writers: "In many ways AIDS has gone off the boil in its public profile and how seriously people take it. People either ignore it, or have a fatalistic approach. We want to show that people can live with AIDS and manage it."[18]

This approach took on added importance because then-President Thabo Mbeki was a known sympathizer with AIDS dissidents, publicly and repeatedly questioning whether HIV in fact caused AIDS. Mbeki resisted the distribution of antiretroviral drugs (ARVs) that prolong the life of patients by preventing the development of AIDS. Until 2003, the health ministry had no national program for distributing ARVs. Thus the network became a tool to educate and inform viewers, challenging pervasive and dangerous beliefs.

Additionally, this storyline demonstrates the ways in which soap operas can transcend the narrative limitation of the actual genre. Would American soap writers have made Genie Francis's wildly popular character of Laura HIV-positive at the peak of her popularity, even though it coincided with the rise of the AIDS epidemic in the United States? Not likely, as that would take the narrative too far out of the realm of fantasy, bringing reality into the text. This *Isidingo* storyline is written with the reality of HIV/AIDS in mind.

The storyline becomes more complex when Parsons has an affair. The headline of the newspaper that breaks the scandal asks if Parsons uses a condom with his mistress. The story states that if he doesn't, and he is HIV-positive, he can pass on HIV/AIDS to her. Nandipha chooses to leave Parsons, realizing that having HIV/AIDS does not mean that she has to deal with a philanderer. The show examines questions about her self-esteem and the real-world concerns about whether someone else will be willing to love her as she ponders her next step.

HIV/AIDS is a constant part of Nandipha's storyline and character construction. S'khumbuzo "Ace" Nzimande (Sisa Hewana) is a world-famous soccer player who retires and "inherits" a co-anchor position on Nandipha's show. He is a good-looking ladies' man, but Nandipha tries to resist his advances. She goes out on a date with a gay friend and uses a dating site for people with HIV to find dates to help keep her mind off Ace. Ace finally wears her down with chivalrous behavior. Yet when Nandipha lets down her guard, Ace rejects her upon learning of her HIV-positive status. Later, he realizes his mistake and pursues her. Unfortunately, he misses out on a chance at true love, as Nandipha chooses to move forward with someone else more accepting.

Nandipha experiences the highs and lows of love, like everyone else, some of them related to her HIV status and some not. Her character experiences the emotions and concerns that people living with HIV/AIDS have, particularly when they are young, dynamic, and desirable. While SABC and the writers of *Isidingo* could play it safe by making a less popular character HIV-positive or pretending it is not a major part of the character's life, they choose to move beyond conventional soap opera narratives and character constructions to create programming that is both entertaining and purposeful. Although these narrative choices are driven by guidelines prescribed by SABC, they are transformative for the soap opera genre itself and the viewers.

Moreover, *Isidingo* challenges soap opera narrative conventions by incorporating current events in the fictional world as they occur in the real world. For example, in 1997, a public servants strike broke out in South Africa. It was the first time that Black South Africans had rebelled against a Black government. The public servants (teachers, nurses and police officers) went on strike because they wanted an increase in pay and better working conditions. They asked for a 12.5 percent raise that was rejected by the government even though government officials had received raises that year. For example, then-President Mbeki received a 57 percent raise but offered public servants only 6 percent.

During the strike, most of the soap operas, including *Generations*, incorporated the strike into the narrative. The characters discussed the strike, with each having a different perspective. On *Isidingo*, two of the characters stayed home from work in support of the strikers. This was communicated through dialogue and their absence from the setting the following day. Soap operas, typically marked by a temporality that can be sluggish and not representative of real time, are updated in real time in South Africa with regard to social issues. The timing that allows U.S. viewers to miss soap operas for weeks at a time and still be able to follow the storyline is subverted when it comes to social issues in South African soap operas.

Another example of this difference is when then-Senator Barack Obama announced that he was running for president in 2008. Characters on *Isidingo* discussed whom they would vote for if they lived in the United States. Barker Haines (Robert Whitehead) said that he would vote for Obama because he is half-African. This surprised some of the characters since Barker Haines is a wealthy white media mogul. Barker's sometimes business partner, Harriet Thompson (Grethe Fox), stated that she would vote for Hillary Clinton, while another character stated that he would vote for John McCain. They discussed why they would vote for each candidate and why this particular election was important in U.S. and South African culture. U.S. soap operas, on the other hand, rarely mention political candidates or elections.

Conclusion

Radio and television have been ascribed multiple and often contradictory roles in the process of democratic transition and consolidation in South Africa. The electronic media have been presented as a pathway of national reconciliation and unification. First conceptualized as a medium of political communication, the mass media were given a pivotal role in the democratic information policy enshrined in the ANC's blueprint for postapartheid transformation. Radio and television were seen as important aspects of symbolic representations of the "rainbow" concept of "One Nation, Many Cultures." According to the scholar Clive Barnett, "Nation-building in the South African context of the 1990s [was] not officially understood merely as a project of constructing a single, overarching national culture or identity. Policy makers have conceptualised it primarily in terms of facilitating processes of exchange and dialogue between South Africa's different cultural, regional, and linguistic communities."[19] This push for exchange has been imagined through the soap opera genre, although its ties to the political agenda of the party in power are extremely problematic. While South African soap operas reflect visions of racial unity and economic empowerment, they are not conflict free—especially when considering the increasingly contentious relationship between SABC and the postapartheid government and the perpetuation of gender stereotypes.

U.S. and South African soap operas share many commonalities in terms of narrative structure, but the complexities in South African storylines and character construction, coupled with the practice of incorporating real-world issues in real time in their narratives, serve as strong distinctions. Even though the

United States has been out of de facto segregation for decades longer than South Africa, the soap opera genre has changed very little from its radio origin.

SABC's mandate to reflect diverse populations, respect diverse cultural practices, including language, and promote ownership among disadvantaged groups clearly adds to the ability of producers and writers to experiment with narratives within the conventions of the soap opera genre. SABC and the soap opera creators, writers, and producers have figured out how to maintain the rules of soap operas (multiple protagonists, narrative enigmas, consistent settings and locations) while adding narrative elements that enhance the genre (multiracial casts, issues of social justice, and real-world current events). While U.S. soap operas are declining in viewership and profits, most South African soap operas are doing the opposite.

One final thing to consider is that eighteen- to thirty-five-year-old viewers of soapies are not particularly enthusiastic about "aspirational" show elements, most specifically in *Generations*. Michele Tager's study of college-aged viewers' beliefs about soap operas in general and *Generations* specifically found that they felt that since the soap opera had gone all-Black, it had become a Black version of the American soap opera *The Bold and the Beautiful*, referring to it as "local Bold." The respondents, a sample of Black South African college students, felt that the network had imposed reversed segregation on the characters, reinscribing a dominant racial model contrary to the "Rainbow Nation" identity. While these viewers like the upward mobility of the characters, they do not like the fact that the soap opera fails to demonstrate how to achieve wealth and status, since most of the characters inherit or just have it. Students are not only looking for their own individual identities on *Generations*; they are seeking a form of collective, national identity as well.[20] Respondents see soap operas as a social and cultural barometer of their place in society. What the networks and government hope to create is not necessarily how viewers will receive the information. Seemingly, these audiences have a negotiated relationship with the soap opera genre. While recognizing that it is fictional, they nevertheless want more of their reality in it.

NOTES

1. Robert B. Horwitz, *Communication and Democratic Reform in South Africa* (Cambridge: Cambridge University Press, 2001), 56, 58.

2. Funso Afolayan, *Culture and Customs of South Africa* (Westport, CT: Greenwood Publishing, 2004), 8.

3. Horwitz, *Communication and Democratic Reform*, 60, 63.

4. Ibid., 62–63.

5. Andrew Worsdale, "Rushes: Worldwide TV: Beyond Realism," *Sight & Sound* 14, no. 5 (May 2004): 6.

6. Hannelie Marx, "South African Soap Opera as the Other: The Deconstruction of Hegemonic Gender Identities in Four South African Soap Operas," *Communication* 34, no. 1 (2008): 83–84.

7. Tania Modleski, *Loving with a Vengeance: Mass-Produced Fantasies for Women* (London: Methuen, 1982), 34.

8. Feminist critics of soap operas include Tania Modleski, Dorothy Hobson, Lynn Spigel, Christine Gledhill, and Marilyn J. Matelski.

9. Michele Tager, "The Black and the Beautiful: Perceptions of (a) New Generation(s)," *Critical Arts: A Journal of South-North Cultural and Media Studies* 24, no. 1 (2010): 113.

10. Horwitz, *Communication and Democratic Reform*, 141, 144, 39, 125.

11. Ibid., 145.

12. Tager, "The Black and the Beautiful," 103.

13. Ibid., 105.

14. Herman Wasserman and Arnold S. de Beer, "Afro-optimism/Afro-pessimism and the South African Media," *Critical Arts: A South-North Journal of Cultural & Media Studies* 23, no. 3 (2009): 389.

15. Tager, "The Black and the Beautiful," 108.

16. Barry Bearak, "Post-Apartheid South Africa Enters Anxious Era," *New York Times*, New York ed., October 6, 2008, A1.

17. "HIV and AIDS in South Africa," Avert.org, http://www.avert.org/aidssouthafrica.htm http://www.avert.org/aidssouthafrica.htm (accessed June 19, 2012).

18. David Blair, "South African Soap Opera Breaks the Taboo on AIDS," *Telegraph*, July 8, 2006, http://www.telegraph.co.uk/news/worldnews/africaandindianocean/southafrica/1523399/South-African-soap-opera-breaks-the-taboo-on-Aids.html.

19. Clive Barnett, "Broadcasting the Rainbow Nation: Media, Democracy, and Nation-Building in South Africa," *Antipode* 31, no. 3 (1999): 275.

20. Tager, "The Black and the Beautiful," 107, 122.

Minority Television Trade as Cultural Journey

THE CASE OF NEW ZEALAND'S
BRO'TOWN

TIMOTHY HAVENS

Four animated, brown-skinned youth are lounging on a porch step in Auckland, New Zealand, when a fierce-looking social worker and police constable approach and insist on knowing where the father of two of the boys is. As the constable raises his nightstick, one of the boys fumbles in heavily accented Māori English, "He went to the pub four days ago and hasn't been back." The authorities quickly cart two of the boys off as wards of the state as another performs a Māori *haka*, or war chant, in mock warning to the police. However, according to script notes for the episode, the *haka* is in fact a "bastardization of a well-known Māori *haka* because of [the boy's] lack of *Māoritanga* [knowledge of things Māori.]" While the general situation of this scene may be familiar enough for foreign viewers to recognize, much of the language, cultural allusion, and humor requires substantial knowledge of New Zealand and Polynesian culture to decode.

This is a scene from *bro'Town* (2004–2009), the first scripted prime-time series in New Zealand television history. Produced by local firm Firehorse Films, it was written and performed by the Polynesian comedy troupe Naked Samoans and funded through both commercial and noncommercial New Zealand sources. *Bro'Town* has also been an unlikely popular export—unlikely not simply because New Zealand television is untested in international markets, but also because the series is so closely tied to New Zealand, especially Polynesian New Zealand culture.

The success of *bro'Town* abroad provides a textbook example of what is, in my opinion, one of the more intriguing and promising trends in the worldwide circulation of commercial minority television programming today: the presence of highly local cultural content in a globally circulated text. While most scholarship on global television to date has assumed that globally popular texts must in some ways reference "shared" or "universal" cultural values,[1] a growing number of television programs steeped in quite particularistic cultural and linguistic allusions seem to be gaining global audiences—from the highly intertextual, politically charged *Chappelle's Show* (2003–2006) to the Japanese mythological anime series *Bleach* (2004–present) to *bro'Town*. This chapter explores the apparent contradiction of widely circulated, culturally specific television programs, arguing that the business practices of postnetwork television around the world lead program buyers to find commercial value in certain highly localized forms of nonwhite cultural expression. While the cultural politics of such programming exchanges are not guaranteed, the example of *bro'Town* gives us insight into emerging global markets that may offer ways to fund culturally specific minority programming in the present era of commercial media globalization.

Including *bro'Town* in an edited anthology on Black television might seem inaccurate or controversial, since the program features Polynesian teenagers living in the Morningside suburb of Auckland, New Zealand, who have no ancestral connection with Africa and are generally not seen as members of the diaspora. Nevertheless, some of the Polynesian populations of New Zealand, in particular members of the indigenous Māori nations, have long found significant resonance with African American cultural and political movements. In part because the master racial narratives and racist legal and cultural strategies that white New Zealanders deployed against the Māori borrowed heavily from American models, Māori political agitators in the 1970s and 1980s deployed the politics and rhetoric of the African American civil rights and Black Power movements to counter legal exploitation. African American cultural imports, especially jazz, R&B, and rap, have long been central to these political movements and to contemporary Māori culture more generally. Some Māori today even self-identify as "Black."[2] For the purposes of this volume, *bro'Town*'s worldwide circulation holds important lessons for Black television in general, including African American television, in an era of globalization.

Globalization and African American Television

Television globalization refers to a wide range of deterritorializing strategies in program funding, trade, and broadcast, all of which have become transnationalized among U.S. television organizations and those in much of the rest of the world. Increasingly, television programs need to attract foreign investors and sell worldwide in order to cover the costs of production. Television broadcasters, on the other hand, require cheap imports to fill out their program schedules in a cost-effective manner. These evolving transnational business structures have created a network of television professionals from around the world who not only think globally but also trade ideas about what kinds of programming tastes are shared across national boundaries and what kinds of textual practices best appeal to those tastes. In other words, while programmers continue to respond to domestic developments and tastes, the global television business culture profoundly shapes their responses as well.[3]

The primary way in which the business networks and cultures of global television influence programmers' perceptions is through what I call industry lore. Industry lore derives from practical business considerations, including how to position a television channel in a market and how much to pay for programming. It addresses such questions as what the desired audience's tastes are and what kinds of programs (within budget constraints, of course) can best appeal to those tastes. For instance, during the era of nationwide, general entertainment, broadcast television industry lore held that dramas with African American characters could not sell abroad, and consequently few such dramas got made. Here, expectations for foreign syndication revenues combined with the drive to reach the widest possible audiences in each market created a perception of the audience as an undifferentiated mass. This mass audience, it was thought, could only be reached by tapping into supposedly universal human themes, like family values or law enforcement. Because most international television syndicators were white and the most lucrative foreign markets were also predominantly white, industry insiders tended to see unique African American experiences, cultures, and values as unsuited for international trade. Consequently, few African American dramas got made. As one senior executive at a major Hollywood distributor put it: "The Black American experience is unique to Black America. It's really not the same experience that Blacks are having in London or having in France . . . So there has to be that broader sense of humanity to the show . . . I think that there is a general sense that if it's too tied to the Black American experience, then it won't work internationally, because nobody else is having specifically that experience."[4] The white American experience, by contrast, was rarely seen as inherently too distinct to appeal abroad.

Because industry lore arises out of particular economic-institutional and historical conjunctures, we would expect the lore to change when conditions change. Herman Gray has specified in some detail the specific conditions that contemporary television series addressing African American themes and experiences face.

> Despite their claims to the contrary, to remain competitive networks long ago abandoned the strategy of aiming the least objectionable programs at the widest possible audiences. Cable operators, new networks, and old-line networks made explicit marketing decisions to use their programming to reach distinct demographics, including black urban markets. Black shows, where they are developed at all, were and are selectively developed and deployed by major commercial networks as part of their overall marketing and branding strategy, a strategy and ideal demographic that in all likelihood does not include black people as a prime market.[5]

These new demands for clearly defined, transnational demographic niches and consistent channel brands with which to hail them constitute the most important institutional changes in television over the past fifteen years.

The altered economic and institutional practices of the television industries have opened up opportunities for new forms of industry lore that understand cultural expression, exchange, and consumption differently than in the past. Specifically, I believe that we can see a shift from talk about "universal themes" to talk about "cultural journeys" among some segments of program brokers. Although shifts in industry lore are difficult to demonstrate because so much business-related talk takes place behind closed doors, only occasionally surfacing in more public forums, I believe that sufficient evidence exists to argue that the metaphor of cultural journeys is a nascent form of industry lore among certain members of the global television business. While these changes in no way guarantee that more multicultural programming gets produced and circulated, it does encourage conditions that are more amenable to that possibility. At the same time, while industry lore about cultural journeys helps diversify the political potentials and routes of minority television trade, it also works to channel that diversity into particular generic and content expectations.

Satire, Adult Animation, and the Cultural Politics of bro'Town

Featuring a core group of five teenage boys, all of whom are of Polynesian decent and one of whom, Jeff da Māori, is of Māori descent, *bro'Town* provides satirical portraits of both brown and nonbrown New Zealanders from a brown perspective; that is, white satirical portrayals of nonwhites have little place in the series. Thus,

Figure 15.1   *bro'Town.* Frame grab.

although the producer of the series claims that it "explores the New Zealand identity just as much (if not more) than the Pacific Island/Māori stuff,"[6] I would argue that the exploration occurs from a decidedly brown subject position.

The episode "A Māori at My Table" offers clear examples of the ethnic minority perspective of the series as well as the ways in which the series remains anchored to local cultures. In addition, it demonstrates how the series appropriates elements of the globally successful adult animation genre in an effort to appeal to foreign viewers, not unlike the animated African American adult series *The Boondocks*, which Deborah Elizabeth Whaley explores elsewhere in this volume.

The episode begins as all episodes do, in heaven, where we see Jesus trying to stop the Māori leader Hone Heke from chopping down heaven's flagpoles. Heke's act references the leader's role in initiating the Flagstaff War with Great Britain in 1845. When God, an Islander wearing a lava-lava skirt, appears, he chastises Jesus for his ignorance of Māori culture and tells him to watch the upcoming episode "and learn a few things about *tangata whenua*, or People of the Land."

The remainder of the episode focuses on Jeff da Māori's trip with his classmates back to his ancestral "homeland," where he discovers that his favorite aunt, the leader of the community, has just died. Jeff is named as the new leader and quickly becomes embroiled in a debate about whether to sell the land to Japanese businessmen who want to develop it into a mall. Uncomfortable with selling the land but unable to win over the other inhabitants, Jeff is visited by a spirit who reminds him of the ancient story that the whales will again return to Kia Ora Bay when the sacred noseflute is played in the proper location. Jeff finds he cannot play the noseflute to summon the whales, but his guitar does the job. Tourists immediately begin to show up to watch the whales, thus saving the land from development. The conclusion of the episode returns us to heaven, where Jesus and Hone Heke have reconciled, even as a new disagreement breaks out between Jeff's dead aunt and the spirit who visited Jeff over which of her nephews she intended to leave in charge.

Both direct and ironic critiques of white New Zealanders, the New Zealand government, global capitalism, and white popular culture in general feature prominently in this episode and mark it as coming from a decidedly minority perspective. Lynn Grey, the boys' teacher and chaperone on their trip, is the main white character in the episode. She is persistently mocked as a Māoriphile, especially through her efforts to incorporate Māori words into her speech and sleep with as many young Māori men as possible. The other white character, a South African immigrant boy named Joost, protests that he needs to carry a handgun on the trip in case "one of Jeff da Māori's relatives tries to rob me." In both cases, stereotypical white views about the Māori are mocked in a way that Māori culture is not, even though the Māori do not fully escape critique.

Meanwhile, the policies of the New Zealand government and their oppression of the Māori people are confronted more directly. This comes across most clearly in two scenes featuring Jeff's aunt. In the first scene, a flashback to when Jeff left to move to Morningside, she explains that he has to leave because they have no more land for him to play on and tries to teach him to say "bloody thieving colonialists." When young Jeff can't say the phrase, she simply tells him to call them "Pākehās," a Māori word for white settlers that can carry negative connotations similar to the American English word *whitey*. At the end of the episode, when we discover that Jeff was wrongly made the new leader of the people, the spirit who visited him protests that he has bad hearing because of "the poor standard of health care available to Māori."

The Japanese businessmen who want to buy and develop theMāori land represent the dangers of global capitalism for contemporary Māori—a danger they are able to thwart because of Jeff's faith in ancient Māori myths. Of course, another form of global capitalism, namely tourism, is what ultimately saves the day. In this way, it is noteworthy that the makers of the series have a difficult time creating narrative closure without appealing to already existing political and economic options, rather than trying to imagine any radical new options for Māori cultural survival.

Finally, the episode's critique of white popular culture, in particular Hollywood, lampoons the conventional practice of using brown-skinned actors to play characters of a variety of ethnic backgrounds. One of Jeff's cousins, Cliff Curtis, is a Māori actor in Hollywood "who gets to act as Latin American drug dealers, terrorists, and Iraqi refugees." At the end of the episode, he proposes using the land to "build a drama school to teach Māori actors how to play other ethnic minorities in Hollywood movies." These comments serve as incisive, if somewhat commonplace, critiques of Hollywood's racial politics. At the same time, they require an insight primarily possessed by the world's ethnic minorities, again positioning the series as a minority text. Moreover, the critique also builds on shared, global minority experiences and knowledge.

While the episode reserves its most scathing critiques for white culture, Polynesian and Māori culture are also satirized. The satire, however, is balanced by more complex portraits of minority people and cultures. That complexity comes across most obviously in the boys' characters as well as the generally respectful treatment of Māori culture that we receive in the episode. However, Māori culture is portrayed as anything but idyllic. Perhaps most scandalously, Jeff and his buddies make frequent reference to the fact that he has "eight dads," all of whom live with him and his mother. The series never makes clear whether Jeff's mother is involved in a polyandrous marriage, whether his "fathers" are mere lovers, or whether they are simply friends or family members. Still, the fact that Jeff's dads are a satirical departure from expected social norms is quite clear and would seem to be intended to poke fun at either Māori sexual or habitation relationships, or both.

The satirizing of both Polynesian and white New Zealander cultures can be read as an attempt to lampoon all cultures and social norms, especially political correctness. Certainly, journalists and television professionals often take this position on the series. But bro'Town does not satirize all groups equally, instead reserving its harshest criticism for white colonialist practices and mindsets, Christian religious elitism, and stereotypical portrayals of nonwhite people in Western cultural products, such as Hollywood films. The pervasive use of satire clearly identifies bro'Town with the global adult animation genre but also alludes to a long tradition of satirizing European colonialism, Christianity, and cultural stereotyping in Polynesian literature and storytelling.[7] Such satirical cultural practices, which parody both dominant and minority groups, have been common in minority cultures around the world for centuries, making them a form of global minority discourse,[8] or "vernacular globalization,"[9] that contemporary television programs such as bro'Town tap into when they travel abroad.

In addition to the use of satire, bro'Town's scatological humor also marks the series as a member of the adult animation genre. In "A Māori at My Table," for instance, in addition to the images of and references to Jeff's perpetually runny nose, we also witness a scene in which Pepelo Pepelo, the father of Vale and Valea and a perpetual drunk, defecates in front of Mack's family. We follow the excrement through the sewers until it reappears at the sewage treatment plant near Jeff's homeland. Scenes such as these have earned bro'Town comparisons to South Park.[10] Meanwhile, the series' mockery of adulthood, family, parenting, religion, school, and polite culture more generally has engendered comparisons to both South Park and The Simpsons. bro'Town is self-consciously aware of its lineage in the long history of globally popular animated television series, though such allusions tend to be far less common than in series such as South Park and Family Guy. Still, in the present episode, one such allusion does appear when Jeff's cousin is finally unmasked as a Japanese businessman who complains, à la villains in Scooby-Doo, Where Are You (1969–1972), "I'd have gotten away with it, too, if it weren't for you meddling kids!" More than mere intertextual tributes, these allusions to globally popular animated series also work to mark bro'Town as a global television text with a distinctly young and male demographic slant.

Through both satirical and respectful treatment, bro'Town manages to articulate a distinctly Polynesian perspective on contemporary life in New Zealand. At the same time, its adherence to the aesthetics of global adult animation helps make the series popular with young adult males of all ethnic groups,[11] while also contributing to its juvenile, masculinist tendencies. Moreover, these generic elements also work with the grain of the contemporary television industries in much of the world, especially the development of animation channels targeting young men.

The Global Syndication of *bro'Town*

Bro' Town has been sold into nine foreign territories including Australia, Canada, the Cook Islands, Fiji, Latin America, Portugal, South Africa, Africa, and the United States. While these are not large numbers when compared with such globally popular exports as the *CSI* franchise, which reportedly airs in two hundred foreign markets,[12] they are, frankly, remarkable given that New Zealand is a small, English-speaking nation. According to every model of global television trade, it should be swamped in Australian, British, and American programming and unable to even produce its own television programs, much less export them.[13] Moreover, *bro'Town*'s cultural specificity should create such a large "cultural discount" that few foreign buyers should even be interested in the series.[14]

International syndication did not come immediately for *bro'Town*, but the series did quickly become an important revenue stream. Adult animation in general is a pricey affair, and given the size of the New Zealand market, *bro'Town*'s production costs were tough to cover. The initial six episodes ran more than three hundred thousand NZD per half hour. Production funding came from a combination of public and private broadcasting sources and extensive product placement. The government funding agency NZ On Air kicked in eight hundred thousand NZD for the first season, and commercial broadcaster TV3, with assistance from Canadian media conglomerate CanWest, provided the remainder. Significant amounts of production work were outsourced to animation houses in India, China, and the Philippines to help defray costs.

Despite its primarily domestic funding, *bro'Town* was a product of media globalization from the outset. The initial idea came from a meeting between a Nickelodeon executive from the United States who had come to New Zealand looking for programming from the region and producer Elizabeth Mitchell. This led Mitchell to begin thinking about internationally marketable television program ideas. Indeed, Mitchell claims to have been thinking of international distribution from the beginning of the development process, even though international sales did not begin until the series' second season.[15]

Bro'Town's buyers have ranged from general entertainment broadcasters to transnational cable channels to indigenous peoples' satellite networks. Consequently, the series has performed a wide range of institutional labors, each of which highlights different textual elements in the series in order to fit the buyer's channel brand. Sales to general entertainment broadcasters have been limited to the immediate geo-linguistic region where cultural proximity seems to be the primary programming consideration. As initially proposed by Joseph Straubhaar, the theory of cultural proximity holds that while viewers prefer domestic programming over imports, smaller nations that cannot afford to produce all of their own programming will tend to import from culturally and linguistically similar countries.[16] As nations with a shared language, histories, and cultures, Fiji and the Cook Islands are natural cultural trading partners for the

Polynesian population in New Zealand, and the fact that the series focused on five Polynesian teenagers certainly helped smooth its exportation.

Broadcasters in Fiji and the Cook Islands programmed the series for a general audience during prime time, emphasizing the program's similarities with their predominantly Polynesian viewers. Jeane Matenga, the CEO of Elijah Communications, brokered the sale to Cook Islands Television. She explained: "What I like about it is that it is made in our region and it's a top quality production."[17] Matenga's emphasis on the regional elements, of course, refers as much to an ethnic and cultural region as a geographic one. In this manner, the exportation of *bro'Town* to predominantly Polynesian nations does little to challenge the perception among program brokers that viewers seek to identify with the universal elements of imported television, even though the similarities that they value come from Polynesian rather than white cultures.

Australia, too, might seem like a natural trading partner for television programs like *bro'Town*, especially given the shared history of ethnic tension between indigenous people and white European settlers and a shared language between the two nations. However, because Australia has a highly active television production industry with extensive exports of its own, the major commercial broadcasters do not program many imports other than Hollywood and British films and series.[18] Consequently, *bro'Town* did not appear on general entertainment channels but was imported by Foxtel's The Comedy Channel and National Indigenous Television (NITV). On The Comedy Channel, *bro'Town* was surrounded by other animated adult programs, including *South Park*. Unlike the general broadcasters in Polynesia, The Comedy Channel exploited the satirical and scatological elements of *bro'Town* to position it as adult humor aimed at men in their late teens and early twenties. While such institutional uses do not erase the Polynesian and ethnic minority elements of the program, they do work to highlight the program's more juvenile aspects and address viewers as young men regardless of ethnicity. Buyers in other parts of the world positioned the series in similar ways, including SIC Radical in Portugal, an entertainment channel aimed at teenagers, and Cartoon Network Latin America, which reaches viewers in Argentina, Brazil, Chile, Colombia, Mexico, and Venezuela. In both of these cases, the series was programmed with similar kinds of adult animation to help brand the channel as youthful and "edgy."

Still, despite the similarity among adult animation programs from around the world, the persistent use of local cultural allusions and linguistic terms in a series like *bro'Town* posed challenges for distributors and programmers. Rather than eliminating or downplaying the specificity of Polynesian youth culture in New Zealand, however, Firehorse Films produced a "bro'Town Glossary" that it distributed to fans and importers to help them translate the series' dialogue into their own cultural frameworks. Moreover, scripts provided for translation are littered with definitions of specific phrases, cultural explanations, and character notes. For instance, a script from the episode "Go Home, Stay Home" contains the following footnotes for translators: "Tineke Bouchier = NZ game show hostess (1970s)—replace with anyone your audience will recognise"; "Taumaranui = name of a NZ town"; "Constable Bababiba desperately wants to be an actor and often misquotes lines from movies."[19]

Not surprisingly, questions about how to deal with the cultural specificity of *bro'Town* and how much confusion television audiences can tolerate became a prime topic of discussion when the series was translated into Spanish and Portuguese for Cartoon Network Latin America. Firehorse Films contracted with Miami-based Hola Entertainment to translate the series, with oversight from a script supervisor from Cartoon Network and frequent input from the producers. E-mail discussions between Firehorse Films, Hola, and Cartoon Network about the word *fa'afafine* offer an interesting glimpse into how these organizations negotiated cultural differences in order to translate the series into Latin American markets.

In Samoan cultures, fa'afafine are boys who are raised as girls and tend to live their lives as women, essentially representing a third gender category. In *bro'Town*, the boys attend a community college whose principal is a fa'afafine, and Hola Entertainment contacted Firehorse Films about translating the word, initially suggesting *gay*. The producer at Firehorse Films, however, objected to this characterization, explaining that "fa'afafine has nothing to do with sex really" and insisting that the character in question was "definitely not gay." The representative from Cartoon Network conducted Internet research and suggested that fa'afafine are perhaps more like transsexuals, but the producer disagreed with this translation as well. Fa'afafine do not transition from one sex to another but rather see themselves as having always been culturally female. Finally, the translators decided to leave the word as is, explaining, "After all, the series is a cultural journey." In an interview, producer Elizabeth Mitchell further explained that "we made the decision to leave Māori words 'un-translated' as they [foreign viewers] were embracing 'the cultural journey' we were embarking on."[20]

The idea that television trade and the viewing of imported programming take us on a "cultural journey" in which we learn what is distinct about other cultures, and our own as well, is a far cry from industry lore about universal values that transcend local cultures. What we see in this exchange and in Mitchell's comment is a different kind of industry lore that recognizes that cultural differences will always frustrate both the translation and viewing processes, and both industry professionals and at-home viewers have to be willing to put up with such difficulties when it comes to importing television programs.

I would suggest that this discourse of cultural journeys is an emerging form of industry lore that originates, in part, from efforts to sell programming created for a particular audience segment, especially audiences outside the conventional mainstream of Hollywood television, and to distribute and program such series for audiences in other parts of the world, particularly nonmainstream audiences.

As mentioned above, it is difficult to specify the existence and extent of a new form of industry lore, but the phrase "cultural journey" has begun showing up more and more frequently in industry talk and publications. Perhaps most prominently, when BET Jazz rebranded itself as BET J, the executive vice president and general manager for BET Digital Networks explained, "The 'J' in our new network name is now more indicative of the complete musical and cultural 'Journey' rather than only jazz" that BET J intended to program.[21] Programmers from the United States to South Africa use the phrase, most commonly to refer to television programming that focuses primarily on a minority or foreign culture.[22]

While industry lore built around the cultural-journey metaphor is arguably more tolerant, even encouraging, of the global circulation of minority programming, the cultural politics of the lore is more ambiguous, encouraging both a cultural tourism and a multicultural orientation depending on channel type and brand, programming practices, and the geopolitical power relations that exist among importing, exporting, and represented cultures. At Foxtel's The Comedy Channel and Cartoon Network Latin America, bro'Town is surrounded by programming from Western nations, especially the United States, which features predominantly white cultural values. Such programming choices encourage comparison with Hollywood and the West in a way that tends not to challenge the supposed universality of Western values and aesthetics. One poster on an Australian discussion forum dedicated to the program complained, for instance, "It's not even in the same league as South Park."[23]

A similar form of cultural tourism got encouraged by the programming of the series in the United States, where it aired on the nonprofit satellite broadcaster Link TV. Link TV operates under the auspices of FCC regulations that require DBS providers to reserve 4 percent of their channel space for noncommercial public service programming. bro'Town aired on Link TV in the mid-2000s at 8 P.M. Pacific Standard Time, sandwiched between world news and a documentary slot. It was one of the few nonnews, noncultural programs aired on Link TV. Consequently, Link TV's identity and programming did not invite the kinds of comparisons to Western programming that we saw above. Instead, the airing of bro'Town fit well the channel's slogan: "Television Without Borders."

The mission of the channel is to "provide a unique perspective on international news, current events, and diverse cultures," and the importation of programming like bro'Town obviously fulfills this mission. However, while such a goal is laudable, Link TV only comes with a subscription to satellite television, reaching less than 30 percent of the U.S. market and charging significantly more for basic service than cable television does. As a result, Link TV's viewers tend to be economically and culturally privileged. The channel can encourage the kind of Eurocentric cultural tourism that bell hooks has called "eating the other," or a desire to consume difference in a effort to "spice up" the "dull dish that is mainstream white culture," without really challenging the assumptions of white supremacy.[24] In other words, it is very easy for privileged white viewers to watch shows like *bro'Town* on Link TV and feel connected with the rest of the world, and superior to their white American compatriots, but still never question their own privilege or cultural values.

By contrast, indigenous peoples' broadcasting networks that air *bro'Town* program it in ways that encourage more comparative, multicultural orientations among viewers. These networks include NITV in Australia and the Aboriginal Peoples Television Network (APTN) in Canada. In both cases, *bro'Town* appears alongside television programs of various genres that feature indigenous cultures from both domestic and foreign lands. Although the majority of both channels' program schedules are made up of domestic indigenous programming, they also rely on imports, specifically imports that "have Aboriginal content, deal with Aboriginal issues and feature actors, directors or producers who are of Aboriginal descent," including "Indigenous Peoples from around the globe."[25] Explaining his decision to acquire *bro'Town*, Jean LaRose, CEO of APTN, called it "a fun and innovative series . . . We are always looking for creative, indigenous programming from not only Canada but from other countries worldwide."[26] While not using the phrase "cultural journey" here, in his talk of "creativity," "innovation," and "indigenous programming," LaRose obviously values imported programming that is culturally different and assumes that his viewers will as well.

The on-screen presence of television programs from both domestic and international indigenous peoples provides what I would argue is a significant multicultural experience, articulating quite different notions of global cultural trade than mainstream television exchanges. Not only do such exchanges force programmers to actively think through the kinds of cultural resonances that imported programming might have in a far more deliberate manner than simple assumptions about universal themes, they also allow programmers and viewers to consider global indigenous cultures side by side, including not only their differences but also the kinds of cultural-adaptive strategies that might be common to a range of indigenous minorities from around the world.

Both the cultural-tourist and multicultural uses of *bro'Town* fit well into the broad metaphor of the cultural journey. While such industry lore in no way guarantees free, respectful, or equal exchanges of cultural programming among diverse populations of the world, it does facilitate a more complex way of thinking through cultural exchange among television insiders than does the mainstream industry lore about universal themes. Still, the producers of *bro'Town* have packaged Polynesian New Zealander culture into a globally recognizable format in order to increase the variety of its institutional uses abroad, even as they champion an industry lore that is more accommodating of the kinds of cultural specificity that also mark the program.

Conclusion

Bro'Town activated a range of transnational distribution circuits, including culturally proximate general entertainment channels and niche channels targeting either
young men or ethnic minorities. In these latter two instances, we saw that the
dominant industry lore about how audiences identify with the universal themes in
imported programming required revisions due to the highly localized nature of the
series. Instead, niche programmers relied on the metaphor of the cultural journey
to explain how and why foreign viewers watch imported programming.

The discourse of cultural journeys is not a significant departure from the
recognition among industry insiders of the appeal of African American youth culture in the 1990s, which helped stoke international sales of sitcoms like *The Fresh
Prince of Bel-Air* and *Moesha*. In both instances, program merchants identified cultural difference as a positive textual feature for some viewers.[27] What is different
in the industry lore about cultural journeys is that it is a flexible metaphor
that can apply to a range of programs as well as a more generalized acquisition
strategy than earlier observations about African American youth series. The
metaphor of the cultural journey permits both buyers and sellers to imagine
television viewing quite differently than the discourse of universal cultural
themes does, encouraging programmers to value cultural difference.

When it comes to recent African American television, those programs that
do make substantial in-group reference, such as *The Boondocks* and *Chappelle's
Show*, tend to get programmed primarily as a form of cultural tourism, aired
on cartoon and comedy channels throughout Europe and Latin America.
Unfortunately, indigenous foreign broadcasters that might program African
American series differently seem to associate African American imports closely
with American cultural imperialism in general and shy away from purchasing
them. Put slightly differently, most program merchants continue to see African
American television as too culturally specific to appeal to universal themes, but
too universal to fit the specific needs of indigenous or ethnic niche channels.

Still, the development of channel identities, trade routes, and, increasingly,
forms of industry lore that permit, even require, programmers to think differently about television and cultural difference on a global scale continues to hold
promise for Black programming, including African American programs. As these
markets and attitudes continue to spread, growing numbers of Black creative
talent might begin to recognize these outlets as genuine markets for their
programming, and ethnic and indigenous programmers might begin to see that
multicultural sensibilities, interests, and politics can extend to oppressed minorities everywhere, including those in the richest nation in the world.

NOTES

1. Chris Barker, *Global Television: An Introduction* (Malden, MA: Blackwell, 1997); Herman
Gray, *Watching Race: Television and the Struggle for "Blackness"* (Minneapolis: University of

Minnesota Press, 1995); Timothy Havens, " 'It's Still a White World out There': The Interplay of Culture and Economics in International Television Trade," *Critical Studies in Media Communication* 19 (2002): 377–398.

2. James Lull, *Media, Communication, Culture: A Global Approach*, 2nd ed. (New York: Columbia University Press, 2000), 246–249.

3. Denise D. Bielby and C. Lee Harrington, *Global TV: Exporting Television and Culture in the World Market* (New York: New York University Press, 2008); Timothy Havens, *Global Television Marketplace* (London: British Film Institute Press, 2006); Timothy Havens, "Imagining Universal Television: Global Television Fairs as Tournaments of Value," in *Negotiating Values in the Creative Industries: Fairs, Festivals and Competitive Events*, ed. Brian Morean and Jesper Pedersen (Cambridge: Cambridge University Press, 2011), 145–168.

4. Executive vice president of international sales at a major Hollywood studio, personal interview, 1999. Name withheld.

5. Herman Gray, *Cultural Moves: African Americans and the Politics of Representation* (Berkeley and Los Angeles: University of California Press, 2005), 84.

6. Elizabeth Mitchell, executive producer, Firehorse Film, personal interview, 2009.

7. Michelle Keown, *Postcolonial Pacific Writing: Representations of the Body* (New York: Routledge, 2005).

8. Abdul R. JanMohammed and David Lloyd, "Toward a Theory of Minority Discourse: What Is to Be Done?" in *The Nature and Context of Minority Discourse*, ed. Abdul R. JanMohamed and David Lloyd (Oxford: Oxford University Press, 1990), 1–16.

9. Arjun Appadurai, *Modernity at Large: Cultural Dimensions of Globalization* (Minneapolis: University of Minnesota Press, 1996), 10.

10. Katalin Lustyik and Philippa K. Smith, "From *The Simpsons* to '*The Simpsons* of the South Pacific': New Zealand's First Primetime Animation, *bro'Town*," *Television & New Media* 11 (2010): 331–349.

11. Matthew Bannister, "Where's Morningside? Locating *bro'Town* in the Ethnic Genealogy of New Zealand/Aotearoa," *New Zealand Journal of Media Studies* 11 (2008): 1–15.

12. Gerard Gilbert, "CSI: The Cop Show That Conquered the World," *The Independent*, December 19, 2006, http://www.independent.co.uk/news/media/csi-the-cop-show-that-conquered-the-world-429262.html.

13. Colin Hoskins, Stuart McFadyen, and Adam Finn, *Global Television and Film: An Introduction to the Economics of the Business* (New York and Oxford: Oxford University Press, 1997); Toby Miller, Nitin Govil, John McMurria, Richard Maxwell, and Ting Wang, *Global Hollywood 2* (London: British Film Institute Publishing, 2005).

14. Hoskins, McFadyen, and Finn, *Global Television*, 32–33.

15. Lustyik and Smith, "From *The Simpsons*"; Mitchell interview.

16. Joseph Straubhaar, "Beyond Media Imperialism: Asymmetrical Interdependence and Cultural Proximity," *Critical Studies in Mass Communication* 8 (1991): 39–59.

17. "Kia Orana Cook Islands!" *bro'Town News*, http://www.brotown.co.nz/ news_15.html (accessed September 30, 2011).

18. Stuart Cunningham and Elizabeth Jacka, *Australian Television and International Mediascapes* (Cambridge: Cambridge University Press, 1996).

19. Firehorse Films, *Go Home, Stay Home*, unpublished television script, 2003.

20. Mitchell interview.

21. "BET Fine Tunes Jazz, Changes Its Name to BET 'J' and Aligns with Directv," *Wireless News*, March 4, 2006, http://www.factiva.com, document: WLNW000020060309e2340000p.

22. "Comcast Celebrates Hispanic Heritage Month with Special On Demand Programming That Highlights the Best of Latin Culture," *Business Wire*, September 21, 2010, http://www.factiva.com, document: BWR0000020100920e69k005k8; Jane Mayne, "The Colour Maroon," *Cape Times*, November 23, 2007, http://www.factiva.com, document CAPTIM0020071123e3bn0000d.

23. Luke, October 2, 2006, 8 p.m., comment on "Forums Archive\TV shows\Bro Town," *Whirlpool* forums, http://forums.whirlpool.net.au/forum-replies-archive.cfm/531328.html.

24. bell hooks, *Black Looks: Race and Representation* (Boston: South End Press, 1992), 21.

25. Aboriginal Peoples Television Network, "Acquisitions," http://www.aptn.ca/corporate/producers/acquisitions.php (accessed November 21, 2010.

26. "*bro'Town* in Canada," *bro'Town News*, accessed November 14, 2010, http://www.brotown.co.nz/archive_10.html (accessed November 14, 2010).

27. Havens, "'It's Still a White World.'"

Notes on Contributors

CHRISTINE ACHAM is an associate professor in the Program for African American and African Studies at the University of California, Davis. She is the author of *Revolution Televised: Prime Time and the Struggle for Black Power* (University of Minnesota Press, 2004) and numerous articles. She is also the co-director of the documentary film *Infiltrating Hollywood: The Rise and Fall of the Spook Who Sat by the Door*. She is currently on the editorial board of *Film Quarterly*.

NSENGA K. BURTON is an associate professor of Communication and Media Studies at Goucher College in Baltimore. Burton's research interests and scholarship focus on the examination of popular culture, specifically television, film, and new media, through the lens of race, class, gender, and sexuality. Her work has appeared in the *Encyclopedia of African American Culture and History*, *FemSpec*, and *Screening Noir*. She serves as an editor-at-large for *TheRoot.com* (a Washington Post/Slate publication), where she contributes to the news section of the site and writes features regularly. She owns BurtonWorks Media and is completing a documentary on the 2007 public servants strike in South Africa entitled *Four Acts*.

ANDRE M. CAVALCANTE is a doctoral candidate in the Department of Communication Studies at the University of Michigan. His research interests include media audiences, the work of identity, and the construction of the ordinary in everyday life. His work has been published in the journal *Critical Studies in Media Communication*. He is currently working on a project that examines the relationship between transgender audiences, popular media representations, and the achievement of the everyday.

ROBIN R. MEANS COLEMAN is an associate professor in the Department of Communication Studies and in the Department of Afroamerican and African Studies at the University of Michigan. She is the author of *African American Viewers and the Black Situation Comedy: Situating Racial Humor* (Routledge, 2000). She is also the editor of *Say It Loud! African American Audiences, Media, and Identity* (Routledge, 2002) and co-editor of *Fight the Power! The Spike Lee Reader* (Peter Lang, 2008). Her most recent book is *Horror Noire: Blacks in American Horror Films from the 1890s to Present* (Routledge, 2011).

MARK D. CUNNINGHAM received his PhD in Radio-Television-Film at the University of Texas at Austin. His dissertation considered narrative, race, and gender in John Singleton's hood trilogy: *Boyz N the Hood, Poetic Justice*, and Baby Boy. His research interests include film studies, literature, popular culture studies, and race studies. His work has appeared in *The Spike Lee Reader* and the *African American National Biography*.

JENNIFER FULLER is an assistant professor in the Department of Radio-TV-Film at the University of Texas at Austin. She is a television historian who focuses on race and gender. Her work has been published in *Cinema Journal, Feminist Media Studies, Media, Culture & Society*, and elsewhere.

RACQUEL GATES is an assistant professor in the Department of Media Culture at the College of Staten Island. Her research focuses on representations of race in popular culture, with specific attention to the importance of disreputable media in discourses of race, gender, and class. Her work has appeared in *In Media Res*, the *Velvet Light Trap*, and elsewhere. Currently, she is working on a book manuscript that examines African American representations of whiteness in popular culture.

REIGHAN ALEXANDRA GILLAM received her PhD in Anthropology from Cornell University and is currently a postdoctoral fellow at the University of Michigan in the Department of Afroamerican and African Studies. Her dissertation examines the struggle to create alternative images of Afro-Brazilians through segmented television production in São Paulo, Brazil. She conducts research on the ways in which Afro-Brazilians deploy media to create spaces for Blackness within public life.

TIMOTHY HAVENS is an associate professor of Communication Studies, African American Studies, and International Studies at the University of Iowa. He is the author of *Global Television Marketplace* (British Film Institute Publishing, 2006) and *Black Television Travels: African American Media Around the Globe* (NYU Press, 2012); co-author with Amanda D. Lotz of *Understanding Media Industries* (Oxford University Press, 2011); and co-editor with Anikó Imre and Katalin Lustyik of *Popular Television in Eastern Europe During and Since Socialism* (Routledge, 2012). His published research has also appeared in numerous academic journals and anthologies.

DEVORAH HEITNER is a visiting scholar at Carnegie Mellon University. Her research focuses on media activism, youth media-making, digital media and learning, mediation of identity, and the workplace culture of media organizations. She is the author of *Black Power TV* (Duke University Press, forthcoming). Her scholarship has been published in journals such as *Television & New Media* and the *Velvet Light Trap*.

KIM M. LEDUFF is an associate professor and associate director of the School of Mass Communication and Journalism at the University of Southern Mississippi.

She holds a PhD in Mass Communication from Indiana University. LeDuff is the author of *Tales of Two Cities: How Race and Crime Intersect on Local TV News* and co-author of *Race and News: Critical Perspectives*. She teaches a course titled "Race, Gender and Media" at both the undergraduate and graduate levels at USM, which reflects her research interests.

NGHANA LEWIS is an associate professor of English and of African & African Diaspora Studies at Tulane University, where she teaches courses on a wide range of subjects including Black literature, Black education, and Black women's health. She is the author of *Entitled to the Pedestal: Place, Race, and Progress in White Southern Women's Writing, 1920–1945* (University of Iowa Press, 2007) and has been published in *Black Music Research Journal*, the *Journal of American Drama and Theatre*, *Law & Literature*, *African American Review*, and *Black Women, Gender & Families*.

ERIC PIERSON is an associate professor and department chair of Communication Studies at the University of San Diego. His work on Black images and audiences has appeared in the *Encyclopedia of African American Business History*, *Screening Noir*, and the *Encyclopedia of the Great Black Migration*. He has also done research in the area of public policy. His most recent work in that area is the co-authored piece "The Rhetoric of Hate on the Internet: Hateporn's Challenge to Modern Media Ethics" which appears in the *Journal of Mass Media Ethics*.

TREAANDREA M. RUSSWORM is an assistant professor in the English Department at the University of Massachusetts, Amherst. She teaches classes in American Studies, post-1950s African American literature, popular culture, and new media. She has written several articles on representations of race in film, media, and video games. Her current book manuscript is on race, popular culture, and psychoanalytic thought during the civil rights era.

BERETTA E. SMITH-SHOMADE is an associate professor and chair of the Department of Communication and director of the Newcomb-Tulane Summer Transition Program at Tulane University. Her books include *Shaded Lives: African-American Women and Television* (Rutgers University Press, 2002) and *Pimpin' Ain't Easy: Selling Black Entertainment Television* (Routledge, 2007). She is a former Fulbright Fellow to Nigeria. Her research, creative, and teaching passions revolve around K–12 media literacy, Black media, and media production. She is on the editorial board of *Velvet Light Trap*.

KRISTEN J. WARNER is an assistant professor in the Department of Telecommunication and Film at the University of Alabama. Her research focuses primarily on the production cultures of casting as it relates to race, representation, and employment within the Hollywood film and television industry.

Her work has appeared in *In Media Res*, *Antenna*, *Flow*, and elsewhere. Currently, she is working on a book manuscript that examines the history and process of color-blind casting in American prime-time television.

DEBORAH ELIZABETH WHALEY is an associate professor of American Studies and African American Studies at the University of Iowa. Her first book, *Disciplining Women: Alpha Kappa Alpha, Black Counterpublics, and the Cultural Politics of Black Sororities* (SUNY Press, 2010), examines the cultural politics and popular practices of the oldest historically Black sorority. Her current book project is titled *Sequential Subjects: Black Women in Comics, Graphic Novels, and Anime*.

Index

Page numbers in italics refer to figures.

ABC: ABC Entertainment, 21; *ABC News Online*, 188; and blindcasting, 52; Broadcast Standards Department, 23; Movies for Television division, 22. *See also titles of ABC programs*
Aboriginals, 243
Abrams, J. J., 58, 64
Academy Awards, 37
accountability, 160–163, 165, 195
Acham, Christine, 3, 10, 176, 247
activism, 135, 176, 194, 198; and *Black Journal*, 78–79, 82–83; and Brazil/Afro-Brazilians, 207–208, 210, 212, 214–215, 217, 218n16; and *bro'Town*, 233. *See also* radical politics
actors. *See* casting
actors' guilds, 51–53, 59–60. *See also individual guilds*
Adult Swim, 12–13, 187, 191, 202n11
Adventures of Flagee and Ribbon, The, 190, 203n14
advertising sponsors, 1, 20; and *Black Journal*, 77, 87; and *bro'Town*, 232–233, 239; and *A Different World*, 37, 39–40; and *Fat Albert*, 97; and *Noah's Arc*, 177; and *The Office*, 63; and *Rich Man, Poor Man*, 32n17; and *Roots*, 29; and South African soap operas, 222; and *TV da Gente*, 216; and webisodes, 63, 72–73
Advocate, The, 174, 176
Africa: "African Renaissance," 224; on *Black Journal*, 78–79, 83–85; and *bro'Town*, 233; in *Roots*, 26–28; and South African soap operas, 224; and *TV da Gente*, 214–215. *See also individual African countries*
Africa Magic (M-Net), 1
African American Studies, 19, 30, 82, 190
African American Viewers and the Black Situation Comedy (Coleman), 3
Africanist vision, 224, 226
Afrikaans, 221, 226
AfroAnime, 189–190, 195, 197, 201
Afro-Brazilians. *See* Brazil/Afro-Brazilians

Afro hairstyle, 81–82; Afro puffs, 198
AIDS. *See* HIV/AIDS
Ajakawe, Michael, 66, 73
Akil, Salim, 159
Alexander, Khandi, 130
Ali, Muhammad, 21
Allen, Anita L., 160–161
Allen, Debbie, 10, 33, 36–41, 43–47, 44, 167
Alley, Robert, 33–34
Amaechi, John, 184
American Dilemma (Myrdal), 92
American Federation of Television and Radio Artists (AFTRA), 52–53, 59
American History Illustrated, 21
America's Next Top Model, 153, 172
Amos 'n' Andy, 10, 20
Angel Heart (film), 39
Angels in America (film), 180
animation, 89–91, 94, 97–101, 189, 202n11; and *bro'Town*, 236, 238–240. *See also* anime
anime, 12–13, 187, 189–204, 191, 196, 232–233; AfroAnime, 189–190, 195, 197, 201
apartheid, 38, 41, 84, 220–222, 225, 229–230
Appadurai, Arjun, 5
Apprentice, The, 142–144, 147–149, 147, 155n14, 155n22
APTN (Aboriginal Peoples Television Network), 243
Araújo, Joel Zito, 209
Arnold, Roseanne, 153
Asante, Molefi K., Jr., 158
Asheru, 202n4
"ashiness," 58, 61n25, 166
Asians, 52, 60n4, 189–190, 196
Asner, Edward, 24
assimilation, 26–28, 28, 109
Atwood, Jensen, 175
audiences, Black, 1–9, 11–14; and *Black Journal*, 77, 82–86; and blindcasting, 58–59; and *The Boondocks*, 195; and *City of Angels*, 58; and *Diary of a Single Mom*, 69–72; and *A Different World*, 37, 40; and

audiences, Black (*continued*)
  Drama Queenz, 68–69; and *Fat Albert*,
    89–91, 94, 99, 101, 102n6, 104n27; and
    Gimme a Break! 112–113, 117; and
    Girlfriends/The Game, 157–158, 161, 164,
    166, 169; and "guilty pleasure," 117; and
    Lee's documentaries, 122–127; and
    letter-writing campaigns, 112–113; and
    Noah's Arc, 177, 179–183; and reality
    television, 144; and *Roots*, 20–22, 26; and
    South African soap operas, 224, 227, 230;
    and *Treme*, 122–124, 127; and TV da
    Gente, 207, 213–215; and *Undercovers*, 59;
    and webisodes, 63–64, 66–74
audiences, mainstream, 2, 7, 11–12, 20; and
    The Apprentice, 147–148; and *Black Journal*,
    82, 84–85; and blindcasting, 53–56, 58–60;
    and *The Boondocks*, 189–192, 195, 199–201;
    and bro'Town, 234, 241, 243; and *City of
    Angels*, 54–56, 58, 60; and *A Different
    World*, 37, 40, 167; and *Fat Albert*, 89–91,
    99, 104n27; and *Flavor of Love*, 152–153;
    and *Gimme a Break!* 106, 108, 113–114,
    116–117; and *Girlfriends/The Game*, 158,
    161, 164, 166, 169, 169n3; and Lee's
    documentaries, 122–135; and *The Office*,
    63; and *The Real Housewives of Atlanta*,
    141; and reality television, 141, 143–148,
    152–154; and *Roots*, 19, 22, 24, 26–27, 29;
    and South African soap operas, 224, 227,
    230; and *Survivor: Fiji*, 144–146; and *Treme*,
    122–127, 129–135; and *Undercovers*, 58–60;
    and webisodes, 63, 65–66, 72
audiences, niche, 65, 67, 72, 234, 244
Australia, 1, 239–240, 242–243
Autobiography of Malcolm X, The, 21

Bachelor, The, 143, 150–153
Bakhtin, 97, 103n19, 188
Banfield, Bever-Leigh, 112–113
Banks, Tyra, 172
Barclay, Paris, 54–58, 61n19
Bargh, John, 124
Barnett, Clive, 229
Batten, Tony, 84
BBC (British Broadcasting Corporation), 221
Beam, Joseph, 184
Beatts, Anne, 10, 33–36, 41–43, 42, 46
Belafonte, Harry, 92
Bell, Darryl M., 38–39
Belushi, John, 34
Bennett, Bonnie, 49
Bennett, Lerone, 85
Bergman, Anne, 56

Berry, Gordon L., 102n6
BET (Black Entertainment Television), 2,
    64, 72, 158, 169, 199, 213, 242; Digital
    Networks, 242
Better Living Through Reality TV (Ouellette
    and Hay), 149
Beulah Land, 31n13
Beulah Show, The, 10, 106, 108–109
Big Brother Africa, 13
bin Laden, Osama, 190, 203n14
Birth of a Nation, The (film), 150
Black AIDS Institute, 176, 179, 185n18
Black Collegian, 148
Black Enterprise, 86, 148
Blackface, 150, 152, 195
Black Family Channel, 213
black fu, 196
Black Gay Pride celebrations, 175
Black History Lost, Stolen, or Strayed, 92–93
Black Is . . . Black Ain't (documentary film),
    15n12, 179
Black Journal, 11, 13, 26, 31n12, 77–87, 80, 86,
    87n13; Addis Ababa bureau of, 84; and
    censorship, 85; critics/criticism of, 81–82,
    85; first episode of, 77–78, 87; fifth
    episode of, 79–80; opening theme of, 79;
    on strike, 79–80, 87
Blackness, 2–5, 9–11, 13–14, 15n12; and *The
    Apprentice*, 148–149; "Black buddy,"
    148–149; "Blackness tour guide," 40; and
    The Boondocks, 200; and Brazil/Afro-
    Brazilians, 207, 213–214; and bro'Town, 14,
    233–234, 244; and *A Different World*, 33,
    35–37, 40–46; and *Fat Albert*, 90, 94, 98,
    101–102; and *Flavor of Love*, 153; and
    Gimme a Break! 107, 110; graphic
    Blackness, 189, 191, 201, 202n11; and
    minstrelsy, 150, 152; and *Noah's Arc*,
    176–177; as Other, 41, 44, 46, 179; and
    reality television, 148–150, 152–153; and
    Tongues Untied, 173. *See also* global
    Blackness
Black Panther Party, 81, 191
Black Perspective on the News, 86
Black Power, 77, 80–81, 158, 165, 233
Blacks and White TV (MacDonald), 2
Black South Africans, 221–223, 225, 227–228,
    230
Black star–white environment shows,
    109–112, 115
Black Television Travels (Havens), 3
"Black world." *See* global Blackness
Blakes, Tifani, 122, 136
Blanchard, Terence, 126–128, 128

Blanchard, Wilhelmina, 127–128
Bleach, 233
blindcasting, 10, 49–60; and *City of Angels*,
    10, 50, 54–60, 61n8, 61n19, 61n25; and *Soul
    Food*, 61n8; and *Undercovers*, 58–60
Blinn, William, 29
blogs, 124, 180–181, 193
Boatman, Michael, 172
Bochco, Steven, 54–58, 61n19
Bodroghkozy, Aniko, 6
Bold and the Beautiful, The, 230
Bonet, Lisa, 33, 35–36, 39, 42
Boondocks, The, 12–13, 187–201, 191, 196,
    202n11, 203n14; *bro'Town* compared to,
    236, 244; "The Fried Chicken Flu," 201;
    Gangstalicious, 198–201; "The Garden
    Party," 192, 195–198, 201; Granddad, 192,
    194, 196–197, 199–200; Huey, 190–192, 191,
    194–197, 199, 203n14; "It's a Black
    President, Huey Freeman," 201; Joe
    Petto, 193–195; "The Return of the King,"
    187–189, 193; Rev. Goodlove, 193–195;
    Riley, 192–194, 197, 199–200; "The Story
    of Gangstalicious," 192, 198–201; "The
    Story of Thugnificent," 192, 198–201;
    "The S-Word," 192–195, 203n18; Uncle
    Ruckus, 192, 194–195, 200
Boondocks, The (comic strip), 189–191,
    202n11
*Boondocks, The: Because I Know You Don't
    Read the Newspaper* (McGruder), 190,
    203n13
Boone, Eunetta, 159
Bourne, St. Clair, 79
Boutte, John, 133
Bowser, Yvette Lee, 159
boycott threat (post-1999), 51, 54
Boykin, Keith, 176, 184
Boyz n the Hood (film), 177
Boyz II Men, 43
Bravo, 141–142
Brazil/Afro-Brazilians, 13, 207–217; and
    colonial period, 208–209; and Law 10.639,
    212, 215; and National Day of Black
    Consciousness, 207; and National
    Program for Affirmative Action (2002),
    212; and racial democracy, 208–211, 213,
    216, 217n5; and SEPPIR (Secretariat for
    Promoting Policies of Racial Inclusion),
    212; and TV da Gente, 13, 207–208,
    211–217, 213; and TV Globo, 209–210
Brent Zook, Kristal, 4
Bright Road, A (film), 92
Brinkley, Douglas, 123

British Petroleum (BP) oil spill, 121, 134
Brock Akil, Mara, 12, 157–160, 163–169,
    169n1
Brook, Vincent, 51–52, 60n4
Brooks, Golden, 162
bro'Town, 14, 232–244, 235; "bro'Town
    Glossary," 240; and "cultural journeys,"
    14, 235, 241–244; and *fa'afafine*, 241; and
    globalization, 232–235, 239–243; "Go
    Home, Stay Home," 241; and industry
    lore, 233–235, 241–244; Jeff da Māori,
    235–238; "A Māori at My Table," 236–238;
    and satire, 235–238, 240; and scatological
    humor, 238, 240; translation of, 241
Brown, Charnele, 39
Brown, Foxy, 158
Brown, Rob, 128
Brown, Tony, 85–87, 86
browns, 209, 232, 235–237
Brown v. Board of Education (1954), 91, 195
Burdick, John, 218n16
Burton, LeVar, 27
Burton, Nsenga K., 13, 220–231, 247
Bush, George H. W., 190
Bush, George W., 190, 192, 198, 203n14
Busselle, Rick, 125, 134

cable networks, 2, 4, 31, 61n8; and *The
    Boondocks*, 187, 189; and *bro'Town*, 239,
    242; and *Noah's Arc*, 173–174, 176–177, 180;
    and webisodes, 64–65, 67. *See also
    individual cable networks*
Calhoun, Monica, 69, 70
call and response, 13, 35, 173, 199
Cambridge, Godfrey, 77
Campbell-Martin, Tisha, 38, 167
Canada, 188, 239, 243; CanWest, 239
Cannick, Jasmyne, 181, 183
capitalism, 2, 84, 97, 103n14, 158, 168; and
    The Boondocks, 198, 200–201; and
    bro'Town, 236–237
Carbado, Devon, 149, 155n21
Cardosa, Fernando, 211–212
Carroll, Diahann, 109
Carter, Nell, 105, 107, 110–114, 117–118
Cartoon Network, 12–13, 187, 189, 202n11,
    240–242
cartoons/cartoonists, 202n11; and *The
    Boondocks*, 190; and *Fat Albert*, 89–91, 94,
    96, 99, 101–102, 102n6, 104n27
casting, 9; blindcasting, 10, 49–60, 61n8,
    61n19, 61n25; and Brazil/Afro-Brazilians,
    209; of *City of Angels*, 10, 50, 54–60, 55,
    61n8, 61n19, 61n25; of *Diary of a Single*

casting (*continued*)
  Mom, 69–70; of *A Different World*, 38–40,
  42–45, *42*, *44*; of *Drama Queenz*, 67–68; of
  Flavor of Love, 143, 150–153; of
  Girlfriends/*The Game*, 160–162, *161*,
  163–165, *168*, *169*; of *Noah's Arc*, 174–175,
  175, 177–178, 181, *182*, *183*, 185n9; "organic"
  process of, 58; of *The Real Housewives of
  Atlanta*, 141–142; of reality television,
  141–146, 150–153; of *Roots*, 10, 19, 22–26,
  31n11; of *Soul Food*, 61n8; of South
  African soap operas, 223–227, 230; of
  Survivor: Fiji, 144–146; of *Treme*, 121, 124,
  127–134; of *Undercovers*, 58–60; of *The
  Vampire Diaries*, 49; of webisodes, 64,
  67–70. *See also names of actors and
  characters*
Cavalcante, Andre M., 10, 11, 33–48, 171n24,
  247
CBS, 20–21; and blindcasting, 50, 52, 54, 56,
  61n15; Paramount Network Television,
  169n1. *See also titles of CBS programs*
CDC (Centers for Disease Control), 179
celebrities, 9, 111–112, 212; local, 121, 132
censorship, 85, 190, 194, 200, 203n14; and
  Brazil/Afro-Brazilians, 208, 211;
  "cultural," 208
Chan, Yau-Man, 144–145, 155n10, 155n12
Chanchez, Hosea, 162
Changeling (film), 183
Channeling Blackness (Hunt), 3
Chaplin, Charlie, 98
Chapman, Mark, 189
Chappelle's Show, 232, 244
Chase, Chevy, 34
Cheney, Dick, 198
Cheng, Anne, 91
Chester, Rodney, 175
children, Black, 4; faceless drawings of,
  92–93, 103n9; and *Fat Albert*, 11, 89–94,
  96–97, 99, 101–102, 103n13, 104n27; and TV
  da Gente, 214–215
Children Now, 51
Chock, T. Makana, 124–125, 136
Christian Century, The, 31n7
Christianity, 238
churches, Black, 38, 179
CIA (Central Intelligence Agency), 190
Cinderella myth, 143, 153
citizenship, 144–150, 201; corporate, 149
City of Angels, 10, 50, 54–60, *55*, 61n8, 61n19,
  61n25
civil rights movement, 80–84; and *The
  Boondocks*, 187–188, 194–195; and

Brazil/Afro-Brazilians, 214–215; and
  bro'Town, 233; and *Fat Albert*, 90–92, 94,
  102, 104n27; and *Gimme a Break!* 108; and
  Girlfriends/*The Game*, 158, 164
Civil War, 38, 108, 114
Clark, Kenneth, and Mamie, 92; doll
  studies of, 92–93
Clark, Robert, 83
class, 1, 3; and *The Boondocks*, 192, 195,
  198–200, 202n2; and *A Different World*, 40;
  and *Girlfriends*/*The Game*, 158; and *Noah's
  Arc*, 177; and reality television, 12, 142,
  144, 153; and webisodes, 73. *See also
  middle class; upper class; working class*
Cleaver, Kathleen, 81–82
Clifton, Jacob, 148
Clinton, Bill, 155n14
CNN, 141–142, 194
Cobb, William Jelani, 189
Coetzee, Greig, 227
Cohen, Andy, 142
Cohen, Nathan, 102n6
Cole, Johnetta, 37
Coleman, Gary, 110, 112
Coleman, Robin R. Means, 3, 10, 11, 171n24,
  247
Coles, Martin, 96
colleges, Black. *See* HBCUs
Collins, Monica, 40–41
Collins, Patricia Hill, 108, 148–149
colonialism, 208–209, 237–238; decolo-
  nization, 84–85
Color Adjustment (Riggs), 5
color-blindness. *See* blindcasting
Color by Fox (Zook), 2–3
Colored People's Time (Detroit), 78, 85
Color Purple, The, 4
Columbia Studios, 21
Combs, Sean, 159
comedy, 20, 24, 30–31; and *The Boondocks*,
  195; and *A Different World*, 34–36, 41, 43;
  and *Gimme a Break!* 105; and
  Girlfriends/*The Game*, 159, 165; and *Noah's
  Arc*, 172, 176–177, 179; and webisodes, 63,
  65–67. *See also names of comedians and
  comedies*
Comedy Channel, The, 240, 242
Come on People (Cosby and Poussaint),
  102n6
comic strips, 12–13, 189–191, 202n11
community, Black: and *Black Journal*, 78,
  80, 82–83, 87n14; and Brazil/
  Afro-Brazilians, 215; and *Diary of a Single
  Mom*, 69–72; and *A Different World*, 38,

45–46; and *Drama Queenz*, 69; and *Fat Albert*, 94, 100; and HBCUs, 38, 45–46; and Katrina (hurricane), 122, 128; and *Noah's Arc*, 174, 176, 179–181, 184, 185n12; and *Roots*, 27, 31n13; and *Treme*, 122, 128; and webisodes, 63, 65–67, 69–73
condoms, 162, 166–167, 170n23, 228
consumers, 5–6, 20, 71, 97, 143, 192, 235
Cook Island Television, 239–240
Cooper, Anderson, 141–142, 154n1
Cosby, Bill: and *To All My Friends on Shore*, 92; and *Black History Lost, Stolen, or Strayed*, 92–93, 103n9; and *The Boondocks*, 194–195, 200; and *A Different World*, 36, 39, 41; and *Fat Albert*, 11, 87n13, 89–102, 102n6, 103n9, 103n13; and *I Spy*, 31n3; stand-up routines of, 89, 93–94, 102, 195. *See also Cosby Show*
Cosby Show, The, 10, 11, 65, 90, 112; and *The Boondocks*, 194–195; *A Different World* compared to, 33, 35–36, 39–41, 167; *Fat Albert* compared to, 102, 102n6, 104n27; *Gimme a Break!* compared to, 115, 117
Cosby Show, The (Fuller), 104n27
Coulter, Ann, 193–195
CSI franchise, 239
Culp, Robert, 31n3
"cultural journeys," 14, 235, 241–244
Cultural Moves (Gray), 2
cultural politics, Black, 2, 109, 207; and *The Boondocks*, 12–13, 189–192, 200–201, 202n2, 202n12, 203n24; and *bro'Town*, 233, 237, 242
cultural specificity, 1–3, 5–7, 12; and *Black Journal*, 77–78; and blindcasting, 49–54, 58–60; and *The Boondocks*, 12–13; and *bro'Town*, 233, 239–241, 243–244; and *City of Angels*, 10, 54, 58–60; and *A Different World*, 10, 33, 35, 40–46; and *Fat Albert and the Cosby Kids*, 11; and *Roots*, 24, 26–28; and *Undercovers*, 58–60; and *The Vampire Diaries*, 49; and webisodes, 73. *See also* difference, cultural
Cunningham, Mark D., 12, 13, 74n8, 172–186, 247–248
CW Television Network, 49, 64, 168

D'Adesky, Jacques, 209
Dallas Morning News, 190, 203n14
Dandridge, Dorothy, 92
Dangerous Minds (film), 46
Daniels, Lee, 159
Danke, Katlego, 226
Danziger case, 130

Dark Ghetto (Clark), 92
Dates, Jannette L., 108, 117
dating shows, 143, 150–154. *See also individual shows*
Davis, Michaela Angela, 166–167
Davis, Miles, 21
Dawson, Paul, 193
Debmar-Mercury, 8
de Certeau, Michel, 98, 101
decision making: and *The Apprentice*, 144–149, 155n22; and *The Boondocks*, 198; and *Girlfriends/The Game*, 160, 167
Dee, Ruby, 22
Deggans, Eric, 57, 60
Delirious, 172
Delvy, Richard, 104n26
democracy: Brazilian racial democracy, 208–211, 213, 216, 217n5; and South African soap operas, 221, 223–224, 229
Dia de Princesa (Princess for a Day), 212
Diary of a Single Mom, 66, 69–72, 70; Bo, 69; Lupe, 69, 70, 71; and "Make It Easy Toolbox," 71; Ocean Jackson, 69–72, 70; Peggy, 69, 70, 71; "Running on Empty," 71–72; viewer commentary on, 70–72
diaspora, African, 13, 35, 83–85, 214–215, 233
Dickerson, Debra, 150
difference, cultural, 1, 3; and *Black Journal*, 81, 84; and blindcasting, 49–51, 53, 59–60; and Brazil/Afro-Brazilians, 212; and *bro'Town*, 241–244; and *A Different World*, 43, 46; and *Fat Albert*, 95–96, 103n9; and *Flavor of Love*, 151; and *Noah's Arc*, 179; and *The Real Housewives of Atlanta*, 142, 154n5; and *The Vampire Diaries*, 49; and webisodes, 66. *See also* cultural specificity
Different World, A, 10, 11, 33–47, 65, 167–168, 171n24; Allen as producer of, 10, 33, 36–41, 43–47, 44, 167; Beatts as producer of, 10, 33–36, 41–43, 42, 46; Denise Huxtable, 33, 35–36, 39, 42; Dwayne Wayne, 39, 42, 44, 46; and *Girlfriends/The Game*, 167–168; Hillman College in, 33, 35, 37–38, 45, 167; HIV/AIDS addressed in, 167; Jaleesa Vinson, 36, 40, 42–43, 45; Kimberly Reese, 39, 41, 45; Maggie Lauten, 35, 39, 42; marching band in, 45; "Monet Is the Root of All Evil," 167; "No Means No," 41; opening credits of, 41–46, 42, 44; "Porky de Bergerac," 36; Ron Johnson Jr., 39, 44; split image in, 41, 47; "A Stepping Stone," 38; theme song of, 41–43; "Time Keeps on Slippin'," 167; Whitley Gilbert, 34, 39, 44, 46

Diff'rent Strokes, 43, 110, 117

Diggs, Taye, 172

Diller, Barry, 22

directors: and Brazil/Afro-Brazilians, 211; casting directors, 49–50; of *City of Angels*, 54, 57; of *Diary of a Single Mom*, 69, 71; of *Noah's Arc*, 173, 175–176; of *Roots*, 30; of webisodes, 64–66, 69, 71. *See also names of directors*

discrimination, racial, 50, 83, 135, 220; and Brazil/Afro-Brazilians, 208–210, 212–213, 218n16

distribution, 5, 13; and *Black Journal*, 86; and *bro'Town*, 234, 239–241, 244; Web, 9, 66

diversity, racial: and *Black Journal*, 80, 87; and blindcasting, 51–59; and Brazil/Afro-Brazilians, 207, 212, 215–217; and *bro'Town*, 235; and *City of Angels*, 54–59; and *A Different World*, 39, 45–46; and diversity executives, 51–53; and *Fat Albert*, 89; and *Noah's Arc*, 174, 176, 185n9; and *The Real Housewives of Atlanta*, 142; report cards on, 52, 60n4; and South African soap operas, 223, 230; and *Undercovers*, 58–59; and webisodes, 66, 73

documentaries, 7, 11–12; on *Black Journal*, 78, 80–82; and *bro'Town*, 242; and *Fat Albert*, 92, 103n9; and female MCs, 158; of Lee, 7, 11, 121–136, 128; and reality television, 143; of Riggs, 12, 15n12, 173, 183–184; webisodes as, 65; of Wolper, 22. *See also titles of documentaries*

Dodson, Antoine, 172

double-dutch rope jumping, 43

Drama Queenz, 65–66, 67–69, 68, 73; Davis, 67–69; Donovan, 67–69; Preston, 67–69; "Simple Little Things," 68–69

Drayton, William, 152. *See also* Flavor Flav

Dreamz. *See* Herd, Andria "Dreamz"

Dr. John, 133

dry-skin condition, 58, 61n25

Duas Caras (Two Faces), 210

DuBois, W.E.B., 192

Dubrofsky, Rachel, 151–152

du Gay, Paul, 143

Duplechan, Larry, 184

Dutton, Charles S., 171n24

Ebony, 21, 111–112

educational programs: *The Boondocks* as, 191; *Fat Albert* as, 89–90, 97; *Girlfriends/The Game* as, 157; *Noah's Arc* as, 179–180. *See also* ETV; NET; *and titles of educational programs*

Edwards, David, 146, 155n13

effeminacy, 177–178, 198

Egoli, 223

Ehrenstein, David, 35, 43

Elie, Lolis Eric, 122–123

Elijah Communications, 240

Elise, Kimberly, 164

elitism, 85, 238, 242–243

Ellen DeGeneres Show, The, 141

Elliott, Missy, 158

Ellis, Nelsan, 173

Ellison, Ralph, 4

Emmy Awards, 24, 29–30, 40

English language, 221, 223, 226–227, 237, 239–240

Entertainment Weekly, 54

equality/inequality, racial, 13, 135; and Brazil/Afro-Brazilians, 207–214, 216–217; equal opportunity, 50–51, 53; and reality television, 149–150; and segregation, 38, 91–92, 108; and South African soap operas, 220, 223, 225; and structural inequities, 102, 108, 148–149, 202n2

Essence, 111–113, 118, 150, 166–167

ETV (educational television), 77–78, 82, 85; Alabama ETV, 85

Evans, Art, 38

Evans, Walker, 83

Facebook, 5

Fales, Susan, 41, 44, 167

fantasy, 109, 118, 118n2, 142; and *Fat Albert*, 91–94, 96, 99–100, 102, 103n13

fashion, Black: and *Black Journal*, 81–82, 85; and *Flavor of Love*, 153–154; and *Girlfriends/The Game*, 164, 167; and *Noah's Arc*, 178

Fashion TV, 1

Fat Albert and the Cosby Kids, 11, 87n13, 89–102, 95; animation of, 89–91, 94, 97–101; Bill, 89, 96, 102; *The Brown Hornet* (cartoon), 96; "buck buck," 96, 100; Bucky, 89, 95; Fat Albert in, 89, 94–97, 95, 99–102, 103n19; and *Fort! Da!* 98–99, 101; Junkyard Gang in, 94–95, 102; laugh track in, 103n19; "Moving," 99–101; music in, 95, 96, 99–101, 103n9, 104n26; and play, 89–94, 96, 98–101, 103n9, 103n13, 103n19; and postmodernism, 91, 95–99, 101, 103n14, 103n19; recycled imagery in, 89, 97, 99; Rudy, 89, 95–96, 100; silhouettes in, 97–99, 101; "The Stranger," 95, 103n9; and superheroes, 90, 101; titles of, 102n5; Weird Harold, 89, 95

Faustino, Oswaldo, 214
favelas/favelados, 209–210
FBI (Federal Bureau of Investigation), 180, 190, 194
FCC (Federal Communications Commission), 30, 85–86, 170n23, 242
femininity, 118, 142, 154, 154n5, 164, 209, 222
feminism, 164, 166–168, 222, 231n8
Feshbach, Seymour, 102n6
50 Cent, 198
Filmation, 89, 98–99
Finke, Nikki, 59
Firehorse Films, 232, 240–241
Fiske, John, 97
Flavor Flav, 143, 150–154, 151, 156n25
Flavor of Love, 3, 142–144, 150–154, 151, 156n25, 156n34; grill as award in, 150, 152, 156n25
Flavor of Love Girls, 153–154
Forbes, 8
Foster, Kevin, 122, 136
Fournier, Ed, 104n26
Fox, Grethe, 229
Fox, Vivica A., 57
Fox Network Television, 2–3, 12, 15n12, 52, 65, 119n14, 126–127, 171n24, 181
Foxtel, 240, 242
Foxx, Jamie, 159
Foxx, Redd, 25
Franklin, Aretha, 43
Fresh Prince of Bel-Air, The, 43, 65, 244
Freud, Sigmund, 98–99, 101, 102n6
Freyre, Gilberto, 208
Friday (film), 177
From G's to Gents, 153
Fuller, Jennifer, 11, 248
Fuller, Linda F., 90, 104n27
Fuqua, Antoine, 159

Gambit, 130–131, 136
Game, The, 3, 10, 12, 64, 74n4, 157–160, 162–164, 167–169, 168, 169n1, 170n15–17; Derwin, 162–163; "Diary of a Mad Black Woman, Redux," 162; "Fool Me Twice . . . I'm the Damn Fool," 162–163; Kelly, 167, 170n15; Malik Wright, 162–164, 170n17; Melanie, 162–163, 167, 170n15; "Punk Ass Chauncey," 170n17; Sabers football team, 163, 170n16; Tasha Mack, 162–164, 167, 170n15; "The Third Legacy," 170n17
gangstas, 153, 192, 198–201
Gardner, Stu, 41, 43
Garrett, Kent, 78–79

Gates, Henry Louis, Jr., 152, 156n31
Gates, Racquel, 12–13, 141–156, 248
gay bashing, 180
gay men, Black, 15n12; and *The Boondocks*, 198, 200–201; and *Drama Queenz*, 65–66, 67–69, 68; and *Girlfriends/The Game*, 166; and HIV/AIDS, 157, 166; and *Noah's Arc*, 12, 172–184, 182, 185n9, 185n12; and South African soap operas, 228
gay men, white, 142
gay pride events, 175–176
gay rights movement, 158
GED, 69–70
gender, 1, 3; and *The Boondocks*, 192, 197–198, 200; and Brazil/Afro-Brazilians, 211; and *bro'Town*, 241; and *Girlfriends/The Game*, 158, 167; and *Noah's Arc*, 177; and reality television, 12, 142–143, 149–154, 154n5, 156n34; and South African soap operas, 222–223, 225–227, 229; and webisodes, 73. See also health: Black women's
Generations, 221, 223–226, 228, 230; Karabo Moroka, 225–226
George, Nelson, 159
George Peabody Fund, 38
Getlein, Frank, 77
ghetto life: and *Fat Albert*, 89–90, 94, 97, 100–101, 103n19; and hip hop, 159; and *Noah's Arc*, 178; and reality television, 141, 151, 154
Gillam, Reighan Alexandra, 13, 248
Gimme a Break! 11, 105–118, 107, 116, 118n1; Adelaide "Addy" Wilson, 113–114, 116; and Aunt Jemima, 105, 110–111, 113–114; and Black maids, 105–111, 113–115, 118, 118n2; Carl Kanisky, 106, 109, 115; critics/criticism of, 106–114, 117–118; first episode of, 105, 111; "Flashback," 113; Grandpa Kanisky, 115–116; industrial context of, 105–106, 109; Kanisky family, 106, 109, 111, 113–116, 118; and a "modern Black woman," 113–114, 118; Nell Harper, 105–118, 107, 116, 119n4; "Nell's Friend," 113–114; professional women in, 106, 108, 111, 113–116, 118; TV One marathon of, 117–118
Girlfriends, 10, 12, 64, 157–169, 161, 169n1; Brian, 165–166; "Buh-Bye," 161–162; Greg, 160–162; Joan, 160–162, 164–167; Lynn, 162, 164–167; Maya, 162, 166–167; *Noah's Arc* compared to, 173, 177; "The Pact," 164–166; Reesie Jackson, 164–166; Toni, 160–167; "Trick or Truth?," 162

Gledhill, Christine, 108, 231n8
global Blackness, 13–14; and *Black Journal*,
    79, 82–85, 87; and *The Boondocks*, 189; and
    Brazil/Afro-Brazilians, 13, 207–217; and
    bro'Town, 14, 232–244; and *The Cosby
    Show*, 90; and South African soap operas,
    13, 220–230
globalization, 3, 13, 232–235, 238–243;
    "vernacular globalization," 238
Glover, Danny, 117
Glover, Henry, 130
Goldberg, Whoopi, 167
Golden Girls, The, 116, 173
Golden Globes, 37
Gone with the Wind (film), 114
gospel music, 8, 57, 110, 162
Gossett, Louis, Jr., 29
Graden, Brian, 174, 176, 181–182
Grammer, Kelsey, 169n1
Grammy Awards, 43
Gramsci, Antonio, 108
Grant, Cary, 58
graphic Blackness, 189, 191, 201, 202n11
Gray, Herman S., 2, 90, 177, 211, 234
Gray, Jonathan, 153
Greaves, William, 79–80, 80, 84–85
Greenberg, Bradley, 125, 134
Greene, Lorne, 25
Grier, David Alan, 172
Griffith, Kristen-Alexzander, 67
Guest, Christopher, 34
Guy, Jasmine, 34, 38–39

Haley, Alex, 21–23, 27, 30, 114
Hall, Christine, 96
Hall, Pooch, 162
Hall, Stuart, 143–144, 150, 210
Hall, Vondie-Curtis, 172
Hardison, Kadeem, 38–39
Hardrict, Tia Mowry, 162
Hardy, Antoine, 151–152
Hardy, James Earl, 184
Harris, E. Lynn, 184
Hasenbalg, Carlos, 209
Hasinoff, Amy Adele, 153
Havens, Timothy, 3, 14, 189, 219n25,
    232–246, 248
Hay, James, 144–145, 149
HBCUs (historically Black colleges and
    universities), 33, 35–39, 44–46, 167
HBO, 7, 121–124, 131, 172–173, 176;
    HBO.com, 122–123, 126–127, 129, 131,
    134–136
health, Black women's, 12, 157–162, 164–169

Heitner, Devorah, 11, 13, 31n12, 77–88, 248
Help, The (film), 105, 118n2
Hemphill, Essex, 184
Hemphill, Shirley, 109
Hepburn, Katharine, 58
Herd, Andria "Dreamz," 144–145, *145*, 148,
    154, 155n10
Hero Ain't Nothing but a Sandwich, A (film),
    92
Hill, Lauryn, 158
Hill Street Blues, 54
Hilton-Jacobs, Lawrence, 25
hip hop, 43, 157–160, 163–169, 170n9; and
    The Boondocks, 188, 191–192, 198–201; and
    Brazil/Afro-Brazilians, 214; and *A
    Different World*, 167; and female MCs,
    157–159, 168; feminist aesthetic of, 164,
    166–168; and *Girlfriends/The Game*, 12,
    157–160, 163–166, 169, 170n15; and *The Real
    Housewives of Atlanta*, 141
HIV/AIDS: and ARVs (antiretroviral
    drugs), 227; in *A Different World*, 167; and
    Girlfriends/The Game, 12, 157, 159–162,
    164–169, 170n9, 171n24; and *Noah's Arc*,
    175–176, 179–180, 185n18; and South
    African soap operas, 220, 227–228; and
    Tongues Untied, 15n12, 173, 183–184
Hobson, Dorothy, 231n8
Hoffman, Dominic, 38
Hogan, Hulk, 97
Hola Entertainment, 241
Hollywood, 8, 49, 52–54, 56, 59–60, 105; and
    bro'Town, 234, 237–238, 240–242; and
    Noah's Arc, 177, 185n12; and webisodes,
    65–66. *See also* titles of movies
Hollywood Shuffle (film), 72
homonationalism, 200–201, 203n24
homophobia, 159, 173, 177, 180, 184
homosexuality, 15n12, 172–173, 177, 180, 220.
    See also gay men, Black
Honey, 166
hooks, bell, 168, 242
Hooks, Benjamin, 86
Hooks, Kevin, 57–58
Hoover, J. Edgar, 194
Hopkins, Telma, 113
House, Lou, 78–80, 82–83, 87n2. *See also*
    Siddiq, Wali
House of Payne, 8–9, *8*
Houston, Whitney, 117
Howell, Mary, 124, 130–131
Hughes Brothers, 177
Human Rights Campaign (HRC), 176
humor, Black, 35–36, 90, 102, 159, 179

Hunt, Darnell, 3, 41
Hunter-Gault, Chuma, 160

Ice Cube, 177
identity, Black, 5; and *Black Journal*, 82; and
   Brazil/Afro-Brazilians, 213, 218n16; and *A
   Different World*, 42, 46; and *Fat Albert*, 96,
   98, 103n9; and *Girlfriends/The Game*, 158,
   163, 165–166; and Katrina (hurricane), 125,
   131–134; and *Noah's Arc*, 175, 179; and
   reality television, 143, 148, 151, 155n21; and
   Roots, 26; and South African soap operas,
   224, 230; and *Tongues Untied*, 173. *See also*
   Blackness
If God Is Willing and da Creek Don't Rise, 11,
   121, 123–124, 126–128, 130–131, 133–136; and
   perceived realism, 126–128, 130–131,
   133–136; police brutality in, 130–131;
   viewer commentary on, 122–123, 126–127,
   133, 135–136
Imitation of Life (film), 114–115
imperialism, 197; cultural, 244
Indian South Africans, 223, 225, 227
indigenous people, 84, 233, 239–240,
   243–244. *See also names of indigenous
   groups*
industry lore, 233–235, 241–244
inequality. *See* equality/inequality, racial
In Living Color, 2, 65, 172, 181; "Men on
   Film" skit, 12, 15n12, 67
"In Search of the African" (*American
   History Illustrated*), 21
interiority, Black, 11, 90, 92–94, 101
Internet, 9; and anonymity, 124; and *The
   Boondocks*, 193; and *bro'Town*, 241; and
   City of Angels, 59–60; and Antoine
   Dodson, 172; and *Girlfriends/The Game*,
   169; and *Noah's Arc*, 176, 180–181, 183–184;
   post-Katrina, 122–124, 126–127, 129,
   131–136, 137n2; predators on, 70; and
   reality television, 141, 148–149; and
   viewer commentary, 59–60, 68–73,
   122–124, 126–127, 129, 131–136, 137n2, 141,
   148–149, 169, 180–181, 183–184; and
   webisodes, 63–64, 67, 70–72 (*see also*
   webisodes)
interracial couples, 39, 119n14, 194, 225
In the Gloaming (film), 180
invisibility, 4–6, 20, 50, 78–79, 168, 217
Invisible Man (Ellison), 4
Iraq War, 197–198
Isidingo, 221, 224, 224, 226–229; Nandipha,
   224, 227–228
iTunes, 63

Jackson, Samuel, 192
Japan/Japanese, 189, 191, 215; and *bro'Town*,
   232–233, 236–238. *See also* anime
Jarvis, Rebecca, 147–149, 155n22
Jay-Z, 159
jazz, 233; BET J, 242
Jeffersons, The, 20, 109–111, 117, 119n14;
   Florence Johnston, 109, 111
Jet, 111–112, 117
Jhally, Sut, 90, 104n27, 117
John, Deacon, 133
Johnson, Earvin "Magic," 167
Johnson, E. Patrick, 178–179
Johnson, Reggie, 36
Jones, Jacquie, 173
Jones, James Earl, 31n11
Jones, Jill Marie, 160
Jones, Quincy, 21
Jordan, Vernon, 19
Joseph, Dane, 66–67, 69, 73
Joyce, Ella, 171n24
Julius Rosenwald Fund, 38
junkies, 51, 56, 90, 92
junkyards, 43, 90, 94, 96–98, 100

Kardiner, Abram, 92
Karenga, Ron, 81
Kate & Allie, 116
Katrina (hurricane), 5, 7, 11–12, 121–136; fifth
   anniversary of, 121–122, 136; and
   perceived realism, 124–125, 127–136; and
   police brutality, 125, 130–131. *See also*
   Treme; *and titles of Lee's documentaries*
Keith, Gregory, 178
Kelley, Venita, 37
Kenyatta, Jomo, 84
Keys, Alicia, 9
King, J. L., 180
King, Mabel, 109
King, Martin Luther, Jr., 21, 78, 80; and *The
   Boondocks*, 187–189, 202n4
King, Regina, 192
Kinoy, Ernest, 29
Klein, Naomi, 5
Knight, Arthur, 150, 152
Kodjoe, Boris, 58, 60
Koonin, Steve, 9
Kraidy, Marwan, 5
Kravitz, Lenny, 39
Krueger, Rex, 189

L.A. Law, 54
Lange, Dorothea, 83
LaRose, Jean, 243

Larry King Live, 194
Last Poets, The, 202n4
Latifah, Queen, 159
Latin America, 217n3, 237, 239–241, 244;
    Cartoon Network, 240–242
Latinas/os, 51–52, 67, 69, 174, 185n9
Leakes, NeNe, 141–142, 154
LeDuff, Kim M., 11–12, 121–137, 248–249
Lee, Hangwoo, 122
Lee, Spike, 7, 11, 38, 46, 121–136, 128. *See also*
    titles of his documentaries
Lemmings, 34
Leo, Melissa, 130
lesbians, 173–174, 180–181, 201
Let There Be Eve . . . Ruff Ryders' First Lady
    (Eve), 158
Levine, Elana, 6
Lewis, Dawnn, 36, 40–41
Lewis, Justin, 104n27, 117
Lewis, Nghana, 10, 12–13, 74n4, 157–171,
    249
LGBT/LGBTQ, 65, 69, 173–174, 201
liberation, Black, 80–81, 84, 87
Link TV, 242–243
Lionsgate, 8
Logo, 67, 173–174, 176, 180–184, 185n9;
    website of, 183
Longtime Companion (film), 180
Los Angeles Times, 110
Los Angeles Web Fest, 73
Lowery, Andrew, 39
Lumumba, Patrice, 215
Lynde, Janice, 69
Lyotard, Jean-François, 101

Maake, Sello, 225
Mackenzie, Robert, 107–108
Madison, Lance, 130
Madison, Ronald, 130
Malcolm X, 21, 80, 198
mammies, 11, 105–106, 108–115, 118, 119n4
Mandela, Nelson, 220–221, 223–226
Manigault-Stallworth, Omarosa, 147–148,
    155n14
Māori culture, 232–233, 235–237, 241
Marc, David, 34, 40
marginalization, 51, 179, 202n2; and
    Brazil/Afro-Brazilians, 207, 209–211, 216;
    and reality television, 144, 148–149
Margulies, Stan, 29
Mark of Oppression, The (Ovesey), 92
Marshall, Pluria W., 107–108
Marx, Leo, 197
Mary Tyler Moore Show, The, 20, 24

masculinity, 97, 152, 164; and *The Boondocks*,
    13, 192, 198, 200; and *bro'Town*, 238;
    hypermasculinity, 178, 198, 200; and
    Noah's Arc, 13, 177–178
Maseko, Tshepo, 227
Masilo-Ferguson, Connie, 225
Masters and the Slaves, The (Freyre), 208
Matelski, Marilyn J., 231n8
Matenga, Jeane, 240
Maude, 20, 109
Mbatha-Raw, Gugu, 58
Mbeki, Thabo, 224–228
Mbembie, Achille, 203n24
Mboya, Hlubi, 224, 227
McClurkin, Donnie, 162
McCullom, Rod, 181
McFadden, Cynthia, 188
McGruder, Aaron, 12–13, 187–201, 202n4,
    203n14, 203n18
MC Hammer, 165
McKay, Jenny, 122, 136
McKenna, Katelyn, 124
McKnight, Brian, 57
McLeod's Daughters, 1
MC Lyte, 158
Meet the Browns, 8–9
Menace II Society (film), 177
Merritt, Theresa, 109
middle class, 7, 115, 117, 127–128, 150, 178,
    220; and *The Boondocks*, 199–200; and
    Brazil/Afro-Brazilians, 209, 211; and
    South African soap operas, 222
Mills, Brett, 34
miscegenation, 39, 109, 208, 210
Mitchell, Elizabeth, 239, 241
Mitchell, Elvis, 35
Mitchell, W.J.T., 168
M-Net (Electronic Media Network), 1, 223
mobility, social, 167, 209, 220, 230
model minorities, 148
Modleski, Tania, 222, 231n8
Moesha, 244
Montana-LeBlanc, Phyllis, 131–134, 132
Moonves, Les, 54
Moore, Michael, 127
Morgan, Joan, 164
Morial, Ernest "Dutch," 133
Morial, Jacques, 133
Morial, Marc, 133
Morris, Phil, 161
Moses, Gilbert, 30
Movimento Negro Unificado (Unified
    Black Movement), 210, 218n16
Moynihan, Daniel, 92

Mozambique Liberation Front, 84
MSM, 166
MTV Network, 173–174, 182, 199–200
Muigai, James, 84
multiculturalism, 215, 223–224, 226, 235, 242–244
multiracialism, 192, 223–226, 230
Murphy, Charlie, 192
Murphy, Eddie, 172
Murray, Susan, 144
Myers, Lou, 45
My Mic Sounds Nice, 158
Myrdal, Gunnar, 92
MySpace, 181

NAACP, 20, 50–52, 54, 60n2; Awards Ceremony (2004), 195; Image Awards, 40
Naked Samoans, 232
Naspers (Afrikaner company), 223
National Black Media Coalition, 107
National Endowment for the Arts, 173
National Lampoon's Lemmings, 34
National Urban League, 19
Native Americans, 52
Native Indians (Brazil), 208
NBA, 167, 184
NBC, 31n13, 56–57; NBC.com, 63. *See also titles of NBC programs*
necropolitics, 201, 203n24
negotiation: and *Gimme a Break!* 106, 108, 113–114, 118; and *Girlfriends/The Game*, 158; and *The Help* (film), 118n2; and *Noah's Arc*, 12; and reality television, 143–144; and South African soap operas, 230
Negritude Júnior (Junior Blackness), 212
neoconservatives, 192, 195, 200, 202n2
neoliberalism, 149, 192, 195
NET (National Educational Television), 77–79, 85, 87, 87n3
Netinho (José de Paulo Neto), 212–213, 216
networks, 2, 4, 6–8; and blindcasting, 49–52, 56–57, 60; and *bro'Town*, 233–234, 239, 243; and *City of Angels*, 56–57, 60; and *A Different World*, 33–34, 39–41; and diversity executives, 51; and *Fat Albert*, 89, 97; global, 1, 13, 233; "postnetwork," 6, 233; and *Roots*, 20–21, 30–31; and South African soap operas, 220; and webisodes, 63–65, 67, 72–74. *See also* cable networks; *and names of networks*
Newcomb, Horace, 33–34
New Orleans, 3, 7, 11–12, 121–136; criminal justice system in, 130–131; Danziger

Bridge, 130; Lakeview, 127; local celebrities of, 121, 132–133; Mardi Gras, 136; mayors of, 133; and music, 121, 126–129, 131–133, 135; New Orleans East, 131, 133; 9th Ward, 127; Plaquemines Parish, 127; Pontchartrain Park, 127–128; St. Bernard Parish, 127; *Treme*, 124
Newton, Huey, 191
New Twenties, The, 66, 73–74
New York Television Festival, 73
New York Times, 35, 79, 85, 151
New York Undercover, 181
New Zealand, 14, 232–244; NZ On Air, 239
Ngubane, Menzi Motlhalaphuti, 225
Nickelodeon, 239
Nielsen ratings, 1, 4, 20, 29, 157
"Niggas." *See* racial epithets
Nightline, 188–189
nihilism, 187–188, 192, 201, 202n2
9/11 terrorist attacks, 5, 188, 190, 196, 201
NITV (National Indigenous Television), 240, 243
Noah's Arc, 12, 67, 74n8, 172–184, 175, 182; Alex Kirby, 175, 177–179, 184; "Baby Can I Hold You?," 180; cancellation of, 174, 180–183; Chance Counter, 175, 177–179, 184; and hate crimes, 180; and HIV/AIDS, 175–176, 179–180, 185n18; "I'm with Stupid," 179; Noah Nicholson, 174–175, 177–178, 180–184, 182, 185n12; Ricky Davis, 175, 177–178, 181, 184; Season One, 177–179; Season Two, 179–180; viewer commentary on, 180–181, 183–184; Wade Robinson, 175, 178, 180, 182, 183; and weddings, 179, 183
Noah's Arc: Jumping the Broom (film), 183
NOLA.com, 122–123, 126–127, 132–136
Nollywood, 1, 13
Not Just the Levees Broke (Montana-LeBlanc), 131
NPR (National Public Radio), 122, 131, 180
nudity, 23, 173, 202n11
Nussbaum, Emily, 39
"N-Word." *See* racial epithets
Nyerere, Julius K., 84–85
NYPD Blue, 54

Obama, Barack, 5, 6, 154n1, 201, 229
obesity: and *Fat Albert*, 90, 94, 99–100; and *Gimme a Break!* 105–107, 111–112, 118
Occupy Wall Street protests, 5, 14n6
Office, The, 63
Ogunnaike, Lola, 151–152

One Economy Corporation, 71–72; The Beehive (website), 71–72
One Eight Seven (film), 46
On the Down Low (King), 180
Oprah, 66, 72, 178
Ortiz, Valery, 69
Other: Blackness as, 2, 4, 41, 44, 46, 179; heterosexual, 178; "othering" / "un-othering," 96, 99, 200
Ouellette, Laurie, 144–145, 149
Out, 174
Overmyer, Eric, 121–122, 125, 134, 136
Ovesey, Lionel, 92
OWN, 72

Pan African Cultural Festival (1969), 84
Pan Africanist Congress, 85
Pantaleo, Sylvia, 96–97
Paramount Pictures, 177
Parker, Sarah Jessica, 34
pastoral aesthetic, 195–197
patriarchy, 97, 108, 158, 168, 227
patriotism, 46, 188, 190, 192
Patterson, Saladin K., 159
PBS (Public Broadcasting System), 77, 80, 85–87; and Tongues Untied, 15n12, 173, 183–184
Peabody Award, 30, 189
People's Choice Awards, 40
Perkins, Ken Parish, 56
Perlmutter, Al, 78–79
Perry, Tyler, 8–9, 66, 159
Peters, Clarke, 128, 129
Pierce, Wendell, 131, 134
Pierson, Eric, 10, 19–32, 249
Pimpin' Ain't Easy (Smith-Shomade), 2
Pinkett, Randal, 147–149, 147, 154, 155n22
Pittsburgh Post-Gazette, 190
"playing the dozens," 40, 95–96
PMRC (Parents Music Resource Center), 200
Poitier, Sidney, 31n11
political correctness, 50, 238
Politics of Reality Television, The, 3
Polk, Patrik-Ian, 159, 173, 175–184
Polynesian culture, 232–233, 235, 237–240, 243
Poniewozik, James, 61n25
Porcella, Flavio, 213
Portugal / Portuguese, 207–208, 213–214; and SIC Radical, 240
postmodernism, 5, 91, 95–99, 101, 103n14, 103n19, 193, 195
Postmodern Picturebooks (Sipe and Pantaleo), 96–97

Poussaint, Alvin, 102n6
P.O.V., 173
Practice of Everyday Life, The (de Certeau), 98
Prejudice and Your Child (Clark), 92
Prime Time Blues, 2
Probst, Jeff, 146
producers, 9, 11, 13–14; amateur, 64; of Black Journal, 77–80, 85; and blindcasting, 49–51, 54–58, 61n19; and Brazil / Afro-Brazilians, 207–208, 211, 214, 217; of bro'Town, 232, 239, 241; of City of Angels, 54–58, 61n19; of Diary of a Single Mom, 69, 71; of A Different World, 10, 33–47; of Drama Queenz, 67, 69, 73; of Gimme a Break! 106, 111, 115–116; of Girlfriends / The Game, 157, 159, 164, 169n1; of hip hop, 158; independent, 63, 66, 174; of Noah's Arc, 174; of reality television, 143–144, 146, 152; of Roots, 10, 19, 21–26, 28–30; of South African soap operas, 220, 230; of Undercovers, 58; of webisodes, 63–67, 69, 71, 73–74. See also names of producers
psychoanalysis / psychology, 11, 90–102, 102n6, 103n9, 103n19
Puar, Jasbir, 201, 203n24
public affairs programs, 10–11, 77–86. See also individual programs
Public Enemy, 150, 165
Public Internet Channel (pic.tv), 71; "Make It Easy Toolbox," 71
public-purpose media, 69–72
public television, 77–78, 81, 85. See also names of public television networks
Punks, 175

Queer as Folk, 173
Quem Sabe Clica! (Who Knows Clicks!), 215
Questão de Direitos (Question of Rights), 215
"Quitting Hip-Hop" (Davis), 166–167

R&B, 57, 110, 233
race relations, 1, 3; and The Adventures of Flagee and Ribbon, 190; and The Apprentice, 147–149; and Black Journal, 78, 81–82, 86; and blindcasting, 49–52, 55–60; and The Boondocks, 187–189, 192, 195, 200–201; and Brazil / Afro-Brazilians, 207–213, 216, 217n1; and City of Angels, 55–60; and The Cosby Show, 90; and A Different World, 35, 40; and Fat Albert, 91; and Flavor of Love, 143, 150–153; and Gimme a Break! 105, 107–110, 112, 118; and

Girlfriends/The Game, 158, 167; and *The Help* (film), 118n2; and Katrina (hurricane), 124, 126–127; and Lee's documentaries, 126–127; and *Noah's Arc*, 173–174, 176–177, 179; and *The Real Housewives of Atlanta*, 141–142; and reality television, 12, 141–154, 155n21; and *Roots*, 19; and South African soap operas, 221–225; and *Survivor: Fiji*, 144–146; and *Tongues Untied*, 173; and *Treme*, 124; and *Undercovers*, 58–60. *See also* racism
Rachel, Cinthya, 214
racial democracy, 208–211, 213, 216, 217n5
racial epithets, 188–189, 193–195, 202n4, 202n11
racism, 13, 26; and *Black Journal*, 85; and blindcasting, 50, 52, 59; and *The Boondocks*, 202n2; and Brazil/ Afro-Brazilians, 207–214, 216–217, 218n16; and *bro'Town*, 233; and *A Different World*, 35, 39–40; and *Fat Albert*, 91–92; and *Flavor of Love*, 150; and *Gimme a Break!* 105, 118; and *Girlfriends/The Game*, 168; inferential, 210; and Katrina (hurricane), 122, 127; and *Noah's Arc*, 173, 181; and reality television, 150; reverse, 39; and *Tongues Untied*, 173
radical politics, 77–78, 86, 191, 194, 198; and *bro'Town*, 233. *See also* activism
radio, 6, 109, 221–222, 229–230
Radio Bantu, 221–222
Rah Digga, 158
"Rainbow Nation," 221, 223–226, 229–230
Ramos, Lazaro, 210
Ramsey, Rey, 72
rape, 226–227; date, 41
rap music, 143, 150, 158, 178, 233; and *The Boondocks*, 187, 194, 198–201. *See also* hip hop
Rashad, Phylicia, 36
ratings, 1, 4; and *The Boondocks*, 189; and *Girlfriends/The Game*, 157; overnight, 20; and *Roots*, 20–21, 28–30
Ratliff, Ben, 45
Reagan, Ronald, 90, 190, 196
Real, Michael, 90
Real Housewives of Atlanta, The, 141–142, 154nn1–2
Real Housewives of New York, The, 141–142
Real Housewives of Orange County, The, 141–142
realism, perceived, 124–131; and identity, 125, 131–134; and Magic Window, 125–127;

and plausibility, 125, 130–131; and probability, 125, 134–136; and social reality, 124–125, 127–130; and utility, 125, 134–136
reality/realism: and *Black Journal*, 80–87; and *A Different World*, 45; and *Fat Albert*, 93, 96–97, 99, 101–102; post-Katrina, 11–12, 121–136; and *Roots*, 23, 27. *See also* realism, perceived; reality television
reality television, 12, 141–154, 183; *The Apprentice*, 142–144, 147–149, 147, 155n14, 155n22; *Flavor of Love*, 3, 142–144, 150–154, 151, 156n25, 156n34; *The Real Housewives of Atlanta*, 141–142, 154nn1–2; subversive readings of, 142–143, 150–154; *Survivor*, 142–146, 145, 146, 148, 155n10, 155n12. *See also individual programs*
Reality TV (Ouellette and Murray), 144
Real World, The, 146, 155n13
Reconstruction, 38, 83
Reed, Robert, 25
Reims, Josh, 58
representation, Black, 2–3, 7, 10–13; and *The Apprentice*, 147–149; and *Black Journal*, 82; and blindcasting, 52–53, 58–60; and *The Boondocks*, 189–190; and Brazil/ Afro-Brazilians, 207–209, 212–217; and *A Different World*, 35–36, 43, 47; and *Drama Queenz*, 69; and *Fat Albert*, 94, 96–97, 99, 101–102; and *Flavor of Love*, 150–151, 153; and *Gimme a Break!* 105, 107–110, 115, 118; and *Girlfriends/The Game*, 159, 167–169; and hip hop, 157, 159, 167–169; and *Noah's Arc*, 184; post-Katrina, 126, 136; and reality television, 142–144, 147–151, 153–154; and *Roots*, 19; and South African soap operas, 224; and *The Vampire Diaries*, 49; and webisodes, 63–64, 69, 72
respectability, 12–13, 43, 148–150, 195
Revolution Televised (Acham), 3
Rhimes, Shonda, 64, 159
Ribeiro, Matilde, 212
Rich Man, Poor Man, 21, 29, 32n17
Rick & Steve, 174
Riggs, Marlon, 5, 12, 15n12, 173, 179, 183–184
Rivero, Yeidy, 3
Robinson, Russell, 53
Robinson, Wendy Raquel, 162
Roc, 171n24
Rock, Chris, 176
Rock 'n' Wrestling, 97
Rolling Stone, 35
Roots (Haley), 20–23, 27, 30, 31n7, 114

Roots (TV miniseries), 10, 19–31, *25*, *27*, *28*; assimilation in, 26–28, *28*; critical acclaim for, 19, 29–31; critics / criticism of, 19, 23, 29; historical accuracy of, 19, 23, 31n7; immigrant narrative of, 26, *28*; Kizzy, 25–26, *25*; Kunta Kinte, 22–23, 27–28; newborn infant presented to heavens in, 27, *27*, 32n15; sexual assaults in, 23–24
Rose, Tricia, 159
Ross, Andrew, 178–179
Ross, Fred, 67
Ross, Tracee Ellis, 160
ROTC, 45–46
Roth, Joshua, 219n26
Roundtree, Richard, *25*, 26, 69
Rucker, Troy Valjean, 67
Ruffins, Kermit, 133
Rumsfeld, Donald, 192
RuPaul's Drag Race / Drag U, 174, 176
Russworm, TreaAndrea M., 11, 87n13, 89–104, 249

SABC (South African Broadcasting Corporation), 220–223, 225–226, 228–230; Board of Control, 221, 223
Sampaio, Teodoro, 215
satellite television, 1, 31, 141, 239, 242
satire: and *The Boondocks*, 193, 195, 200–201; and *bro'Town*, 235–238, 240; and *Flavor of Love*, 143, 150–154; and Katrina (hurricane), 131
Saturday Night Live, 34
Sawyer, G. M., 38
Say Brother, 78
Say It Loud! (Coleman), 3
scheduling: "back 9," 61n15; and blindcasting, 51, 54, 56–57, 61n15; and challenge programming, 56–57; of *City of Angels*, 54, 56–57, 61n15; of *Rich Man, Poor Man*, 29, 32n17; of *Roots*, 10, 19–21, 29–30
School Daze (film), 38–39, 46
school reform, 81–82, 90, 92, 212, 215
Schoon, Curtis, 59–60
Scooby-Doo, Where Are You, 238
Screen Actors Guild (SAG), 51, 59
screenwriters. *See* writers / screenwriters
segregation, racial, 38, 91–92, 108, 195, 209, 222, 230. *See also* apartheid
Seiphemo, Rapulana, 226
self-esteem, Black, 92–93, 214, 228
Semoko, Keketso, 227
September 11, 2001. *See* 9 / 11 terrorist attacks
Sesame Street, 85, 89

sex addiction, 161, 178
Sex and the City, 34, 173
sexism, 159, 168, 226
sex / sexuality, 12, 13, 53, 73, 119n4; and *The Boondocks*, 189, 192, 198, 200–201; and Brazil / Afro-Brazilians, 210; and *bro'Town*, 237, 241; and *Girlfriends / The Game*, 157–158, 160–167, 169; and hip hop, 157–158, 164, 169, 170n9, 200–201; and *Noah's Arc*, 173–174, 177–178, 180, 184; and South African soap operas, 220. *See also* gay men, Black
Shaded Lives (Smith-Shomade), 2
Shapiro, Michael, 124–125, 136
Sharpley-Whiting, T. Denean, 158
Sharpton, Al, 189
Shephard, Chaz Lamar, 162
Sheriff, Robin, 208
Showtime, 61n8
Showtime at the Apollo, 36
Sibeko, David, 85
Siddiq, Wali, 84, 87n2. *See also* House, Lou
Silva, Hédio, 215
Silva, Luiz Inácio "Lula" da, 212
Silva, Nelson do Valle, 209
Silverman, Fred, 20–21, 24, 29
Simmons, James O., 102n6
Simon, David, 121–122, 125, 134, 136
Simpsons, The, 238
Sinclair, Madge, 110–111
single mothers: and *Diary of a Single Mom*, 65–66, 69–72; and *The Game*, 163–164, 170n17; and *Gimme a Break!* 118
Singleton, John, 177
Sipe, Lawrence, 96–97
slavery, history of, 23–26, 38, 40, 108, 114; and Brazil / Afro-Brazilians, 207–209, 215, 217, 218n16
Slotkin, Richard, 197
Smith, Henry Nash, 197
Smith, Jada Pinkett, 159
Smith, Roger Guenveur, 38
Smith, Will, 159
Smith-Shomade, Beretta E., 1–15, *2*, 249
Snoop Dog, 198
Snow, Phoebe, 41
Soap, 109–110
soap operas, Brazilian (novelas), 209–210
soap operas, South African, 13, 220–230, *224*; as aspirational models, 220–221, 223–224, 226, 230; and current events, 228–230; *Egoli: Place of Gold*, 223; *Generations*, 221, 223–226, 228, 230;

Isidingo, 221, 224, *224*, 226–229; and racial
purity, 225; and social control, 221, 223
soap operas, U.S., 179, 220, 222–223,
227–230; as webisodes, 65–66, 69. *See also*
titles of U.S. soap operas
social justice, 193, 220, 225, 230
Soul! 85
Soul Food, 61n8
Sounder (film), 21
South (U.S.): and *Black Journal*, 82–84; and
A Different World, 34, 39, 45; and *Gimme a*
Break! 105, 108
South Africa: Afrikaner Nationalist Party,
220–223; ANC (African National
Congress), 221, 223, 225, 229; and
apartheid, 38, 41, 84, 220–222, 225,
229–230; BEE (Black Economic
Empowerment Act, 2003), 224–225;
on *Black Journal*, 84; Broadcasting
Act, 221; Broadcasting Amendment
(1960), 222; Department of Native
Affairs, 221; health ministry, 227; IBA
mandate, 226; Independent Broadcasting
Authority Act (1993), 223; soap operas, 13,
220–230
South Park, 238, 240, 242
Spearman, Doug, 175
Spigel, Lynn, 231n8
Spillers, Hortense, 154n4
Split Image (Dates and Barlow), 108
Square Pegs, 34–35, 43
Squires, Catherine, 77, 87n14
Staiger, Janet, 90
Steinberg, Steven, 202n2
Stephens, Darryl, 174
stereotypes, 20; and Brazil/Afro-Brazilians,
209–210; and *bro'Town*, 236, 238; and *A*
Different World, 43; and *Fat Albert*, 95–96;
and *Gimme a Break!* 105–111, 113–115,
117–118, 119n4; and *Girlfriends/The*
Game, 164; and *I Spy*, 31n3; and Lee's
documentaries, 126; and *Noah's Arc*, 172,
174, 177–178, 184; and reality television,
143, 147, 149, 151; and South African soap
operas, 222, 226, 229
Stevenson, Richard, 41
St. Patrick, Mathew, 172–173
Strabhaar, Joseph, 239
Strickland, Arvarh, 31n7
strikes, 79–80, 87, 228–229
students, Black, 82, 92, 117, 193–194; and
Brazil/Afro-Brazilians, 211, 215; and
South African soap operas, 230
Style Network, 1

subjectivity: and *A Different World*, 33, 46;
and *Fat Albert*, 90, 96, 98; and
Girlfriends/The Game, 158, 164, 169; and
Noah's Arc, 178
suicides, 69
Summer, Cree, 39
Sundance Channel, 174
Super Fly T.N.T., 22
Survivor, 142–146; Fiji, 144–146, *145*, *146*, 148,
155n10, 155n12
Sutherland, Meghan, 14n1
Sutton, Percy, 86
Sweet, Dolph, 106, *107*, 115

Tager, Michele, 230
Target (Montgomery), 31n13
Taylor, Ron, 23–24
Taylor, Schatar "Hottie," 151
Taylor, Tracy, 66, 73
TBS, 8
tele-evangelical ministries, black, 7–8
Television Critics Association, 58
Television Culture (Fiske), 97
Television Studies After TV, 3
That's My Mama, 109
Thinking Outside the Box, 3
Third World Conference on Racism, Racial
Discrimination, Xenophobia, and
Related Intolerance (2001), 212
Times-Picayune, 122
TNT, 9
To All My Friends on Shore, 92
tokenism, 79, 87
Tomei, Marisa, 35, 39
Tongues Untied, 15n12, 173, 183–184
Tony Brown's Journal, 87
Tonys, 37, 110
Torres, Sasha, 106
tourism, 135, 236–237; cultural, 242–244
Toussaint, Allen, 133
Townsend, Robert, 69, 71–72
transsexuals, 241. *See also* LGBT/LGBTQ
Trapper John, M.D., 110–111
Treme, 7, 11, 121–136, *129*, *132*; Albert
Lambreaux, 128–129, *129*; Antoine
Batiste, 131–134; Desiree, 131–134; Mardi
Gras Indians in, 121, 127;
musicians/music in, 121, 126–129, 131–133,
135; and perceived realism, 124–136; police
brutality in, 130–131; viewer commentary
on, 122–123, 126–127, 129, 131–136
Trevor Project, 69
Trump, Donald, 147–149, *147*, 155n22
Tshivenda, 223

Tucker, Ken, 54
Tuning Out Blackness (Rivero), 3
Turminha da Hora (Class Hour), 214–215;
    Tio Bah, 214–215
Turner, Kriss, 159
Turow, Joseph, 53
Tutu, Desmond, 221, 223–226
TV da Gente, 13, 207–208, 211–217, *213*
TV Globo network, 209–210
TV Guide, 107–108
TV One, 2, 4, 72, 117–118
TV3, 239
20th Century Fox Studios, 21
227, 115–116

Uggams, Leslie, 25, *25*
Undercovers, 58–60, 64
United Negro College Fund, 38
universalism, 101; and blindcasting, 50,
    53–54, 58; and *bro'Town*, 232, 234–235,
    240–244; and *City of Angels*, 54, 58; and
    Fat Albert, 90; and *Roots*, 22, 24, 27
uplift, 12, 150, 200
UPN (United Paramount Network), 41, 51,
    64–65, 157
upper class, 7, 115, 142, 151, 199–200
U.S. (United Slaves), 81
USA Today, 40, 153

Variety, 79–80
Vereen, Ben, 28
VH1, 150, 153
Vibe, 166
Vibrations for a New People, 78
Villarejo, Amy, 5
Vincent, Christian, 175, 181
violence: and *The Boondocks*, 189, 197–200,
    203n24; frontier, 197; of hate crimes, 180;
    sexual/domestic, 159; of war, 198
Voting Rights Act, 83

Wade, Adam, 86
Waite, Ralph, 24
Walker, Dave, 122
Wall, Melissa, 124
Warner, Kristen J., 10, 49–62, 249–250
war on terror, 192, 201
Washington Post, 151
watchdog groups, 50–52, 54, 56, 60n2.
    See also individual groups
Watching Race (Gray), 2
Watkins, Mel, 150
Wayans, Damon, 172
Wayans, Keenan Ivory, 15n12

WB (Warner Bros. Television Network),
    41, 51, 64–65
webisodes, 10, 63–74; *Diary of a Single Mom*,
    66, 69–72; and direct action, 69; *Drama
    Queenz*, 65–66, 67–69, 73; financing of,
    73–74; *The New Twenties*, 66, 73–74; *The
    Office*, 63; viewer commentary on, 68–73;
    and Web festivals/conferences, 73–74; as
    webtopia, 73–74; *Who . . .*, 66, 74
Webster, 110
"We Fall Down" (McClurkin), 162
West, Cheryl L., 69
West, Cornell, 202n2
West, Mae, 153
Whaley, Deborah Elizabeth, 12–13, 187–204,
    236, 250
What's Happening?, 109
When Chickenheads Come Home to Roost
    (Morgan), 164
When the Levees Broke, 11, 121–123, 126–128,
    128, 130–132, 134–136; and perceived
    realism, 126–128, 130–132, 134–136; police
    brutality in, 130–131; viewer commentary
    on, 122–123, 126–127, 132, 134–136
White, Persia, 162
Whitehead, Robert, 229
whites/whiteness, 1–4; and *The Apprentice*,
    147–148; and *Black Journal*, 77–83, 85–86;
    and blindcasting, 50–51, 53–55, 57–58, 60;
    and *The Boondocks*, 192–195, 197, 199; and
    Brazil/Afro-Brazilians, 208–211, 216; and
    bro'Town, 233–238, 240, 242–243; and *City
    of Angels*, 54–55, 57–58, 60; and *A Different
    World*, 10, 33, 35, 37–39, 43, 45; and *Flavor
    of Love*, 150, 152; and *Gimme a Break!*
    105–106, 108–111, 113–115, 118; and
    Girlfriends/The Game, 159; and HBO, 7;
    and *The Help* (film), 118n2; and *If God Is
    Willing and da Creek Don't Rise*, 130; and
    Julia, 109; and *Noah's Arc*, 174, 176, 185n9;
    and reality television, 142, 147–148, 150,
    152; and *Roots*, 22–24, 26, 28; and South
    African soap operas, 221–222, 224–225,
    229; and *Undercovers*, 58, 60; and
    webisodes, 65, 73; white supremacy, 108,
    192, 195, 243. *See also* audiences,
    mainstream
Whitfield, Dondre T., 160
Who . . ., 66, 74
Wickham, DeWayne, 153
Wiley, Richard E., 30
Will and Grace, 172
Williams, Billy Dee, 31n11, 69
Williams, Larry, 81, 159

Williams, Michael Kenneth, 173
Williams, Patricia J., 50
Williams, Sherley Anne, 170n9
Williams, Stephen, 146, 155n13
Wiltz, Teresa, 151
Winfrey, Oprah. *See* Oprah
Winnicott, D. W., 93–94, 96, 99, 102n6
Wire, The, 7, 173
WLBT case, 85
Wolper, David L., 19, 22, 24, 29–30
working class, 7, 65, 109, 115, 195
writers/screenwriters, 9–10; and
    blindcasting, 49, 51, 56–58, 60; and
    Brazil/Afro-Brazilians, 211; British, 36; of
    bro'Town, 232; of *City of Angels,* 56–57; of
    Diary of a Single Mom, 69, 71; of *A
    Different World,* 33–34, 36, 41, 46; of
    Gimme a Break! 111–113; of *Girlfriends/The

Game, 157, 164; of *Noah's Arc,* 173; of
    Roots, 10, 21–23, 29; of *Saturday Night
    Live,* 34; of South African soap operas,
    220, 227–228, 230; of *Treme,* 122; of
    Undercovers, 58; of webisodes, 10, 64–67,
    69, 71. *See also individual writers/screen-
    writers*

Xuxa, 209

Young, Andrew, 81
Your World with Neil Cavuto, 155n22
YouTube, 68–69, 193
Yo-Yo, 158

Zook, Kristal Brent, 2–3
Zuma, Jacob, 226
Zumbi dos Palmares, 207, 212

CPSIA information can be obtained at www.ICGtesting.com
Printed in the USA
BVOW02s0348161013

333807BV00001BB/3/P

9 780813 553863